THE CAMBRIDGE COMPANION
AMERICAN GOTHIC

The Cambridge Companion to the American Gothic
view to both the breadth and depth of the American Gothic tradition. This subgenre features works from many of America's best-known authors: Edgar Allan Poe, Toni Morrison, Stephen King, Anne Rice, Henry James, Edith Wharton, William Faulkner, and Flannery O'Connor. Authored by leading experts in the field, the introduction and sixteen chapters explore the American Gothic chronologically, in relation to different social groups, in connection with different geographic regions, and in different media, including children's literature, poetry, drama, film, television, and gaming. This *Companion* provides a rich and thorough analysis of the American Gothic tradition from a twenty-first-century standpoint, and will be a key resource for undergraduates, graduate students, and professional researchers interested in this topic.

JEFFREY ANDREW WEINSTOCK is author or editor of twenty books. These include *The Age of Lovecraft* (co-edited with Carl Sederholm), which won the 2017 Ray & Pat Browne Award for Best Edited Collection in Popular Culture and American Culture from the Popular Culture Association/American Culture Association, *The Ashgate Encyclopedia of Literary and Cinematic Monsters*, which won the 2014 Rue Morgue magazine award for "Best Non-Fiction Book," and *The Vampire Film: Undead Cinema*, which won the 2013 International Association of the Fantastic in the Arts Lord Ruthven Assembly Award for Best Non-Fiction title.

A complete list of books in the series is at the back of this book.

THE CAMBRIDGE
COMPANION TO
AMERICAN GOTHIC

THE CAMBRIDGE COMPANION TO
AMERICAN GOTHIC

EDITED BY
JEFFREY ANDREW WEINSTOCK
Central Michigan University

CAMBRIDGE
UNIVERSITY PRESS

University Printing House, Cambridge CB2 8BS, United Kingdom

One Liberty Plaza, 20th Floor, New York, NY 10006, USA

477 Williamstown Road, Port Melbourne, VIC 3207, Australia

314–321, 3rd Floor, Plot 3, Splendor Forum, Jasola District Centre,
New Delhi – 110025, India

79 Anson Road, #06–04/06, Singapore 079906

Cambridge University Press is part of the University of Cambridge.

It furthers the University's mission by disseminating knowledge in the pursuit of education, learning, and research at the highest international levels of excellence.

www.cambridge.org
Information on this title: www.cambridge.org/9781107117143
DOI: 10.1017/9781316337998

© Cambridge University Press 2017

This publication is in copyright. Subject to statutory exception and to the provisions of relevant collective licensing agreements, no reproduction of any part may take place without the written permission of Cambridge University Press.

First published 2017

Printed in the United States of America by Sheridan Books, Inc.

A catalogue record for this publication is available from the British Library.

ISBN 978-1-107-11714-3 Hardback
ISBN 978-1-107-53978-5 Paperback

Cambridge University Press has no responsibility for the persistence or accuracy of URLs for external or third-party internet websites referred to in this publication and does not guarantee that any content on such websites is, or will remain, accurate or appropriate.

This volume is dedicated to Diane Long Hoeveler.

CONTENTS

List of Contributors	*page* ix
List of Figures	xiii
Acknowledgments	xiv

Introduction: The American Gothic   1
JEFFREY ANDREW WEINSTOCK

PART I PERIODS

1 Early American Gothic (Puritan and New Republic)   15
FAYE RINGEL

2 Romanticism and the American Gothic   31
ALFRED BENDIXEN

3 American Gothic Realism and Naturalism   44
MONIKA ELBERT AND WENDY RYDEN

4 Modernist American Gothic   57
JOHN PAUL RIQUELME

5 Contemporary American Gothic   71
JUSTIN D. EDWARDS

PART II IDENTITIES AND LOCATIONS

6 Race and the American Gothic   85
ELLEN WEINAUER

7 American Female Gothic   99
DIANE LONG HOEVELER

CONTENTS

8	Queer American Gothic ARDEL HAEFELE-THOMAS	115
9	American Frontier Gothic ELIZABETH JANE WALL HINDS	128
10	Southern American Gothic CHARLES L. CROW	141
11	Urban American Gothic LEONARD CASSUTO	156

PART III GENRE AND MEDIA

12	The Gothic in American Children's Literature KAREN COATS	171
13	Gothic American Poetry TRAVIS D. MONTGOMERY	184
14	Gothic American Drama HEATHER S. NATHANS	201
15	Gothic American Film & TV CAROL MARGARET DAVISON	215
16	Gothic American Gaming TANYA KRZYWINSKA	229
	Index	243

CONTRIBUTORS

ALFRED BENDIXEN teaches at Princeton University and is best known as the founder of the American Literature Association, which he continues to serve as Executive Director. His most recent work focuses on the development of genre in a democratic society and includes several edited and coedited volumes: *The Cambridge Companion to American Travel Writing* (2009); *A Companion to the American Short Story* (2010) and *A Companion to the American Novel* (2012); and most recently, *The Cambridge History of American Poetry*, coedited with Stephen Burt of Harvard (2015).

LEONARD CASSUTO is Professor of English and American Studies at Fordham University, and the author or editor of eight books on American literature and culture. The most recent of these are *The Graduate School Mess: What Caused It and How We Can Fix It* (2015) and *The Cambridge History of the American Novel* (2011), of which he was General Editor. He is also a prize-winning journalist who writes on subjects ranging from science to sports. Visit him at www.lcassuto.com.

KAREN COATS is a professor of English at Illinois State University, where she teaches children's and young adult literature. She is author of *Looking Glasses and Neverlands: Lacan, Desire, and Subjectivity in Children's Literature* (2004) and coeditor of *The Gothic in Children's Literature: Haunting the Borders* (with Anna Jackson and Roberick McGillis, 2007) and *Handbook of Children's and Young Adult Literature* (2011). Her most recent book is *The Bloomsbury Introduction to Children's and Young Adult Literature* (2017).

CHARLES L. CROW, Professor Emeritus of English at Bowling Green State University in Ohio, now lives in California. In the Gothic field, his publications include *American Gothic* (2009), *American Gothic: An Anthology* (1999, second edition 2012), *A Companion to American Gothic* (2014), *The Palgrave Companion to the Southern Gothic* (with Susan Castillo Street, 2016), and articles on Gothic aspects of such authors as W. D. Howells, Charles Chesnutt, Edith Wharton, and Jack London.

LIST OF CONTRIBUTORS

CAROL MARGARET DAVISON is Professor of English at the University of Windsor, Canada. A former Canada-U.S. Fulbright scholar, she is the author of *History of the Gothic: Gothic Literature 1764–1824* (2009), *Anti-Semitism and British Gothic Literature* (2004), the editor of *The Gothic and Death* (2017), and co-editor with Monica Germanà of *Scottish Gothic: An Edinburgh Companion* (2017). In addition to publishing dozens of commissioned articles about the Gothic, she has edited a special issue of *Gothic Studies* devoted to the Gothic and addiction, and a special issue of *Women's Writing* devoted to the work of Marie Corelli. She is currently at work on a novel about Edinburgh's Burke and Hare serial murders.

JUSTIN D. EDWARDS is Chair of Gothic Studies at the University of Stirling. He is the author or coauthor of several books, including *Grotesque* (2013), *Mobility at Large* (2012), *Postcolonial Literature* (2008), *Gothic Canada: Reading the Spectre of a National Literature* (2005), *Gothic Passages: Racial Ambiguity and the American Gothic* (2003), and *Exotic Journeys: Exploring the Erotics of U.S. Travel Literature* (2001). He is also the coeditor of *Other Routes: 1500 Years of African and Asian Travel Writing* (2006), *Downtown Canada: Writing Canadian Cities* (2005), *Postcolonial Travel Writing: Critical Explorations* (2010), *Pop Goth: Gothic in Contemporary Literature and Popular Culture* (2012), and *Gothic Technologies in Literature and Culture: Technogothics* (2015).

MONIKA ELBERT is Professor of English and Distinguished University Scholar at Montclair State University, Montclair, New Jersey. She has published widely on the Gothic, including on such authors as Hawthorne, Wharton, Poe, Spofford, and Alcott. Her *Haunting Realities: Naturalist Gothic and American Realism* (coedited with Wendy Ryden) recently appeared (2017) and her *Hawthorne in Context* is forthcoming (Cambridge University Press). She has recently coedited and contributed to *Transnational Gothic: Literary and Social Exchanges in the Long Nineteenth Century* (2013) and *Romantic Education in Nineteenth-Century American Literature: National and Transatlantic Contexts* (2014).

ARDEL HAEFELE-THOMAS holds a doctorate in Modern Thought and Literature from Stanford University and is currently Chair of Lesbian, Gay, Bisexual, and Transgender Studies at City College of San Francisco. Their book, *Queer Others in Victorian Gothic: Transgressing Monstrosity* was published in 2013. Currently, Haefele-Thomas is finishing *Introduction to Transgender Studies*, which will be the first introductory book to the field of study. They are also coauthoring *Transgender: A Reference Guide* with Dr. Aaron Devor from the University of Victoria Transgender Archives and acting as guest editor for *Victorian Review*'s forthcoming edition entitled *Trans Victorians*.

LIST OF CONTRIBUTORS

ELIZABETH JANE WALL HINDS is Professor of English at the State University of New York, Brockport. She is author of *Private Property: Charles Brockden Brown's Gendered Economics of Virtue* and the edited collection *The Multiple Worlds of Pynchon's Mason & Dixon: Eighteenth-Century Contexts, Postmodern Observations*. Her other publications encompass the fields of animal studies and the eighteenth century, American Gothic fiction, and popular culture.

DIANE LONG HOEVELER was Emeritus Professor of English at Marquette University, Milwaukee, Wisconsin, before her passing in 2016. She authored most recently the books *The Gothic Ideology: Religious Hysteria and Anti-Catholicism in British Popular Fiction, 1780–1870* (2014) and *Gothic Riffs: Secularizing the Uncanny in the European Imaginary, 1780–1820* (2010). She was author, coauthor, or editor of over a dozen scholarly and reference books, and some sixty-five articles on a variety of literary topics. She will be deeply missed.

TANYA KRZYWINSKA is Professor in Digital Games and Director of the Games Academy at Falmouth University, Cornwall, UK. As well as a director of Round Table Game Studies, she is the author of several books and many articles on different aspects of digital games, most recently writing a monograph, *Gothic Games*, about the particularities of Gothic tropes in games. She is also currently working on a Lovecraft-inspired game with Round Table Game Studios entitled *Deal with the Devil* and is researching the Gothic affordances of augmented reality.

TRAVIS D. MONTGOMERY is Associate Professor of English at Oklahoma Christian University. His primary research interest is antebellum literature, and he has published essays about the writings of Edgar Allan Poe.

HEATHER S. NATHANS is Professor and Chair of the Department of Drama and Dance at Tufts University. Her publications include *Early American Theatre from the Revolution to Thomas Jefferson* (2003); *Slavery and Sentiment on the American Stage, 1787–1861* (2009); *Shakespearean Educations: Power, Citizenship, and Performance*, coeditor and contributing author (2011); coeditor and contributing author, *The Oxford Handbook of America Drama* (2013); and the forthcoming *Hideous Characters and Beautiful Pagans: Performing Jewish Identity on the Antebellum American Stage*, as well as numerous book chapters and journal articles. She is the past-president of the American Society for Theatre Research. She is also editor of the *Studies in Theatre History and Culture* series. She has received over twenty-five grants and fellowships, including ones from the Guggenheim Foundation and the Mellon Foundation.

FAYE RINGEL, Professor Emeritus of Humanities at the US Coast Guard Academy, New London, Connecticut, holds the doctorate in Comparative Literature from Brown University, Providence, Rhode Island. She is the author of *New England's*

Gothic Literature: History and Folklore of the Supernatural and many articles on fantastic medievalism in literature and history.

JOHN PAUL RIQUELME, Professor of English at Boston University and Cochair of the Modernism Seminar at the Mahindra Humanities Center (Harvard), has published, in addition to his work on modernist writers from Joyce to Beckett, essays on *Frankenstein* and science fiction, *Dorian Gray* and aestheticism, *Dracula*'s stylistic excesses from a post-structuralist perspective, and both modernist Gothic and Gothic of the long nineteenth century. He has edited *Gothic & Modernism: Essaying Dark Literary Modernity* (2008) and a case studies edition of *Dracula* (2nd edition, 2016). He is currently at work on a book concerning modernist Gothic and one about Oscar Wilde's place in literary modernism.

WENDY RYDEN is Professor of English and Coordinator of Writing across the Curriculum at Long Island University, Post. She is coauthor with Ian Marshall of *Reading, Writing, and the Rhetorics of Whiteness* and coeditor with Monika Elbert of *Haunting Realities: Naturalist Gothic and American Realism* (2017).

ELLEN WEINAUER is Dean of the Honors College and Associate Professor of English at the University of Southern Mississippi. She is coeditor, with Robert McClure Smith, of *American Culture, Canons, and the Case of Elizabeth Stoddard* (2003), and author of articles on Hawthorne, Melville, Frederick Douglass, William and Ellen Craft, and others. Her manuscript in progress examines the relationship between marriage, ownership, and the Gothic in mid-nineteenth-century American literature.

JEFFREY ANDREW WEINSTOCK is Professor of English at Central Michigan University and an associate editor for *The Journal of the Fantastic in the Arts*. This edited collection is his twentieth book. Among his other book publications are *The Age of Lovecraft* (2016, edited with Carl Sederholm); *Goth Music: From Sound to Subculture* (2016, authored with Isabella van Elferen); and *Return to Twin Peaks: New Approaches to Materiality, Theory, and Genre on Television* (2016, edited with Catherine Spooner). His 2008 book publication, *Scare Tactics: Supernatural Fiction by American Women*, was reissued in 2016 in paperback. Visit him at www.jeffreyandrewweinstock.com.

FIGURES

1 Characteristic American Gothic preoccupations   *page* 7

ACKNOWLEDGMENTS

I would like to thank Alfred Bendixen for recommending me to Cambridge University Press as editor for this project, as well as Ray Ryan and the staff at Cambridge University Press for their assistance. Projects such as this one tend to develop slowly, so I also extend my thanks to the contributors, not only for their erudition but their patience. Finally, a special thank you to Justin Wigard, who stepped in at the last minute and so ably assisted with the index.

JEFFREY ANDREW WEINSTOCK

Introduction
The American Gothic

In Leslie Fiedler's seminal study of American literature, *Love and Death in the American Novel*, first published in 1960, Fiedler makes bold claims for the significance of the Gothic[1] genre to American literature. He asserts, for example, that "It is the gothic form that has been most fruitful in the hands of our best writers" (28), that the tradition of American literature "is almost essentially a gothic one" (142), and that "Until the gothic had been discovered, the serious American novel could not begin; and as long as that novel lasts, the gothic cannot die" (143). Symptomatic of its historical moment, Fiedler's study limits itself almost exclusively to white male authors. His conclusion, however, is one that arguably could be extended much more broadly: "our greatest writers sought out gothic themes" (142). The American literary tradition, which for Fiedler more or less begins with Charles Brockden Brown at the turn of the eighteenth century and extends to Nabokov but that we could extend today to include Shirley Jackson, Toni Morrison, Joyce Carol Oates, Stephen King, Bret Easton Ellis, Gloria Naylor, Louise Erdrich, Anne Rice, Cormac McCarthy, Peter Straub, and many others, is at its core a Gothic one. An understanding of American culture and character, therefore, must include as part of its consideration the Gothic impulse as it manifests in both literary and popular culture.

While Fiedler's claims about the centrality of the Gothic form to American letters seem difficult, if not impossible, to dispute, they do introduce some curious problems. As developed first in literature starting in the eighteenth century and later in film and other narrative media, the Gothic is a genre that focuses on the past and immoderate, ungovernable passions. What correspondences then could a literary form emphasizing medieval history, ghosts in crumbling castles, emotional extremes, and a debased aristocracy possibly have in the late eighteenth and nineteenth centuries with a new country lacking an entrenched class structure and founded on the principles of Enlightenment rationalism, and why does it retain its hold over the American imagination today? The answers to these questions are complicated ones explored by the contributors to this volume in two ways: first, by taking issue with the premise that America ever was a place free from history, class relations, and, one might add, other forms of social antagonism including race, gender, and religion; and second, by showing the ways in which the Gothic goes beyond elaborating and redeploying a specific set of identifiable clichés (ghosts, castles, monsters, and so forth) as it gives shape to culturally specific anxieties and tabooed desires.

Transgression and Power

The Gothic, as explained by Fred Botting, is an artistic form fascinated with transgression (see Botting 6–12). All cultures inevitably have boundaries – dividing lines between where different people may and may not go, and between what is acceptable and what is off-limits for those occupying different subject positions – and as soon as there are boundaries, there are anxieties and fantasies about crossing them. All communities, therefore, will have their own Gothic tales and traditions: narratives about the desires to and consequences of violating legal rules and transgressing social expectations. Such stories function in a dual capacity. On the one hand, they can act as tools for teaching and socialization – fairy tales frequently function in this capacity: wander off the path of virtue and risk getting lost in the dark woods and eaten up by the big bad wolf. On the other hand, such stories can also function as forms of vicarious liberation for readers and viewers as they follow along with protagonists who disregard established rules and expectations and venture into forbidden territory. The flirtation with the taboo is, of course, a large part of the appeal of the Gothic – we read breathlessly or hold our hands over our eyes while peeking through our fingers as the Gothic hero or heroine confronts the horrifying monster or uncovers the dark history of murder, incest, and/or usurpation on which the present order rests. We enjoy the *frisson* of that which is almost – but not quite – too horrible to be shown or described.

Another way to say that the Gothic takes as its focus transgression of cultural boundaries is to say that the central topic thematized by the Gothic is inevitably *power*: who is allowed to do what based upon their subject position within a particular society at a specific moment in time. This is implicit in Fiedler's thumbnail sketch of the late eighteenth-century Gothic novels of British author Ann Radcliffe:

> Through a dream landscape, usually called by the name of some actual Italian place, a girl flees in terror and alone amid crumbling castles, antique dungeons, and ghosts who are never really ghosts. She nearly escapes her terrible

persecutors, who seek her out of lust and greed, but is caught; escapes again and is caught; escapes once more and is caught ... finally breaks free altogether and is married to the virtuous lover who has all along worked (and suffered equally with her) to save her. (127)

In Radcliffe's novels such as *The Mysteries of Udolpho* (1794) and *The Italian* (1797), virtuous young heroines are preyed upon by unscrupulous and lecherous aristocrats. While the plucky young female protagonists possess a certain capacity to resist the advances made upon them, they nevertheless find themselves in difficult positions as older, rich, white men within Italian patriarchal society are free to do as they like almost without restraint while they, as young women within that same society, are dependent for their sustenance on first fathers and then husbands. Part of the uniquely Gothic quality of these novels derives from the tenuous positions of their disempowered heroines who find themselves both literally imprisoned in castles and convents, and figuratively confined by social expectations that limit their autonomy and circumscribe their options.

What the example of Radcliffe makes clear is that, while the Gothic is always about inequities in distributions of power and contests for control, the specific permutations it takes depend on the configuration of the society that births it and which it reflects. Radcliffe's Gothic romances about disempowered young women attempting to defend their virtue against lascivious and scheming aristocrats find their footing, for example, in a Western cultural setting in which wealth and title permit men wide latitude of action and movement, and which operates according to a sexual "double standard" that allows – even celebrates – men who have many female lovers or "conquests" but that considers a woman's chastity as a primary virtue. As we will see, the American Gothic, reflecting the specific power dynamics of the United States and its difficult history of slavery and racial antagonism, draws much of its energy from anxieties over racial difference.

Before turning to the specific character of the American Gothic and its distinguishing features, however, it is useful to note that the contests for control at the core of the Gothic can be divided into two broad categories: the individual contending against impersonal forces directly, and the individual contending with a specific other or others (a human villain or monster) that itself is the symptom or reflection of larger impersonal forces. Impersonal forces against which Gothic protagonists must contend directly include weather, war, pandemics (zombie producing and otherwise), and, in some cases, God. To a certain extent, these forces can be considered as what literary and cultural theorist Timothy Morton calls "hyperobjects," things "massively distributed in time and space relative to humans" (Morton 1) with which we are entangled and which force upon us the awareness of our own insignificance. In Gothic tales in which protagonists contend with hyperobjects, basic survival rather than victory is generally the goal. This is often the case, for example, in American Naturalist works such as Jack London's "To Build a Fire" (1908), in which the unnamed protagonist contends with (and loses to) extreme cold, and in Frank Norris' "The Open Boat" (1897), in which four men in a small lifeboat try to survive on the open ocean. This is also the situation in the works of twentieth-century American horror author H. P. Lovecraft that seek to elicit what Lovecraft calls in his treatise on "weird fiction," *Supernatural Horror in Literature* (1927), "cosmic fear" (15) – dread evoked by the proposition that the universe is governed by powers and forces that dwarf the human capacity to comprehend, much less resist.

An important variant of the Gothic contest against impersonal forces is the theme of the divided self, in which protagonists are motivated by unconscious desires and irrational impulses. Within the American Gothic tradition, this strain is arguably introduced by late eighteenth-century Gothicist Charles Brockden Brown, notably in his 1799 novel *Edgar Huntly, Or, Memoirs of a Sleepwalker*, in which the eponymous protagonist turns out to be a stranger to himself – compelled by forces of which he is completely unaware, he performs various actions while asleep, the evidence of which then confuses and unnerves him while he is awake. This model of human psychology depicted by Brown in which individuals are acted upon by unconscious forces and in which irrational appetitive desires conflict with rational decision-making was then powerfully developed in antebellum American by Edgar Allan Poe. Not only are insanity and the mind divided against itself recurring themes in Poe's work, but in two separate texts, "The Black Cat" (1843) and "The Imp of the Perverse" (1845), Poe explicitly addresses what he refers to as "perverseness," the human propensity to desire to do things for the sole reason that we know we should not. Although unconscious action and irrational compulsion emerge from within, they create the impression that one is controlled by irresistible, impersonal external forces. Psychological Gothic narratives such as those developed by Brown and Poe in antebellum America and refined by later authors (Chuck Palahniuk's novel *Fight Club* [1996], for example, is a psychological Gothic tale updating Poe's "William Wilson" [1839]), therefore, can be considered as variants of the Gothic contest against overwhelming external powers.

In contrast to things like war, weather, and the unconscious – impersonal forces that act without intentionality and outside of systems of morality – to contend against specific others is, at least on the face of it, to confront comprehensible, if frequently immoral, antagonists. When Radcliffe's heroines, for example, seek to evade the snares of their insidious captors, they are most immediately up against specific villains. Similarly, when Mary Rowlandson in her 1682 captivity narrative, *The Sovereignty and Goodness of God*, details her experience of being held against her will, the antagonists are her captors, the Narragansett, Wampanoag, and Nashaway Indians of Massachusetts. In *'Salem's Lot* (1975), Stephen King's updating of Bram Stoker's *Dracula* (1897), the antagonist is the monstrous vampire Barlow, while in the science fiction film *Alien* (Ridley Scott, 1979), a relocation of the Gothic castle into space, the specific other Warrant Officer Ripley (Sigourney Weaver) must defeat is the monstrous double-mouthed xenomorph. On the face of it, the scope of works such as these seems more circumscribed as the threat presented is specific and localized – such narratives are less immediately allegories of the fragility of human existence and more focused on literal confrontations between protagonist and antagonist. Put differently, there seems to be less of the sublime associated with a protagonist attempting to track down a serial killer as in 1991's *The Silence of the Lambs* (Jonathan Demme, adapted from the 1988 novel by Thomas Harris) than with one man fighting for survival against the elements in the wilds of Montana and South Dakota as in the 2015 film *The Revenant* (Alejandro G. Iñárritu, adapted from the 2002 novel by Michael Punke).

It is important to note, however, that even in Gothic narratives in which protagonists contend against specific others, conflicts are inevitably structured by meshes of more diffuse impersonal forces. Radcliffe's protagonist Emily in *The Mysteries of Udolpho* is held captive by the villainous Montoni but, as mentioned above, Montoni materializes broader cultural forces having to do with class and gender. Rowlandson is taken captive by Indians, but the context for her confinement was King Philip's War – the violent response by New England Indian tribes in 1675–76 to the steady encroachment on their territory by white British colonists. Similarly, the context for Hugh Glass' (Leonardo DiCaprio) tale of survival in *The Revenant* is white encroachment on Native American land, appropriation of their resources, and atrocities committed against them excused by racist ideology. Barlow is the monstrous vampire antagonist of King's *'Salem's Lot*, but King – undercutting romanticized representations of the virtues of small-town life such as in Thornton Wilder's famous play *Our Town* (1938) – makes clear through the shifting focus on different members of the town of Jerusalem's Lot, Maine, that Barlow is in effect the materialization of the peevish and petty immorality already present in the town. And Warrant Officer Ripley must fight off the goo-dripping H. R. Giger-designed xenomorph in *Alien*, but the true villain of the film is capitalism, as reflected through "The Company," the Weyland-Yutani corporation that desires a living alien specimen and considers the crew of the spaceship *Nostromo* expendable in this quest. In keeping with literary romanticism in general – of which the Gothic is arguably a subset (on the debate over this point, see Hume) – Gothic works almost inevitably shade toward being allegories of human insufficiency as protagonists confront specific manifestations of broader cultural forces. Just which forces are at play and the extent to which they are confronted directly or obscured are what will vary from text to text – which now brings us to the American Gothic tradition.

Power and Prohibition: American Gothic Preoccupations

The basic underlying premise structuring this *Companion to the American Gothic* collection is that Gothic narratives give shape to culturally specific anxieties and tabooed desires, and that those anxieties and desires will always have to do with power and prohibition – what is forbidden to whom based on their subject positions within a particular social context. With this in mind, the American Gothic tradition arguably clusters around four interconnected primary loci, each with its particular boundaries: religion, geography, racial and sexual otherness, and rationality. While far from all-inclusive, anxieties and desires related to God, the devil, and the legacy of Puritanism; the frontier; racial otherness and sexual otherness; and the capacity of individuals to draw logical and accurate conclusions based on sensory data are structuring preoccupations of the American Gothic tradition (Figure 1).

As Faye Ringel (Chapter 1) discusses in her contribution to this volume, predating the development of the Gothic novel in the eighteenth century was the intensely Gothicized religious rhetoric of the North American Puritans, which offered striking portraits of apocalyptic end times, eternal damnation, and the snares that the devil lays for the unsuspecting and naïve. Puritan minister Michael Wigglesworth's bestselling poem *The Day of Doom or a Poetical Description of the Last Judgment* (1662), for example, offers the reader an extensive and lurid picture of the terror that awaits the unrepentant and unsaved on the day of the Last Judgment. Exemplifying the Gothic contest against overwhelming force, sinners stand no chance as "All kindreds wail: all hearts do fail: / Horror the world doth fill" (Wigglesworth 85–86). Jonathan Edwards' 1741 sermon, *Sinners in the Hands of an Angry God*, similarly has recourse to intensely Gothicized imagery in its representation of an omnipotent deity who detests sinners and dangles them over the flames of perdition "much as one holds a spider or some loathsome insect, over the fire" (Edwards). For his part, Minister Cotton Mather makes clear in his 1693 defense of his role in the Salem Witch Trials, *Wonders of the Invisible*

Introduction: The American Gothic

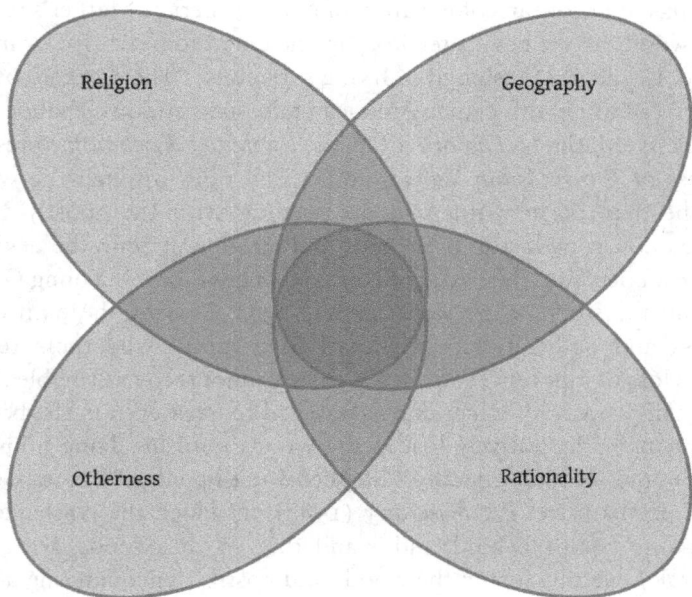

Figure 1 Characteristic American Gothic preoccupations

World, his belief that the Puritans are God's people settled in the devil's territories and that the devil, together with a "dreadful Knot of *Witches*," has worked to vex the New Englanders (Mather xiii). The successful 2015 film, *The Witch* (Robert Eggers), which focuses on accusations of witchcraft among seventeenth-century New England Puritans, shows that religious zealotry together with a fascination with the devil and witchcraft remain fertile veins to be mined by the American imagination.

Cotton Mather's description of New England as the *"Devils* Territories" (Mather xi) highlights the role of another central element of the American Gothic: American geography and particularly the role of the frontier. Addressed in this volume particularly by Elizabeth Jane Wall Hinds (Chapter 9), the American imagination arguably follows the contours of the country's topography, with an emphasis on the frontier as a liminal zone of contact between civilization and wilderness. "I just know I'm going to get lost in those woods again tonight" speaks the voice of murder victim Laura Palmer (Sheryl Lee) from beyond the grave on a cassette tape in episode 1 of David Lynch and Mark Frost's famous television series *Twin Peaks* (episode 1, "Traces to Nowhere," aired 12 April 1990); however, Gothic anxieties about getting lost in the woods – and encountering the supernatural creatures that live there – are anxieties that stretch back to the beginnings of European colonization of North America. Mather's reflections on the woods as the devil's territory is one taken to heart, for example, by Ichabod Crane in Washington Irving's famous "The Legend of Sleepy Hollow" (1820); in this classic American tale, superstitious Ichabod's favorite book is Mather's *History of New England Witchcraft* (presumably *Wonders of the Invisible World*) and, as he rides through the woods at night, he may or may not end up tangling with the ghostly Headless Horseman. Getting lost in the woods and meeting up with the devil is also both the anxiety and the desire of Nathaniel Hawthorne's Young Goodman Brown in the story of the same name (1835). Leaving the path of righteousness and dallying with the devil in a moral wilderness results in Brown's loss of innocence – from which he cannot recover. Unable to accept the human propensity to sin that is revealed to exist even in the best of us, Brown remains figuratively lost in the woods until his dying hour, which "was gloom" (Hawthorne 289). Stephen King updates "Young Goodman Brown" in his novel *Pet Sematary* (1983), in which the consequences of leaving one's faith behind and wandering in the woods are dire (see Magistrale). Getting lost in the woods and possibly encountering a witch is also the premise of Eduardo Sánchez and Daniel Myrick's *The Blair Witch Project* (1999; on the film, see Higley and Weinstock). The forest is where one walks with the devil, witches reside, and ghosts, demons, and other supernatural creatures roam. To go there is to leave civilization behind, to forsake faith and family, to flirt with danger, and to return changed – if one returns at all.

An important variant on the theme of the Gothicized American wilderness – particularly in the nineteenth century – is the sea tale. In works such as James Fenimore Cooper's *The Pilot: A Tale of the Sea* (1823), Edgar Allan Poe's *The Narrative of Arthur Gordon Pym* (1838), Richard Henry Dana, Jr.'s *Two Years Before the Mast* (1840), and most especially the novels of Herman Melville, the ocean replaces the forest as a kind of wilderness that alienates individuals from civilization and licenses barbarity as the protagonists literally and figuratively attempt to navigate a safe course through dangerous and turbulent waters. Whether getting lost in the woods or going to sea, however, leaving civilization behind and traversing the frontier in the American Gothic imagination imperils one's safety by putting one at the mercy of powerful forces ranging from natural threats such as panthers and waterfalls and whales to supernatural monsters including witches and the devil.

Demonstrating, however, how quickly anxieties concerning geography get mixed up with fantasies of race and racial difference, "at the heart of the American Gothic wilderness," writes Alan Lloyd-Smith, "is the savage Indian" (44). In her captivity narrative, Mary Rowlandson represents the

Introduction: The American Gothic

Indians as "hell hounds" in league with the devil (Rowlandson); Cotton Mather not only wrote an account of the Salem Witch Trials but, in *A Brief History of the Warr with the Indians in New-England* (1676), an account of King Philip's war, he characterizes the Indians as Godless, treacherous enemies. In Charles Brockden Brown's *Edgar Huntly*, "savages" are at war with civilized white settlers and Edgar, himself surprisingly adept at using a tomahawk as a weapon, dispatches several without a second thought. In James Fenimore Cooper's Leatherstocking Tales, including *The Last of the Mohicans* (1826), Indians are divided into good and bad based on their attitude toward Anglos, but all are supernaturalized as spirits of the forest able to hunt and track with preternatural adroitness. "There may be a devilish Indian behind every tree," thinks Goodman Brown to himself setting off on his unspecified "present evil purpose" in "Young Goodman Brown" – and then, making the connections between Indians, the forest, and the devil clear, he adds, "What if the devil himself should be at my very elbow!" (Hawthorne 277).

While the indigenous presence as forest spirits possibly in league with the devil remains present in later American Gothic works (see Bergland), the emphasis shifts in the nineteenth century and later to what Toni Morrison refers to in *Playing in the Dark: Whiteness and the Literary Imagination* as the Africanist presence in American history as Gothic works grapple with slavery, its legacy, and with deep-seated anxieties over racial mixing. Indeed, as suggested by several excellent studies on the American Gothic, including Teresa A. Goddu's *Gothic America: Narrative, History, and Nation* and Justin Edwards' *Gothic Passages: Racial Ambiguity and the American Gothic*, anxieties about race, white/black miscegenation, and the legacy of slavery may in fact function most immediately to differentiate the American Gothic from other Gothic traditions. Morrison attends to issues of race in relation to Poe's *The Narrative of Arthur Gordon Pym*, a novel that culminates in the discovery of a hither-to-unknown island populated by a tribe of black-skinned people who turn out to be "among the most barbarous, subtle, and bloodthirsty wretches that ever contaminated the face of the globe" (1150). As Ellen Weinauer develops in her contribution for this collection (Chapter 6), however, the issues of race, racism, and miscegenation are central Gothic elements not only of antebellum captivity and slave narratives and narratives explicitly addressing issues of race such as Harriet Beecher Stowe's *Uncle Tom's Cabin* (1852), but are at the heart of many of America's greatest literary works, including William Faulkner's *Absalom, Absalom!* (1936), Richard Wright's *Native Son* (1940), Ralph Ellison's *Invisible Man* (1947), and Toni Morrison's *Beloved* (1987).

In addition to issues of race and ethnicity, the American literary tradition has also used the Gothic mode as a means to reflect on anxiety, discrimination, and disempowerment related to other forms of social otherness including sexual difference, sexuality, and class. As addressed by Diane Hoeveler (Chapter 7) in her contribution to this volume, American women such as Edith Wharton, Charlotte Perkins Gilman, Shirley Jackson, and Joyce Carol Oates have used the Gothic to explore the terrors of marriage, the demands of motherhood, and the forms of exclusion suffered by women within a patriarchal culture. Ardel Haefele-Thomas (Chapter 8) considers here how American authors and playwrights such as Truman Capote and Tony Kushner have made use of Gothic conventions to foreground and critique sexual norms and the kinds of violence and exclusion visited upon those who do not identify with those expectations. And, as several of the chapters here make clear, issues of race, sex, and sexuality are inextricably interconnected with class – to be disempowered is often also to be either deprived of access to capital and/or dependent on others for support.

Finally, as Allan Lloyd-Smith observes, a significant "pressure" (4) on the development of the American Gothic has been anxieties about popular democracy and the Enlightenment principles upon which the founding of the American Republic rested. Can people govern themselves and make rational decisions based on logical evaluation of empirical data? Or, asks the American Gothic, are they instead prone to religious mania, driven by superstition, easily manipulated by confidence men, and compelled by irrational impulses into betraying not only themselves but the vision of the Founding Fathers? The suspicion, if not the final answer, of the American Gothic is of course the latter as American Gothic works repeatedly thematize the ways in which not only are human senses fallible and decision-making compromised by irrational and unconscious impulses, but that the premise of "all men are created equal" enshrined in the American *Constitution* was undercut from the start by institutionalized racism and sexism. As discussed above, in relation to human psychology, Brown, for example, demonstrated in *Edgar Huntly* the ways in which human beings are driven by unconscious forces. Henry James' *The Turn of the Screw* (1898) leaves unanswered the question of whether ghosts exist or whether the narrating governess is psychologically disturbed – a question reprised with certain twists in Shirley Jackson's *The Haunting of Hill House* (1959) and Stephen King's *The Shining* (1977). And questions about democracy in the "land of the free" are ones forcefully raised by American Gothic authors that highlight the inconsistency between vision and realization – between the rhetoric of liberty and the reality of slavery, sexism, bigotry, and discrimination of all stripes. In this way, American Gothic, according to Goddu, exposes the "cultural contradictions of national myth" (10).

This *Companion to the American Gothic* tracks the way that the Gothic developed in American literature and culture. It is divided into three broad parts: periods, identities and locations, and genre and media. The first attends to the development of the Gothic in relation to the generally accepted chronological developmental schema of American literature. Part II includes contributions that explore the American Gothic in relation to questions of identity and geography. The third part considers the American Gothic in connection with specific genres and media. Some occasional overlap of discussions of texts or authors is inevitable and serves to highlight not only the centrality of those texts and authors, but the interconnections among issues addressed in Gothic texts – the way discussions of geography shade into discussions of race, discussions of religion become questions about rationality, and so forth. Taken together, the inclusions offer broad coverage of the American Gothic tradition. They substantiate Fiedler's claims concerning the centrality of the Gothic to American literature and showcase the ways in which the Gothic, focused as it is on the transgression of cultural boundaries, inevitably focuses on the inequitable distribution of power. Despite its broad coverage, any companion such as this one will inevitably fall short of being comprehensive; the hope is that students and researchers can then utilize the contributors' insights to address additional texts and authors omitted from the present survey.

NOTE

1. For the purposes of this companion to the Gothic, the word "gothic" will be capitalized when it refers specifically to the genre or artistic movement; it will be left lowercase when it is used as a more general adjective.

WORKS CITED

Bergland, Renee L. *The National Uncanny: Indian Ghosts and American Subjects*. Hanover, NH: University Press of New England, 2000.
Botting, Fred. *Gothic*. London: Routledge, 1996.
Edwards, Justin D. *Gothic Passages: Racial Ambiguity and the American Gothic*. Iowa City: University of Iowa Press, 2003.
Fiedler, Leslie. *Love & Death in the American Novel*. 1960. New York: Anchor Books, 1992.
Goddu, Teresa A. *Gothic America: Narrative, History, and Nation*. New York: Columbia University Press, 1987.
Hawthorne, Nathaniel. "Young Goodman Brown." *Tales and Sketches*. New York: Library of America, 1982. 279–89.

Higley, Sarah and Jeffrey Andrew Weinstock, eds. *Nothing That Is: Millennial Cinema and the Blair Witch Controversies*. Detroit: Wayne State University Press, 2004.
Hume, Robert D. "Gothic Versus Romantic: A Revaluation of the Gothic Novel." *PMLA* 84.2 (March 1969): 282–90.
Lloyd-Smith, Alan. *American Gothic Fiction: An Introduction*. New York: Continuum, 2004.
Lovecraft, H. P. *Supernatural Horror in Literature*. 1927. New York: Dover Publications, Inc. 1973.
Magistrale, Tony. "Stephen King's *Pet Sematary*: Hawthorne's Woods Revisited." *The Gothic World of Stephen King: Landscape of Nightmares*. Bowling Green, OH: Bowling Green State University Popular Press, 1987. 126–34.
Mather, Cotton. *Wonders of the Invisible World. Observations as Well Historical as Theological, upon the Nature, the Number, and the Operations of the Devils (1993)*. 1693. Electronic Texts in American Studies. Paper 19. PDF. http://digitalcommons.unl.edu/etas/19.
Morrison, Toni. *Playing in the Dark: Whiteness and the Literary Imagination*. Cambridge, MA: Harvard University Press, 1992.
Morton, Timothy. *Hyperobjects: Philosophy and Ecology After the End of the World*. Minneapolis: University of Minnesota Press, 2013.
Poe, Edgar Allan. *The Narrative of Arthur Gordon Pym of Nantucket*. 1838. *Poetry and Tales*. New York: The Library of America, 1984. 1003–1182.
Wigglesworth, Michael. *The Day of Doom or a Poetical Description of the Last Judgment*. 1662. Electronic Text Center, University of Virginia Library. Dec., 1999. Web. 1 Aug., 2016.

PART I
Periods

I

FAYE RINGEL

Early American Gothic (Puritan and New Republic)

The United States of America was born in the Age of Reason, but, as the etchings of Spanish Romantic painter and printmaker Francisco Goya show, the Sleep of Reason can produce monsters. This chapter's title might seem at least partially anachronistic since colonization of the Americas predates use of the term "Gothic" by Horace Walpole in reference to *The Castle of Otranto* (1764), his horrific romance of the Middle Ages. However, American Gothic is inherently ahistoric: It "revives" a time and place that never existed. New World peoples did not share Europe's medieval period; Great Britain's colonies had no Inquisition (though New Spain did), nor other trappings of the first Gothic Revival – no decadent aristocracy, castles, dungeons, ruined abbeys.[1] But these trappings are but the outward show; there are other Gothic suits of woe. From the first contacts, explorers and conquistadores painted the New World landscape in the colors of the European imagination. They sought legends: Here would be found the Celtic Land of Youth, the Golden Cities of Cibola, the Amazons, the Lost Tribes of Israel. They reported sea monsters and mermaids. Later, the Puritans would impose their demonology upon the land and its inhabitants. These Puritan legacies and folk beliefs would stand in for European feudalism and the Black Legend of Catholic conspiracy in the later American Gothic imaginary.

The treatment by European settlers of the New World's inhabitants became one of America's Gothic secrets; African slavery was the other. Both can be seen as barbaric survivals, completely opposed to the Puritans' City on a Hill or the Enlightenment ideals that culminated in the *Declaration of Independence*. The foundations of American Gothic can thus be traced to Columbus' enslavement of the Arawak in 1492, to the first Africans sold in Jamestown in 1619, to the near-feudal conditions of South Carolina's Low Country, the colony of a colony, Barbados. These Gothic secrets, narratives, and histories are what John Clute calls "Taproot Texts" for later writers of the American Gothic, from Charles Brockden Brown to Toni Morrison.

Clute's term refers to literary works such as Classical epics, traditional ballads, Shakespeare plays such as *The Tempest* (1610-11), and so on composed before the rise in the eighteenth century of literary fantasy and the Gothic romance, which provided the supernatural elements that animated those works (921).

In America's Federal period, 1790–1820, coinciding with Britain's First Gothic Revival, citizens consumed British as well as American Gothic fiction, reenchanting the New World with European myth and fantasy. At the same time, writers were concerned with differentiating the new country from the old, while employing the language, themes, and techniques of English literature. Studying the origins of the Gothic in America means studying the foundation of a distinctly American literature, supporting Leslie Fiedler, whose *Love and Death in the American Novel* first declared in 1960 that all American literature was Gothic (142).

America's Dual Gothic Vision

According to Nathan Drake's "On Gothic Superstition" (1800), Gothic romances fulfilled the yearning for the sublime through "the awful ministration of the Spectre or the innocent gambols of the Fairy" (139). Readers of Gothic romances could find both horror and transcendence through medievalism.[2] This dual vision of an imaginary Middle Ages, at once Golden and Dark, may explain how the Gothic mode can be both conservative and revolutionary. Recreating the romance of the Middle Ages requires reinstating the hierarchy of the feudal system – it's difficult to have heroic knights or absolute tyrants in a democracy, difficult to imagine knights and "damozels" without barons and kings. Yet readers and writers of Gothic romance – from the first generation of the Republic to the present – may themselves have liberal politics. Critics agree that the popularity of Gothic fiction in the 1790s in England and America reflects anxieties raised by the French Revolution. Gothic fiction at once evokes real-world terrors, and reassures us that they are unreal.

Another dual vision emerges from the Puritans' attitude toward New England and to their "errand into the Wilderness": They saw Hell and the Garden of Eden, the Apocalypse and Utopia. American Gothic in the Colonial period can be simultaneously Utopian and dystopian. The Puritans who attempted to found an ideal commonwealth in New England saw its inevitable Fall and the end of the world – or at least the end of the narrator's own world. Writing in 1692, Cotton Mather sees his own generation as fallen from what he calls in *Wonders of the Invisible World* "a true *Utopia*" (12), that is, the "City on a Hill" to which John Winthrop in 1630 compared New England. Puritan hymns and poetry such as Michael Wigglesworth's popular *Day of Doom*

(1662) remind audiences of their inevitable fate. Wigglesworth's verse describes Hell in graphic detail, though he inquires, "But who can tell the plagues of hell,/ and torments exquisite?" (212.1–2).

This dual vision also characterizes the jeremiad, called by Puritans "the political sermon," delivered by ministers who functioned as leaders of Church and State. They preached that sinners will inevitably be punished, but God will bring prosperity to the elect in the new world, if only they repent, just as the Bible linked trial in the wilderness with a Promised Land. Sacvan Bercovitch defines the genre in *American Jeremiad*, showing its continuing influence on American literature and political thought. Increase Mather is the most famous preacher of jeremiads, including "The Day of Trouble is Near" (1674) and his sermon on King Philip's War (1676).[3] In the latter, he blames the war on the falling away of the present generation from the example of the founders: God has punished them using the Indians as his agent. Still, he comforts his listeners: "Jesus Christ ... hath taken possession of this Land for himself. Now, shall we think that Christ will suffer the Devil to drive him out of his possession again?" ("Earnest" 25). Samuel Hooker emphasizes material reward for increased piety in his jeremiad "Righteousness Rained from Heaven" (1677), predicting a Utopian prosperity for his Connecticut flock, while warning that Christ "may shortly come down" (28).

The jeremiad re-emerged as a literary form during the Great Awakening of the 1740s, most famously in the sermons of Jonathan Edwards. "Sinners in the Hands of an Angry God" (1741) provides the nightmare image of God who "abhors" the sinner, holding him over the Pit of Hell, "as one holds a Spider or some lothsom Insect over the Fire" (16). Edwards addresses his listeners intimately, reminding them of that slender, singed thread in God's hand, knowing no "Reason why you don't this very Moment drop down into Hell" (17).[4]

The passions unleashed by the Great Awakening led some New Englanders to commit suicide, while others participated in New London's 1743 Bonfire of the Vanities, where an extreme New Light preacher, James Davenport, condemned established churches, calling on his followers to burn books by the Mathers and other divines, along with their periwigs. Diarist Joshua Hempstead recorded the event after which Jonathan Edwards convinced Davenport of his errors in "the awful Affair of Books and Cloaths [sic]" (Hempstead, 379; Davenport 55).

Even as New England experienced a religious revival, European Enlightenment thinkers began to envision Britain's American colonies as a reasonable successor to an exhausted "Old World," a theory that became known as the "transfer of empire." Such a vision of America simultaneously Utopian and apocalyptic is found in Bishop Berkeley's "Verses on the

Prospect of Planting Arts and Learning in America," composed in 1726, though not published until 1752 (Bercovitch 113). These lines appear to be an optimistic paean to the New World, but may prefigure an apocalypse: "In happy climes, the seat of innocence, / Where nature guides and virtue rules, (9–10).... Westward the Course of Empire takes its Way; / The four first Acts already past, / A fifth shall close the Drama with the Day; / Time's noblest Offspring is the last" (21–24) (365–66). If America is "Time's noblest Offspring," the poem supports Manifest Destiny, with America bestriding the continent, supplanting Europe. But if America is the "last" empire that closes the drama of history, this is the Gothic vision of decadence and fall.

Timothy Dwight, minister, poet, and one of the self-styled "Hartford Wits," composed America's first lengthy Utopian poem, *Greenfield Hill* (1794), locating his ideal commonwealth in the present and future of his Fairfield, Connecticut, home. The seventh part, "The Vision," defines American exceptionalism: Guarded by the Atlantic from the decadence and wars of Old Europe, it is a bastion of democracy based on commerce: "Where man least vice, and highest virtue, knows; / Where the mind thrives; strong nerves th' invention string;/ And daring Enterprize uplifts his wing" (7.131–33). Yet despite this optimism, the poem reminds us of the new nation's Gothic past, drawing on narratives of Indian wars and captivities and praising those who massacred the "Pequods."

Traces of a different sort of Gothic medievalism may be found in the Southern colonies, whose settlers traced their ancestry (accurately or not) to the English aristocracy. Plantation owners in Maryland, Virginia, and South Carolina staged jousting tournaments in the eighteenth and nineteenth centuries – jousting in fact remains Maryland's state sport. The "First Families of Virginia" prized the legend of the sole American order of chivalry: The Knights of the Golden Horseshoe, whose exploits inspired Southern novelist William Carruthers. The cult of the "Virginia Cavalier" continues to this day.

America's Dark Gothic History: Witches, Apparitions, Indian Massacres

Of all the taproot texts from America's Colonial period, the Salem Witch Trials are the best known. A belief in and fear of witches was shared by many colonists, a clear example of the Gothic heritage brought from Europe. The panic and trials in Essex County, Massachusetts, in 1692–93 represented the largest witch hunt in the Colonies; its causes still generate scholarly debate. The Puritan fear of Satanic conspiracy emerges clearly from the transcripts of the Salem Witch Trials, with their accounts of women and men pledging their souls to Satan and inflicting harm on their neighbors. The accusations by the

Early American Gothic (Puritan and New Republic)

"afflicted girls" were proof, according to Cotton Mather, of *"an Horrible PLOT against the Country by WITCHCRAFT"* (*Wonders* 14). Though the exact number of those accused, tried, and condemned may never be known, more accurate records do exist for Colonial New England than for the much larger witch hunts of Britain and the Continent. Over thirty cases of witchcraft in Massachusetts and over twenty in Connecticut were recorded before 1692; more than 150 men and women were charged and jailed during the outbreaks that year in both states. Of the many accused of witchcraft, twenty were executed in Salem in 1692; at least fifteen were hanged prior to that time in Massachusetts and Connecticut. This eruption of the Gothic into everyday life has caused reverberations in literature and popular culture that can be felt to this day in Salem, which resembles a Gothic theme park.[5]

But what of the other colonies?

Virginia records several accusations of witchcraft, but no executions. The earliest case was tried at Jamestown in 1626, antedating the first witchcraft trials in Connecticut and Massachusetts (Horn 412). The Virginia colony's House of Burgesses, apparently not believers, dismissed lower court indictments, and no witch panic resulted. In a 1706 case, Virginia Beach residents accused Grace Sherwood, known as the Witch of Pungo. Amazingly, their victim survived the "water trial" in a pond today known as "Witch Duck Point," retained her property, and lived to old age.

New Hampshire had several Witch Trials, though no executions; Vermont and the future state of Maine, none. Rhode Island, founded by Roger Williams who had been expelled from the Massachusetts Bay Colony for his unorthodox approach to Calvinism, did not accept the narrative of Satanic pact and civil prosecution, so there were no Witch Trials in that colony – in fact, some of the accused from Massachusetts and Connecticut fled to Rhode Island. New York also provided refuge to some fleeing Salem; even before English control, Dutch governor Peter Stuyvesant rescued his sister-in-law, accused of witchcraft in Connecticut. As in the other middle colonies, civil courts and secular governments did not prosecute witchcraft cases. Court records of Maryland and Virginia show judgments for slander against those who called their neighbors "witch."

Many colonists who were not Puritans shared old-world beliefs in witchcraft, omens, and apparitions. Though after Salem no witches were executed, belief in their powers did not die, and folktales from Maine to Georgia tell of witches' curses, fortune-telling, and remedies for witchcraft such as silver bullets. WPA Federal Writers' Project workers collected similar stories in the Virginia mountains in the 1930s.

The seventeenth century saw the transition from the magical paradigm to the scientific method: Isaac Newton, pioneer of modern physics and mathematics, also practiced alchemy and studied other occult sciences.[6] In *Prospero's America*, Connecticut's state historian, Walter Woodward, details the connections between John Winthrop, Jr., whose father founded the Massachusetts Bay Colony, and alchemists in England and on the Continent. Winthrop eventually became Governor of the Connecticut colony. One of Winthrop's correspondents, described as America's first recognized scientist, George Starkey, also learned alchemical arts at Harvard, but left the colonies to work with the Royal Society's chemists (Newman xiii). These practitioners of "natural magic" inspired Hawthorne's depiction of Roger Chillingworth in *The Scarlet Letter* (1850) as well as the representation of twentieth-century horror author H. P. Lovecraft's necromancer Joseph Curwen in *The Case of Charles Dexter Ward* (1927), a Rhode Island secret history.

Fears of conspiracies, natural and preternatural, were manifested by Puritan settlers in ways other than the persecution of witches. Cotton Mather, in addition to participating in and chronicling the Salem Witch Trials, included tales of possession, apparitions, and other wonders in *Magnalia Christi Americana or, the Ecclesiastical History of New England* (1702), making him the New World's first writer of folkloric horror. He was an inveterate collector of monsters, in the original sense of the word – that is, beings that "show forth" or de*monstr*ate the power of God – or the Devil. Mather was a member of the Royal Society, founded in the 1660s: To them he communicated sightings of such "hopeful monsters" as a Triton, or Merman. There could be danger in these first-person accounts: After a description in *Magnalia Christi* of monstrous births occasioned by the Antinomian heresies of Anne Hutchinson, he notes that, "my study where I was writing, and the chamber where my wife was sitting, shook, as we thought, with an earthquake, by the space of half a quarter of an hour. We both perceived it, ... My wife said it was the devil that was displeased that we confer about this occasion" (2.520).

Cotton Mather's history includes apparitions, human and otherwise. He sees a clear indication of God's Providence in the New Haven Colony, which in the 1630s outfitted a ship to open trade with Britain. A few years later, many New Haven residents saw a vision of the ship sail through the clouds above the harbor and disappear into the sunset. This was assumed to be a representation of the ship's fate, for it was never seen again in life (Cotton Mather, *Magnalia Christi* 1: Chap. 6). This ghost ship and others sailing forever off Block Island and the Maine Coast were taproot texts for nineteenth-century poet John Greenleaf Whittier.

In the same year that witches were hanged in Salem, soldiers in the garrison at Cape Ann reported attacks by French Canadians or perhaps by devils in human shape, though no physical evidence of these "phantom leaguers" was ever found. Documented by Cotton Mather in *Magnalia Christi*, this episode reflects the extreme tension of that year, when the fate of the colony seemed uncertain. During a similarly tense period, the 1750s, with threats of French and Indian attack, the militia of Windham, Connecticut registered a similar false alarm. They stood to arms on the town green, but the attacking phantoms with their harrowing cries were identified the next morning as bullfrogs leaving a dried-up pond, and the incident passed into local history as the "Windham Frog-Fight."[7]

The native inhabitants of the New World were literally demonized by the settlers. The Puritan vision of Indians as devil-worshippers lasted into the eighteenth century. As Cotton Mather wrote in 1692, "New-Englanders are a People of God settled in those which were once the Devil's Territories" (*Wonders* 13). Resistance to conquest by such foes was seen in apocalyptic terms. Even the hard-headed Captain John Mason, narrating his victory in the Pequot wars, saw God's hand in his burning of their fort, "who laughed his Enemies and the Enemies of his People to Scorn, making them as a fiery Oven" (30).

Those who were captured during the Indian wars of the seventeenth century and survived were the subjects or authors of captivity narratives, taproot texts for later Frontier Gothic literature (on the Frontier Gothic, see Hinds [Chapter 9] in this volume). Like other providence tales, they demonstrate God's power through depiction of horrors and wonders. Mogen, Sanders, and Karpinski's *Frontier Gothic* collection defines that frontier broadly, subsuming the Puritans' fear of the American wilderness into a tradition of finding horror at the margins of civilization (20–21). According to David Mogen, "the original frontier narratives present the journey into the wilderness not as a quest but as a captivity, the ordeal of the first American heroes, usually female, struggling to keep the light of faith aglow in heathen darkness" (96). The most famous North American captive in Colonial times, Mary Rowlandson, relayed her experience during King Philip's War in her 1682 captivity narrative in terms familiar to readers of Gothic horror: describing the initial attack, "like a company of sheep torn by wolves, all of them stripped naked by a company of hell-hounds," and the next day, "Oh the roaring, and singing and dancing, and yelling of those black creatures in the night, which made the place a lively resemblance of hell" (The First Remove). Her narrative ends in redemption, and she returns from the wilderness transformed, appreciating God's providence.

Rowlandson attempted to assuage her captors, sewing for them in exchange for food; Hannah Dustan took the opposite tack. Cotton

Mather narrates her experience in *Magnalia Christi Americana* (Vol. 2). Taken captive along with the midwife who had attended her only a week earlier, her infant murdered, she and her nurse kill – and scalp – their Indian captors with their own hatchets. J. Hector St. John de Crèvecoeur sounds the same notes a century later as he gothicizes the Indians. *Letters From An American Farmer* (1782) includes letters from "a frontier man," who in Letter XII relates his fear both of the scalping-knife and midnight raids, as well as his fear that if he escapes the American Revolution by moving into the wilderness, "the imperceptible charm of Indian education, may seize my younger children, and give them such a propensity to that mode of life" (168). Living on the frontier, Crèvecoeur observes in Letter III, turns Europeans into Gothic villains, "a mongrel breed, half civilized, half savage" (42). Readers of these letters – or the captivity narratives – could view the Other with fascination mingled with horror.

Gothic Literature in the Federal Period

In the last decade of the eighteenth century, the French Revolution, the Napoleonic Wars, and the revolution in Haiti led to fears for the security of the new Republic, expressed in literature as fear of villainous conspirators, including the Illuminati, who still figure in conspiracy theories.[8] Gothic romances in Britain and in America condemned the excesses of the French Revolution and were nostalgic for the manners and morals of the Old Regime. One "Lady from Massachusetts," later identified as Sally S. B. K. Wood of the new state of Maine, placed a spunky American heroine in the clutches of a Revolutionary atheist and member of the Illuminati in *Julia, and the Illuminated Baron* (1800). Wood proudly proclaims in the Preface to another Gothic romance, *Dorval, or The Speculator* (1801), "The following pages are wholly American" and the characters drawn from life ("A Lady," *Dorval* v). The title villain disguises himself as an astrologer and fortune-teller to dupe the heroine (93); he also succeeds in financial speculations until his evil influence is unmasked. Wood's other novels of this period – *Amelia* (1802) and *Ferdinand and Elmira* (1804) – are melodramatic, but lack explicitly Gothic elements.

The new nation's fears may have inspired its first "horror boom," the best-selling "shilling shockers," short paperbacks containing the most exciting scenes of Gothic novels. During the first twenty years of the Republic, pundits, politicians, and clergy condemned the reading of these texts and of sentimental novels as leading to vice. Enos Hitchcock, in *Memoirs of the Bloomsgrove Family* (1790), an epistolary novel-polemic, decries "the dangerous tendency of bad books." He blames the corruption of young American women on "foreign writings and foreign manners" (2:186–87). Figures from booksellers and the catalogs of circulating libraries support these contentions: According to Donald Ringe, Gothics were the most popular printed imports of the 1790s (14). Bercovitch argues that the jeremiad took secular forms during this period, including the condemnation of Gothic novels: "the overthrow of imperial power ... set loose a libertarian spirit that terrified moderate and propertied democrats" and both the spirit and the anxieties can be found in their "tales of violated taboos (parricide, incest, idolatry)" (134). This displacement of anxiety at the ending of empire reminds us of today's popularity of zombie apocalypse tales coinciding with the end of the Cold War and the rise of terrorism.

Despite attempts at censorship, readers of all classes in the Federal period consumed Gothic fiction. In the preface to *The Algerine Captive* (1797), Royall Tyler, who wrote America's first produced play, *The Contrast* (1787), blames Gothic romances for corrupting the nation's literate peasantry. "Dolly the dairy maid and Jonathan, the hired man, threw aside the ballad of the cruel stepmother, over which they had so often wept in concert, and now amused themselves into so agreeable a terrour, with the haunted houses and hobgoblins of Mrs. Ratcliffe [sic] that they were both afraid to sleep alone" (1.viii–ix). Instead, Tyler offers his new version of the captivity narrative, drawn from the headlines of America's anti-terrorist actions against the Barbary Coast pirates.

One startling approach to creating Gothic terror in the New World was to import the Old World's castle along with dungeons, cruel aristocratic fathers, loyal *famuli*, simple peasants, conspiracies, and the dead hand of the past. *The Asylum: Or, Alonso and Melissa. An American Tale, Founded on Fact* was as popular upon its appearance in 1811 as it is obscure today. The apparent author was Isaac Mitchell, a journalist of Poughkeepsie, New York. In this novel, which blends the sentimental with the Gothic, a father parts the titular lovers by immuring his daughter in an abandoned castle on Long Island Sound near Branford, Connecticut. "The mansion was of real Gothic architecture, built of rude stone with battlements" (Mitchell 2.59). Within its walls, Melissa is tormented by frightening apparitions. Mitchell shows his affinity for Mrs. Radcliffe by explaining the events as the work of a gang of smugglers and thieves. A footnote warns readers that the castle had been destroyed in the Revolutionary War.

Charles Brockden Brown

The most famous figure to emerge from America's revolutionary-reactionary 1790s is Charles Brockden Brown, considered in his own time – and today – the new nation's first professional novelist (on Brown and the Frontier Gothic, see also Hinds [Chapter 9] in this volume). Weinstock argues that Brown in his four Gothic novels defined four subgenres that remain prominent in Gothic fiction, film, and criticism: Frontier, Urban, Psychological, and Female (6). More astonishing is that Brown created these subgenres in a two-year frenzy of writing and publishing: *Wieland* (1798); *Arthur Mervyn* (1799–1800); *Edgar Huntly* (1799); and *Ormond* (1799).[9] During this time he also published the first parts of *Alcuin*, a philosophical dialogue inspired by Mary Wollstonecraft's *Vindication of the Rights of Women*; Parts 3 and 4 were published posthumously (see Dunlap, *The Life*). The backstory of *Wieland*'s antagonist, *Memoirs of Carwin the Biloquist*, appeared in *The Literary Review*, which Brown edited from 1803–1805. Brown published two other novels and essays on literature, history, political philosophy, and other subjects.

Brown's Gothic novels can be seen as proto-science fiction, influenced like Mary Shelley (who read his work) by the philosophical novels of her father, William Godwin, and the feminism of her mother, Mary Wollstonecraft. Like Shelley's *Frankenstein* (1818), Brown's novels extrapolate from contemporary science – biloquism, mesmerism, and spontaneous combustion – and from political philosophy – republicanism, Utopianism, and apocalypticism. They respond to the anxieties and issues of their times. Brown dismisses the European Gothic in the Philadelphia *Weekly Magazine* that in 1798 serialized *Arthur Mervyn*: "Take an old castle ... provide the owls and bats ... among the ruins. ... Convey to this castle a young lady; ... after the lady has been dissolved to a jelly with her fears, let her be delivered by the man of her heart, and married – " ("Anti-Ghost"). Also in these issues are articles on sleepwalking, ventriloquism, and confidence men, which in Brown's novels replaced the Gothic medievalist clichés. Likewise in the Preface to *Edgar Huntly; or, Memoirs of a Sleepwalker*, Brown disdains "Puerile superstition and exploded manners; Gothic castles and chimeras," and declares that, "The incidents of Indian hostility, and the perils of the Western wilderness are far more suitable" for novels set in America (iii–iv). He delivers on these promises. This first novel in the lineage of American Frontier Gothic derives its horrors from Indian attacks and the caves and cataracts of Western Pennsylvania, site of popular captivity narratives more sensational than the New England accounts. Yet Brown, perhaps influenced by a Quaker upbringing, makes Huntly the true demon in the forest; while in a somnambulistic state, he enters the wilderness, kills and devours a panther (166–67) and, like Hannah Dustan, slaughters Indians with a "tom-hawk" (172–203).

Arthur Mervyn and *Ormond* are set in Philadelphia, inaugurating the genre of Urban Gothic. They deal with contemporary issues – confidence men, financial speculation, immigration, crime. The mean streets of these novels look ahead to the Philadelphia mysteries of George Lippard (see Bendixen [Chapter 2] in this volume), while the ambiguous investigator Arthur Mervyn prefigures the noir detective, the disillusioned dark knight. Urban Gothic combines the subversive, undermining received history and consensus reality, with the revanchist rejection of the Illuminati (*Ormond* 252) and revolutionary ideology.

Both novels are also plague narratives of the 1793 yellow fever epidemic, which coincided with the Reign of Terror in Paris, linking these fears. Philadelphia is transformed into a city of the dead. Smith-Rosenberg argues that yellow fever in *Arthur Mervyn* symbolizes the corruption of the body politic that is slavery; it turns white men's bodies yellow and mud-colored, they vomit black bile, and die. Yellow fever was blamed on trading ships and refugees from the island of Santo Domingo; ironically, the Atlantic slave trade had imported the disease-causing mosquito from Africa.

Although the term is more often applied to works *by* women, Brown pioneered the Female Gothic's critique of patriarchal power (on the Female Gothic, see Hoeveler [Chapter 7] in this volume). In *Alcuin*, the "Paradise of Women" section abolishes all distinction between the sexes and denounces the current form of marriage in favor of one based on equal friendship and separate dwellings. Similar ideas are expressed by Clara in *Wieland*, who treasures her single state, even when threatened by attackers, and by *Ormond*'s Constantia, who declares that, "Homely liberty was better than splendid servitude" (85). To narrate *Ormond*'s complex plot, Brown chooses a female voice: Sophia Westwyn, friend of Constantia (224), who like Clara, the narrator of *Wieland*, confronts a maniac in her bedroom. Unlike other Gothic heroines, Constantia kills her attempted rapist, Ormond, and is rescued by Sophia to live with her – Brown equally disdains the sentimental novel's marriage plot. This passionate friendship may be the first Gothic novel to explore female same-sex desire. Brown's unfinished *Memoirs of Stephen Calvert* (1799) deals even more explicitly with male homosexuality.

Brown's works have been called "explained Gothic," in the tradition of Mrs. Radcliffe. In *Wieland*, Brown's first novel, the title character murders his family, defending his actions in court as commanded by God. Yet, as Weinstock argues, some apparently supernatural elements are not explained. Readers never learn whether the deceitful ventriloquist Carwin produced the voice heard by Wieland, or if he was mad, or if it *was* God commanding him – like Abraham – to prove his faith (Weinstock 95). Unexplained also is the death, apparently by spontaneous combustion, of Wieland, Sr. (16–19). Epitomizing the Psychological Gothic subgenre, *Wieland*'s narrator Clara clings to sanity despite the manipulations of Carwin, but breaks down when her brother threatens to kill her. Contemporary Gothic novelist Patrick McGrath notes that from its origins in *Wieland*, American Gothic examines insanity through the voices of unreliable narrators (McGrath). *Edgar Huntly*, too, explores insanity through the Gothic trope of the double, using sleep-walking as a metaphor for the divided self. Hinds observes that, while Brown substitutes contemporary American settings for the castles and dungeons of European Gothic romance, his cities can be seen as "a wilderness disguised" (114). Whether in the alleys of Philadelphia or the caves and forests of the frontier, Brown's characters are astray. They, not their houses and landscapes, are haunted. Their minds are their own dungeons.

Gothic Drama and Conclusion

The Gothic mode – both explained and supernatural – was also popular in the early American theatre (on American Gothic theatre, see Nathans [Chapter 14] in this volume). Although Puritan restrictions hampered theatre's development in New England, the 1790s saw theatres from New York to Philadelphia to Richmond presenting imported and American productions of Gothic drama. William Dunlap, a close friend of Charles Brockden Brown, was a pioneer. In *A History of the American Theatre from Its Origins to 1832*, he describes the success of his translations from the German Romantic playwright Kotzebue's Gothic dramas. His own verse drama *Fountainville Abbey* (1795) was based on Ann Radcliffe's *The Romance of the Forest* (1791), set in seventeenth-century France. Several of his other plays reworked such Gothic tropes as endangered heroines, mad monks, and foreign villains.[10]

The shilling shockers and native Gothic romances of Wood and Mitchell seem to have been read to death, leaving little trace of their popularity save for condemnations by more respectable voices. Similarly, the Gothic dramas of Dunlap's contemporaries were ephemeral: Their scripts rarely saw print. The taproot texts of Colonial America's Gothic history and the novels of Charles Brockden Brown, however, inspired writers of the American Renaissance – James Fenimore Cooper, Washington Irving, Nathaniel Hawthorne, and Edgar Allan Poe (all addressed in the next chapter) – and shaped the future of the American Gothic mode.

Early American Gothic (Puritan and New Republic)

NOTES

1. The Gothic Revival was a British architectural movement that began in the eighteenth century and sought to revive medieval Gothic architecture as represented by cathedrals and castles. Aristocrats built country houses that included sham ruins, dungeons, and chapels.
2. For further information about these dark and light sides of Gothic medievalism, see Ringel, *New England's Gothic Literature* (10).
3. In King Philip's War (1675–76), a confederation of Algonkian and other tribes united by the Indian sachem Metacom, called by the English "King Philip," attacked colonists in Massachusetts and Rhode Island. After many casualties on both sides, combatant and noncombatant, the colonists and their Native allies captured and executed Philip. For further information see Lepore.
4. Susan Stinson's historical novel *Spider in a Tree* (2013) imagines Edwards' life and that of the slaves in his household.
5. Transcripts of the Witch Trials may be read on the Web or in Hall, *Witch-hunting*; historical analyses of the Colonial witch belief are found in Demos; Hall, *Worlds of Wonder*; and Karlsen. Rosenthal's *Salem Story* covers literature and popular culture. Schiff's is a recent accessible account.
6. While Newton never published his alchemical experiments, the original documents have been digitized by The Newton Project. Thorndike's *A History of Magic and Experimental Science* discusses the persistence of occult belief and practice throughout "The Scientific Revolution" of the seventeenth and eighteenth centuries.
7. The event is commemorated on the town seal and in huge statues of golden-eyed frogs guarding a bridge in the town. For further information, see Philips (207–10).
8. The Illuminati were real: A secret order founded in 1776, their name means "The Enlightened Ones." They sought reform and reason, but early Gothic fiction portrayed them as atheists and Satanists. They have achieved new prominence thanks to the Internet and the novels of Dan Brown.
9. Citations from the Bicentennial Edition; Brown appears in the Library of America. For analysis of Brown's Gothic novels see Christophersen; Kafer.
10. For further information on Gothic drama see Anthony; Fisher.

WORKS CITED

Anthony, M. Susan. *Gothic Plays and American Society 1794–1830*. Jefferson: McFarland, 2008.

Bercovitch, Sacvan. *The American Jeremiad. Studies in American Thought and Culture*. Madison: University of Wisconsin Press, 1978.

Berkeley, George. *The Works of George Berkeley...: Miscellaneous works, 1707–50*. Vol. 4. Ed. Alexander Campbell Fraser. Oxford: Clarendon Press, 1901.

Brown, Charles Brockden. *Alcuin: A Dialogue*. Ed. Lee R. Edwards. 1970. New York: Grossman, 1971.

["Anti-Ghost"]. "Receipt for a Modern Romance." *The Weekly Magazine*. 2.22 30 June 1798: 278. Web. 23 Oct. 2015.

Arthur Mervyn; or, Memoirs of the Year 1793. First and Second Parts. 1799–1800. Bicentennial Edition. Eds. Sydney J. Krause and S. W. Reid. Kent: Kent State University Press, 1980.
Edgar Huntly; or, Memoirs of a Sleepwalker. 1799. Bicentennial Edition. Eds. Sydney J. Krause and S. W. Reid. Kent: Kent State University Press, 1984.
Ormond; or, The Secret Witness. 1798. Bicentennial Edition. Eds. Sydney J. Krause and S. W. Reid. Kent: Kent State University Press, 1982.
Three Gothic Novels: Wieland, Arthur Mervyn, Edgar Huntly. Ed. Sydney J. Krause. New York: Library of America, 1998.
Wieland; or, The Transformation An American Tale and Memoirs of Carwin the Biloquist Bicentennial Edition. Eds. Sydney J. Krause and S. W. Reid. Kent: Kent State University Press, 1977.
Christophersen, Bill. *The Apparition in the Glass: Charles Brockden Brown's American Gothic*. Athens: University of Georgia Press, 1993.
Clute, John. "Taproot Texts." *The Encyclopedia of Fantasy*. Eds. John Clute and John Grant. New York: St. Martin's, 1997.
Davenport, James. "Confession and Retractions, 1744." *The Great Awakening: Documents on the Revival of Religion, 1740–1745*. Ed. Richard L. Bushman. Chapel Hill: University of North Carolina Press, 1989. 53–55.
de Crèvecoeur, J. Hector St. John. *Letters From An American Farmer*. Web. 23 Oct. 2015.
Demos, John Putnam. *Entertaining Satan: Witchcraft and the Culture of Early New England*. New York: Oxford University Press, 1982.
Drake, Nathan. "On Gothic Superstition." *Literary Hours: Sketches Critical and Narrative*. 2 vols. London: Sudbury, 1800. Web. 23 Oct. 2015.
Dunlap, William. *A History of the American Theatre from Its Origins to 1832*. Ed. Tice L. Miller. Urbana: University of Illinois Press, 2005.
The Life of Charles Brockden Brown: Together with Selections from the Rarest of His Printed Works, from His Letters and from His Manuscripts Before Unpublished. 1815. Web. 23 Oct. 2015.
Dwight, Timothy. *Greenfield Hill: A poem in seven parts. The prospect. The flourishing village. The burning of Fairfield. The destruction of the Pequods. The clergyman's advice to the villagers. The farmer's advice to the villagers. The Vision, or Prospect of the future happiness of America*. New York: Childs and Swaine, 1794. Web. 23 Oct. 2015.
Edwards, Jonathan. *Sinners in the Hands of an Angry God. A Sermon Preached at Enfield, July 8th, 1741*. Edinburgh, 1745. Web. 23 Oct. 2015.
Fiedler, Leslie. *Love and Death in the American Novel*. New York: Stein and Day, 1960.
Fisher, Benjamin Franklin. "Early American Gothic Drama." *A Companion to American Gothic*. Ed. Charles Crow. Chichester: Wiley Blackwell, 2014. 96–109.
Hall, David D., ed. *Witch-hunting in Seventeenth-Century New England: A Documentary History 1638–1692*. Boston: Northeastern University Press, 1991.
Hempstead, Joshua. *Diary of Joshua Hempstead of New London, Connecticut, covering a period of forty-seven years, from September 1711 to November, 1758*. New London: New London County Historical Society, 1901. Web. 23 Oct. 2015.

Hinds, Elizabeth Jane Wall. "Charles Brockden Brown and the Frontiers of Discourse." *Frontier Gothic: Terror and Wonder at the Frontier in American Literature.* Eds. David Mogen, Scott P. Sanders, and Joanne B. Karpinski. Rutherford, NJ: Fairleigh Dickinson University Press, 1993. 109–25.

Hitchcock, Enos. *Memoirs of the Bloomsgrove Family: In a series of Letters to a Respectable Citizen of Philadephia. Containing Sentiments on a Mode of Domestic Education, Suited to the Present State of Society, Government, and Manners in the United States of America: And on the Dignity and Importance of the Female Character.* 2 vols. Boston: Thomas and Andrews, 1790.

Hooker, Samuel. *Righteousness rained from heaven....* Cambridge, MA: Samuel Green, 1677.

Horn, James J. *Adapting to a New World: English Society in the Seventeenth-Century Chesapeake.* Chapel Hill: University of North Carolina Press, 1994.

Kafer, Peter. *Charles Brockden Brown's Revolution and the Birth of American Gothic.* Philadelphia: University of Pennsylvania Press, 2004.

Karlsen, Carol F. *The Devil in the Shape of a Woman: Witchcraft in Colonial New England.* New York: Vintage/Random House, 1989.

"Lady from Massachusetts" [Sally S.B.K. Wood]. *Julia, and the Illuminated Baron: A Novel Founded on Recent Facts which have Transpired in the Course of the Late Revolution of Moral Principles in France.* Portsmouth, NH: Oracle Press, 1800.

"A Lady" [Sally S.B.K. Wood]. *Dorval: Or, The Speculator. A Novel, Founded on Recent Facts.* Portsmouth, NH: Ledger Press, 1801. Web. 23 Oct. 2015.

Lepore, Jill. *The Name of War: King Philip's War and the Origins of American Identity.* New York: Knopf, 1998.

Mason, John. *Brief History of the Pequot War.* 1736. Bedford, MA: Applewood Books, n.d. Web. 23 Oct. 2015.

Mather, Cotton. *Magnalia Christi Americana or, the Ecclesiastical History of New England.* In Seven Books. 1702. Vol. 2. Hartford: Silas Andrus, 1820. Web. 23 Oct. 2015.

— *The Wonders of the Invisible World: Being an Account of the Tryals of Several Witches Lately Executed in New-England.* 1692. London: John Russell Smith, 1862.

Mather, Increase. *Remarkable Providences Illustrative of the Earlier Days of American Colonisation.* 1684. London: Reeves and Turner, 1890.

— *AN EARNEST EXHORTATION To the Inhabitants of New-England.* 1676. Electronic Texts in American Studies. Lincoln, NE: University of Nebraska—Lincoln. Web. 19 Oct. 2015.

McGrath, Patrick. "Method to the Madness." *New York Times Sunday Book Review* 28 June 2013. Web. 23 Oct. 2015.

Mitchell, Isaac. *The Asylum: Or, Alonso and Melissa. An American Tale, Founded on Fact,* 2 vols. Poughkeepsie, New York: Joseph Nelson, 1811.

Mogen, David. "Wilderness, Metamorphosis, and Millennium: Gothic Apocalypse from the Puritans to the Cyberpunks." *Frontier Gothic: Terror and Wonder at the Frontier in American Literature.* Eds. David Mogen, Scott P. Sanders, and Joanne B. Karpinski. Rutherford, NJ: Fairleigh Dickinson University Press, 1993. 94–107.

Newman, William R. *Gehennical Fire: The Lives of George Starkey, an American Alchemist in the Scientific Revolution*. 1994. Chicago: University of Chicago Press, 2003.
The Newton Project. Web. 23 Jan. 2016.
Rowlandson, Mary. *Narrative of the Captivity and Restoration of Mrs. Mary Rowlandson*. 1675. Project Gutenberg. Web. 23 Oct. 2015.
Philips, David. *Legendary Connecticut: Traditional Tales from the Nutmeg State*. Hartford, CT: Spoonwood Press, 1984.
Punter, David. "Gothic, Theory, Dream." *A Companion to American Gothic*. Ed. Charles Crow. Chichester: Wiley Blackwell, 2014. 16–28.
Ringe, Donald. *American Gothic: Imagination and Reason in Nineteenth-Century Fiction*. Lexington: University Press of Kentucky, 1982.
Ringel, Faye. *New England's Gothic Literature: History and Folklore of the Supernatural from the Seventeenth Through the Twentieth Centuries*. Studies in American Literature 6. Lewiston: Edwin Mellen Press, 1995.
Rosenthal, Bernard. *Salem Story: Reading the Witch Trials of 1692*. Cambridge: Cambridge University Press, 1993.
Schiff, Stacy. *The Witches: Salem, 1692*. Boston: Little, Brown, 2015.
Smith-Rosenberg, Carroll. "Black Gothic." *Possible Pasts: Becoming Colonial in Early America*. Ed. Robert Blair St. George. Ithaca: Cornell University Press, 2000. 243–69.
Stinson, Susan. *Spider in a Tree: A Novel*. Easthampton: Small Beer Press, 2013.
Thorndike, Lynn. *A History of Magic and Experimental Science*. 8 vols. New York: Columbia University Press, 1923–58.
Tyler, Royall. *The Algerine Captive: Or, The Life and Adventures of Doctor Updike Underhill, Six Years a Prisoner Among the Algerines*. Walpole, New Hampshire [sic]: David Carlisle, 1797. Web. 23 Oct. 2015.
Van Der Beets, Richard, ed. *Held Captive by Indians: Selected Narratives, 1642–1836*. Nashville: University of Tennessee Press, 1973.
Weinstock, Jeffrey Andrew. *Charles Brockden Brown*. Gothic Authors: Critical Revisions. Cardiff: University of Wales Press, 2011.
Wigglesworth, Michael. *The Day of Doom, Or, A Poetical Description of the Great and Last Judgment*. 1662. New York: American News, 1867. Web. 23 Oct. 2015.
Woodward, Walter. *Prospero's America: John Winthrop, Jr., Alchemy, and the Creation of New England Culture, 1606–1676*. Chapel Hill: University of North Carolina Press, 2010.

2

ALFRED BENDIXEN

Romanticism and the American Gothic

Throughout the early nineteenth century, aspiring American authors faced numerous obstacles, ranging from the lack of a healthy publishing industry to the unsuitability of most of the current literary models. Almost all the available literary traditions seemed mired in the trappings of the aristocratic cultures that had produced them. For example, the English novel usually relied on and upheld both conservative values and a fairly rigid class structure. Novels of manners often seemed to equate social class with moral virtue, and the central plot of the British *Bildungsroman* usually focused on orphans who had to find their true place within an established hierarchy, not on individuals struggling to create new identities in a fluid, rapidly growing nation. The formation of a distinctively American tradition of fiction making during the first half of the nineteenth century ultimately rested on the adaptation of literary Romanticism to the specific qualities of the American experience and on the creation of the short story by a number of writers, most notably Washington Irving, Edgar Allan Poe, and Nathaniel Hawthorne, all of whom turned to and transformed the Gothic into a flexible, multifaceted form capable of raising fundamental questions about the possibilities and limitations of national life. The Gothic mode liberated American authors of fiction, playing a decisive role in the emergence of an original and vital tradition of storytelling in the United States.[1]

***

The Gothic is crucial to the exploration of American identity that distinguishes Washington Irving's "Rip Van Winkle" (1819) and "The Legend of Sleepy Hollow" (1820). Although he is generally credited with establishing the short story as a new literary form, Irving does not have the commitment to a strong plot that is one of the defining features of the romantic tale and of most Gothic fiction. In his most significant statement of literary values, Irving reduced "story" to "a frame on which to stretch my materials" and declared his chief goals to be "the play of thought, and sentiment, and language; the weaving in character, lightly, yet expressively delineated; the familiar exhibition of scenes of common life; and the half-concealed vein of humor that is often playing through the whole" (Bendixen, "Emergence" 6).[2] Nothing in this description supports a commitment to the Gothic mode. Indeed, his two best stories are marked by meticulously rendered pictures of rural peace embedded in the natural landscape and embodied in the inhabitants of Old Dutch New York. These works evoke the sense of terror characteristic of the Gothic only briefly, but the treatment of supernatural elements in both tales highlights two specifically American markers of our national Gothic: a source of terror rooted in a loss of identity and a plunge into Nature as the liminal space of transformation.

Rip Van Winkle leaves his nagging wife to retreat into the woods where his encounter will leave him falling asleep for twenty years, during which the American Revolution takes place. He awakes to find himself older and his familiar world replaced by the new values of a bustling democracy. When he sees the young son he left years ago occupying his place as the town's ne'er-do-well, Rip experiences the central nightmare of the American Gothic, the loss of identity, proclaiming: "I'm not myself – I'm somebody else – that's me yonder – no – that's somebody else got into my shoes – I was myself last night, but I fell asleep on the mountain, and they've changed my gun, and everything's changed, and I'm changed, and I can't tell what's my name, or who I am!" (Irving 781). By immersing himself in a nature cut off from the dramatic events of history and politics, he has slept through time and lost his place in the world. In the simplest terms, Rip reflects the plight of Americans who emerged from their revolution aware that everything's changed but not fully aware of who they now were. Irving's genial mood certainly does not permit the kind of gloomy tragedy that will appear when Hawthorne rewrites Rip's journey into the woods in "Young Goodman Brown" (1835). In fact, Rip ultimately creates a new place for himself in the town by becoming a storyteller, which may be Irving's clearest affirmation of the power of storytelling to help Americans understand their new position in the world.

Irving's creation of the short story as an important American form is inextricably interwoven with both the idea of nature as a place where one can become lost and an understanding of the fragility of identity in the new democratic world. In aristocratic cultures, identity is generally fixed within the boundaries established by birth and social class. In the new democratic culture, identity was more fluid, offering individuals the chance to rise in the world and the danger of falling. The fundamental myth of the United States rests on the idea of opportunity and the possibility of self-made men and women, individuals who create new identities in a new world. The Gothic challenges that mythology by depicting an American landscape in which it is easy to become irrevocably lost. This relationship between the fragility of identity and the natural world shapes the Gothic foundations of other early tales, particularly William Austin's "Peter Rugg, the Missing Man" (1824), which Americanizes the Flying Dutchmen story by depicting a Boston man doomed to run his coach frantically all over the country in a desperate attempt to return home, and William Cullen Bryant's unjustly neglected "The Indian Spring" (1830), in which a stroll into the forest becomes a nightmare confrontation with native America. The fullest treatment of the fluidity and fragility of identity in the American Gothic is Robert Montgomery Bird's 1836 novel of metempsychosis, *Sheppard Lee*, which features a protagonist who occupies a series of different bodies.[3]

Irving's "The Legend of Sleepy Hollow" focuses on conflicting views of nature that point to larger social, economic, and political issues. Brom Bones and Ichabod Crane are not only rivals for the hand of Katrina Van Tassel but also representatives of opposing values. Brom Bones is part of the Dutch community whose possession of the land is marked by easy contentment and prosperity. In contrast, Crane's gluttonous lust manifests in his perverse desire to devour both Katrina and her family's farmlands, converting the natural world into cold hard cash to launch a series of real estate speculations that will uproot his family. The abundance of American natural resources has always evoked contradictory responses: The desire to appreciate the spectacular beauty of forests, rivers, and mountains is in conflict with a powerful commercial urge to cut down the woods, dam the rivers, and mine the mountains. At stake in the tale is the future identity of a nation that might be composed of either farmers or financial speculators. Irving speaks for the Hudson River Valley tradition that is hostile to rampant capitalism and finds the latter fundamentally unnatural.[4] In fact, in Irving's tale, the supernatural is nature's response to an unnatural act. On the most superficial level, Brom Bones defeats Crane by appealing to his superstitious nature and creating a headless horseman. On the most important level, Bones transforms a harmless item from nature – a pumpkin – into a weapon to arouse a fear of the supernatural in the man who wants to commit an unnatural act, a man whose lust for wealth is explicitly defined as a lecherous and gluttonous assault on the natural.

Irving's tale also reflects the alienating nature of an unhealthy capitalism that fragments and divides human beings. In his allusions to a headless horsemen and a man named Bones, Irving anticipates the moral failures of those who separate head from heart, mind from body as Crane does and as many of the protagonists in tales by Poe and Hawthorne do. The American Gothic is particularly concerned with the divided self, which is almost always defined as a division between head and heart or head and body and usually points to a fear of the physical body that leads to acts of repression or self-destruction. The loss of the head, the rational side, is also the underlying subject of Irving's "The Adventure of the German Student" (1824), set in the period of the French Revolution. The economic and political issues underlying "The Legend of Sleepy Hollow" are critiqued more bluntly and fiercely in Irving's "The Devil and Tom Walker" (1824), which portrays an American money lender who sells his soul to the devil, and in many of the stories collected in James Kirke Paulding's unjustly neglected *The Book of St. Nicholas* (1836). Poe and Hawthorne would give the short story a greater sense of architectural form and provide much grimmer, darker visions, but Irving led the way in establishing the Gothic possibilities of the American tale.

***

As theorist, poet, and master of the short story form, Edgar Allan Poe made the Gothic into a central part of American literary romanticism. He was the first to articulate a set of critical principles that emphasize a unity of effect in which every carefully crafted detail moves the reader to a specific response. His emphasis on literary craftsmanship requires works short enough to be read in a single sitting and long enough to allow for significant development of mood and theme. Poe's fiction relies on elaborate plotting, a heightened literary language in which mood is established as much by sound as by visual imagery, and the creation of imagined realms that usually exist outside of normal time and space, almost always leading to the depiction of symbolic and psychological landscapes. He was the first American author of fiction fully to grasp the potential of the unreliable narrator, and the first to transform masochism into an art form. His protagonists usually tell their own stories, but their tales almost always focus on acts of seemingly inexplicable violence, revealing a divided self engaged in various acts of repression and a desire for self-torture and self-destruction.

Poe sometimes explicitly notes his fascination with the spirit of perverseness, "this unfathomable longing of the soul *to vex itself*, – to offer violence to its own nature – to do wrong for wrong's sake only" ("The Black Cat" 599), but he refuses to locate this theme in the specific details of history or geography. In one famous statement he proclaimed, "that terror is not of Germany, but of the soul" ("Preface" 129). In fact, Poe is the only major nineteenth-century American author who did not root his fiction in the specific details of his own time and place. Scholars, however, have placed his tales of terror into appropriate cultural contexts, noting that his general avoidance of Southern settings and the slavery that defined this region may have freed him from the clumsy political defensiveness that marks much antebellum Southern prose, but not from the powerful impact of slavery.

For these critics, Poe's almost relentless obsession with absurd acts of violence and self-destruction stems from the evils of racism and slavery, which stifle honest expression, promote acts of violent cruelty, and must be sustained by forms of repression. Thus, Eric Savoy writes that "several of his most celebrated texts are rightly understood now as profound meditations upon the cultural significance of 'blackness' in the white American mind" ("Rise" 182), and goes on to describe "The Black Cat" (1843) as "an abolitionist allegory" (183).⁵ It is also possible to place Poe within a larger American context by emphasizing his rejection of the expansive freedom that marks much American writing. His major biographer, Kenneth Silverman, notes that while others "were creating a feeling of space and self-reliant freedom, he was creating in his many accounts of persons bricked up in walls, hidden under floorboards, or jammed in chimneys a mythology of enclosure, constriction, and victimization" (228). If the Gothic's chief purpose in a democratic culture is to warn that identity can be lost, then Poe's repeated treatment of the dissolution of the self in tales narrated by murderers and others who fail to understand the meaning of their own stories constitutes the most American version of that mode even when his stories seem to evade specific national identity.

The Gothic represents only one facet of this remarkable writer who also invented the detective story, which he called the tale of ratiocination, a genre that seems to oppose Gothic terror in its fundamental faith in the power of human reason as represented by the detective who perceives truth, discovers meaning, and restores order. He also wrote a significant number of satiric and comic pieces, including the immensely clever "How to Write a Blackwood's Article" and its accompanying sample, "A Predicament" (1838), which combine to provide a satiric survey of the conventions of the Gothic tale. Poe was also among the foremost literary critics of his day and a major poet, probably the most important writer of Gothic poetry in the English language. His current reputation rests largely on his short fiction, especially the Gothic tales and a handful of detective stories.

Critics tend to focus on one aspect of Poe's artistry, usually exploring the psychological dimensions of his work or the political and racial undercurrents. However, his best story, "The Fall of the House of Usher" (1839), illustrates the capacity of the Gothic to move in multiple directions, suggesting a wide number of interpretations that can exist in surprising harmony with each other. Our best guide to the complexity of this work may be in the theory of craftsmanship expressed most fully in "The Philosophy of Composition" (1846), the essay in which Poe offers a detailed analysis of his own craftsmanship in creating "The Raven" (1845). Although he begins by emphasizing the importance of the unity of effect which requires that each element contribute to the denouement, his concluding section notes that: "Two things are invariably required – first, some amount of complexity, or more properly adaptation; and, secondly, some amount of suggestiveness – some undercurrent, however indefinite of meaning. It is this latter, in especial, which imparts to a work of art so much of that richness (to borrow from colloquy a forcible term), which we are too fond of confounding with the ideal" ("Philosophy" 24). In Poe, and other masters of the literary Gothic, it may be the multiple forms of suggestiveness that matter the most. Thus, the analysis of "The Raven" begins by emphasizing his commitment to the "intense and pure elevation of *soul*" that comes from the contemplation of Beauty (16) and concludes with "the human thirst for self-torture" (24) of a speaker emblematic of *"Mournful and Never-ending Remembrance"* (25), indicating the remarkable way in which Poe covers the full range of human possibilities but usually ends in pain and grief.

The artistry and complexity of "The Fall of the House of Usher" emerges in its opening sentence, which is remarkable for its intricate syntax and almost excessive emphasis on the "O" and "R" sounds that Poe has defined as most effective means to evoke the mood of melancholy: "During the whole of a dull, dark, and soundless day in the autumn of the year, when the clouds hung oppressively low in the heavens, I had been passing alone, on horseback, through a singularly dreary tract of country; and at length found myself, as the shades of the evening drew on, within view of the melancholy House of Usher" (317). It is easy to get lost in the convoluted syntax that buries its subject alive in the middle of the sentence, keeping the pronoun, "I," separated from the most important verb, "found," and its object, "myself." Poe thus warns us that this is another story about the loss of identity, about a narrator who has actually failed to find himself and will be unable to understand the story he has just started to tell. For most scholars, the narrator is the true subject of the story, which is, among many other things, about the failed confrontation with a divided self, represented by Usher and his sister, Madeline. The name, Usher, easily breaks down into "us" and "her." The narrator's and Usher's burial of his sister while she is actually alive thus becomes a powerful symbol of repression, and her final emergence from the tomb becomes the literal embodiment of Freud's return of the repressed. Poe's form of suggestiveness requires that he never really specify the source of anxiety or injury, leaving it up to the reader to deduce the causes of division and sources of repression. Thus, readers can find Usher and Madeline representative of the conflict between Freudian Super-ego and Id, or the Death Wish and Pleasure Principle, or Nietzsche's Apollonian versus Dionysian, or the Male and Female, or the Rational and Irrational. For Poe, the male relationship with women can involve a fear of animal sexuality ("The Black Cat") or an inability to reconcile the ideal with the real ("Ligeia" [1838]), but these texts generally share a sense of unhealthy or perverted sexuality that is repressed in some form and an inability to come to terms with the reality of the physical body and the fact of mortality.

Various scholars have read "The Fall of the House of Usher" as an incest story, or a vampire tale, or a fable of the Fall of the South. Some of Poe's symbols, however, seem quite clear. The Usher house with its eye-like windows is clearly an image of the human mind, an idea reinforced when we are given Usher's poem, "The Haunted Palace," which speaks of "the monarch Thought's Dominion" ("Usher" 326). Nevertheless, Poe can also be quite tricky and a bit playful. He had himself published that poem, and his detailed physical description of Usher's face (321) appears to be Poe's self-portrait in words. Thus, he almost seems to invite the autobiographical readings of his work that have proliferated over the years. Yet, Usher's bizarre paintings, limited range in music, and poor health all suggest that Poe is playing with the idea of the artist in complicated ways, perhaps offering us an elaborate allegory of the misunderstood or failed artist who is unable to pull together the divergent parts of himself into a coherent, creative, and healthy self. The narrator's failure to understand the plight of his supposed friend is exemplified in the final scenes in which he tries to calm Usher's disturbed spirits by reading works selected at random while utterly failing to make the obvious connections between the works and their current experience. The narrator clearly and improperly believes that the function of reading is to put us to sleep, while Poe understood that literature's real role was to awaken us to heightened experiences. In the intimate connection between Usher and his house, Poe also seems to include a jab at the Transcendentalists who repeatedly insisted on a process of perception that united the individual and Nature, the me and the not-me. If Usher is a failed artist, as some believe, he may be a failed Transcendentalist whose perverted fusion with Nature creates only gloom and blight. As both Usher and his house collapse at the end of the tale, Poe leaves us alone with the narrator, who seems closed to almost all of the multiple possibilities embedded in the tale. For Poe, the great horror is the human failure to understand the world in front of us. (For more on Poe, see also Hinds [Chapter 9], Cassuto [Chapter 11], and Montgomery [Chapter 13] in this volume.)

***

Nathaniel Hawthorne shared Poe's commitment to endowing the Gothic with literary artistry through a complexity of characterization that included explorations of aberrational psychology and a carefully structured plot that often moves the reader into a nightmare world. Characters can become as lost in

Hawthorne's New England forests as they do in Poe's symbolic realms, but they remain rooted in the real facts of history and geography. The loss of identity and the dissolution of the self are central dangers in many of Hawthorne's tales but these ends are not inevitable as they are in most of Poe's Gothic masterpieces. While Poe's typical narrator is a man of questionable sanity trying desperately to explain the inexplicable or compelled to reenact and perpetuate in words the perverse deeds he has committed in life, Hawthorne's favorite narrator is a historian recounting a young man's initiation into a complex world that will destroy his innocence. Nevertheless, Hawthorne also offers the possibility that individuals can emerge from a spiritual crisis with the ability to create a new identity and embrace both the limitations and possibilities of life.

The Gothic played its greatest role in the early historical tales with which Hawthorne launched his literary career and the late romances that mark his final phase. The early works were originally intended to appear in book collections shaped either around New England history or American geography as reflected in the travels and tales of an itinerant storyteller. What this means is that grim stories of failed initiation, like "Young Goodman Brown," the most famous, most anthologized, and most representative of the early Gothic tales, were not intended to stand alone but to appear as part of a broader representation of the possibilities and dangers of the American experience. If we gather the other major historical narratives together, we have a combination of dark masochistic tales of self-destruction ("The Gentle Boy" [1837] and "Roger Malvin's Burial" [1846]), stories in which characters lose their innocence but end with the possibility of refashioning new identities ("My Kinsman, Major Molineux" [1832] and "The Maypole of Merry Mount" [1837]), and some remarkably patriotic affirmations of New England as the cradle of liberty ("The Gray Champion" [1837] and "Endicott and the Red Cross" [1837]). This collection thus represents and balances both the bright and dark moments of the American historical experience. Hawthorne clearly and repeatedly expressed his sense of New England history as shaped around a dialectical process in which the fundamental contradictions between the ideals of freedom and democracy and the realities of persecution and intolerance move forward from the Puritan beginnings to culminate in the American Revolution. In this process, the Gothic played a crucial role in delineating a perverse, masochistic capacity for self-destruction in the New England psyche and acknowledging a long history of repression and cruelty as central aspects of the American experience. Nathaniel Hawthorne transformed the Gothic mode by rooting it in the details of history and geography, moving it to a more honest exploration of the most treacherous parts of the American historical landscape. In this respect, he is the founder of an American school of historical fiction that relies heavily on the Gothic and culminates in such masterpieces as William Faulkner's *Absalom, Absalom!* (1936) and Toni Morrison's *Beloved* (1987).[6]

Hawthorne thus solidifies a clearly American Gothic tradition in which the great danger is becoming lost in the dark wilderness of a new world whose underlying mythology embraces renewal and rebirth but whose history includes repression and failure. The early tales generally follow a pattern that moves carefully and dramatically from historical fact into an increasingly symbolic and psychological landscape, and ultimately culminates in a nightmare vision that destroys or transforms the protagonist. Most of these short fictions focus on the initiation of young men; women are usually either cast as victims or moral touchstones whose main function is to reveal the moral strengths and weaknesses of the protagonist. In his later romances, however, Hawthorne moved to a richer and more complex Gothic structure that focused on multiple characters who respond in different ways to the revelation of some sin or crime that occurred in the past but whose consequences haunt the present. In these works, both male and female characters are much more fully developed than in his short stories and usually undergo significant change in response to Gothic trauma and their interactions with each other. Some characters clearly evolve and grow, sometimes gaining the capacity to express love and compassion, while others regress, sometimes becoming deformed into Gothic villains. The Gothic devices in the four major romances (*The Scarlet Letter* [1850], *The House of the Seven Gables* [1851], *The Blithedale Romance* [1852], and *The Marble Faun* [1860]) include family curses, mysterious wizards, and suggestions of the supernatural. All rely on the revelations of secrets, which either transform or destroy individual characters.

Although women characters are invariably placed in the role of Gothic victim, they tend to resist victimization in a variety of ways, sometimes even achieving a moral high ground through a significant symbolic rebirth. Part of the achievement of Hawthorne's romances stems from its development of a Gothic sensibility that encompasses female power and growth as central elements of a mythic framework rooted in the specific details of time and space. The underlying myth of initiation into experience grounds a complex plot that ultimately affirms a multiplicity of possible responses to the inevitable Gothic discovery of human frailty, which can lead to symbolic rebirth and redemption or to misery and self-destruction.

***

The Gothic mode also inspired two other authors who remain undervalued in our own time even though they once had significant reputations, Fitz-James O'Brien and Harriet Prescott Spofford. In her introduction to the two volume collection, *The Supernatural Tales of Fitz-James O'Brien*, Jessica Amanda Salmonson revealed that O'Brien was gay, a fact that invites us to read his fiction in the context of queer theory as well as the American Gothic's fundamental concern with the loss of identity. The central source of terror for gay Americans has been rooted in the need to hide or repress one's true identity, to remain invisible or risk losing one's place in society. O'Brien's most anthologized story, "What Was It?" (1859), relies on the presence of an invisible creature who remains both threatening and mysterious, a motif later used in such classics of the horror tradition as F. Marion Crawford's "The Upper Berth" (1894), Guy de Maupassant's "The Horla" (1887), and Ambrose Bierce's "The Damned Thing" (1893). In this tale, the invisible man in the bed clearly incarnates the fears and desires of gay men in a world that denies their reality, a theme further developed through the story's metaphors of entrapment and starvation as well as the final allusion to a freak show. The fear of sexuality and the concern with what remains unseen also emerge in the references to the microscope in "The Diamond Lens" (1858), one of the most important works of Gothic science fiction in the nineteenth century. O'Brien's finest story, "The Lost Room" (1858), focuses on a man who leaves his room to go into a garden where a mysterious stranger informs him that he lives in a "queer" house and does not really know its occupants. The protagonist returns to discover that the room that has been his home and defined his identity has been transformed and occupied by others who soon succeed in dispossessing him, leaving him lost and alone in the final paragraph. The fear evoked in "The Lost Room" is a queer variant of the characteristically American terror of losing one's place in the world.

The early fiction of Harriet Prescott Spofford represents both the final flowering of romantic prose in New England and the beginnings of a feminist Gothic tradition in the United States (see Hoeveler [Chapter 7] in this collection). Her lush prose and daring innovations invigorated the romantic tale in the late 1850s and the 1860s, culminating in a handful of masterpieces that enlarged the Gothic mode with a complex exploration of the female voice. In "Circumstance" (1860), a woman finds herself entrapped by a savage beast that has hauled her up into a tree and demands that she sing endlessly in order to survive; the story gave Emily Dickinson nightmares. "The Amber Gods" (1863) is a poetically rich, fully developed monologue detailing the triumphs and ultimate defeat of a passionate and sensuous woman who violates all of the expected norms of New England society as she speaks with a voice so powerfully self-obsessed that it seems to triumph over death. The narrator of "Her Story" (1872) is a woman in an asylum who details how her husband's infatuation with another woman led to her own madness and imprisonment in the hopes that telling her story will lead to her release. "The Moonstone Mass" (1868) is a feminist revision of the traditional adventure story that emphasizes the destructive absurdity of men who cut themselves off from women and reality. Spofford's best tales revise the trope of the Gothic female victim in significant ways, emphasizing the female voice as a potential source of power and liberation. Her stylistic flamboyance was a way of asserting her own place in the literary world and helped transform the Gothic into a form that could speak for and about women as well as men. She is a formative influence on a tradition of American female Gothic that includes Louisa May Alcott's *Behind a Mask* (1866), E.D.E.N. Southworth's *The Hidden Hand* (1859), and impressive short fiction by most of the major women writers of New England throughout the rest of the nineteenth century.[7]

***

The Gothic liberated and empowered American writers of fiction, providing them with a flexible and adaptable mode capable of asking a wide range of challenging questions about life in a fluid democratic society in which identity could be lost or destroyed as well as created and enabling them to establish a set of conventions that would form the foundation of our fiction. There are crucial Gothic moments in virtually every important novel produced by Americans throughout the nineteenth century, including Herman Melville's *Moby-Dick* (1851), Harriet Beecher Stowe's *Uncle Tom's Cabin* (1852), Mark Twain's *Adventures of Huckleberry Finn* (1884), and Henry James's *The Portrait of a Lady* (1881). In short, the Gothic is a crucial building block in the house of American fiction.

NOTES

1. The importance of the Gothic to the development of American fiction has been recognized by scholars since it became one of the central themes of Leslie Fielder's *Love and Death in the American Novel*. The most widely acclaimed recent studies of the Gothic are Teresa Goddu's *Gothic America* and the collection of essays edited by Martin and Savoy, *American Gothic*, which includes Eric Savoy's valuable summary of recent critical approaches: "The Face of the Tenant: A Theory of American Gothic" (3–19).
2. Irving's comments appear in his letters to Henry Brevoort and are quoted in Alfred Bendixen's "The Emergence and Development of the American Short Story," which provides a fuller account of Irving's impact on American fiction. The best study of Irving remains William Hedges's *Washington Irving*. Much of the best scholarship has been collected in Ralph M. Aderman's *Critical Essays on Washington Irving*.
3. The essays collected in *Frontier Gothic: Terror and Wonder at the Frontier in American Literature*, edited by Mogen, Sanders, and Karpinski, argue that the

danger of becoming lost in the American wilderness constitutes the chief theme of much Gothic writing in the United States. Renée Bergland's *The National Uncanny* provides the fullest exploration of the use of Native Americans as sources of terror.
4. For a discussion of this New York tradition, see Alfred Bendixen's chapter, "The Emergence of Romantic Traditions," in the *Cambridge History of American Poetry*, especially pages 178–79.
5. Poe also receives substantial treatment in Toni Morrison's *Playing in the Dark*. For a fuller account of Poe scholarship and of the ways of reading his fiction, especially "The Fall of the House of Usher," see Benjamin F. Fisher's "Poe and the American Short Story." My treatment of Poe is also deeply indebted to the work of Daniel Hoffman and G. R. Thompson cited below.
6. For a fuller sense of Hawthorne's view of history see Michael Bell's *Hawthorne and the Historical Romance of New England* and Alfred Bendixen's "Towards History and Beyond: Hawthorne and the American Short Story." Monika M. Elbert and Bridget M. Marshall's preface to the special issue of the *Nathaniel Hawthorne Review* on the Gothic contains an invaluable and thorough review of scholarship.
7. Alfred Bendixen's edition of Spofford's *The Amber Gods and Other Stories* is the main source for general information on Spofford. For an excellent account of Spofford and other American women writers of the supernatural, see Jeffrey Andrew Weinstock's *Scare Tactics*.

WORKS CITED

Aderman, Ralph M. ed. *Critical Essays on Washington Irving*. Boston: GK Hall, 1990.

Bell, Michael. *Hawthorne and the Historical Romance of New England*. Princeton: Princeton University Press, 1971.

Bendixen, Alfred. "The Emergence and Development of the American Short Story." *A Companion to the American Short Story*. Eds. Alfred Bendixen and James Nagel. Oxford: Wiley-Blackwell, 2010. 3–19.

"The Emergence of Romantic Traditions." *The Cambridge History of American Poetry*. Eds. Alfred Bendixen and Stephen Burt. New York: Cambridge University Press, 2015. 177–91.

"Introduction." *The Amber Gods and Other Stories* by Harriet Prescott Spofford. Ed. Alfred Bendixen. New Brunswick, NJ: Rutgers University Press, 1989. ix–xxxiv.

"Towards History and Beyond: Hawthorne and the American Short Story." *A Companion to the American Short Story*. Eds. Alfred Bendixen and James Nagel. Oxford: Wiley-Blackwell, 2010. 50–67.

Bergland, Renee L. *The National Uncanny: Indian Ghosts and American Subjects*. Hanover: University Press of New England, 2000.

Elbert, Monika M. and Bridget M. Marshall, "Haunted Hawthorne, Hawthorne's Hauntings." *The Nathaniel Hawthorne Review* 38.2 (Fall 2012).

Fiedler, Leslie A. *Love and Death in the American Novel*. 2nd edn. New York: Stein and Day, 1966.

Fisher, Benjamin F. "Poe and the American Short Story." *A Companion to the American Short Story*. Eds. Alfred Bendixen and James Nagel. Oxford: Wiley-Blackwell, 2010. 20–34.

Goddu, Teresa A. *Gothic America: Narrative, History, and Nation.* New York: Columbia University Press, 1987.
Hawthorne, Nathaniel. *Collected Novels.* New York: Library of America, 1982.
Hedges, William L. *Washington Irving: An American Study.* Baltimore: Johns Hopkins University Press, 1965.
Hoffman, Daniel. *Poe Poe Poe Poe Poe Poe Poe.* Garden City, New York: Doubleday, 1972.
Irving, Washington. "The Legend of Sleepy Hollow." *History, Tales, and Sketches.* New York: Library of America, 1983. 1058–88.
——— "Rip Van Winkle." *History, Tales, and Sketches.* New York: Library of America, 1983. 767–85.
Martin, Robert K. and Eric Savoy, eds. *American Gothic: New Interventions in a National Narrative.* Iowa City: University of Iowa Press, 1998.
Mogen, David, Scott P. Sanders, and Joanne B. Karpinski, eds. *Frontier Gothic: Terror and Wonder at the Frontier in American Literature.* Rutherford, NJ: Fairleigh Dickinson University Press, 1993.
Morrison, Toni. *Playing in the Dark: Whiteness and the Literary Imagination.* Cambridge, MA: Harvard University Press, 1992.
Poe, Edgar Allan. "The Black Cat." *Poetry and Tales.* New York: The Library of America, 1984. 597–606.
——— "The Fall of the House of Usher." *Poetry and Tales.* New York: The Library of America, 1984. 317–36.
——— "The Philosophy of Composition." *Essays and Reviews.* New York: The Library of America, 1984. 13–25.
——— "Preface to *Tales of the Grotesque and Arabesque.*" *Poetry and Tales* New York: The Library of America, 1984. 129–30.
Salmonson, Jessica Amanda, ed. *The Supernatural Tales of Fitz-James O'Brien.* 2 vols. Garden City, New York: Doubleday, 1988.
Savoy, Eric. "The Face of the Tenant: A Theory of American Gothic," *American Gothic: New Interventions in a National Narrative.* Eds. Robert K. Martin and Eric Savoy. Iowa City: University of Iowa Press, 1998. 3–19.
——— "The Rise of the American Gothic." *The Cambridge Companion to the Gothic.* Ed. Jerrold E. Hogle. New York: Cambridge University Press, 2002. 167–88.
Silverman, Kenneth. *Edgar A. Poe: Mournful and Never-ending Remembrance.* New York: HarperCollins, 1991.
Spofford, Harriet Prescott. *The Amber Gods and other Stories.* Ed. Alfred Bendixen. New Brunswick, NJ: Rutgers University Press, 1989.
Thompson, G. R. *Poe's Fiction: Romantic Irony in the Gothic Tales.* Madison: University of Wisconsin Press, 1973.
Weinstock, Jeffrey Andrew. *Scare Tactics: Supernatural Fiction by American Women.* New York: Fordham University Press, 2008.

3

MONIKA ELBERT
AND
WENDY RYDEN

American Gothic Realism and Naturalism

As American Realism and Naturalism supplanted Romanticism in the nineteenth century, the American Gothic mode morphed accordingly to represent a literary focus on the horrors of quotidian reality in the home and marketplace and the biological determinism that haunted the popular imagination. Although the high point of American Gothic might have been in the Romantic period of the American Renaissance, the period of American Realism was rife with possibilities for investigation into Gothic horror. While Romantic Gothic deals with the sins of the fathers in the shape of aristocratic privilege and their abuse of those disempowered or outcast on the periphery of society (Native Americans, African Americans, and the servant class), the Realist Gothic visits the commonplace in the shape of horrors inflicted upon factory workers, recent immigrants, city dwellers, rustic isolatoes, social climbers, wounded Civil War soldiers, disabled and diseased veterans, fallen or mad women, and African Americans newly emancipated but still disenfranchised. Such hauntings usually revolved around inequalities in wealth and the vagaries of the economic market. As Karl Marx described with vampiric metaphors in *Capital* (1867), parasitic business owners and industrialists exploited overworked laborers, but consumers mesmerized by mass-marketed material goods also contributed to a vampirism associated with commodity fetishism. As Realism's commonplace focus gave way to lurid determinism in the work of Naturalist authors, Gothic tropes and imagery disrupted even these most scientific attempts at rendering human behavior.

Adam Smith's notion of the "invisible hand" of capitalism and the free market, developed most fully in his *The Wealth of Nations* (1776), would more than a century later haunt the Realist landscape of authors such as Henry James, Mary W. Freeman, Sarah Orne Jewett, and Edith Wharton who exoticize Realism with ghost stories, ironically a popular genre during a period characterized by belief in social Darwinism, scientific truths, and an interest in the everyday and ordinary that would seem to exclude the supernatural or paranormal. In such Realist texts, unscrupulous or failed business deals can catalyze the appearance of a ghost, as in Edith Wharton's "Afterward" (1910) in which a spirit reveals the dark truth that underwrites a couple's leisured existence. In some Realist plots, attempts to deny the powers of the Romantic imagination through an emphasis on logical certainty result in the appearance of an apparition as a Gothic backlash against positivist tyranny. The novel *Characteristics* (1910) by S. Weir Mitchell (proponent of the infamous "rest cure" for depression and hysteria attacked by Charlotte Perkins Gilman in "The Yellow Wallpaper" [1892]) captures the contradictions of Gothic Realism in Mitchell's depiction of Owen North, a physician caught between the scientific realm and a desire for a life beyond the body. North's near death experience during the Civil War causes him to question doctors and the discourse of science as he develops an interest in the supernatural.

Despite the zeitgeist of scientism at century's end, interest in the paranormal was high, and indeed the two contradictory threads reconciled themselves via the impulse to study and catalogue ghostly and other supernatural phenomena as subjects of scientific investigation. The American Society for Psychical Research was founded in America in 1885 and included American philosopher and psychologist William James on its charter. The documentation of ghostly encounters appears to have influenced his brother Henry James's novella, *The Turn of the Screw* (1898), as he describes his dilemma in composing the narrative within a Realist tradition that sought to free itself of sensationalism and sentimentality. James bemoans the strictures of the "new type" of ghost story that is a "mere modern 'psychical' case, washed clean of all queerness as by exposure to a flowing laboratory tap" (226). In order to compose his Gothic tale he had "simply to renounce" the "copious psychical record of cases of apparitions" (230).

In abandoning fidelity to the "psychical case," Henry James produced a narrative structure renowned for its profound ambiguity in point of view, inspiring much debate as to whether the governess's ghosts exist or are merely the hallucinations of a frightened and marginalized servant. James' tale positions itself at the crossroads of Realism and the Gothic, toggling between the sensationalism of the supernatural and the modern psychology that finds the irrational a fit subject of methodical study. He further probes class and sexuality through Gothic convention by placing an unspeakable secret at the heart of the tale. What transgression, the reader is left to wonder, could cause the expulsion of Miles from boarding school? What horrors so great that they remain unnameable? Like the infinite reflections of two facing mirrors, James' use of Gothic here reveals only to reconceal, creating an "epistemological puzzle" (Crow 74).

James' take on haunting makes a decidedly modernist turn in "The Beast in the Jungle" (1903), in which the effete protagonist, Marcher, feels the existential abyss of failed romanticism, as he vainly and somewhat perversely awaits a robust tragic fate only finally to discover that the tragedy is missed opportunity for human connection and his own narcissistic alienation. James uses the same Gothic device of the embedded secret to propel the action. Replete with romantic Gothic imagery that functions almost ironically to mock Marcher, the psychological haunting of this text becomes more metaphysical as he prostrates himself on his friend May's grave. As with *The Turn of the Screw*, the hint of repressed sexual difference hovers over the story to the point that Marcher sees himself in uncanny disconnection from himself and others, which James describes through grotesque mask imagery: "What it had come to was that he wore a mask painted with the social simper, out of the eye-holes of which there looked eyes of an expression not in the least matching the other features" (487).

Certain late nineteenth-century writers (e.g., Charlotte Perkins Gilman, Charles W. Chesnutt) gothicize in order to explore social causes such as women's independence/suffrage and African American rights. Although the age of the True Woman began to give way to the age of the New Woman in the 1890s, Charlotte Perkins Gilman, in both "The Yellow Wallpaper" and her sociological treatise *The Home* (1903), gothicizes the domestic space to show its nefarious effects. Mitchell's rest cure, which Gilman endured, seemed merely an extension of the typical banal existence of the lonely and isolated middle-class or upper middle-class woman. The first-person protagonist in "The Yellow Wallpaper" is an Everywoman who, denied any creative activity or fulfilling work outside the home, goes mad. In *The Home*, Gilman describes with Gothic imagery a claustrophobic, suffocating atmosphere of fetishized commodities: "There is ... a repulsive horror, in the mass of freakish ornament on walls, floors, chairs, and tables, on specially contrived articles of furniture, on her own body and the helpless bodies of her little ones, which marks the unhealthy riot of expression of the overfed, and underworked lady of the house" (220). Gilman saw the feminine addiction to commodities as particularly debilitating since it enslaved not just the woman but also the husband, forced to provide for extravagant material desires. Indeed, in many Realist texts, the seductive material object looms large. Just as Marx's view of the vampiric relationship between labor and capital is inherently Gothic, so too is his concept of the commodity fetish that posits an object inhabited by the spectral presence of an invisible producer.

The stultifying domestic realm of the home becomes a favorite haunted location for Mary Wilkins Freeman, Sarah Orne Jewett, Harriet Spofford, Elizabeth Stuart Phelps Ward, Henry James, and Edith Wharton (see also

Jeffrey Andrew Weinstock on the use of Gothic as a political or empowering device used by women writers). In Mary Wilkins Freeman's ghost stories, domesticity and maternity are embroiled in uncanny hauntings that reveal troubled gender roles for the protagonists. In "The Lost Ghost" (1903), Mrs. Bird, a widowed kindly woman who epitomizes True Woman selflessness but has not fulfilled her role of childbearing, is haunted by a dead child abandoned by a profligate mother. Similarly, in "The Wind in the Rose-bush" (1903), a spinster, Rebecca Flint, who "unconsciously" holds her shawl in a canvas bag on her left hip "as if it had been a child" (4), feels compelled to search for and adopt her niece, Agnes, the daughter of her deceased sister who has fallen victim to an uncaring stepmother. Trapped in her role of caretaker, Rebecca is a victim of her own good nature as she succumbs to "fatigue and nervous strain" and is "not able to move from her bed" with a "species of low fever induced by anxiety and fatigue" (36). Maternal neglect transforms into the opposite extreme in Freeman's "Luella Miller" (1902), in which the protagonist, in an effort to resist the domestic roles of teacher or wife/mother, stays the eternal child, devouring vampire-like all who would try to subdue her. Luella is described in Gothic (as distinct from Romantic sentimental) child imagery as a spoiled baby, "a baby with scissors in its hand cuttin' everybody without knowin' what it was doin'" (97). Following the deaths of Luella and the narrator, the story ends with the Gothic convention of the burning house that cleanses the town, exorcising the haunting that has imperiled it.

The setting of Dunnet Landing in Sarah Orne Jewett's *The Country of the Pointed Firs* (1896) is a veritable ghost town in which the dead and the living are both haunted and haunting. Mrs. Todd tells the story of Poor Joanna as if she were still alive, even though Joanna died, isolated on an island after being jilted. The frame narrator, who makes pilgrimage to the island, concludes that "there is a place remote and islanded, and given to endless regret or secret happiness; we are each the uncompanioned hermit and recluse of an hour or a day" (65). The supernatural and natural converge in Dunnet Landing, with characters unaware this is a ghost town, themselves sequestered and perhaps as good as dead. Captain Littlepage, who enjoys funerals, tells a fantastic story about ghostlike figures he met on a polar expedition, in the "Waiting Place." Another seafaring character, the widowed Mr. Tilley, is lashed to his wife's memory by her prized items of home décor, such as china and tea sets, which he morbidly maintains and fetishizes.

Dunnet Landing is a ghost town of old or widowed sailors, relics of the largely defunct maritime trade. The town is blighted too by the former slave trade and illicit global commerce, as evoked in the separately published tale "The Foreigner" (1900). The xenophobic town rejects Captain Tolland's

French wife, whom he rescued during a journey to the West Indies – a trip that was most likely part of the timber-sugar trade between the two regions and an evocation of the industry's slavery-tainted origins (Walsh 310). After her husband's death, the exotic Catholic widow who bears the stigma of the Creole is ostracized further for the impropriety of her music and dancing. Upon the widow's death, witnessed by Mrs. Todd, the ghost of the French mother comes to fetch her daughter and, in a matrifocal act that reverses the earlier masculinist rescue by Captain Tolland, saves her from her friendless existence in life. Mrs. Todd inherits the widow Tolland's home, although the house tragically burns down as a consequence of the actions of Mrs. Todd's avaricious uncle who is obsessed with the belief that gold is hidden in the home. Mrs. Todd, it seems, is haunted by the story of widow Tolland. Indeed, as with other tales that Mrs. Todd narrates, the characters appear locked in a past relived through retelling to an auditor who, as the outsider and frame narrator of the stories, identifies with and captures the isolation of the town.

The search for ill-gotten gold witnessed in "The Foreigner" becomes a motif in various Jewett ghost stories that hinge upon a material fetish or commodity culture (also a notable element of Naturalist texts like Frank Norris' *McTeague* [1899]). In "In Dark New England Days" (1890), two hard-working old-maid sisters rejoice over their prospective inheritance. Captain Knowles leaves a chest of foreign money and exotic goods plundered from China and India, but the rival Captain Enoch Holt robs the sisters of the treasure, as proved by supernatural means. Both seafaring men plundered other cultures: by rumor, Captain Knowles' wealth "'t was n't no honest gains; most on 't was prize-money o' slave ships, an' all kinds o' devil's gold was mixed in" (38). Hannah Knowles, surmising Enoch Holt's theft of their legacy, curses Enoch Holt and his family when, at trial, she curses "the right hand" of all the Holts who follow. The curse comes to fruition: One Holt loses his right hand in a frontier battle, and Captain Enoch loses his right arm.

Harriet Spofford's "The Amber Gods" (1863) brings together the Gothic themes of ill-gotten wealth – in this case, the slave trade and exploitation of the "Asian imp" servant – and the middle-class woman's dangerous lassitude attacked by Gilman. Georgione, or Yone, the protagonist, a predecessor to the New Woman type, resists conventional domestic traditions but exhibits an egocentric and atavistic sense of self (cf. Freeman's "Luella Miller"). She is heir to a set of cursed amber beads belonging to the servant whom the family patriarch had imported into the household like one of his exotic home ornaments. The servant, who proves unsatisfactory, is returned, but, in a plot twist, becomes the attendant of an Italian mistress, who then becomes the beloved wife of the American patriarch's son. The union produces the seductive and self-absorbed Yone, whose rupture of domestic codes aligns her with the Asian servant still serving the family in Italy. After Yone's Italian mother dies during a trip to the Caribbean, the amber beads, having been blessed by the Pope and thus a symbol of Gothic (Catholic) patriarchal power, are cursed by the servant with the edict they never be returned to America. Ultimately, the beads return to Yone in America who, in claiming them, curses herself. The curse plays out in the form of a punishment of Yone's sensuality, as she has seduced her cousin's beau only ultimately to be rejected by him for her violation of the traditional feminine role. Yone lies in bed dying, and in grim Dickinsonian fashion, announces, "I must have died at ten minutes past one" (83).

The ornaments characteristic of consumer culture become haunted for Gothic women writers who represent the feminine imagination through domestic interior landscapes that both inspire and madden the captive female protagonist, as iconically shown in Gilman's "The Yellow Wallpaper" (1892; see also Dara Downey on Gothic domestic objects). In Madeline Yale Wynne's enigmatic tale "The Little Room" (1895), wallpaper and other domestic commodities become even more ambiguously associated with women's repression and liberation vis-à-vis the masculine world as two spinster sisters appear to manipulate the other characters' perceptions in a "gaslight" plot regarding the existence of a room in their old New England house. The "little room," with such domestic trappings as ladies magazines, a sea shell, and pretty flowered wallpaper, mysteriously presents itself as either a magical haven of domestic delight, or as a mere china closet devoid of wonder and containing only the banal imprisoning elements of the feminine household. The latter reality is perhaps inflicted on the female characters who have exchanged the virginal free state of their imagination for the servitude of marriage and accompanying social obligations metonymically represented in gilt-edged china dishes. As with Jewett's "The Foreigner," the colonial past intrudes on the domestic sphere – in this case through a textile gift of India chintz from a sea captain who courted one of the spinster sisters. The crones' tyrannical power over material reality and the irreconcilable existence of the two opposing domestic spaces are resolved in good Gothic fashion: The house burns down.

In addition to the cursed commodity, the horrors of displaced workers certainly loom large in Gothic Naturalist and Realist texts and are depicted in such works as Rebecca Harding Davis' early Realist story, "Life in the Iron Mills" (1861) and Herman Melville's "The Paradise of Bachelors and The Tartarus of Maids" (1855). But with its astonishing number of casualties, the Civil War became a foundational source of horror that haunted the American imagination and the texts of Gothic writers. The Union rent asunder is depicted through the image of a broken home. Elizabeth Stuart Phelps, whose immensely popular novel, *The Gates Ajar* (1868), shows an afterlife in which those lost in the Civil War are united with loved ones, and Ambrose Bierce, whose own Civil War experience as a soldier informed his writing, work within a Gothic framework of ghostly soldiers to renew a sense of nation-(re)building through a call, not to arms, but to the domestic hearth. Ghostly troops point to the home, women's sphere, as the place for recovery and healing, and mourning women reanimate the dead through parlor mementoes and memories of the lost. What one critic has said of Bierce is true of Phelps: "[The Civil War] was a soul-shattering experience that required an exorcism" (Thomsen 7). Both Bierce and Phelps move toward the otherworldly to make sense of battlefield carnage, and it is the domestic parlor that brings a semblance of normalcy back to the Gothic revenant, although the juxtaposition between domestic space and bloody battlefields ultimately makes the home that much more *unheimlich* and the war experience that much more grotesque.

Bierce's most famous Civil War ghost stories include "The Affair at Coulter's Notch" (1889) and "An Occurrence at Owl Creek Bridge" (1890), both of which expose the ghastly demise of the family and the shocking effect on the returning or dying soldier. Perhaps his most allegorical yet sentimental ghost story is "Chickamauga" (1889), which recounts a deaf mute six-year-old child imitating his military father by playing soldier in the forest. Upon realizing he is lost, however, the boy "cries for his mother, weeping, stumbling" (317). An approaching army of Union soldiers in "the haunted landscape" who "crept like babies" has been firing upon the child's house, now engulfed in flames. The child discovers his dead mother in a most horrible manner: "The greater part of the forehead was torn away, and from the jagged hole the brain protruded, overflowing the temple, a frothy mass of gray, crowned with clusters of crimson bubbles – the work of a shell" (318). The maternal image offers no solace to the boy or hope to the nation of soldiers. Not just a sacrificial victim, she is an inversion of the sentimental maternal figure, an object of horror, indicating the profundity of the psychic and cultural rupture that has occurred in this motherless universe. The child shrieks – "something between the chattering of an ape and the gobbling of a turkey – a startling, soulless, unholy sound, the language of a devil" (318).

The devastation of the Civil War was graphically captured by Matthew Brady through the emerging art of photography, as he depicted a battlefield on which corpses were blatantly and promiscuously strewn. Jacob Riis would later use the same medium to reveal the horrors of the work world and the pain of newly arriving immigrants in his photojournalistic *How the Other Half Lives* (1890). Stephen Crane's, "In the Depths of a Coal Mine," a journalistic piece written for *McClure's Magazine* in August, 1894 that Crane felt had been unduly "whitewashed" through editorial deletion, conveys the Gothic horrors of the mine nonetheless: "the infernal dins" (122) and "an inscrutable darkness, a soundless place of tangible loneliness" (123); his work here is comparable to Norris' ghostly depiction of the poverty-stricken worker in "A Deal in Wheat" (1902), wherein the machinations of a spectral Chicago Board of Trade deprive the working class of livelihood and humanity. Jack London also depicted ghostly survivors populating the streets of working-class London in his *The People of the Abyss* (1903), based on his own journalistic observations of life in the East End.

Charlotte Perkins Gilman, as a journalist and creative writer in her journal *The Forerunner* (1909–1916), was critical of exploitive voyeuristic journalism, as she understood the appeal of mass catastrophes and sensationalist images that haunted the onlooker. In two of her stories, she targets the world of yellow journalism. In "The Giant Wistaria" (1891), a journalist wants to discover the mystery of a haunted house he is vacationing in with his wife and two other couples, as he sees the potential popular appeal to the masses of a lurid discovery concerning a dead woman and her baby and a conjectural account of a punishing father. In "The Rocking-Chair" (1893), two journalist friends are mesmerized by a beautiful ghost who invites them into her lodgings. Both men seem too rational to be in love with a ghost, but the one bedazzled journalist, perhaps looking for a salacious story, is seduced to his peril. As with the scientific study of paranormal phenomena, research and documentation in an age of positivism found themselves enmeshed in the bizarre, fantastic, and grotesque, and journalism itself takes on a Gothic tenor. This generative contradiction at the intersection of Realism and the Gothic mode would continue into Naturalism as attempts to render dark truths objectively erupt into Gothic expression.

Naturalist Gothic writers, like Ambrose Bierce, Stephen Crane, Frank Norris, and Jack London appalled at the bestial and atavistic qualities embodied in soldiers, workers, and hunters struggling in a social Darwinian/Spencerian environment or dehumanized by a mechanistic world, employed grotesque Gothic imagery to expose what appears as an essentially unaware, animalistic human nature bent on inevitable devolution. William Dean Howells, the great champion of Realism, envisioned a literary emphasis on ordinary life as anti-Romantic and redemptive, but Naturalists such as Dreiser, Norris, and Crane saw the everyday as a kind of pornography, in which humans manifest their depraved essence dictated by a fundamental biology warped through circumstance. While anti-Romantic, such depictions ironically tap into the same Gothic sensationalism of Romanticism, an aesthetic vision about which Norris was unapologetic in "A Plea for Romantic Fiction" (1901), the essay in which he charges that Realist obsession with the mundane, such as that espoused by Howells, makes for dull literature, "the drama of a broken teacup" (215). By contrast, in Norris' *McTeague*, an ordinary dentist becomes a murdering beast in his banal descent from middle-class aspirations. The vicissitudes of market capitalism symbolized in his wife Trina's randomly bestowed, unearned lottery winnings, the catalyst for McTeague's fall, coupled with the modern bureaucracy that deprives the uncredentialed McTeague of his practice, awaken the murderous beast in the man, who kills his wife and ultimately his best friend. The final nihilistic, Gothic image, McTeague in the Death Valley landscape chained to a cadaver, is a less than subtle reminder of the trapped, caged condition of the human animal whose aspirations to control nature are continually foiled.

Stephen Crane's work reveals a similar fascination with decay, such as his focus on Civil War corpses in *The Red Badge of Courage* (1895). Crane, too, relies on animal imagery to identify the perceived human tendency toward atavistic degeneration (see Monnet). His perhaps most overtly Gothic work, "The Monster" (1898), is a fascinating ontological exploration of racialization and disability in a small Progressive Era town. Exceeding a critique of middle-class hypocrisy, "The Monster" plumbs "a general anxiety about the nature of human identity permeating late Victorian and Edwardian culture, an anxiety generated by scientific theories of degeneration and the abhuman" (Michaud 81), as Crane juxtaposes the African American horse groomer Henry with the middle-class white Dr. Trescott, who becomes the groom's caretaker after Henry nobly sacrifices himself to rescue the doctor's son from a house fire. Henry's resultant "monstrous" physical and mental condition challenges the community's commonplace notions of human normality characterized by suburban lawn care and tea parties. The parody of the courtship ritual performed by the monstrous Henry becomes grotesque as the same words and actions of the dandy Henry before the accident that marked him as suave and desirable are now uncannily repeated by the damaged Henry and are seen by his fiancée and the reader as hideous caricature. Relying on the Gothic to mine this slippage in definitions of human normality, Crane also imbricates post-Reconstruction conceptions of race and implicitly questions the essence of racial distinctions that rely on the color line, for after Henry's accident, the stigma of disability becomes a more powerful modifier and eclipses his racial identity altogether, as he becomes a phantom that the townspeople vainly try to hide and remove from public view.

The construction of the color line is a subject richly explored in American Realism and its Naturalist offshoots, notably by Charles W. Chesnutt. Perhaps in many ways a Howellsian Realist as described above, Chesnutt sometimes moves into the arena of Naturalist determinism even as he complicates the stability of racial categorization. He, along with such writers as Kate Chopin and Pauline Elizabeth Hopkins, expresses through the Gothic the contradiction of American progress and racism. Chesnutt's incorporations of "local color" in such stories as the Julius tales, found in his collection *The Conjure Woman* (1899), for example, which feature old plantation stories with supernatural motifs, have been lauded as sophisticated moral challenges to narratives of progress under deceptively simple guises of entertaining regionalism. In such stories, the horrors of the nation's past haunt the present and mar hopes for a modern future free of slavery's burden. Such a scenario epitomizes the Gothic relationship of the present to the past as it erupts in inconvenient ways to reveal "what is hidden, unspoken, deliberately forgotten, in the lives of individuals and of cultures" (Crow, *Companion* 2). Gothic elements of the repressed are featured in other stories such as "The Sheriff's Children" (1899), where the sheriff and the reader discover the existence of an African American descendant in addition to the sheriff's acknowledged white child. The disparity in treatment of the two offspring and the tragedy that ensues as a result of that inequity exemplify the lingering reality of America's racial failure and its inescapable effects on the nation's moral character.

The theme of passing present in Chesnutt's work resonates with the Gothic's emphasis on repression and Naturalism's concern with biology and destiny. "The Wife of his Youth" (1899), a seemingly quaint tale about moral choice, becomes an allegory for atavism explored through Gothic imagery, in which the dark-skinned slave wife left behind by light-skinned Mr. Ryder uncannily resurfaces from the past to make stubborn claim on him as he prepares to embrace a future in which she is forgotten and erased. This fear of atavism and its devastating social consequences appears in a more literal sense in Kate Chopin's "Desiree's Baby" (1893). The birth of a dark-skinned offspring suggests to a wealthy Creole that his wife's heritage is dubious only for him to discover, after her tragic suicide, that he in fact is the carrier of the suspected genetic contamination.

This fear of biological latency lurking within established identity is the subject of Pauline Elizabeth Hopkins' short mystery "Talma Gordon" (1900), which similarly steeps its tragedy in a husband's discovery of his wife's impure bloodline after the birth of a dark-skinned child. This causes Mr. Gordon to disinherit the other children born by this wife who have in effect been passing unbeknownst to them. Hopkins consciously drapes her story in Gothic conventions of old mansions and fallen aristocracy, connecting the stain from the past with biologically determined race. As is typical of the genre, the secret must be revealed in order to out the racist, hypocritical characters as well as identify the victims of racism's arbitrary oppression. But Hopkins adds an optimistic twist that locates the past's evil in Mr. Gordon's shady connection to the exploitive East India Company. Rather than a condemned heroine, as demanded by the tragic mulatta plot, Hopkins' victim marries the doctor who is the narrator of the frame tale. His surprise revelation of this at the story's end makes an interesting counterpoint to Chesnutt's Mr. Ryder's more ambiguous unveiling of his former wife and also suggests a possibility where, through intermarriage, America might transcend the injustices of the imperialism it was embarking upon.

As Modernism emerged from the Gilded Age, literary concerns with economic and social inequalities were subsumed by a focus on the solipsism of the entrapped self. Edith Wharton's trajectory as a writer epitomizes this movement and spans the period from Realism to Modernism in her Gothic stories. Earlier Gothic tales such as Wharton's "Afterward" (1910) and "The Triumph of Night" (1914) feature swindles and bad business deals that haunt the Gothic protagonists, much as Howells' Silas Lapham is haunted by his victim in *The Rise of Silas Lapham* (1885). In other Wharton stories, marital strife begets Gothic marriages such as in "The Lady's Maid's Bell" (1902), "Kerfol" (1916), and "Bewitched" (1925). But in her later stories, horror manifests itself in existential dread, such as in "The Looking Glass" (1936), in which the protagonist, stripped of family, servants, and friends, finds herself deluded by false spirits, or in the posthumously published "All Souls" (1937), which perhaps reflects Wharton's own increasing fears of mortality. This shift in emphasis from the spectral economy to the monstrosities of the mind is exhibited in works such as Twain's "Mysterious Stranger" (1916) or L. Frank Baum's *The Wonderful Wizard of Oz* (1900). Oz's witches, monsters, and too real wizard, who loses the power to manipulate the economy, seem effete in the face of the terror of a dispossessed girl unmoored and perhaps forever lost in the world of her imagination. The destabilization of society's strictures becomes even more terrifying than its mechanistic determinism and the prison of the human mind perhaps more frightening than any external structure that haunted the Gothic texts of Realist and Naturalist writers.

WORKS CITED

Bierce, Ambrose. "Chickamauga." *The Complete Short Stories of Ambrose Bierce*. Compiled by Ernest Jerome Hopkins. Foreword by Cathy N. Davidson. Lincoln: University of Nebraska Press, 1970. 313–18.

Chesnutt, Charles. W. "The Sheriff's Children." *Chesnuttarchive.org*. Web. 1 Aug. 2016.

"The Wife of His Youth." *Chesnutt: Stories, Novels, and Essays*. Ed. Werner Sollors. New York: Library of America, 2002. 101–12.

Chopin, Kate. "Desiree's Baby." *The Norton Anthology of American Literature, 1865–1914. Vol. C.* Eds. Nina Baym and Robert S. Levine. New York: Norton, 2012. 551–57.
Crane, Stephen. "In the Depths of a Coal Mine, 1894." *A Documentary Reader: The Gilded Age and Progressive Era.* Eds. William A. Link and Susannah J. Link. Malden, MA: Wiley-Blackwell, 2012. 120–24.
— "The Monster." *Crane: Prose and Poetry.* Ed. J. C. Levenson. New York: First Library of America, 1996. 389–448.
Crow, Charles. *American Gothic.* Cardiff: University of Wales Press, 2009.
Downey, Dara. *American Women's Ghost Stories in the Gilded Age.* New York: Palgrave Macmillan, 2014.
Freeman, Mary E. Wilkins. "Luella Miller." *The Wind in the Rose-Bush and Other Stories of the Supernatural.* Ed. and Afterword Alfred Bendixen. Chicago: Academy Chicago Publishers, 1986. 75–106.
— "The Wind in the Rose-bush." *The Wind in the Rose-Bush and Other Stories of the Supernatural.* Ed. and Afterword Alfred Bendixen. Chicago: Academy Chicago Publishers, 1986. 3–40.
Gilman, Charlotte Perkins. *Herland, The Yellow Wall-Paper, and Selected Writings.* Ed. Denise Knight. New York: Penguin, 1999.
— *The Home: Its Works and Influence.* 1903. Intro. Michael S. Kimmel. New York: Rowman and Littlefield, 2002.
Hopkins, Pauline E. "Talma Gordon." Spartanburg, SC: Hornpipe Vintage Publications. Web. 1 Aug. 2016.
James, Henry. "The Beast in the Jungle." *The Norton Anthology of American Literature, 1865–1914. Vol. C.* Eds. Nina Baym and Robert S. Levine. New York: Norton, 2012. 477–506.
— "Henry James's Preface to the 1908 Edition." *The Turn of the Screw.* 3rd edn. Ed. Peter G. Beidler. New York: Bedford/St. Martin's, 2010. 225–32.
Jewett, Sarah Orne. "In Dark New England Days." *Lady Ferry and Other Uncanny People.* Ed. Jessica Amanda Salmonson. Ashcroft: Ash-Tree Press, 1998. 26–41.
— *The Country of the Pointed Firs and Other Stories.* Ed. Alison Easton. New York: Penguin, 1985.
— "The Landscape Chamber." *Lady Ferry and Other Uncanny People.* Ed. Jessica Amanda Salmonson. Ashcroft: Ash-Tree Press, 1998. 74–88.
Michaud, Marilyn. *Republicanism and the American Gothic.* Cardiff: University of Wales, 2009.
Mitchell, S. Weir. *Characteristics.* New York: Century, 1910.
Monnet, Agnieszka Soltysik. "'His face ceased instantly to be a face': Gothicism in Stephen Crane." *Haunting Realities: Naturalist Gothic and American Realism.* Eds. Monika Elbert and Wendy Ryden. Tuscaloosa: University of Alabama Press, 2017. 90–102.
Norris, Frank. "A Plea for Romantic Fiction." *The Responsibilities of the Novelist and Other Literary Essays.* London: Grant Richards, 1903. 211–20. Openlibrary.org. 3/1/2015. Web.
— *McTeague.* New York: Signet, 1964.
Phelps, Elizabeth Stuart. *The Gates Ajar.* (1868). In *Three Spiritualist Novels.* Intro. Nina Baym. Urbana: University of Illinois Press, 2000.
Riis, Jacob A. *How the Other Half Lives.* 1890. New York: Penguin, 1997.

Spofford, Harriet Prescott. *"The Amber Gods" and Other Stories*. Ed. Alfred Bendixen. New Brunswick, NJ: Rutgers University Press, 1989. 37–83.

Thomsen, Brian M. Introduction to *The Civil War Writings of Ambrose Bierce*. Ed. Brian Thomsen. New York: Tom Doherty Associates, 2002.

Walsh, Rebecca. "Sugar, Sex, and Empire: Sarah Orne Jewett's 'The Foreigner' and the Spanish-American War." *A Concise Companion to American Studies*. Ed. John Carlos Rowe. Chichester: Wiley-Blackwell, 2010. 303–19.

Weinstock, Jeffrey Andrew. *Scare Tactics: Supernatural Fiction of American Women*. New York: Fordham University Press, 2008.

Wharton, Edith. *The Ghost Stories of Edith Wharton*. New York: Charles Scribner's Sons, 1973.

4

JOHN PAUL RIQUELME

Modernist American Gothic

The Convergence of Gothic and Modernism

Literary modernism seems at first glance far removed from Gothic writing. Writers who were identified retrospectively as literary modernists were considered avant-garde because their challenging works seemed intended for an elite audience. The Gothic, by contrast, has typically been considered part of popular culture, meant for readers, sophisticated or not, in search of a thrill and escape. But, in fact, key literary modernists on both sides of the Atlantic produced important works that belong to the Gothic tradition and to literary modernism. Modernist American Gothic is part of transatlantic modernism. It has international affiliations, but it also exhibits recognizably American dimensions, at times in its settings and narrative events, at times in the history that informs those settings and events, and at times in its resemblance to works by antecedent and contemporary American writers. America's history of race relations is often a significant element in modernist American Gothic, while it typically is not in Irish or English modernist Gothic. The reader is always important in Gothic writing, which is oriented toward making a striking impact. In modernist American Gothic, reader engagement is often at issue as part of the challenging of boundaries that occurs not only within the narratives but also because of them as an effect of their delivery to the audience. Direct implication of the reader is considerably less evident in modernist Gothic produced by writers with roots in English-speaking countries on the other side of the Atlantic. Joseph Conrad, for example, does not address the reader directly in *Heart of Darkness* (1899), but T. S. Eliot, who was influenced by Conrad, does in *The Waste Land* (1922).

Broadly speaking, modernism involves a culturally critical reaction against Victorian and earlier nineteenth-century attitudes and literary forms, central among them realism in fiction. It reacts against the culturally dominant belief in progress, which conceives history as linear and always improving, and the belief in reason as dominant in the human makeup. It questions the assumption that a person's identity is stable and singular. In fiction, the narratives associated with it tend to be fragmented and nonlinear, often without determinate closure. The language is often highly stylized and tends to draw attention to itself, whereas the language of realism tends to be self-effacing. These and other features provided a basis for a crossover between modernism and Gothic, which also tends to be highly stylized, to swerve from realism, to be temporally strange, and to present characters who are not stable psychological presences. Gothic narratives in the eighteenth century often involved the incarceration of a character in a castle in a plot that is structurally a journey into a dark situation involving an enigmatic space or landscape from which escape seems unlikely because a villain is behaving monstrously. Later Gothic narratives frequently retain that kind of structure without a literally ruined castle as the threatening space; for example, in *Heart of Darkness*, there are movements into literally and figuratively dark spaces of living, thinking, and behavior. That kind of narrative structure occurs as well in modernist American Gothic writing – for example in Djuna Barnes' *Nightwood* (1937), Truman Capote's *Other Voices, Other Rooms*, and Ralph Ellison's *Invisible Man* (1952), in which questions arise concerning the central character's ability to turn the situations to advantage in the endings, which tend to be enigmatic or open to opposing readings.

Literary modernism is sometimes treated in narrow terms as a fifty-year period of intense literary experimentation on both sides of the Atlantic, from 1895 until WWII, but those dates are too limiting to do justice to the several waves of modernist writing that occurred from 1890 until well after WWII. An early wave that made it clear that something decidedly post-nineteenth century had developed included such major figures as Conrad, who was Polish but became a British citizen, James Joyce, who was Irish but spent his adult life in Europe, Virginia Woolf, who was English, and Eliot, an American who became a British citizen at age 39. Writing in English but with roots in various countries, these writers had international audiences. As a consequence, American modernist Gothic needs to be understood in transatlantic and international contexts as well as national ones. Two key figures of Gothic modernism that I discuss below, Eliot and Barnes, were expatriates during the 1920s and 30s (Eliot for much longer), but their roots and their audiences on the American side of the Atlantic make them part of American literature. They share in Oscar Wilde, who was Irish, a common Gothic modernist forebear.

Frequently, there are dark threads in literary modernism. All the writers whom I have named participate significantly, though in varying degrees, in the disturbing literary discourse of modernity that we call the Gothic, a discourse that changed markedly after the French Revolution – a kind of explosion of society. It changed again during the nineteenth century in response to questions about what it means to be human that arose because of evolutionary thinking about race, the increasing contact of white Europeans and white Americans with non-European people, and, in America, issues regarding slavery. The Civil War and its aftermath play a large role in some prominent American modernist Gothic narratives, but for understandable reasons, not in English writing of the same period, in which WWI and its aftermath are often significant.

Despite national differences, the convergence of modernism and Gothic on both sides of the Atlantic involves challenges to hierarchical thinking and behavior, specifically to attitudes relying on clear boundaries that support exclusionary practices. Hierarchies of value and power separate one type of human being from others (based on gender, race, ethnicity, class, and other considerations) in ways that distinguish people and groups as better and worse, or, in an extreme version, good and evil. This kind of contrast informs representations in Gothic narratives that both call up the hierarchy and question it regarding what constitutes the fully human and valuable. Other contrasts separating animals and machines from the human often mimic and evoke hierarchical social thinking that considers some people or groups to be less human, or even nonhuman, and, as a consequence, expendable, as if they were animals or mere instruments. The significant place of such hierarchical thinking in modern history during the modernist period, with horrific events (such as the genocide attempted by the Nazis against the Jews during WWII) underlines the importance, as well as the historical and moral relevance, of its prominence in modernist literature. As we shall see, modernist Gothic frequently challenges prejudicial thinking by means of contradictions, ambivalences, and the coexistence of opposites that blur boundaries and make the maintaining of hierarchies difficult.

A significant part of the modernity of modernist American Gothic is its attention to violence in Western culture, whether literal violence in which people are injured and blood is shed or the figurative violence that frequently accompanies the differential treatment of individuals and groups within society because of hierarchies of power. One of the most highly regarded American modernists who wrote Gothic narratives, William Faulkner, commented memorably on the pervasive dread of violence in the modern world. In his speech accepting the 1949 Nobel Prize in Literature, Faulkner remarks on our situation: "Our tragedy today is a general and universal physical fear ... There is only the question: When will I be blown up?" (Faulkner, "Nobel"). He is referring, of course, to the dread that all of us face as a determining context for our lives in a highly technological violent world, a dread that crossed a threshold of intensity with WWI and that has increased since then. Most of Faulkner's audience in 1949 would have recognized a reference to the threat of atomic holocaust, but today we understand the fear as relevant as well to terrorist attacks. Injury and death by explosion of various kinds occur in modernist Gothic texts from *The Secret Agent* (1907) by Conrad, an author who influenced Faulkner, through *Mrs Dalloway* (1925) by Virginia Woolf, which is in part about a psychologically damaged soldier after WWI, to *Invisible Man* by Ellison, whose protagonist is injured in an explosion. Shadrack in *Sula* (1973) by Toni Morrison is also a former soldier who returned from WWI psychologically damaged.[1] The works I focus on here are part of the modernist Gothic heritage that Morrison draws on in this and her other late modernist Gothic works, which lie chronologically but not conceptually beyond the limits of my sketch.

The convergence of Gothic and modernism began almost half a century before Faulkner wrote *Absalom, Absalom!* (1936). Modernist Gothic's character emerges in an anticipatory way from the intersection that began in the last decade of the nineteenth century in writings by Bram Stoker and Oscar Wilde, who were Irish. I call the convergence *anticipatory* because modernism had not yet emerged sufficiently to receive a name, as it eventually would, based on works published in the two decades following WWI. It is no insignificant coincidence that writers on the margins of the dominant English imperial culture were instrumental in making such an important merger possible through the production of culturally critical works with troubling casts. In writing *The Picture of Dorian Gray* (1891), Oscar Wilde was influenced by the Scottish writer Robert Louis Stevenson's Gothic narrative *The Strange Case of Dr. Jekyll and Mr. Hyde* (1885) and by the American Gothic writer, Edgar Allan Poe – in particular, his story about doubles, "William Wilson" (1839). Later, Poe's writings are frequently an implied backdrop for American modernist Gothic narratives in a way that is not regularly the case or not as evident in narratives by authors after Wilde with roots in Ireland or the UK.

The mingling of Gothic and modernism involved a bidirectional process across the Atlantic. Poe influenced the French writer Charles Baudelaire, whose own disturbing writings and translations of Poe influenced Wilde, who then influenced (along with Poe and Baudelaire themselves) such American writers as Eliot, Barnes, Faulkner, and Capote (see Cassuto [Chapter 11] in this volume), whose works span the range of literary modernism from early to late, from the years following WWI into the period following WWII. Wilde's dialogue essays concerning the character of art and literature set directions that modernist writers on both sides of the Atlantic would pursue, and his memorable Gothic narratives, the revenge tragedy *Salome* (1893) and the queer modernist *Bildungsroman* (German for "novel of development") *The Picture of Dorian Gray*, are major works of Gothic and of modernism that were attended to by later writers. By contrast with many earlier novels of development, the modernist *Bildungsroman*, which starts with Wilde, involves a young protagonist whose formative experiences result in a life that is significantly flawed from the perspective of society's expectations. Dorian undergoes a Gothic *Bildung*, a dark education. Later protagonists of the modernist *Bildungsroman* also undergo Gothic educations, including Quentin Compson in *Absalom, Absalom!*, Joel Knox in *Other Voices, Other Rooms*, and the invisible man in Ellison.

The convergence of Gothic and modernism in Bram Stoker's *Dracula* (1897) also points backward and forward in the literary history relevant to modernist American Gothic but with distinctly different emphases from Wilde. Its Gothic literary genealogy goes back through the English sensation novels of the 1860s by Wilkie Collins and Mary Elizabeth Braddon to Mary Shelley's *Frankenstein* (1818). His narrative about a monster and the monstrous behavior of the humans who pursue him puts pressure on conventional attitudes toward the human in his time, and his fragmented, multiperspectival narration anticipates later nonlinear modernist narratives. Monsters emerge in nineteenth-century Gothic with Victor Frankenstein's creature early in the century and the vampire later. These Gothic monsters raise questions about conceptions of the human and exclusionary limits. Works of Gothic modernism sometimes include behavior that can reasonably be called monstrous, in the sense of villainous, despicable, or repulsive, as in the behavior of Thomas Sutpen in *Absalom, Absalom!* They also frequently question limits imposed by social attitudes toward conditions, identities, and behavior that some readers might regard as monstrous, perverted, or repulsive, as in the case of some of the queer characters in Barnes and Capote. These aspects involving the monstrous in modernist writing extend and develop elements of earlier Gothic into twentieth-century forms.

From its beginning, Gothic has been a deeply affective literary form, one that depends on audience response. Characters and readers often experience thrills of a dark kind, dread, or confusion, if not all three. Modernism also emphasizes literature's affective dimension through writing that invites and requires active engagement by readers more emphatically than was the case in dominant nineteenth-century forms, which tended to stress the mimetic, or referential, dimension of literature (its presentation of apparently preexisting details, as in realism) or the expressive dimension (the central place of the author, as in Romantic poetry of the early nineteenth century). This shared emphasis on affect provides an important element in the crossover between Gothic and modernism, for example, in works such as *Nightwood* and *Absalom, Absalom!*, in which the reader experiences persistently confusing language that is at or beyond the limit of reason's ability to clarify and that focuses on strange thinking or behavior. Such works present us with enigmas and with the experience of an unusual literary form that remains irresolvable and disturbing. That effect is part of literary modernism's permanently revolutionary aspect, which it attains in its greatest works, and it is also part of the Gothic's disquieting relation to its readers.

Modernist American Gothic: Eliot to Ellison

In the history of modernism, including its convergence with Gothic, T. S. Eliot holds a special place as a preeminent critic, poet, and editor who became a director at Faber & Faber, a leading London publishing house. From 1925 onward, Eliot significantly influenced publishing decisions at Faber. By then Eliot had already channeled considerable positive attention to sixteenth- and seventeenth-century revenge tragedy, or tragedy of blood, a highly stylized type of drama characterized by violence that was largely neglected or disparaged in the nineteenth century. He did so in prominently placed essays on Elizabethan drama and in *The Waste Land*, where he included the words of an ostensibly mad character, Hieronymo, from a revenge tragedy that influenced Shakespeare, Thomas Kyd's *A Spanish Tragedy* (ca. 1657). Eliot was focusing on precursors that he felt would invigorate contemporary literature by providing models different from nineteenth-century Romanticism and realism. In effect, he became a conduit for a troubling kind of writing that challenged self-congratulatory, optimistic thinking about culture and human identity.

Besides revenge tragedy, Eliot focused on authors who are key figures in the nineteenth-century genealogy of modernist Gothic mentioned above. He admired, in particular, Poe, the sensation novelist Wilkie Collins, and Charles Baudelaire, translator of Poe and author of the volume of poems *Les Fleurs du mal* (*Flowers of Evil*, 1857). Eliot also acknowledged the importance of his older modernist contemporary, Joseph Conrad. The epigraph for Eliot's "The Hollow Men" (1925) comes from *Heart of Darkness*, a narrative that concerns an insufficiently acknowledged dimension of human history and behavior at the time, the violence that accompanied imperial expansion. *The Waste Land* itself concerns the darkness of a threatening, shadowy landscape at odds with spaces and attitudes oriented toward reason and a conventionally ordered daytime world. We are invited to come into a rock's shadow to see fear in a handful of dust (l.30). The title of Barnes' *Nightwood* evokes a similarly threatening landscape marked by shadow. In *Nightwood*, a character modeled on Wilde, Dr. O'Connor, asserts that, "A man is whole only when he takes into account his shadow as well as himself" (Barnes 127). He also refers to himself as "the god of darkness" (134).

The closing verse paragraph of part one of *The Waste Land* (ll. 60–76) includes details that make the poem's Gothic character evident. Beginning "Unreal City," the passage suggests a descent into an underworld aligned with Dante's descent into hell and with the urban Gothic atmosphere of Baudelaire and other late nineteenth-century French poets. The undead in London on their way to work in the morning are zombies before that term began to be used to identify the walking dead. The poem was written in the immediate aftermath of WWI, when the English had become familiar with the historical precursors for zombies in mentally and physically crippled soldiers who returned home. The poem's context is Gothic history. The terrifying fantastical imaginings of earlier Gothic narratives have found a real counterpart in history, with senseless violence on a massive scale and an atmosphere of dread.

The verse paragraph closes with a memorable address to the reader in a combination of English words and phrases in French taken from Baudelaire's *Les Fleur du mal*: "You! *Hypocrite lecteur! – mon semblable, – mon frère!*" (l. 76). Eliot insists on the poem's affective dimension – its engagement with the reader – and on the reader's involvement in the poem's often disturbing perspectives. *The Waste Land* calls up extreme moments of violence (as in the mutilation of Philomel, ll.97–106), another descent into an underworld (involving the blind seer of Greek myth, Tiresias, ll.215–56), and at its end the mad revenger Hieronymo as a counterpart for the poem's speaker. These details create a troubling effect that is amplified by the poem's fragmented form and often-enigmatic language. The poem's heavily allusive character makes it a literary counterpart of Frankenstein's creature, since it is constituted from previous literary works that have been, in effect, dismembered and stitched together.

In his role at Faber & Faber, Eliot strongly supported publication of Barnes' *Nightwood*, a queer Gothic post-Wildean post-surrealist narrative that had been rejected by numerous other presses. In his introduction, Eliot links the book to the "horror and doom" of "Elizabethan tragedy" (xxii). *Nightwood* has no revenge plot, but Eliot suggests that the book's strongly affective dimension resembles revenge tragedy. Also regarding the book's effect, Eliot warns the reader, as he does in *The Waste Land*, not to respond hypocritically to the characters as "a horrid sideshow of freaks" (Barnes xxii), rather than recognizing them as people with whom we share a common mortal condition. We can extend Eliot's point by recognizing the book's focus on issues involving hierarchies of value and exclusions, beginning with the mention of Jews on the first page and running through the prominent place of gay and lesbian characters to the closing scene, in which a woman engages on all fours with a dog. Part of *Nightwood*'s Gothic aspect is its dissolving of conventional boundaries, both between kinds of people and between the human and the animal. Eliot additionally rightly emphasizes Barnes' highly poetic style. It is a small step from Eliot's comment about style to the point that Barnes' often enigmatic writing is both modernist and Gothic in drawing attention to itself, by contrast with realism's more transparent, unobtrusive style. We experience stylistically a densely textured, highly rhythmical literary obscurity.

Night is as central to *Nightwood* as darkness is to *Heart of Darkness*. Barnes presents it discursively and nondiscursively in, respectively, Dr. O'Connor, who, like Oscar Wilde, is loquacious, and Robin Vote, who tends toward somnambulism and is often out at night. In the final chapter (of eight), "The Possessed," Robin has a violent though not injurious encounter with her former lover Nora's dog during the night in a chapel in the New York State countryside. The strange ending is a deeply revealing moment of night that significantly effaces the boundary between human and animal. Robin is the occasion for O'Connor's lengthy discourse about *night* in the crucial fifth chapter, "Watchman, What of the Night?" in which the homosexual and transgender cross-dressing O'Connor responds at length during the night to Nora's request that he explain the *night* – that is, Robin's temperament and the way she understands and experiences the world. Nora is baffled and remains so, including at the end, when she is unconscious from hitting her head accidentally outside the chapel during Robin's encounter with the dog. Robin's experiences lie outside Nora's cognitive ambit. The reader also remains at least partially in the dark concerning Robin, who is both fluid and not subject to being possessed by anyone else. Neither modernism nor the Gothic frequently provides closure or tidy endings.

Although both the Dr. and Robin represent alternatives for institutionally generated attitudes toward identity and knowledge, Robin's closing experience is beyond or below O'Connor's discursive formulations. They both provide options that differ from the sense of self induced by a market economy. The Dr. aligns himself with "paupers and bums ... because they are impersonal with misery" (36). This is a forward-looking moment that anticipates Beckett's tramps in *Waiting for Godot* (premiered in 1953) and the American black community as Toni Morrison presents it in works such as *Sula*, especially in the opening of its second part. A lack of institutional support has given the paupers and presumably also the Dr. (as well as Morrison's blacks) an alternative sense of identity that does not take misery personally.

Robin ends the narrative "in a fit of laughter, obscene and touching" (179) that becomes "grinning and crying" (180). This conjoining of laughter and tears embodies a truth in art as Wilde describes it in "The Truth of Masks," whose title refers to the twin dramatic masks of laughing and crying: "A Truth in art is that whose contradictory is also true" (Ellmann 432). The coexistence of opposites undermines hierarchies and the contrasts on which they rely. Early in "Watchman," the Dr. refers specifically to "Life, the permission to know death" (90), not the *obligation* or the *unavoidable fate of knowing* death, but a gift enabling us to understand our own mortality. He blurs the boundary between ostensible opposites, life and death, implicitly responding to the pervasive denial of death in the West, the refusal to recognize and actively accept human transience without feeling misery. Unresisting acceptance undercuts all hierarchies of value and power within the human species because it reminds us that we are all the same. Everyone, rich or poor, young or old, queer or straight, performs the dance of death; as a consequence, boundaries that support exclusionary hierarchies are insupportable.

At issue in the closing chapter is the species hierarchy between human and nonhuman creatures. Robin does not perform a dance of death with the dog, but she and the dog do engage in a performance of their mutuality in an unforgettable, enigmatic challenge to the notion that humans differ from animals in ways that make the human a master. Instead, Robin and the dog, while not the same, resemble one another, though neither *communication* nor *recognition* captures what happens. Both partners "gave up" (Barnes 180) the text says, in an act of letting go reflected and expressed as well in the book's style. Barnes reaches escape velocity, and not just at the end, by linking humans with animals, expressing an understanding of life as a way of knowing death, and presenting queerness as no more perverse than the night.

Eliot suggests that some readers may react wrongheadedly to Barnes' characters as freaks or monsters. As already mentioned, monstrous behavior by villainous humans is important in the Gothic. In *Absalom, Absalom!*, monstrous behavior occurs prominently in the context of the coexistence of opposites. Its modernist Gothic narrative, stylistically as poetic as Barnes', focuses on Thomas Sutpen, sometimes referred to as a demon, whose monstrous behavior contributes to a death and leads to the family's collapse. There are no Gothic monsters in *Absalom*, but its narrative core is in salient ways congruent with the narrative of *Frankenstein*. It carries *Frankenstein*'s concerns with monstrosity, domination, and hierarchy forward in a modernist, nonlinear, multiperspectival form in order to present an historically later but congruent situation that is quintessentially American in its racial aspect.

Poe's "The Fall of the House of Usher" is a more obvious precursor for *Absalom, Absalom!* than *Frankenstein* because of the literal and figurative fall of houses (buildings, families) common to both. Faulkner was also influenced by his older modernist contemporary James Joyce, whose *Ulysses* (1922) anticipates in an enabling way Faulkner's handling of myth. Faulkner, however, goes beyond Joyce by aligning his narrative not only with Biblical and classical narratives but also with the modern Gothic myth of Victor Frankenstein and his creature. That mythic narrative had recently been the basis for the American director James Whale's *Frankenstein* (1931). Before Whale, Thomas Edison produced the first film of *Frankenstein* in 1910. Mary Shelley's *Frankenstein* (1818) is an English narrative, but Faulkner is part of a recasting of it by Americans for an American audience that was well under way by the 1930s.[2]

Unlike Victor Frankenstein, a scientist and inventor, Sutpen invents himself as an adult in what turns out to be a monstrous way, mastering both the landscape and the slaves who are his instruments. His hierarchy of value and power extends to social attitudes, including racial ones, but the merging of opposites in the narrative reveals the hierarchy's flaws. Supposedly distinctly different races are variously mixed in Sutpen's world, including in his offspring, with miscegenation and incest becoming indistinguishable in a situation in which Henry, Sutpen's son, feels both heterosexual and same-sex desire for his half-brother and his sister. Faulkner stages the logic of hierarchies inherent in the story of Frankenstein and his creature. Scorned as a child, as was the creature, Sutpen's biracial son, Charles Bon, desires to be recognized. Like the creature, Bon relentlessly applies pressure to his progenitor when recognition does not occur. The result for Sutpen is the collapse of his house and the undermining of the hierarchy supporting it in the contradictory moment in which the white son kills the biracial son, who were simultaneously on the same side during the Civil War and on opposite sides in the family dispute. As is regularly the case in Gothic narratives, there is no resolution, and the difficulties repeat themselves into the future for younger characters, such as Quentin Compson, whose extended encounter with Sutpen's story is part of a Gothic education.

Modernism does not end with WWII. Among the new generation of American late modernists writing immediately after WWII, Truman Capote and Ralph Ellison are particularly significant and distinctive. Both *Other Voices, Other Rooms* and *Invisible Man* are examples of the modernist *Bildungsroman*, and both the white queer Joel Knox and the black unnamed invisible man experience, like Quentin Compson, a Gothic education that results in an identity that does not conform to societal expectations. Like Joyce's Stephen Dedalus in *A Portrait of the Artist as a Young Man* (1916), whose story also has significantly dark, even infernal, moments, their development reaches only ambiguous, provisional closure.

Capote is better known for his masterly "nonfiction novel" (his term) *In Cold Blood* (1966), a true crime novel, than for *Other Voices, Other Rooms*. The later work is evidence for the Gothic genealogy of Capote's career. Though distinctly American and of its time, it looks back implicitly to the sensation novel that emerged in England a hundred years earlier as a development from earlier Gothic. Often central to sensation novels were crimes that had received newspaper coverage.

Capote's earlier novel is a queer Southern Gothic late modernist *Bildungsroman* with a disabled aspect whose original dust jacket was controversial because the photograph of Capote showed him in a pose that some considered perversely sexually inviting. One of the characters is less than able-bodied, Joel's father, who is a quadriplegic, but some readers might consider the able-bodied protagonists of modernist novels of development, including Joel Knox (age 13), to be figuratively disabled – that is, developmentally challenged in a social way, because they do not accept conventional attitudes. As with Robin Vote, identity is fluid rather than stable for both Joel and the older, cross-dressing Randolph who, in trying to seduce Joel, educates him about fluidity. Structurally, the narrative is Gothic in its shift from the city, New Orleans, where Joel is comfortable with his surroundings, to an isolated house in the corner of the rural South, where Joel finds the situation disconcertingly strange. The strangeness reaches a climactic moment in chapter eleven (of twelve), when Joel encounters the midget carnival performer, Miss Wisteria, who tries to seduce him. When Joel falls ill in the next chapter, the narration's feverish style points back to earlier modernist experiments in rendering unusual states of mind, including Stephen's fevered consciousness in Joyce's *A Portrait* and Benjy's developmentally challenged thinking in Faulkner's *The Sound and the Fury* (1929).

Joel's illness is a descent into an underworld figuratively, as are some of his other experiences, including the visit with Randolph following his illness to the decrepit Cloud Hotel deep in the swamps. Out of these experiences, Joel develops a distinctive identity that, like Randolph's, is fluid and queer, but the ending is ambiguous concerning the extent to which his new sense of identity is enabling or disabling. As so often in Gothic and in modernism, the conclusion is open. In the final paragraph, Joel seems to be responding to the invitation represented by the window in which Randolph, dressed as a woman, has watched him: "he knew he must go" (Capote 231). He could be going literally to Randolph as the queer lady, or he could be going away. He may be doing both. Like Joel's identity, the ending is fluid and open.

The conclusion is also open in *Invisible Man*, a book whose modernist and dark literary heritages are evident. We encounter a quotation from the end of Joyce's *A Portrait* in chapter sixteen, when the invisible man considers his statement in a speech that he has become "more human," a claim that he does not understand, though he knows that his new identity has emerged from others "kicking me into the dark" (Ellison 354). There are emphatic evocations of Dostoevsky's *Notes from Underground* (1864), as well as references to Dante's descent into the underworld (Ellison 9) and to the South as a Conradian "heart of darkness" (Ellison 579). The protagonist's transition into adulthood is Gothic and punctuated with violence and betrayal, as is his adulthood. The violence starts with the battle royal that he experiences as a youth, in which he is forced to fight with other blacks as part of a spectacle organized by whites when he is being honored for his scholastic achievements. The president of the college he attends betrays him by sending him to New York City with a letter of recommendation that makes it impossible for him to find work. In a climactic incident in chapter ten in the book's middle, he struggles, apparently for his life, in "a deep basement" (Ellison 207) several levels below ground with an older black supervisor at a factory. When an explosion stops the struggle but sends the protagonist to the hospital, his experience there is rendered in chapter eleven in a bizarre hallucinatory style that points back in modernist literary history to the hallucinatory and infernal fifteenth episode (called by critics either Nighttown or Circe) of Joyce's *Ulysses* and to the other modernist texts that provided Capote with models for Joel Knox's feverish thoughts. To quote Faulkner's Nobel speech again: "There is only the question: When will I be blown up?" His injuries, however, are far from the end for the invisible man, who undertakes a long unsuccessful search for a meaningful daylight identity that drives him to the underground lair where we encounter him in the prologue and the epilogue. The space is well lit, though by a perverse number of light bulbs, 1369, a number that yokes the unlucky 13 with the sex position sometimes called *soixante-neuf*. When he states interrogatively "I speak for you?" in the book's last sentence, as in Eliot's evocations of the reader, he invites us to recognize ourselves in the disturbing reflections of his thoughts and his narrative.

It is unclear whether the protagonist's gothic education will enable a meaningful exercise of agency in the future, since in the epilogue he finds himself in a state of uncertainty, not knowing whether he is "in the rear or in the *avant-garde*." In that state, he has moved beyond binaries, including "good and evil, honesty and dishonesty," which are just "shifting shapes" (Ellison 572). He has learned "to live without direction" (Ellison 577), that is, without a specific direction but also not in response to directions from others, in a world defined by "possibility" (Ellison 576). No longer interested in conventional success, he knows that "humanity is won by continuing to play in face of certain defeat" (Ellison 577), a statement that is simultaneously about heroism and mortality, gambling and music, in which the word *won* suggests *one*. Instead of being disabling, a state of unknowing and uncertainty can be a precondition for freedom that recognizes contradictions rather than ignoring them. Having decided to come out despite his continuing invisibility, Ellison's protagonist, like all the authors discussed in this essay, has turned what he knows about darkness to advantage, in this case into a generative recognition that threats of being blown up or subjected to violent exclusionary attitudes need not be paralyzing.

The recognitions that emerge for characters and readers in modernist American Gothic arise from narratives that put pressure on realism's stylistic conventions and on its assumptions and implications; on continuities of narrative, narration, and identity; on boundaries that mark hierarchical separations; and on the possibility of reaching determinate closure concerning the often enigmatic meaning of the narrative's troubling events and sometimes turbulent style. We find ourselves neither guided by the light of reason and sanity nor faced with a daylight world characterized by domestic order. Instead, we encounter a threatening world of at times explosive violence framed by twentieth-century history as itself a Gothic narrative. That history is not narrowly American, but often prominent aspects of it are, especially regarding race relations. As in earlier Gothic literature, the reader is memorably affected by the antirealistic elements of modernist American Gothic, but now with insistent implications about our complicity, as part of the dissolving of hierarchical boundaries. We see such implications in Eliot's and Ellison's direct addresses to the reader, in Eliot's warning not to pretend we are better than Barnes' characters, and in our alignment with characters in *Absalom, Absalom!* who are, like us, attempting to piece together the events and their meaning. The invisible man suggests that, in telling his story, he speaks for (and implicitly about) us. He does so with an American accent.

NOTES

I wish to acknowledge with deep thanks the help of my two undergraduate research assistants in preparing this essay, Lauren Shapiro and Andrew Garcia.

1. Although *Sula* falls outside the time period of this essay, it is a late modernist American Gothic narrative, whose title and central character's name, Sula Mae Peace, refer implicitly to Oscar Wilde's violent, self-destroying Salome.
2. Concerning the significant place of the Frankenstein narrative in American culture, see Elizabeth Young, *Black Frankenstein: The Making of an American Metaphor*. Young does not comment on *Absalom*.

WORKS CITED

Barnes, Djuna. *Nightwood*. 1937. New York: New Directions, 2006.
Capote, Truman. *Other Voices, Other Rooms*. 1948. New York: Vintage International, 1994.
Eliot, T. S. *Selected Poems*. New York: Harcourt, Brace & World, 1967.
Ellison, Ralph. *Invisible Man*. 1952; New York: Vintage International, 1995.
Ellmann, Richard, ed. *The Artist as Critic: Critical Writings of Oscar Wilde*. Chicago: University of Chicago Press, 1969.
Young, Elizabeth. *Black Frankenstein: The Making of an American Metaphor*. New York: New York University Press, 2008.

5

JUSTIN D. EDWARDS

Contemporary American Gothic

In the United States, the words "contemporary" and "Gothic" go together like zombies and brains. Like a swarming hoard, Gothic is ubiquitous: It is in our novels, our TV programs, on our computer screens, and in our movie theatres. It has spread throughout literary and popular culture like a virus, infecting us with a contagion of tropes, figures, and images. Gothic consumes and it is consumed by the feeding frenzy of audiences with insatiable appetites. This is seen in the best-selling novels of Stephen King, Anne Rice, Stephenie Meyer, L. J. Smith, and Charlaine Harris, as well as in their mutated progeny: films such as *The Shining* (1980), *Interview with a Vampire* (1994), *Twilight* (2008), or TV series such as *True Blood* (2008–2014) and *The Vampire Diaries* (2009-). Yet there is also a significant continuity in the aesthetics of the American Gothic from the late eighteenth century to the present. For instance, there is a continuum between the psychological breakdowns of characters in Edgar Allan Poe's Gothic stories and those found in Stephen King's novels. The vampires in works by Rice and Harris are the heirs of the pseudo-vampiric creatures found in H. P. Lovecraft's "The Hound" (1924) and "The Outsider" (1926). And the generic hybridization of Gothic and Romance in the sagas by Meyer and Smith mirror the blending of Gothic with Romanticism in Nathaniel Hawthorne's *Scarlet Letter* (1850) and *House of the Seven Gables* (1851). Gothic never dies: It just morphs into different forms at different historical moments.

Contemporary US Gothic is not homogenous. Nor is it unified through a specific body of texts. Rather, there are multiple strands of contemporary Gothic that range from, among many others, the paranormal romance of Meyer's *Twilight* saga to the queer Gothic of Poppy Z. Brite's *Lost Souls* (1992) to the eco-Gothic of Cormac McCarthy's *The Road* (2006) to the Gothic SF of Richard Matheson's *I Am Legend* (1954) to the apocalyptic Gothic of Max Brook's *World War Z* (2006). Contemporary Gothic is, like that which came before it, an adaptable mode. It is a shape-shifter: It transforms into different beasts to match the demands of new audiences while simultaneously reflecting the deep-rooted personal, social, and cultural anxieties of the day. These are myriad fears, which include, but are not limited to, new forms of advanced technology, ecological devastation, the migration of people, the speed of hypercapitalism, and the powerful forces of globalization. These phenomena threaten to unsettle the homely American nation, transforming it into an unhomely place, an alien nation.

Sympathy for the Undead

One way of assuaging these fears is by domesticating them. If the monster is sympathetic, then it can be safely integrated into the home. In Isaac Marion's *Warm Bodies* (2010), the zombie makes a good boyfriend; in Harris' *Dead Until Dark* (2001), the vampire makes an excellent lover and a potential father figure; in Andrew Fox's Fat *White Vampire Blues* (2003), we laugh at the obese, lazy vampire who is forced to go on a diet; and in Christine Pope's *Darkangel* (2014), we are invited to sympathize with a witch who is faced with embracing her clan and supernatural powers or giving them up for a mysterious man and the possibility of a "normal" family. Zombies have cell phones, vampires feel guilt, and witches have biological clocks. The Gothic monster is not necessarily an icon of terror, threatening humanity by consuming blood or brains or creating more of the undead. In contemporary Gothic, these figures are often humanized and engender sympathy, rather than the fear inspired by confronting the otherness of the undead rotting corpse or the bloodthirsty vampiric cannibal. "As monsters are sought out," writes Fred Botting, "radical difference is diminished: they become familiar, recognized, expected, 'normal' rather than 'monstrous' monstrosities, domesticated to the point of becoming pets" ("Monsters" 500).

This marks a paradigm shift in Gothic: Monsters are invited into the home. Nowhere is this more apparent than in recent representations of the American zombie, a figure that once reminded audiences that the human condition always ends in rotting flesh. The zombie hoard once signaled a loss of the self and individuality, just as it unveiled the dark side of mass consumer culture and the fragility of humanity in a social structure underpinned by the dehumanizing impacts of hyperglobalization. The zombie lacked cognition and was motivated only by the base instinct of its ravenous appetite for human flesh. Yet this "most abject and inhuman of Gothic monsters" has been transformed: It is now often a sentient and emotional being that is used as "a metaphor for alienated otherness" (Spooner 183). For instance, in S. G. Browne's *Breathers: A Zombie's Lament* (2009), the newly revived zombie, Andy, tells his own tale of living in his parents' basement, attending Undead Anonymous meetings, falling in love with another zombie, and seeking to find a place in a world where zombies aren't marginalized as outcasts. Likewise, in Carrie Ryan's post-apocalyptic young adult novel *The Forest of Hands and Teeth* (2009), the main protagonist, Mary, reflects on how other characters choose to become zombies and, as the plot develops, her attitude to the undead is increasingly sympathetic, even envious; after all, zombies have, from her perspective, uncomplicated lives. And in Jonathan Maberry's *Rot and Ruin* (2011), the zombie hunter, Benny, must confront his hatred of zombies when, as in Mary Shelley's *Frankenstein* (1818), he discovers that sometimes the worst monsters are humans. Zombies, it would seem, are people too.

Robin Becker's *Brains: A Zombie Memoir* (2010) is a significant contribution to the sentient zombie narrative. Here, the English professor and B movie aficionado, Jack Barnes, is bitten when the zombie apocalypse hits small-town Missouri. Once undead, Barnes realizes that he has retained information and knowledge: He has not lost his understanding of Walt Whitman, the New Testament, zombie films, the best recipes for piecrusts, or the cultural significance of Freud ("as massive as his cigar") (1). He also has some control over his craving for brains and, although he does not have speech, he can read and write. "In death," he explains, "I am a flesh-eating zombie with a messianic complex and these superpowers: I can think and I can write" (1). He heads north to Chicago to seek out Dr. Howard Stein, the inventor of the chemical compound that produced the virus, and prove his sentience so the good doctor will give him the antidote. Along the way, he meets several other thinking zombies – Joan, a zombie nurse who can suture wounds; Ros, a gun-slinging zombie who can speak; and Guts, a young zombie with a quick sprint – all of whom form a bedraggled band of undead who embark on a shuffling pilgrimage to the Jewel of the Midwest, the Heart of America. The zombie narrative tropes of hordes of staggering corpses and the consumption of tasty human victims are not abandoned, and yet Becker's text also illustrates how a lack of appropriate social infrastructure leaves the nation vulnerable to large-scale catastrophes. Moreover, by adopting Barnes' point of view, Becker explores the zombie as a misunderstood minority commenting on the political drive for human rights. Barnes does not just want to eat human brains; he wants to sound his barbaric yawp to the living and undead citizens of the world.

The reference to Walt Whitman's yawp (section 52 of *Song of Myself*) is just one of the text's many allusions to literary and popular culture. Barnes names two of the militarized zombie hunters Ros and Guil, and when they are bitten Barnes proudly announces that Rosencrantz and Guildenstern are undead (72). When he laments being hunted as a zombie, Barnes paraphrases Rodney Dangerfield: "monsters can't get no respect" (5). There are direct references to Edmund Spencer's *Faerie Queene* (1590), George Romero's zombie series (1968-), Thomas Kuhn's *Structure of Scientific Revolutions* (1962), Boris Karloff in *Frankenstein* (1931), Max Brooks' *Zombie Survival Guide* (2003), Stephen King's *'Salem's Lot* (1975), as well as many other novels, poems, TV programs, and musicians. Even the protagonist's name, Jack Barnes, is a thinly veiled allusion to Ernest Hemingway's narrator and protagonist, Jake Barnes, in *The Sun Also Rises* (1926). Likewise, the scientist Howard Stein echoes the name of the American shock-jock Howard Stern, just as Dr. Stein is a short hand reference for Dr. Frankenstein.

These allusions appear alongside the political assertions of liberty, freedom, and civil rights. Seeing himself as a leader in an emerging zombie rights movement, Barnes calls for the nation's "zombietariat" to unite and fight for the "pursuit of life, liberty, and brains" (62). What Barnes calls his "Zombie Army" and "Operation Zombie Shield" are not meant to be aggressive attacks on humanity. Rather, he sees his movement as having a revolutionary politics that is aligned with Thomas Paine, Mary Wollstonecraft, and Martin Luther King. In fact, he describes his manifesto, "A Vindication of the Rights of the Post-Living," as "revolutionary as the Magna Carta, the Treaty of Versailles, *The Feminine Mystique*, The Declaration of Independence and the Bill of Rights" (177, 167). A self-declared freedom fighter, Barnes' story turns the figure of the zombie as a devolved form of humanity, a decayed and reanimated corpse, on its head: "Zombies are the next step in human evolution," he declares; zombies are us and we are "determined to gain our rightful place in the world" (155, 104–5). Here, Barnes' voice reverberates with Henry Thoreau's assert of the right of revolution, as well as the right to resist or challenge governance that is ineffective, inadequate, or tyrannical (383–85). For behind its humor, the text asks pressing questions about political rights and the relations between sentient beings: What beings should be feared? Who should be cared for? Who should be restrained or locked up? The zombie's physical and mental impairments speak, with tongue firmly planted in cheek, to what Barnes calls the plight of the undead. But the symbolic logic of the text extends to the political rights of other beings who might have imitations due to disability, age, illness, or incapacity. The memoir poses a significant question: What does it mean to be human? And Barnes provides the answer: the human should not be conflated with the humane.

A sympathetic zombie like Barnes complicates the relationship between self and other. After all, if the reader sympathizes with the zombie, then there is an intimate connection between the self and the monster. This in turn resists the representation of the monster as the other in relation to the self, and it also gestures to the possibility of the human as being othered, thus inverting the self-other dynamic that is often invoked in Gothic representations of monstrosity. Such an inversion might include the individual human (a person who is demonized as inhumane in relation to the monster) or it might include the structures of society (the inhumane conditions of social structures that marginalize the monster). However, this is not always a simple inversion of self and other. For while we often conceive of the relationship between human and zombie as a dichotomy, the sympathetic zombie often demonstrates how this relationship is a continuum: The zombie's cognition does not necessarily diminish its appetite for, or consumption of, human flesh. Moreover, the zombie might have retained certain aspects of its former self and lost others; Barnes, for instance, retains his memory and capacity for self-reflection, but loses his ability to move quickly or to speak. This continuum and the zombie's call for equality and civil rights force us to reflect on where we draw the line between the human and the zombie. The other is always constructed through artifice; or, as Barnes puts it, "Go ahead and sympathize. Construct me as the 'other'" (12).

It is in this context that song of myself, to again reference Whitman, becomes song of myself-as-zombie. The human condition is shadowed by its monstrous creation: the post-industrial global economy that is perpetually restructured around the latest speculative financial scheme, maintained by national and transnational government subsidies, and enforced by a massive military industrial complex that profits from a so-called war on terror. The American industrial economy of the past is simply the latest detritus to be disposed of in the landfill of history and those made redundant by outsourcing – the zombietariat – are relegated to the margins of society, made into pariahs and outcasts by the demands of a high-speed capitalist Empire that circumnavigates the globe. When Barnes laments the loss of humanity, "Oh, hateful, hateful humans" (68), he mourns the death of compassion, altruism, self-reflection, and empathy at the hands of those who have exceeded humanity by adapting to the new world order. These lead to ethical and ontological questions: What if being zombie is more ethical than being human? And what if being undead is preferable to being dead? Perhaps the zompire, a collective body politic made up of an egalitarian new species, is more desirable than a human empire wherein the humane aspects of humanity are dead. In fact, Barnes' "zombie self" comes to the realization that his human self was part of a dehumanized state that he finds in the ubiquitous shadow of life: "It took zombiedom," he confesses, "to give me a soul, death to make me 'human'" (112). This is echoed by Ros, who comes to realize that mortality is overrated and that human life is not necessarily humane or a form of living: "Perhaps life as a zombie is better than no life at all" (71).

JUSTIN D. EDWARDS

High-Tech Gothic

The industrial age that died alongside the monstrous zombie has been replaced by a post-industrial era underpinned by digital and communication technologies that have transformed contemporary life. In a society where the service sector generates more wealth than the manufacturing sector, the economic structure has transitioned from the production of goods to the provision of services. As a result, knowledge becomes a valued form of capital – human capital – as the production of ideas is a main driver of the American economy. Globalization and automation have led to the decline of manual labor in the United States, and the rise of professional work in the sciences, the creative industries, engineering, IT, and computing has grown in prevalence and value. This has had a profound impact on the dissemination of information sciences and technologies so that the hyperdevelopment of advanced technology plays an increasing role in contemporary culture and society. Ever faster and more powerful, computer systems and telecommunications have converged to engender a sea change wherein new technologies store and process information and communicate it instantaneously across the globe.

Ghosts and specters are sometimes associated with a pre-modern and pre-industrial past, relegated to "under-developed" cultures that rely on superstition rather than the rationality associated with science, technology, and modernity. This distinction is challenged by French philosopher Jacques Derrida, who suggests that advancements in technology produce ghosts: Daguerreotypes and photographs produce ethereal and liminal images of people as spectral figures, audio-recordings and telephones disembody human voices, and cinema presents the actions of people who may be deceased (the walking dead). New technologies engender new anxieties. This is consistent with a strand of Gothic wherein technology generates specters and monsters that include, for instance, the biotechnology of Dr. Frankenstein, the transformative chemistry of Dr. Jekyll, and the grotesque medical experiments of Dr. Moreau.

The widespread dissemination of the internet through personal and home computing has produced its own ghosts and fiends who, according to internet lore, linger in the shadows and wait for a chance to haunt, possess, curse, or infect users. These digital ghosts and ghouls appear on web-series, podcasts, creepypasta, and social media sites, and include, among many others, threatening and spectral figures such as the Rake, the Midnight Man, and the figure perhaps most exemplary of the digital age, Slender Man. A tall and thin figure in a black suit, Slender Man's face is featureless and his head is white and black. His presence is signaled through audiovisual distortion on the screen; sometimes this is the only way of detecting him (Oliver 253–70). He is provoked by attempts to document or understand him, and he haunts those who try to gather information about him by appearing as a dark shadow in your room or disrupting the flow of information to your computer. He demonizes information transfer and threatens those who seek him out. In this, he is a manifestation of Gothic that reflects contemporary social and cultural concerns about technology and its significant changes to everyday practices and attitudes. But like other internet monsters, the absent presence of Slender Man encourages us to reflect upon an ontology based on the necessity of absence in order to image presence, and challenges our ideas about the divisions between past, present, and future.

In fiction, Gothic has been adapted for a technologically defined context in novels such as *Neuromancer* (1984), *Count Zero* (1986), and *Mona Lisa Overdrive* (1988) by William Gibson, and his co-authored pieces with Bruce Sterling, "Burning Chrome" (1982) and "Red Star, Winter Orbit" (1983). These texts hold a mirror to contemporary techno-social relations, the advanced consumer culture of late capitalism and their impacts on contemporary subjectivity, consciousness, and human behavior. In so doing, they recycle and reappropriate Gothic tropes such as the undead, decaying bodies, spectral presences, claustrophobic spaces, and fluid movements between past and present. In *Neuromancer*, for instance, characters such as McCoy and Dixie Flatline traverse the borders separating technology from the organic body, life from death. After his physical death, McCoy is reconstructed through his brain patterns, a ghostly revival that is mirrored in the regeneration of Dixie, who, according to name and history, is simultaneously alive and dead. By crossing these borders, the text dislodges the being and non-being from their homely settings through a process of organic and technological mongrelization. Bodies and brains are manipulated through new technologies to engender Frankenstein-esque creations that re-map human and nonhuman conditions.

In *Gothic High-Tech* (2011), a collection of twelve short stories by Bruce Sterling, we find the end of postmodernism and the rise of a post-postmodern era wherein wealthy North Atlantic societies are gradually crumpling and others are anarchically emerging. "We are into an era," Sterling writes in an essay in *Wired*, "of decay and repurposing of broken structures, of new social inventions within networks, a world of 'Gothic High-Tec' and 'Favela Chic', a crooked networked bazaar of history and futurity, rather than a cathedral of history, and a utopia of futurity" ("Atemporality"). In this context, he asserts, time and space must be reconceived and re-presented as atemporality in order to remain sensitive to the convergence of "the symbol of the ruined castle," the "ruins of the unsustainable" (represented in "Gothic High-Tech"), and the "informalized, illegalized, heavily networked structure of the emergent new order" (represented in "Favela Chic"). This convergence has not been domesticated or brought into sociality in the first two decades of the twenty-first century, and this has led to an unhomely state-of-being and new aesthetics in creative productions – including fiction – that he calls "Frankenstein Mashups," which "take elements of past, present, and future and just collide 'em together, in sort of a collage. More or less semi-randomly, like a Surrealist 'exquisite corpse'" ("Atemporality").

One of the stories in *Gothic High-Tech* that captures Sterling's Frankenstein mashup aesthetic is "The Hypersurface of this Decade," which is set in an area called the Silicon Roundabout in the neighborhood of Hackney, East London. Located near Old Street Station, the first-person narrator's abode is a gentrified space that was once an industrial sweatshop and which now makes features of the Victorian redbrick walls, Edwardian Girders, and shrapnel from the Blitz. This space is wired and networked to form a "Web-Squared situation" where "no effort need be made to reconcile the differing scales of the virtual and the material. They can simply exist in raw form" (60). Within this atemporal setting, the ghosts of the past merge with the specters of the present and future hauntings. The "ghost-host of time-layered East End urban phantoms" are traces within the bricks and mortar; here, "possessions are over" and have been replaced by data so that "dematerialization is defined by its surfaces" (59–60). Materiality is supplanted by zones of interactive transactions, network docks, social-software communities, Twitter streams, blog posts, and the "hypermodern Web"; this disembodies communication, separating data from corporeal and material contexts, and transforms it into a series of spectral traces that flicker across a screen (62). The "multimodal urban landscape" and "urban futurity" of the story is haunted by the "dead past's invisible hand" and by future collapse: the collapse of financial infrastructures, branding, and copyright (60, 61). It is haunted by nostalgia for a lost future.

Many of the stories in *Gothic High-Tech* represent the collapse of postindustrial societies and imagine a future within a post-postindustrial world. In "White Fungus," for instance, a guerrilla urbanist rejects new reward systems to redesign "junkspaces," the postindustrial detritus of the future, into homely places to live. Likewise, in "The Exterminator's Want Ad," the first-person narrator describes his life in jail after the fall of a hypercapitalist and hypertechnological America that is now ruled by a socialist government. As a self-proclaimed "political prisoner," the narrator is an advocate of what has been lost: the neoliberal capitalist system driven by profit, self-interest, and greed. But the economy has tanked and reverted to preindustrial poverty. Hyperinflation has transformed the suburbs into a dead "Permanent Foreclosure Zone" surrounded by abandoned highways and areas with "constant power blackouts" (75–76). Former financial centers are the Gothic ruins of advanced capitalism: "burnt-out skyscrapers, lotta wreckage, junk, constant storms and no air conditioning" (84). Killing bugs is the only thing left for the narrator to do. In both of these stories, Sterling reflects on how new technologies and economic changes alter the world and conceptions of personal identity, but his texts are also concerned with the shape of the future. How will new technology alter social relations? How will economic institutions respond to these changes? And how will political structures and governments transform in relation to techno-economic changes? These questions lead to a haunting presence in the texts: the stories are haunted not just by the past or the present but by the future. This convergence engenders atemporality, a state of temporal, historical, and ontological disjunction, wherein the immediacy of presence is replaced by the metaphoric figure of the ghost that is neither present nor absent, neither dead nor alive, but which is situated in a contemporary culture that is haunted by its own futurity (Derrida 116–22).

Uncanny Textuality

Gothic has never been impeded by new technologies. After all, early Gothic fiction was mass-produced by advancements in the printing press and was often circulated in newly founded circulation libraries. Nineteenth- and early twentieth-century Gothic novels are no longer restricted by copyright and can be read on open-access websites. Previously inaccessible Gothic texts have become more widely read as archives are digitalized. New technologies have led to new ways of accessing and reading texts. Gothic novels are now often read on tablets and e-readers, resulting in dire predictions about the future of paperback and hardcover books, and contemporary Gothic is particularly well placed to address changes in access to texts. For Gothic fiction has always been self-reflexive about its own textuality. It is littered with discovered manuscripts, counterfeits, inset tales, false translations, narrative fragmentation, structural contradictions, as well as dubious claims to authenticity.

Contemporary American Gothic novels continue to explore uncanny textuality: Elizabeth Kostova's *The Historian* (2005) interweaves a series of letters and oral accounts to link the narratives of Vlad the Impaler and Count Dracula to protagonists living in the 1930s, 1950s, and 1970s; Jennifer Egan's *The Keep* (2006) is primarily set in a dark and mysterious castle, which includes a series of secret underground passages that have their textual corollary in the distorted and haunted perceptions of the main character; and in Glenn Cooper's *Library of the Dead* (2009), the secret identity of a New

York serial killer can only be found in a mysterious and dangerous medieval library that lies underneath an eighth-century monastery. One of the most critically acclaimed recent Gothic texts to engage in uncanny forms of textuality is Mark Z. Danielewski's *House of Leaves* (2000), which follows Will Navidson and his family after they move to a typical suburban house and discover a mysterious labyrinth. The novel uses unique typography to map out embedded narratives – a textual labyrinth – that requires the reader to manipulate the text by turning it sideways or reading it upside down. Written in the Gothic tradition of Edgar Allan Poe and H. P. Lovecraft, Danielewski's novel is structured across rhizomatous pathways so "the hunt for prey is the quest for a transcendental signified that will ground the other signifiers towards one united meaning; a signification that will cure the horror of the unreadable text, ensuring that the multiplicity of endless pathways is mastered and mapped" (Watkiss 12). Yet the measure of disorder and randomness in the closed system of *House of Leaves* is based on the impossibility of this kind of reading practice.

A striking example of how contemporary Gothic is linked to textual experimentation is J. J. Abrams and Doug Dorst's *S* (2013), which is sold in a black case embossed with the capital letter S in a Gothic font. Inside the case is what looks to be an old library book, *Ship of Theseus*, which has been extensively annotated by two readers using different colored pens. This leads to several layers of narrative: The novel *Theseus* tells one story, the penned annotations comprise another, while the translator's note, foreword, and footnotes help to construct the story of the mysterious and elusive author of the novel, V. M. Straka. The notes in the margin tell several stories, but they are focused on uncovering the academic mystery surrounding the fictional book's author. Text and paratext are self-consciously blurred so that it is difficult to distinguish one from the other, thus calling attention to the materiality of the book and highlighting the text as a physical object through the insertions that are placed between the pages: letters written in Swedish and English, postcards from Brazil, newspaper clippings, and other documents that supplement the layering of the stories.

In the fictional paratext of the foreword to *Ship of Theseus*, the scholar F. X. Caldeira, a character who may have been created by Straka, presents the author as a mysterious and unknowable figure. Straka could have been murdered; he might have committed suicide; he may still be alive; perhaps he never existed. This mystery is amplified by the rumors that have circulated about his life: Some stories claim he was involved in the attempted assassination of Mussolini, others assert he was involved in the murder of Trotsky and the 1920 bombing of Wall Street. This raises questions about the life and death of the author and calls attention to the materiality of the text by gesturing back to medieval manuscripts wherein the collaborative efforts of the author, scribe, illuminator, and commentators in the margins obscured the notion of a text being the work of a single writer. Like the medieval manuscript, the author of *Ship of Theseus* remains unclear, and *S* is the work of a creator, Abrams, a modern "scribe," Dorst, the commentators in the margins, Jen and Eric, as well as "illuminations" by a New York graphic design company.

From this perspective, there is a continuum between *S* and Horace Walpole's *The Castle of Otranto* (1764). For the paratext of Walpole's seminal Gothic novel presents the work as a newly discovered medieval manuscript that has been translated for an English audience. Moreover, in the first edition, Walpole concealed his authorship, engendering a sense of mystery surrounding the source of the text and its writer. This leads the literary critic Jerrold Hogle to assert that counterfeit or "the ghost of counterfeit" is central to Gothic: "the 'Gothic revival' in the eighteenth century, the remnant of 'obligatory' or 'natural' meaning," he writes, "is replaced as the sign's point of reference by counterfeits of that remnant: portraits or armour hung on walls ... illustrations of the medieval 'Gothic' in books, performances or editions" (501). Such counterfeit speaks to Abrams and Dorst's presentation of *Ship of Theseus* as a 1949 translation of a mysterious author's last work, and the appearance of authenticity is conveyed in the worn binding, the library catalogue number, as well as the seeming real postcards, articles, and letters.

Contemporary Gothic in the United States does not shy away from textual experimentation, new technologies, or new forms of monstrosity. Rather, American Gothic adapts to social and cultural changes (and related fears and anxieties) by shaking-up the signifying process and invoking defamilarization by offering the writer access to a nonrealistic mode that resists documentary verisimilitude and discursive practices. These texts, then, underscore the slippery nature of language and map out new territories to explore the uncharted character of new sociocultural phenomena that are not immediately intelligible. This is not to say that contemporary American Gothic breaks with a tradition that began in the eighteenth century. After all, Gothic has always relied on uncanny disruptions, liminal states of being, monstrosity, grotesquery, and tensions between the real and the unreal. Yet the rise of new technologies and digital culture in the information age has engendered fruitful material for understanding the specters and monsters of contemporary modernity while also reflecting on a past that continues to haunt the present and the future.

WORKS CITED

Becker, Robin. *Brains: A Zombie Memoir*. New York: HarperCollins, 2010.
Botting, Fred. "Love Your Zombie: Horror, Ethics, Excess." *The Gothic in Contemporary Literature and Popular Culture: Pop Goth*. Eds. Justin D. Edwards and Agnieszka Soltysik Monnet. New York: Routledge, 2012. 19–36.
———. "Post-Millennial Monsters: Monstrosity-no-more." *The Gothic World*. Eds. Glennis Byron and Dale Townshend. New York: Routledge, 2014. 498–509.
Danielewski, Mark Z. *House of Leaves*. London: Doubleday, 2001.
Derrida, Jacques. *Spectres of Marx*. Trans. Peggy Kamuf. New York: Routledge, 1994.
Gibson, William. *Neuromancer*. New York: Ace Books, 1984.
Hogle, Jerrold E. "The Gothic Ghost of Counterfeit and the Progress of Abjection." *A New Companion to the Gothic*. Ed. David Punter. Oxford: Blackwell, 2015. 496–509.
Oliver, Marc. "Glitch Gothic." *Cinematic Ghosts: Haunting and Spectrality from Silent Cinema to the Digital Era*. Ed. Murray Leeder. London: Bloomsbury, 2015. 253–70.
Spooner, Catherine. "Twenty-First-Century Gothic." *Terror and Wonder: The Gothic Imagination*. Ed. Dale Townshend. London: British Library, 2014. 180–207.
Sterling, Bruce. "Atemporality for the Creative Artist." *Wired*. 25 Feb. 2010. Web. 6 Dec. 2015.
———. *Gothic High-Tech*. Burton, MI: Subterranean Press, 2011.
Thoreau, Henry David. "Civil Disobedience." 1849. *Walden and Civil Disobedience*. New York: Penguin, 1986. 383–414.
Watkiss, Joanne. *Gothic Contemporaries: The Haunted Text*. Cardiff: University of Wales Press, 2012.

PART II

Identities and Locations

6

ELLEN WEINAUER

Race and the American Gothic

It takes only a brief glance at a sampling of texts to realize the pervasive, significant, and persistent link between race and the Gothic in US literature. From Gothic precursors such as Mary Rowlandson's captivity narrative (1682) to classic Gothic texts such as Poe's *Narrative of Arthur Gordon Pym* (1838), from Melville's *Benito Cereno* (1855) to the short stories of Charles Chesnutt and Paul Laurence Dunbar, from antislavery texts such as *Uncle Tom's Cabin* (1852) to Toni Morrison's prizewinning 1987 novel, *Beloved*, we have ample evidence that Gothic forms, tropes, and traditions have functioned to help writers tell the story of race in America. D. H. Lawrence seems to have recognized this link early on, noting in 1923 the dark energies at work in the writings of Poe, Hawthorne, and others. But it is Leslie Fielder – a "paradigm shifter," according to Charles Crow (*Companion* xvii) – from whose work the ongoing critical conversation about race and the Gothic truly emerges. Having famously declared in 1960 in *Love and Death in the American Novel* that the "tradition of the American novel" is "almost essentially a gothic one" (142), Fiedler went on to explain why: In the US, he asserts, "certain special guilts awaited projection in the gothic form"; although a "dream of innocence had sent Europeans across the ocean to build a new society immune to the compounded evil of the past," that dream was quickly (and remains) troubled by such "abominations" as the decimation of indigenous peoples and the slave trade (143). Fiedler, Charles Crow has noted, "defined a single broad tradition of American Gothic comprising the culture's dark, repressed, and oppositional elements." "All subsequent discussions of American Gothic," Crow goes on, "were shaped by this insight" (*Companion* xvii).

In exploring how American literature is fueled by "special [racial] guilts," Fiedler took a primarily psychological approach: The Gothic, he observes, "was the West's chief method for dealing with the night-time impulses of the psyche" (140), the vengeful psychic return of the repressed truths of the American experience. But as critics following from Fiedler began increasingly to wrangle with the Gothic as a (if not *the*) central American literary form, their discussions took an historical turn. Influenced by Toni Morrison's groundbreaking treatment of the "dark, abiding, signing Africanist presence" that haunts American literature (*Playing* 5), critics such as Kari Winter, Justin Edwards, and, most significantly, Teresa Goddu have established the historical conditions out of which the Gothic emerged and to which the US Gothic has most persistently spoken.[1] We are now able to recognize that, as Goddu has recently asserted, "the Gothic as a genre emerged simultaneous to and in dialogue with the rise of New World slavery and the construction of racial categories" (Goddu, "African American Slave Narrative" 71).[2] And in a nation that is founded on principles of freedom – a nation that dared to base itself on ideas rather than on bloodlines – the existence of slavery, and the increasingly important role of racial categories in justifying that existence, gives the Gothic a unique and special function. In the US context, in short, the Gothic tells the "true" story of race in America – a story that points not only to the existence of substantive national "unfreedoms" but also of the strenuous effort to create racial categories that distinguish free from unfree, civilized from savage, white from black. Eric Savoy has asserted that the "entire tradition of American gothic can be conceptualized as the attempt to invoke ... the specter of Otherness that haunts the house of national narrative" (13–14). That tradition testifies as well to the (failed) effort to keep the "specter of Otherness" in check – to deny the brutal truths of America's complex racial story.

Paradoxically, the role of the Gothic in managing the "specter of Otherness" in America can be seen to predate the rise of the Gothic as a recognizable literary form. Long before Horace Walpole inaugurated and Ann Radcliffe popularized the literary Gothic in England, long before Charles Brockden Brown would consciously revise the Gothic for an American audience, white colonists were drawing on proto-Gothic metaphors, tropes, and techniques to capture the anxieties provoked by life in a strange and forbidding land. Of course, colonists arriving in North America discovered not a "new" world but one already inhabited by diverse communities of indigenous peoples, a world saturated by culture, political structures, and religious belief systems that were dizzyingly unfamiliar and often deeply perturbing. In addition, violent clashes between and among Anglo colonists and Native American communities, whether in the form of local skirmishes or prolonged warfare, provoked efforts to explain a world of profound uncertainty and upheaval and to justify the dispossession and extermination of native peoples in the name of Puritanism (and, later, democracy).

Those efforts frequently involved what Jeffrey Andrew Weinstock has called the "monsterizing of indigenous peoples" (42) – the effort to manage cultural anxiety through the invocation of "othering" figures and tropes that would, as the years progressed, become staples of American Gothic. This "othering" can be seen throughout colonial American writing, from the secular to the sacred. In works by such writers as John Smith, William Bradford, and Thomas Morton, native people are figured as strange and inexplicable at best, savage instruments of the devil at worst. Mary Rowlandson's 1682 captivity narrative offers perhaps the most famous example of such "monsterizing" (for more on Rowlandson, see Ringel [Chapter 1] in this volume). The process begins in the "Preface," where "Amicum" (believed to be Increase Mather), reflects that "none can imagine, what it is to be captivated, and enslaved to such Atheistical, proud, wild, cruel, barbarous, brutish, (in one word,) diabolical Creatures as these, the worst of the heathen" (24). Rowlandson draws on similar language throughout her narrative, describing her native captors as "Barbarous Creatures" and "ravenous Beasts," "black creatures" and "hell-hounds" (28–29). Among the key elements of Rowlandson's captivity is her own descent into barbarism. Rowlandson describes, for instance, how food that she had once deemed "filthy trash" became "pleasant" to her palate (36–37); at one point in the narrative, Rowlandson's hunger drives her to devour a boiled horse's hoof, seized from a child who "could not bite it"; "savoury it was to my taste," she admits (53).

Rowlandson's descent into bestial behavior, of course, works against the narrative's efforts to delineate the categorical otherness of her Indian captors. Indeed, although Rowlandson is redeemed from captivity – and, presumably, from her circumstantial savagery – she tells her readers in the last line of the narrative that she has been forever changed by her experience: "Oh! the wonderfull power of God that mine eyes have seen, affording matter enough for my thoughts to run in, that when others are sleeping mine eyes are weeping" (6). In this line, Rowlandson claims the role of a modern-day Job, redeemed by God so that she can, in turn, help redeem a fallen Puritan community. Yet we can also read in this final line traces of an otherness from which Rowlandson cannot be fully "restored." In the end, the lines that Rowlandson and "Amicum" attempt to draw between Anglos and Indians are unreliable, far more fluid than they are fixed.

While certainly a precursor text, Rowlandson's *Narrative* establishes many key ideas that will function in Gothic literature to follow: an encounter with (and entrapment by) mystifying, monstrous "others," the association of those others with supernatural power, the frightening descent into otherness on the part of the "victim" herself, and an often incomplete restoration to the previous social order. A "violent, sensational, disturbing, and racially complex genre," the captivity tale exemplified by Rowlandson's *Narrative* "constitutes," in the words of Matthew Sivils, "one of the most important influences for what would eventually become American Gothic" (85). From Edgar Huntly's descent into savagery in Charles Brockden Brown's *Edgar Huntly* (1799) to the eponymous protagonist's journey into a dark wilderness inhabited by Satan and his Native American minions in Hawthorne's "Young Goodman Brown" (1835), writers of American Gothic have mined narratives such as Rowlandson's for depictions of harrowing, life-changing encounters with a native other. "[C]reated by and on behalf of the continent's non-Native population," Michelle Burnham remarks, these demonizing depictions perform significant cultural work, suggesting the "triumphant yet guilty history of white violence against the indigenous peoples of the Americas" (228). At the same time, the narratives in which they are embedded point to how quickly self can become other, "civilized" can become "savage," white Christian become native Indian.[3]

"A convenient first step in running roughshod over someone is always to label that person or group as a monster," Weinstock wryly observes (42). If the "monsterizing" of native peoples helped justify the history of white violence, so too did the effort to depict those of African descent as radically other, as monstrous, justify the institution of slavery, particularly as the debate over that institution intensified. While a history of race theory in the United States is, of course, beyond the scope of this essay, it is important to note the instrumental role such theory played in defending the existence of slavery in a nation based on the idea of freedom.[4] At its founding, the upstart United States predicated itself on a radical idea: the natural rights of the individual. Yet what was such a nation to do with the institution of slavery, which had grown in force and influence from the arrival of the first shipload of African slaves in 1619? Evolving theories of race and racial difference would eventually become important tools in the effort to resolve this contradiction – the continuing existence (indeed, the growth) of slavery in a "free" nation. Such theories worked in several ways to help bolster the institution of slavery: first, by depicting race as something innate and inheritable; second, by depicting whites as essentially superior to all other "races," particularly blacks; and third, by depicting the enslavement of blacks by whites as a natural result of black inferiority. Slavery, in short, is saved from contradiction when those who are enslaved are categorically different from those who enslave them – when they are, essentially, less than human.

At the risk of oversimplification, it is fair to say that, until the late eighteenth century, most race theorists were convinced that climate and/or environmental conditions were responsible for perceived racial differences. In

1787, for example, Samuel Stanhope Smith noted the numerous and complex environmental factors at work in creating differences between human beings, insisting finally that, "It is impossible to draw the line precisely between the various races of men or even to enumerate them with certainty"; to try to create an "accurate system of classification of races" would involve "useless labor" (qtd. in Gossett, 40). Even Thomas Jefferson qualifies his notorious statements regarding black inferiority in *Notes on the State of Virginia* (1781) by acknowledging his own uncertainty about what "makes" race. Although he asserts that the "inferiority [of blacks] is not the effect merely of their condition of life" (190), he hedges his bets: "I advance it ... as a suspicion only, that the blacks, whether originally a distinct race, *or* made distinct by time and circumstances, are inferior to the whites in the endowments of both body and mind" (emphasis mine; 192–93).

But while theories regarding the "essential unity of all human races" persisted, as the new century dawned and as slavery exerted increasing economic and political influence, "Racial theory explaining inherent inferiority and superiority would make great inroads not merely in popular thought but also in that of the scientists and scholars" (Gossett 55, 53). Using ostensibly scientific tools (cranial measurement, physiognomy, phrenology), theorists such as Louis Agassiz, Samuel Morton, George Gliddon, and Josiah Nott insisted that race was something innate and that whites were *in essence* superior to blacks. The law of hypodescent, which determined that any child of "mixed" racial heritage would be designated as "black," the debates over racial admixture and "miscegenation" (a term coined in 1863), the uses in literature and law of terms such as "mulatto," and "quadroon" – these developments all point to the growing belief that race was, as Shawn Smith puts it, an "heirloom rooted in the blood" (30). Managing the lines of inheritance, determining who was "white" by blood and who was "black," became increasingly important as race-based slavery gained centrality in the American economy and in social and political life.

Gothic literature of the nineteenth century registers this newfound and growing obsession with race "heritage," and with the policing of the "natural" boundaries between white and black, free and enslaved. Although on the surface a typical tale of seafaring adventure, Edgar Allan Poe's *Narrative of Arthur Gordon Pym of Nantucket* (1838) provides ample evidence of the close tie between the Gothic and race in this period. *Pym* is at once replete with what had become familiar Gothic tropes (live burial, rotting corpses, madness, incarceration) and obsessed with race, which plays a role in many of its most horrifying moments.[5] On the one hand, Pym, the novel's first-person narrator, points repeatedly to distinct and seemingly indelible "color lines." He carefully delineates the racial identity of his shipmates, including a black cook, "who in all respects was a perfect demon," and the ship's first mate, Dirk Peters, the son of a white man and an "Indian squaw of the tribe of Upsarokas"; indeed, Pym describes Peters, "one of the most ferocious-looking men I ever beheld," using the sort of othering language we have encountered elsewhere. The novel's obsession with racial delineation heightens on the mysterious island of Tsalal, where Pym and his shipmates eventually land. There, the crew encounters "jet black" "savages," several "perfectly white" animals (with "blood red" eyes and "scarlet claws"), and water "made up of a number of distinct veins, each of a distinct hue" that never "commingle" (189, 188, 194). But the novel also indicates that color lines and racial categories are neither as reliable nor fixed as they first appear. In *Pym*'s course, "civilized" white men engage in savage acts of cannibalism, white bodies become black under the duress of starvation and in death, and, after Pym and Peters narrowly escape an ambush by the islanders, Peters suddenly "becomes" white. Pym's appalled declaration after the ambush that "We were the only living white men upon the island" (212) points both to the shifting nature of racial identity and to the ways in which whiteness is, as Toni Morrison asserts, contingent, "bound to" and dependent upon "Africanism" (*Playing* 57–58). The novel's inscrutable final plot detail – on a small boat, Pym, Peters, and a black Tsalalian are sucked into a chasm, presided over by a figure whose skin is "perfectly" white – and its unfinished business ("the few remaining chapters which were to have completed his narrative" are "irrecoverably lost") suggest that the story of race and its meanings is far more uncertain and unsettling, far more Gothic, than the science of the day would have it.[6]

While invoking fewer conventional Gothic figures and tropes than *Pym*, Herman Melville's 1855 *Benito Cereno* deploys the psychic bewilderment typical of Poe's work to offer a similarly unsettling (non)ending to the story of race in America. Based on a number of true accounts, *Benito Cereno* tells the retrospective story of a shipboard slave revolt. The mastermind of the revolt is the African Babo, whose ability to orchestrate not only the revolt but also its elaborate cover-up gives the lie to scientific claims regarding black inferiority. Indeed, *Benito Cereno* is concerned not with the revolt itself, which has occurred before the events of the story take place and of which we are informed after those events have concluded, but rather with Babo's elaborate and successful plan to dupe American captain Amasa Delano into misunderstanding what has happened aboard the *San Dominick*. Moreover, because the story is told from the third-person limited point of view (a technique common to Gothic fiction by Ann Radcliffe and others), readers are both restricted to knowing only what Delano knows and implicated in what Delano thinks and assumes. *Benito Cereno* thus becomes an elaborate and complex trick that relies for its effects on the racist assumptions of the American captain *and* of Melville's own (white) readers.

Delano is, as it turns out, an easy mark. Encountering the *San Dominick* on a morning on which "everything" is "gray" (the sky, the "troubled ... fowl," the "troubled ... vapors," the water [35]), the good-natured Captain sees much that is conceptually gray, ambiguous, and shadowy when he boards the ship: He is troubled by its "slovenly" condition (37), by the evident lack of order on board, by the eponymous ship captain's "half-lunatic" behavior (41) and feeble passivity. This passivity has led, Delano assumes, to the "noisy indocility" of the blacks on board and the "sullen inefficiency of the whites" (40). Yet, although he struggles to explain these mysteries, Delano defaults to a predetermined racial script that prevents him from realizing what is actually afoot. Drawing on paternalistic notions made familiar not only by race "scientists" but also by pro-slavery apologists, Delano reads the relationship between Don Benito and Babo as a "beautiful" one involving "fidelity on the one hand and confidence on the other" (45). During a tense scene in which Babo shaves Don Benito, Delano reflects complacently on the innate propensities of blacks: They are "natural valets and hair-dressers," characterized by "a certain easy cheerfulness," and a "docility arising from the unaspiring contentment of a limited mind"; indeed, we are told, like "most men of a good, blithe heart, Captain Delano took to negroes, not philanthropically, but genially, just as other men to Newfoundland dogs" (70–71).

Babo proves to be a shrewd manipulator of such racist assumptions, masquerading as a slow-witted, dog-like "faithful slave," all the while holding Cereno's and Delano's lives in his hands. Only when Babo drops his mask, revealing a "lividly vindictive countenance" as he attempts to stab Don Benito in the heart, does Delano (and do we) finally experience a "flash of revelation" (85). In the deposition attached to the end of the narrative, Don Benito recounts the harrowing events aboard the ship: the uprising, the murder of the slave owner, Alexandro Aranda, the "fictitious story" (95) that Babo authors for the purposes of duping Delano, and to which Cereno and the other whites on board are forced to adhere. Having ourselves finally experienced a "flash of revelation," we are then able to go back and reread the narrative, the horror of which is revealed retroactively, uncannily.

Even as the events of the mutiny are resolved, however, and order is restored (Babo is brought to trial and executed, his head, a "hive of subtlety, fixed on a pole" [102]), *Benito Cereno* leaves Gothic traces of unease. Earlier in the narrative, long before Delano (or Melville's reader) is aware of what has truly occurred on the *San Dominick*, Delano and Don Benito discuss the death of Alexandro Aranda, Don Benito's friend and the owner of the slaves. As Delano gently probes Cereno's grief, the latter reacts with "horrified gestures, as directed against some specter": "This poor fellow now," thinks Delano, "is the victim of that sad superstition which associates goblins with the deserted body of man, as ghosts an abandoned house. How unlike we are made!" (49). Later, of course, Delano learns that Cereno's is no "sad superstition": Aranda is a sort of "goblin" aboard ship, his skeleton having replaced the ship's figurehead as a terrifying reminder of who is really in charge.

But what truly haunts Cereno, along with the story that bears his name, is not Aranda, nor even Babo, but rather the idea of race itself. Like Mary Rowlandson before him, Don Benito is forever changed by his traumatic experience on the *San Dominick*. In the aftermath of that experience, Delano implores Cereno to leave his haunted past behind him. More knowledgeable than he once was about what took place, but not any more enlightened, Delano cannot understand why Cereno remains gloomy: "you are saved; what has cast such a shadow upon you?" (101). Cereno's enigmatic answer, "The negro" (101), gestures not just to Babo but to the unsettling of racial meanings that Babo has unleashed. Delano is seemingly untouched, for his narrative of the "natural" inferiority and docility of blacks is apparently too entrenched. Cereno, however, is not. The story of race in America, *Benito Cereno* suggests, is indeed a haunting and dangerous one, full of false "truths" and blind assumptions; we would do well to heed its ghosts.

Like white authors such as Poe and Melville, black authors too draw on the uncertainty regarding seemingly fixed racial meanings and categories to haunt their readers and fuel their Gothic tales. Efforts to depict the shifting meaning of race, and the white effort to contain and control it, can be seen, for example, in such Gothically inflected texts as William Wells Brown's *Clotel* (1853) and Harriet Wilson's *Our Nig* (1859), and in Hannah Crafts' more explicitly Gothic novel, *The Bondwoman's Narrative* (ca. 1850s). Obsessed as is Poe's *Pym* with the ever-moving color line, *The Bondwoman's Narrative* offers numerous light-skinned African Americans who are taken to be white, and in one case a white woman who uses a "beautifying powder" that turns her face "as black as Tophet" (170, 171). Indeed, so dizzyingly fallacious is skin color as a marker of racial identity that it requires a "bloodhound"-like lawyer, the terrifying Mr. Trappe, to "scent out" "African blood" and ensure that social order is maintained. While Crafts thereby suggests that race is a fiction created in the name of slavery, *The Bondwoman's Narrative* also makes plain that the fiction has real and costly effects. Crafts' novel is punctuated by scenes of bloody violence: a linden tree whose roots have been "many a time ... manured" with the blood of tortured slaves (21); a white slave-owner who slits his own throat upon learning that he has married a black woman, his blood seeping through the floor to the room beneath (76); a slave mother, threatened with separation from her infant, who stabs her baby, then herself, "bathing" the white father's feet "in her blood" (183). Such graphic violence bears witness to the brutality of slavery as an institution and, at the same time, to the terrifying lengths to which white society will go to protect the idea of "race" itself.

In using the Gothic explicitly to indict both slavery and the idea of race that underwrote it, Crafts is certainly not alone. As white and black writers alike understood, "The Gothic's focus on the terror of possession, the iconography of imprisonment, the fear of retribution, and the weight of sin provide a useful vocabulary and register of images by which to represent" slavery and its horrors (Goddu, *Gothic America* 133). In Harriet Beecher Stowe's *Uncle Tom's Cabin*, for example, Cassy orchestrates her escape from the hell that is Simon Legree's plantation by creating an "Authentic Ghost Story" (594): Preying on Legree's superstitions and his awareness of his own guilt – "a human soul is an awful ghostly, unquiet possession, for a bad man to have" (595) – Cassy (along with Emmeline, a slave girl she has befriended) simply walks away from the plantation, the web she has spun around Legree having driven him to drink and to madness.

But while the Gothic provided a ready array of tropes, figures, and plots by which to represent the atrocities of slavery, it was also a dangerous political tool, particularly for African American writers seeking to tell their true stories of slave life. Cassy's "authentic" ghost story is not, of course, authentic, but the stories told by such slave autobiographers as Frederick Douglass and Harriet Jacobs are manifestly so. For these writers, as Goddu has amply demonstrated, the Gothic was both powerful and treacherous, "its narrative construction" threatening to "empty slavery of history by turning it into a gothic trope" (*Gothic America* 135). While aware that the Gothic could cut both ways, however, the narratives of Douglass, Jacobs, and others nevertheless draw readily and in many respects subversively on its tropes. In *Incidents in the Life of a Slave Girl* (1861), for example, Jacobs, writing as Linda Brent, inverts the "othering" process, turning her white tormentors into monsters, "fiends who bear the shape of men" (27). A victim of relentless stalking by her master, Linda uses Gothic conventions to expose slavery's darkest secrets: the sexual predation at its heart, the tortures inflicted on men, women, and children alike, the psychological abuses, the corruption of innocence, the "perversion" of the "natural feelings of the human heart" (142). Linda, who hides for seven years in her grandmother's attic in order to escape from slavery, turns the Gothic tables, showing that a self-chosen imprisonment in a "living grave" is better than a life in slavery (147). Although Linda ostensibly escapes that grave and reaches freedom in the north, she also indicates that she never feels truly safe, for slavery's grasp is long. Here, in Goddu's words, Jacobs "haunts back," indicting the supposedly "free nation" for its cruel hypocrisy, and revealing that "the gothic shadows of slavery encompass the entire nation" (*Gothic America* 151). "It is a sad feeling to be afraid of one's native country" (186), Jacobs writes, in a profound statement that transforms the nation itself into the true Gothic villain.

In discussing the relationship between race and the Gothic, this chapter has focused on the nineteenth century, when theories of race took recognizable, enduring shape and when diverse writers responded to those theories, and the institutions they underwrote, with particular fervor. While slavery would officially come to an end in 1865, the ideas about race that were used to justify it remained in place; beliefs about the innate superiority of whites obviously persisted and have continued to shape economic, political, and social life in the years after the Civil War and into the twentieth and twenty-first centuries. The Gothic has thus remained a useful tool with which diverse writers explore and expose the story of race in America. William Faulkner, for example, draws on the Gothic for his anatomies of southern society, both during and after slavery, depicting the entangled lines of ancestry that slavery has produced: the haunted history it has left behind. But it is perhaps in the work of African American writers that the Gothic takes its most potent form in later periods. Charles Chesnutt's stories of conjure, hoodoo, black magic, and racial transformation – "Mars Jeems's Nightmare" (1899), for example – are certainly Gothic descendants, as are many of the short stories and poems of Paul Laurence Dunbar. Indeed, three of the twentieth century's most groundbreaking African American novels – *Native Son* (Richard Wright, 1940), *Invisible Man* (Ralph Ellison, 1947), and *Beloved* (Toni Morrison, 1987) – are rooted in, and indeed draw much of their emotional energy from, the Gothic.

In his introduction to *Native Son*, for example, Wright explains that he intended to expose the unjust racial structures at the nation's heart by writing a book "so hard and deep" that readers "would have to face it without the consolation of tears" (xxvii). Certainly Bigger Thomas, Wright's antihero, induces fears rather than tears: His life in soul-crushing and relentless poverty leads him to kill and dismember one (white) woman and rape and kill another (black) woman. The final scene of the novel recounts the last conversation between Bigger, now on death row, and Max, the attorney who has fought to convince a jury that Bigger is a "native son": The product of a racist society, Max argues, he should not be executed for his crimes. But although well meaning, Max can neither fathom nor face what an enlightened Bigger tries to tell him: "It must have been good!" Bigger declares in a voice "full of frenzied anguish": "When a man kills, it's for something ... I didn't know I was really alive in this world until I felt things hard enough to kill for 'em"

(392). These words strike Max with "terror," and he cannot look at Bigger as he says his final goodbye. Like Max, Wright's readers are left to confront Bigger's chilling valorization of his crimes; begotten by the violence of his own dispossession in a racist society, Bigger's violence is the only "good" thing available to him. It is no wonder, then, that Wright invokes the American Gothic tradition in his introduction. Alluding to the shadowy truths of race liked those exposed in *Benito Cereno*, Wright states that "we have in the oppression of the Negro a shadow athwart our national life dense and heavy enough to satisfy even the gloomy broodings of a Hawthorne ... And if Poe were alive, he would not have to invent horror; horror would invent him" (xxxiv). (On Wright, see also Cassuto [Chapter 11] in this volume.)

A few years later, another African American writer, Ralph Ellison, will launch his own expose of the true, "uninvented" horrors of America's racial structures with a direct reference to *Benito Cereno* (he uses Delano's final question to Don Benito, "what has cast such a shadow upon you?" as an epigraph) and an invocation of Poe. "I am an invisible man," declares our eponymous narrator in the novel's opening lines: "No, I am not a spook like those who haunted Edgar Allan Poe; nor am I one of our Hollywood-movie ectoplasms. I am a man of substance, of flesh and bone, fiber and liquids – and I might even be said to possess a mind. I am invisible, understand, simply because people refuse to see me" (3). Like Wright, Ellison invokes Poe to suggest the difference between dematerialized Gothic trappings ("Hollywood-movie ectoplasms") and the Gothic reality of race in America that has forced Ellison's unnamed narrator underground. Yet, as we have seen, Poe's Gothic seems closer to Ellison's (and to Wright's) than the latter might recognize: Both writers address the uncanny enigma of race in America, at once "invisible" but palpable, a false construct that has bred unceasing violence, damaged millions upon millions of lives.

While Ellison and Wright are both interested in how the troubled legacies of the nation's racial past haunt the contemporary moment, Toni Morrison's *Beloved* reaches back to that past to tell the story of Sethe, Paul D, and other former slaves who are struggling to find a way to acknowledge the horrors of their past enslavement while living whole, free, and with love in the present. Based on the true story of Margaret Garner, a fugitive slave who killed her daughter rather than allow her to be carried back into slavery, *Beloved* relies fully on Gothic forms and conventions: The house where Sethe lives is haunted by Beloved, the child that Sethe killed – "124 was spiteful. Full of a baby's venom," the novel begins (3) – and that child eventually becomes an enigmatic "flesh and blood" presence in the lives of Sethe and her loved ones. In the course of the novel, these damaged characters must learn to accept their past without being possessed by it, to repossess and reclaim the humanity that slavery has denied them. But while the ghost of Beloved is exorcised so that Sethe and Paul D can claim "some kind of tomorrow" (322), hints and whispers of the past she represents are left behind: "the rustle of a skirt" that "hushes" when someone wakes, or the footprints "down by the stream" that "come and go, come and go" are reminders of the indelible legacies of slavery and its traumas. The Gothic enables Toni Morrison to tell a story that exists in a kind of ghostly in-between: "This is not a story to pass on," the narrator repeats in the novel's final pages, yet neither is it a story that should ever be forgotten.

In Paul Laurence Dunbar's 1904 story, "The Lynching of Jube Benson," a character named, interestingly, Dr. Melville is haunted by his participation in the lynching of a black man, falsely accused of murdering a white woman: "Why did I do it? I don't know. A false education, I reckon, one false from the beginning. I saw his black face glooming there in the half light, and I could only think of him as a monster. It's tradition" (486). As we have seen, the "tradition" of racist belief to which Dr. Melville refers, and the social, political, and economic structures that such belief fuels, goes back to the earliest encounters between white colonists and indigenous people and is evident in literary production from the period of encounter to the contemporary moment. That "tradition" is indeed a haunting one, appropriate to and for a literary form that resides above all in disquietude.

NOTES

1. Morrison's *Playing in the Dark* follows from her remarkable "Unspeakable Things Unspoken," first delivered as a lecture at the University of Michigan in 1988, then published in the *Michigan Quarterly Review* (1989). Also see Winter, *Subjects of Slavery*; Edwards, *Gothic Passages*; and Goddu, *Gothic America*. In a recent study, Siân Silyn Roberts takes a different tack to the historically interventionist role of the Gothic, taking issue with the "guilt thesis" (21) and asserting that the American Gothic produces nothing less than a "complex and wholly distinct theory of the political subject" (6) in the new and developing nation.
2. The significance of Goddu's work in the domain of the Gothic, history, and race cannot be overestimated. With *Gothic America*, Goddu firmly established the ways in which the Gothic must be understood as a historically responsive genre that tells a complex and often vexed story of the nation's failures to deliver on its political and social promises.
3. Michelle Burnham argues suggestively for the recognition of an indigenous Gothic, one produced by and reflecting the worldviews of native populations rather than colonial settlers, and extending well into the twenty-first century. Drawing on the Gothic trope of the haunted house, Burnham writes, "if we think of the land, of the continent, as itself a house that belongs to its indigenous peoples, then the identities of landlord and tenant change radically, and in ways

that invert the traditional racial dynamics of American Gothic. In this view, it is the settler colonist whose face has taken up an unwelcome tenancy in the Native American home, and whose threatening presence haunts American Indian narrative" (227).
4. Thomas Gossett's *Race: The History of an Idea in America* (first published in 1963, and republished in 1997), remains an excellent source. See also Bruce Dain, *A Hideous Monster of the Mind*.
5. For slightly longer treatment of *Pym* in this context, see my essay, "Gothic Fiction."
6. Similarly complex engagements with the issue of race can be seen throughout Poe's corpus, in such texts as "The Black Cat" (1843), "The Gold-Bug" (1843), and "Hop-Frog" (1849).

WORKS CITED

Burnham, Michelle. "Is There an Indigenous Gothic?" *A Companion to American Gothic*. Ed. Charles L. Crow. Hoboken, NJ: John Wiley & Sons, 2014. 225–37.

Crafts, Hannah. *The Bondwoman's Narrative*. New York: Warner Books, 2005.

Crow, Charles L. *A Companion to American Gothic*. Hoboken, NJ: John Wiley & Sons, 2014.

Dain, Bruce. *A Hideous Monster of the Mind: American Race Theory in the Early Republic*. Cambridge, MA and London: Harvard University Press, 2002.

Dunbar, Paul Laurence. "The Lynching of Jube Benson." *American Gothic, From Salem Witchcraft to H.P. Lovecraft: An Anthology*. Ed. Charles L. Crow. 2nd edition. Malden, MA: Wiley-Blackwell, 2013. 483–87.

Edwards, Justin D. *Gothic Passages: Racial Ambiguity and the American Gothic*. Iowa City: U of Iowa P, 2003.

Ellison, Ralph. *Invisible Man*. 1947. New York: Vintage International, 1990.

Fiedler, Leslie. *Love and Death in the American Novel*. 1960. Normal, IL: Dalkey Archive Press, 1997.

Goddu, Teresa. "The African American Slave Narrative and the Gothic." *A Companion to American Gothic*. Ed. Charles L. Crow. Hoboken, NJ: John Wiley & Sons, 2014. 71–83.

Gothic America: Narrative, History, and Nation. New York: Columbia University Press, 1997. Print.

Gossett, Thomas F. *Race: The History of an Idea in America*. 1963. New York: Oxford University Press, 1997.

Jacobs, Harriet. *Incidents in the Life of a Slave Girl*. Cambridge, MA: Harvard University Press, 1987.

Jefferson, Thomas. *Notes on the State of Virginia*. *The Portable Thomas Jefferson*. Ed. Merrill D. Peterson. New York: Penguin, 1977. 23–232.

Melville, Herman. *Benito Cereno*. *Melville's Short Novels*. Ed. Dan McCall. New York: WW Norton, 2002. 34–102.

Morrison, Toni. *Beloved*. New York: Penguin, 1987.

Playing in the Dark: Whiteness and the Literary Imagination. Cambridge, MA: Harvard University Press, 1992.

"Unspeakable Things Unspoken: The Afro-American Presence in American Literature." *Michigan Quarterly Review* 28 (1989): 1–34.

Poe, Edgar Allan. *The Narrative of Arthur Gordon Pym of Nantucket*. New York: Penguin, 1999.

Roberts, Siân Silyn. *Gothic Subjects: The Transformation of Individualism in American Fiction, 1790–1861*. Philadelphia: University of Pennsylvania Press, 2014.

Rowlandson, Mary. *A True History of the Captivity and Restauration of Mrs. Mary Rowlandson*. *Classic American Autobiographies*. Ed. William L. Andrews. New York: Signet, 2003. 19–69.

Savoy, Eric. "The Face of the Tenant: A Theory of American Gothic." *American Gothic: New Interventions in a National Narrative*. Eds. Robert K. Martin and Eric Savoy. Iowa City, IA: University of Iowa Press, 1998. 3–19.

Sivils, Matthew Wynn. "Indian Captivity Narratives and the Origins of American Frontier Gothic." *A Companion to American Gothic*. Ed. Charles L. Crow. Hoboken, NJ: John Wiley & Sons, 2014. 84–95.

Smith, Shawn Michelle. *American Archives: Gender, Race, and Class in Visual Culture*. Princeton, NJ: Princeton University Press, 1999.

Stowe, Harriet Beecher. *Uncle Tom's Cabin; or, Life Among the Lowly*. New York: Penguin, 1981.

Weinauer, Ellen. "Gothic Fiction." *American History through Literature, 1820–1870*. Eds. Janet Gabler-Hover and Robert D. Sattelmeyer. New York: Charles Scribner's Sons, 2005. 475–81.

Weinstock, Jeffrey Andrew. "American Monsters." *A Companion to American Gothic*. Ed. Charles L. Crow. Hoboken, NJ: John Wiley & Sons, 2014. 41–55.

Winter, Kari. *Subjects of Slavery, Agents of Change: Women and Power in Gothic Novels and Slave Narratives, 1790–1865*. Athens: University of Georgia Press, 1992.

Wright, Richard. *Native Son*. 1940. New York: Harper & Row, 1966.

7

DIANE LONG HOEVELER

American Female Gothic

The subgenre of the Female Gothic refers generally to Gothic works written by women that use specific themes, tropes, and conventions of the Gothic to reflect and address female concerns such as marriage, childbirth, inheritance laws, and patriarchal disempowerment. As Jeffrey Andrew Weinstock observes in his *Scare Tactics: Supernatural Fiction by American Women*, the United States has its own tradition of supernatural writings by women in which hundreds of female authors made use of the Gothic mode in order to express their frustration with and anger at the circumscribed roles available to them. Their fiction frequently condemned the forms of discrimination and violence to which they were exposed. This chapter will consider Gothic themes as developed by a number of representative female authors who specialized in the composition of the short Gothic tale, a subgenre that has been particularly effective as a means by which female writers can express a variety of political, social, religious, and sexual critiques.

New England Female Gothic

The American Female Gothic can be considered to have originated in the stories of a number of female authors associated with the New England schools of local color realism and consolation writing, particularly as seen in the works of Sarah Orne Jewett and Mary E. Wilkins Freeman.[1] Jewett's *The Country of the Pointed Firs* (1896) concerns a polar netherworld as described by a castaway named Gaffett, a stranded survivor of an earlier polar expedition, who tells his tale to Captain Littlepage. For the Captain, who in his turn relates the tale to female auditors, this mysterious netherworld needs to be rationally understood, mapped, and managed by a masculinist system of knowledge. For the female auditors of the tale, however, this netherworld is easily understood as an extension of their own world with its mysterious boundaries between life and death. Clearly influenced by the theosophical theories of Emanuel Swedenborg, Jewett attempted to present the material world as a reverse image of the spiritual, transcendent realm – what a number of critics have seen as a form of "feminized Christianity" (Gentile 210). Maintaining fluid boundaries between the two worlds provides some comfort to the living who fear the nothingness of an unknowable afterlife. As Carpenter and Kolmar have noted, female authors, unlike male writers, did not draw a sharp distinction between the natural and the supernatural worlds, instead seeing the two spheres as continuous, able to be "accepted, connected with, reclaimed" ("Introduction" 12). In taking this position, they acknowledge Rosemary Jackson, who has also explored this theme in female supernatural fiction. Jackson writes, "Women writers of the supernatural have overturned many of these assumptions and definitions [about the sharp divide between life and death] – not, as with some of their male counterparts, to investigate 'horror' for its own sake, but in order to extend our sense of the human, the real, beyond the blinkered limits of male science, language, and rationalism" (xviii).

Wilkins Freeman is another one of the best known of the New England school of writers, with her short story "Luella Miller" being one of her most frequently anthologized Gothic tales. Generally read as a critique of Coventry Patmore's "angel in the house" ideal (or what was known in America as "The Cult of True Womanhood"),[2] the story focuses on a woman who, while supposedly helpless, actually preys on and vampirically sucks the life out of everyone who cares for her. It is only when an older woman refuses to do her bidding that Luella herself dies and her ghost presides over a procession of all of the previous victims of her vampirism. Freeman's other Gothic tales frequently featured ghosts, children, and unhappy, unfulfilled ordinary people. Her tales "The Wind in the Rose-bush" (1902) and "The Lost Ghost" (1902) both concern child abuse; the first depicts the ghost of the young Agnes who haunts her aunt Rebecca. Years earlier, Rebecca had failed to rescue Agnes in time from the neglect of Agnes' stepmother, an act of neglect that directly caused Agnes' death. Whereas the familial relations are somewhat distanced in "The Wind in the Rose-bush," they are very direct in "The Lost Ghost." This story focuses on the recounted tale of Mrs. Bisbees, a mother who physically and verbally abuses her five-year-old daughter before finally locking her in a room to starve and freeze to death. The mother is later murdered by her husband when he learns the truth of their daughter's death. It is the ghost of this dead girl who haunts the house, now inhabited by the narrator and two childless widows, Mrs. Dennison and Mrs. Bird, the latter of which is especially sensitive to the sufferings and cold that the ghost of the dead girl still experiences. One morning, the narrator and Mrs. Dennison see what appears to be Mrs. Bird walking with the child, only to discover Mrs. Bird dead in her bed with her arm crooked in a protective manner, as if shielding the little girl. As Voller has observed, the ghosts in the fiction of Wilkins Freeman are not "denizens of some malefic otherworld but (dis)embodied projections of the human psyche and the complex socio-cultural cross-currents in which [they are] caught" (122–23). As Voller notes, the supernaturalism of these stories is naturalized, domesticated, and situated in the realm of the quotidian and the psychological, making the horror in the tale all the more direct and immediate to the readers of these tales. The story clearly critiques both those who fail at the task of motherhood and those who are consumed by its demands. Such a double-edged position, however, was uncomfortable for the readers of the late nineteenth century, who generally preferred their ideology clear-cut. Confronting the disappointing realities behind the façade of marriage made for uneasy reading, hence the marginalization of a number of these New England Gothic stories.

Charlotte Perkins Gilman's "The Yellow Wallpaper" (1892) is undoubtedly the most famous and widely reprinted example of a New England Female Gothic tale. Written as a first-person case study that documents a young mother's descent into madness, the story is famously based on the wrong-headed treatment that Gilman herself received for postpartum depression from Dr. S. Weir Mitchell.[3] In addition to critiquing the patriarchal medical establishment, the story also condemns the stultifying effects of marriage and motherhood as ruinous to a creative woman's needs to write and think for herself. Only when the nameless heroine succeeds in peeling off the wallpaper in her bedroom-nursery does she confront her other buried self, a doubled or split-off version of herself that she names "Jane": Whether this is a repressed artist or a ghost is left ambiguous. Recalling the doppelgänger motif used by Edgar Allan Poe in "William Wilson" (1839) or Charlotte Brontë's madwoman in the attic in *Jane Eyre* (1847), Gilman's "Yellow Wallpaper" presents the American woman as hopelessly split by the conflict between her duties in the public and private spheres.

Gilman's other major Gothic tale, "The Giant Wistaria" (1891), is structured around two events occurring over one hundred years apart. In the first part of the tale, a Puritan unwed mother is physically abused and perhaps eventually murdered by her father, who cannot forgive her for bringing shame on the Dwining family name and refusing to marry an oafish cousin who would have made an "honest woman" out of her. The second part of the tale concerns a group of young people, three couples, who rent the house one summer only to begin seeing a ghostly mother trying to flee the house with a bundle of goods (or the baby?) on her back but continually circling back to the dank and deep well on the property. It is only when the young people excavate the well that they find the skeleton of an infant and the implication is that either the girl's father drowned the baby and the mother attempted to rescue it before she too was killed by her father, or, more horrifically, the mother killed the baby herself rather than desert it and then committed suicide. After more exploring, the young renters discover the mother's skeleton, identified by the red stone cross around her neck, entangled in the roots of a wisteria tree that the Dwining mother had brought over with her from England. The story is dominated by two contrasting symbols that encode the ambiguity of the tale, the patriarchal house juxtaposed against the large blooming wisteria bush that the young mother and her mother planted one hundred years earlier. While the house does continue to stand, it is gradually being overtaken by the strangling growth of the tree's roots, which now have almost swallowed the foundations of the house. Pitting masculine and feminine forces against each other, the tale suggests that the edifices that men build will eventually be undercut by female generative power, as well as the ability to expose male crimes, no matter how ancient and buried they appear to be.

Edith Wharton

Edith Wharton has frequently been discussed by critics as a member of the New England supernatural school, but given the cosmopolitan settings of most of her ghost tales, it is possible to see her, like Henry James, as an expatriate writing in a decidedly Anglo-American voice. A wealthy American who spent the majority of her life in England and France, Wharton sets many of her tales in Europe and in some ways her stories rely more on British and French Gothic techniques than on American.[4] In her supernatural short story "Afterward" (1910), Wharton writes of her protagonist Mary Boyne: "There were ... moments of weariness when, like the victim of some poison which leaves the brain clear, but holds the body motionless, she saw herself domesticated with the Horror, accepting its perpetual presence as one of the fixed conditions of life" (*Ghost Stories* 84). This description sums up much of the Gothic ambience of Wharton's stories, suffused as they are with suffocating houses, paralyzing codicils and wills, and crimes motivated by patriarchal privilege and power.[5]

The twenty-two short Gothic stories written by Wharton can be divided into three groups that reflect her shifting attitudes toward marriage, the patriarchal family, and the usually victimized female body.[6] While it is impossible to provide summaries for all of these stories, it is possible to draw some conclusions about a number of trends that emerge from examining them as a series of groups. The earliest ghost stories (1893–1906) generally focus on the power of an absent husband or father over a weaker or dependent woman. A crime or the threat of a crime occurs, and the guilt of the survivor pervades the tale.

Included in this group are "The Fullness of Life" (1893), "The Duchess at Prayer" (1900), "The Angel at the Grave" (1901), "The Moving Finger" (1901), "The Lady Maid's Bell" (1902), "The House of the Dead Hand," (1904), and "The Hermit and the Wild Woman" (1906). The second grouping (1910–1926) shifts the focus away from the victim and onto the perpetrator of the crime. In these tales, the victim(s) are not exclusively female and the inability to articulate the story is often at the heart of the matter. These tales include "Afterward" (1910), "The Eyes" (1910), "The Triumph on Night" (1914), "Kerfol" (1916), "Bewitched" (1926), "A Bottle of Perrier" (1926), and "The Young Gentlemen" (1926). The last grouping of stories includes "Miss Mary Pask" (1925), "Mr. Jones" (1928), "Dieu D'Amour" (1930), "After Holbein" (1930), "The Pomegranate Seed" (1931), "The Looking Glass" (1935), and "All Souls" (1937). In these, the victim has not only found her voice and been able to record the story of her imprisonment or oppression, but such records, if buried, are recovered in order to reconstruct the tale of abuse. The last two stories focus on an older woman's fears of aging and her dependence on the assistance of servants. Like the ghost stories of Henry James, Wharton's tales trace her shifting personal anxieties throughout her long life.

In her very first attempt to write a ghost story, Wharton produced a work that she herself considered heavy-handed in its critique of marriage: "The Fullness of Life." This story introduces us to a ghostly narrator, a just-dead woman who tells her tale from beyond the grave. Most critics view this story as a fairly overt depiction of Wharton's view of her marriage to Teddy Wharton, and the frustrations that resulted from it. When the Spirit of Life offers to unite her with a true soul mate who understands fully her artistic nature, she declines in order not to abandon her first husband at his death. She imagines a befuddled newly dead man wondering why his ever-dutiful wife is not there to welcome him into the afterlife. As Weinstock notes, the tale is "a caustic commentary about gender roles in American culture ... [W]omen are expected to sacrifice their personal fulfillment for the sake of the happiness of others, while men are free to pursue personal satisfaction even when it may affect negatively those around them" (117). Just as the wife in "The Fullness of Life" says of free choice, "Choosing! ... Do you still keep up here that old fiction about choosing? ... How can I help myself?" (242), Wharton suggests in a number of these early tales that women are so thoroughly socialized that they have no free choice in any matter, even after their deaths. "The Fullness of Life" also employs the Keatsian idea of life as symbolized by a house: "like a great house full of rooms: there is the hall, through which everyone passes in going in and out; the drawing room, where one receives formal visits; the sitting room, where the members of the family come and go as they list; but beyond that, far beyond, are other rooms, the handles of whose doors perhaps are never turned; ... and in the innermost room, the holy of holies, the soul sits alone and waits for a footstep that never comes" (Wharton in Bendixen, *Haunted Women* 234). This domestication of the spiritual world recalls the works of Jewett and several of the other New England Female Gothic writers.

But clearly Wharton was influenced by the short tales of a number of French authors. For instance, Honoré de Balzac's "La Grande Bretêche" (1832) was praised by Wharton as the "that most perfectly- composed of all short stories" (Wharton, *The Writing of Fiction* 67). Her "The Duchess at Prayer" is an attempt to rewrite Balzac's story, complete with an exploration of the psychology of adultery and live burial as punishment. In Wharton's version, the Duchess Violante is virtually entombed by her scholarly husband, the Duke Ercole II, when she is installed in his country villa. With no company aside from her servants, it is not surprising that she becomes entangled with the Duke's young cousin Cavaliere Ascanio. Suspecting that his wife and cousin are cuckolding him in the crypt where St. Blandina's relics are kept, the Duke has a huge statue of the Duchess at prayer placed over the entrance to the vault, thereby trapping Ascanio underground to suffocate. The Duchess herself dies the same night after drinking poisoned wine. The monumental statue of the Duchess, with a look of "frozen horror ... hate, revolt and agony" (154) on her face, stands as a visual totem to Wharton's indictment of the corrupt patriarchal family and the hollow and hypocritical institution of marriage.

Wharton's 1901 story, "Angel at the Grave," reads as a rewrite of Henry James' *The Aspern Papers* (1888), another tale of the power of the past over the present lives of the heirs of creative people. Wharton's protagonist, Paulina Anson, is the granddaughter of a famous philosopher, Orestes Anson. She returns to the family estate and becomes an historian and a biographer of her grandfather, eventually rejecting marriage to Hewlitt Winsloe in order to continue to serve as a caretaker of her grandfather's estate. Although the townspeople believe Paulina's choice to be a result of her aunts' pressure, the narrator explains that "such disapproval as reached her was an emanation from the walls of the House, from the bare desk, the faded portraits, the dozen yellowing tomes," which represent Orestes' estate and literary legacy (*Wharton's New England* 28). It seems as if Paulina Anson's isolation is a choice rather than enforced, but her decision results at least partially from the "disapproval" (28) she senses as emanating from the walls of the house itself. Her shame derives from the grandfather rather than from with Paulina herself. It is her diligence in preserving Orestes' legacy that provides for the still extant manuscript on the fish *amphioxus* that the scientist Mr. Corby comes seeking. This story is also rare in its explicit statement of theme in Paulina's warning to Mr. Corby that, "I gave up everything ... to keep *him* alive. I sacrificed myself – others – I nursed his glory in my bosom and it died – and left me – left me here alone" (*Wharton's New England* 37).

In "The House of the Dead Hand," Sybilla is also isolated, but, rather than geographically distant on a country estate, she lives within her family's home in Siena, marked by "an antique hand of marble which for many hundred years has been above the door" (361). Sybilla Lombard has had an opportunity to escape from the family house and marry a young man of good family, the Conte Ottaviano Celsi. However, her father, Dr. Lombard, has "forbidden the lovers to meet or correspond" (370); thus, Count Ottaviano must rely on the touring Englishman Wyant as a messenger in delivering notes to Sybilla, encouraging her to escape with him. Sybilla is held captive via a family legacy, compelled by her father to "invest ... her whole inheritance in the purchase of [a painting by Leonardo]" (364), one which it is the father's goal to keep secretively locked away in the house, kept only for private viewing. However, Sybilla needs to sell the painting in order to recoup her dowry and marry the Count. While Wyant refuses to aid Sybilla and Ottaviano in duping Dr. Lombard and locking him within the chamber with the painting so that Sybilla may escape to marry Ottaviano, Wyant expects, upon hearing that her father has died a month later, that she would have married the Count. When Wyant revisits Siena about five years later, however, he discovers that Sybilla is still unmarried, and living at the House of the Dead Hand. Despite the fact that Sybilla claims to hate the painting, which is very sensual in nature, she tells Wyant that she has not sold it; "he [her father] wouldn't let me – he will never let me now," and she repeats, "he prevented me; he will always prevent me" (376–77). She adds, "he was always in the room with me ... I can't lock him out; I can never lock him out now" (377). The dead hand of the father presides over the house as thoroughly as it did while he was living. There is no escaping the power of the patriarchy in these tales because, ultimately, the father has invaded the mind of the daughter through socialization. Because of this ambivalent devotion to the father, Wharton's feminist themes do seem to "lurk" in these Gothic tales rather than proclaim themselves in an explicit or aggressive voice. Her female characters may attempt at times to combat the oppressive forces of patriarchy, marriage, and limited horizons, but they rarely succeed. The supernatural on the edges of these tales sometimes functions as an enabling force but more frequently as an extension of the father's continued allure and power.

Shirley Jackson

Jackson herself observed that, "I have had for many years a consuming interest in magic and the supernatural. I think this is because I find there so convenient a shorthand statement of the possibilities of human adjustment to what seems to be at best an inhuman world." Later, she noted that she loved eighteenth-century novels because they "preserv[ed] and insist[ed] on a pattern superimposed precariously on the chaos of human development" (qtd. in Oppenheimer 125). But in spite of Jackson's insistence on the importance of the Gothic for her style and vision, literary critics have been wont to see in her works something very different, very "proto-postmodern" (Hattenhauer 2). In fact, if one were to recognize a constant refrain in the literary criticism of Shirley Jackson, it is that she deserves to be appreciated as something other than a writer of "horror" tales, or stories about witchcraft, or Gothic fiction.[7] One would think, in fact, that these critics are embarrassed by this particular strain in Jackson's work, or that if they could only absolve her of her Gothic tendencies, they could rehabilitate her reputation as a serious writer of contemporary fiction. This anti-Gothic tendency in the criticism of Jackson's works has been countered most effectively by the publication of Darryl Hattenhauer's *Shirley Jackson: American Gothic*, a critical study that places the Gothic impulse at center in Jackson's life and works. It is impossible to ignore the Gothic quality of her novels *The Haunting of Hill House* (1959) and *We Have Always Lived in the Castle* (1962). Less examined is the Gothic impulse in her late short fiction. As she herself observed, everything that she wrote was concerned with the struggle between chaos and pattern: "the sense which I feel, of a human and not very rational order struggling inadequately to keep in check forces of great destruction, which may be the devil and may be intellectual enlightenment" (qtd. in Oppenheimer 125). By examining a couple of her late short stories – "My Uncle in the Garden" (1995) and "Home"(1998) – we can, I think, see how Jackson handled Gothic tropes in her short fiction. As she herself noted, her recurrent concern was "an insistence on the uncontrolled, unobserved wickedness of human behavior" (qtd. in Oppenheimer 125).

In Jackson's version of the Fall, the posthumously published "My Uncle in the Garden," two bachelor uncles exude eccentricity and, indeed, one of them admits to dancing with the devil in the garden at night. But perhaps this is just one of the strange acts they have committed. Narrated by a naive innocent who in fact is not related by blood to the two men, the story presents uncle Oliver and uncle Peter as brothers who have lived together all their lives, except for the one year that Oliver spent married to Mrs. Duff. An odor of perversion fills the air as the two old men fuss over Peter's gray cat, Sandra

Williamson, in their static, perpetually frozen little rose-covered cottage (209). One evening, over dinner, the brothers lapse into a quarrel over the absence of tomatoes on the table, and Oliver confides to his young visitor that Peter has "been consorting with the devil" in the garden at night (211). But in addition to these nocturnal visits, the devil has also been invited to lunch and, over this cozy repast the devil has requested a "tribute," for which the tomatoes have been offered. After an absence of several weeks, the tomatoes suddenly reappear, as does the offering of "a little boy" (214).

All this could be read as a harmless and inconsequential matter, a tale about nothing much and certainly nothing very important. But in the last few paragraphs, the other shoe drops and we realize, with a sickening thud, that the men are something other than innocent bachelor uncles. As they turn to each other, reconciled by the reappearance of ripe tomatoes at their table, they wax nostalgic by musing about a trip into the city that they have never made. Talking about making this trip, leaving their sheltered abode for an adventurous foray into the urban unknown, has always been "their favorite mutual whimsy" (214). But now we hear the ominous suggestion that this "whimsy" is second only to talking about "the death of Mrs. Duff" (214), Oliver's bride for only one year. The implication that immediately flashes into the reader's mind is that the brothers conspired to kill Mrs. Duff for her inheritance, and they have been happily living off of it ever since. In fact, to go yet the next step, it would appear that perhaps the devil had appeared to the insane Peter earlier and had requested a "tribute" then as well, and that the "tribute" offered earlier had been the life of Mrs. Duff. To take the implications yet another step further, it would appear that Mrs. Duff had been an inconvenient woman who had stood in the way of primal male-bonding and the earlier, intense relationship between the brothers. These men, so pleasant and mild that generations of neighbors entrust their children to them for strolls in the park and zoo, appear to be members of some sort of ancient fertility and satanic cult that practices human sacrifice, substituting crops when humans are not readily available.[8] This mild-mannered tale actually presents a hyperbolic version of the capitalistic and patriarchal logic that operates in so many of Jackson's stories, for this tale presents men as vampiric, homosocial, murderous, satanic worshippers of an ancient fertility that produces life forms that they do not need or want. And the major female character, mature and wealthy, is offered up as expendable and consumable by the man she has foolishly admitted into her life.

Just as "My Uncle in the Garden" focuses on a rural retreat that turns out to be based on human sacrifice, so does "Home" present rural life as a recurrent nightmare. Ethel Sloane, the protagonist of "Home," is a recent transplant to country living and after only one day's occupancy she considers herself "acquainted with most of the local people" through her numerous trips to the hardware store. But Ethel, like all of Jackson's smug female characters, has more than a little to learn before the day is finished. In Ethel's case, she is unaware of the fact that there are also "local people" who are not living and not met in the hardware store. Indeed, she and her husband have just bought a house that is considered by the locals to be haunted. The old Sanderson place was the site of a kidnapping and double drowning some sixty years before, and local legend has it that on rainy days it is best to avoid the creek where the disaster occurred. But Ethel has no time to hear warnings or village history from the owner of the hardware story, who tries in vain to warn her to avoid the route. So she proceeds to take the haunted road and even stops to pick up the two mysterious and bedraggled "figures standing silently in the rain by the side of the road" (400). An old woman and little boy are shivering, and the "child was sick with misery, wet and shivering and crying in the rain" (400). Although the old woman speaks only to ask for directions to "the Sanderson place," she clearly is controlling the child and putting him in harm's way. Ethel is shocked when she sees the condition of the boy, barefoot, wearing "thin pajamas," and wrapped in a wet and dirty blanket (400). The boy never speaks, but the old woman informs Ethel that "he wants to go home" and home is the Sanderson place (401). Ethel, of course, can hardly imagine how these two can intend to visit her and her husband, and she "felt oddly feudal with pride. We're the lords of the manor" (401). But when she arrives at the home, the woman and boy have vanished from the back seat of her car.

Ethel receives the explanation she seeks from her husband Jim, who has heard the legend about a "crazy old woman" (401) who kidnapped and disappeared with the little Sanderson boy. As the night was rainy and the creek had risen, it was believed that the two had drowned. Pride, elation, ownership of the "ghosts" initially fills Ethel with happiness, and she intends to tell the story of her recent encounter with her very own ghosts in town the next day. But when she next enters her car she once again has company, for the ghosts are back and are complaining that they could not go "home" because there "were strangers in the house" (403). Desperate, Ethel proposes to take the two back to where she found them yesterday, next to the creek. But her passengers have another idea. As the car skids on the wet road and almost plunges into the creek, Ethel hears the young boy's "horrible laughter," and she realizes that the two of them intend to take her with them into the dark waters (404).

We might recall here the Nietzchean or Kierkegaardean theories of the "eternal return," the notion that we will repeat and return over and over again to certain moments within our lives. For the boy and the old woman, the eternal return will be to the site of the betrayal, the kidnapping, and its violent denouement in drowning. Forever kept out of a home to which the boy can never return, the two of them seek to dispossess others as they were dispossessed, by poverty and victimization. For Jackson there is an afterlife, but it is just like "home," a place where we will be returned in order to be wounded and betrayed yet again. And there are no parents at "home," only a crazy old woman who takes us with her into the dark waters of death. Jackson's worldview is predicated again on the dysfunctional family, a site where victimization, abandonment, disappointment, and abuse lurk around every corner. "Home" is not a cheery vision of families gathered around their fireplaces, providing moral and emotional support to one another, and Jackson's vision of the afterlife suggests that if there cannot be good parents in this life, what hope can we have that they will exist in the next life?

John G. Parks has observed: "Jackson's gothic fiction is an effective mode for her exploration of the violations of the human self – the aching loneliness, the unendurable guilt, the dissolution and disintegrations, the sinking into madness, the violence and lovelessness" (28). But Jackson writes out of concern for more than the personal. She is deeply invested in exploring the persistence of evil in communities and institutions. More violent than the fiction of Jewett, Freeman, or Wharton, Jackson's works reveal the influence of World War II and the Holocaust on the consciousness of her reading public. Inexplicable acts of brutality occur and history is presented as a pattern of repetitive violence from which there is no real escape.

Joyce Carol Oates

Joyce Carol Oates is such a prolific writer that any attempt to provide a listing of her Gothic works is immediately outdated. Her short Gothic tales are collected in a number of collections, but at this point it is fair to say that her most successful volume of short Gothic tales is *Haunted: Tales of the Grotesque* (1995), a collection that contains several unforgettably strange and perverse tales (most noticeably "The White Cat," a postmodern rewrite of Poe's "The Black Cat," "Poor Bibi," a rewrite of Kafka's "The Metamorphosis," "The Doll," and "The Accursed Inhabitants of the House of Bly," the last a very precise and detailed rewriting of Henry James' 1898 *The Turn of the Screw* told from the perspective of the ghosts). In the tradition of postmodern rewrites of earlier classic works, Oates' "Accursed Inhabitants" stands out as both a creative and a critical response to her source in James. In this story, Oates answers the questions the reader cannot resolve after reading James, and she answers them in ways that are not comfortable or pleasant, but she is honest about the dark and unspoken urges in James' text: pedophilia, trauma, and fantasy. And in addition to pedophilia, Oates explores erotic melancholia, the kind of frustrated, infinite erotic suffering, the kind of loss and pain that is so intense that it exists even after we die, the kind of insatiable longing that would constitute hell should there be such a place.

"The Doll" presents an exquisitely successful professional woman haunted by her childhood memories of a dollhouse and one particular doll who could not control her bodily functions. Years later, as a university president visiting a small town, Florence Parr finds herself confronted by an exact replica of her childhood dollhouse complete with a Raggedy Andy man sitting in the parlor. After making her way into the house, the man suddenly confronts her with the charge that she "smells"; "[y]ou did something nasty on the floor there. On the carpet" (45). He then slaps her across the face and screams at her: "Liar! Bad girl! Dirty girl!" (46). The contrast in the story between the cowering girl and the masterful professional woman could not be greater, suggesting again the female Gothic concern with the yawning gulf between the private and public realm for women.

Other stories in *Haunted* specifically concern anxieties connected to the female body. For instance, "Extenuating Circumstances" examines the psychopathology of infanticide, while "Don't You Trust Me?" looks at abortion from a viewpoint that is very similar to Margaret Atwood's *The Handmaid's Tale* (1985). "Phase Change" presents a particularly unpleasant dream about rape, while "The Premonition" depicts dismemberment fantasies connected with anxieties about menstruation. In short, the tales are graphic and unsettling and focus on a woman's fears about the changes inherent in the female body.

Oates' most extensive postmodern attempts to reconfigure the Gothic as a genre, however, can be found in her four novels *Bellefleur* (1980), *A Bloodsmoor Romance* (1982), *Mysteries of Winterthurn* (1984), and *My Heart Laid Bare* (1998). Oates herself labeled these works "an immense design: America as viewed through the lens of its most popular genres" ("Five Prefaces" 373). *Bellefleur* is a multigenerational tale that can be read as an allegory of American history. Each generation pushes the family and its property holdings further until the inevitable dramatic crash: Germaine Bellefleur's father aims a dynamite-filled airplane into the family estate. *A Bloodsmoor Romance* traces the lives of the five Zinn sisters, and, as Susan Ford observes, it reads like "a parodic version of *Little Women*" (309). The third novel in the series, *Mysteries of Winterthurn*, presents a post-modern version of Edgar Allan Poe's master detective, Dupin, in the character of Oates' detective Xavier Kilgarvan. Structured as three novellas, each concerns a particular nineteenth-century Gothic trope: "The Virgin in the Rose-Bower; or, the Tragedy of Glen Mawr Manor" explores father-daughter incest and infanticide; "Devil's Half Acre; or the Mystery of the Cruel Suitor" features Valentine Westergaard, a wealthy psychopathic murderer of women who uses religion to escape his crimes, and "The Bloodstained Bridal Gown; or Xavier Kilgarvan's Last Case" presents Xavier's marriage to the possible murderer Perdita. The fourth and final novel in the series, *My Heart Laid Bare*, concerns the issue of race in America by examining the lives of Adam Licht and his sons Abraham and Elisha.

Conclusion

As we have seen, the earliest works of Jewett, Freeman, and Gilman situate their female characters in the claustrophobic patriarchal home. Here the terror is marriage and the suffocating demands of motherhood. The psychological toll that mothering presents to women causes a split or rupture to appear in a number of these texts. Women either conform to being "angels in the house" or they rebel and become demons, outcasts, even murderers. This dichotomy is spelled out more fully in the works of Wharton, who traces dozens of different permutations in the private/public split that women are forced to navigate. In Jackson and Oates, both of them firmly situated in the historical realities of the twentieth century, we can see the toll that large-scale war and genocide have taken on their literary visions. Both present women as scapegoats to be sacrificed by a capitalistic economy intent on eliminating redundant or noncontributing members of the society. If women are valuable only for their reproductive capacities, then the aging female body becomes the ultimate embodiment of Gothic horror.

The American Female Gothic is a complex meta-narrative that explores a variety of specifically female concerns. That it has persisted for more than a century and that it continues to proliferate suggests its power to speak to its audience about the challenges that face women in a masculinist society.

NOTES

1. Carpenter and Kolmar list the other major practitioners of New England Gothic as Alice Cary, Harriet Beecher Stowe, Elizabeth Stuart Phelps, Rose Terry Cooke, Annie Trumbull Slosson, Charles Craddock (aka Mary Ann Murfee), and Mildred Haun (8). Weinstock has expanded that list considerably to include discussions of the tales of Harriet Prescott Spofford, Anna Hoyt, Harriet Beecher Stowe, Edith Wharton, Madeline Yale Wynne, Elia Wilkinson Peattie, Mary Austin, Louise Stockton, Olivia Howard Dunbar, Josephine Daskam Bacon, Georgia Wood Pangborn, Alice Brown, Helen Hull, Charlotte Perkins Gilman, and Gertrude Atherton.
2. Coventry Patmore's "Angel in the House," a poem published in England in 1857, established the Victorian ideology of a wife and mother as goddess of the middle and upper-class domestic hearth. This notion was popular in America under the

category of "the cult of true womanhood," an ideal that stressed purity, piety, domesticity, and submission to one's husband (see Welter).
3. Mitchell's "rest cure" prescribed a heavy diet, a lack of intellectual work or writing, and a complete removal from all sources of stress. The regime almost drove Perkins Gilman to a complete breakdown after the birth of her daughter. See Golden for a detailed analysis of the "cure" and its use in the story.
4. Wharton lists Walter Scott, Poe, LeFanu, R. L. Stevenson, and Henry James as the major influences on her ghost stories (*The Writing of Fiction* 36–37).
5. Helen Killoran, in her review of the critical reception of Wharton's work, frames her discussion of Wharton's ghost stories to show that Wharton's "dual text" (5) emerges when she inserts a subversive feminist message within a text that in other ways seems to conform to or support the dominant patriarchal social mores. This double-voiced technique is similar to what Blake Nevius (85) and later Jenni Dyman define as the "lurking feminism" (xviii) in her Gothic tales. Margaret McDowell reads them as a social commentary on marriage and divorce, while other critics most often interpret the ghost stories as being mirrors of the biographical facts of Wharton's life, either working through her personal attitudes to marriage and divorce (see Lawson), or her ambivalence about writing (see Murray; Singley and Sweeney). Fedorko sees Wharton's use of the conventions of the ghost story as providing her with a "psychic theater" (x) in which to explore, via the use of supernatural events occurring in a domestic setting, the results of unnatural acts that can occur in a Gothic ambience. Other critics have read the social context of her Gothic works in Marxist terms (Stengel; Elbert), while Waid examines the psychosexual implications in certain stories. Barbara A. White suggests that Wharton may have been a victim of father-daughter incest (40–50) and that her personal history of sexual abuse is the source of most of the covert or hidden subtext in the short Gothic tales, particularly the early ones (40–41). I am indebted for background material on Wharton to Nancy Metzger's "Edith Wharton and Father-Daughter Incest," a graduate paper prepared for my "Female Gothic" course at Marquette University (Fall 2000).
6. A full listing of Wharton's short stories generally excludes her quasi-pornographic incest tale "Beatrice Palmato" 1918.
7. Friedman, for example, discounts Jackson's Gothic strain, while her humor and proto-feminism are emphasized by Carpenter ("Domestic").
8. Note the blatant similarity between the references to food and the young boy and the annual practice of human sacrifice as depicted in Jackson's most famous short story "The Lottery" (1948). Jackson was a serious student of mythology and anthropology, both of which informed her understanding of the ritualistic practice of stoning a human sacrifice in order to ensure the fertility of crops for a rural community. See Murphy (75–90) for a fuller analysis of this theme.

WORKS CITED

Bendixen, Alfred, ed. *Haunted Women: The Best Supernatural Tales by American Women Writers*. New York: Ungar, 1985.
Carpenter, Lynette. "Domestic Comedy, Black Comedy, and Real Life: Shirley Jackson, a Woman Writer." In *Faith of a (Woman) Writer*. Eds. Alice Kessler-Harris and William McBrien. Westport, CT: Greenwood Press, 1988: 143–48.

Carpenter, Lynette, and Wendy K. Kolmar. "Introduction." In *Haunting the House of Fiction: Feminist Perspectives on Ghost Stories by American Women.* Eds. Lynette Carpenter and Wendy K. Kolmar. Knoxville: University of Tennessee Press, 1991. 1–25.

Dyman, Jenni. *Lurking Feminism: The Ghost Stories of Edith Wharton.* New York: Peter Lang, 1996.

Elbert, Monika. "T. S. Eliot and Wharton's Modernist Gothic." *Edith Wharton Review* 11.1 (1994): 19–23.

Fedorko, Kathy A. *Gender and the Gothic in the Fiction of Edith Wharton.* Tuscaloosa: University of Alabama Press, 1995.

Ford, Susan Allen. "Joyce Carol Oates." In *Gothic Writers: A Critical and Bibliographical Guide.* Eds. Douglass H. Thomson, Jack G. Voller, and Frederick S. Frank. Westport, CT: Greenwood, 2002. 303–14.

Friedman, Lenemaja. *Shirley Jackson.* Boston: Twayne, 1975.

Gentile, Kathy Justice. "Supernatural Transmissions: Turn-of-the-Century Ghosts in American Women's Fiction: Jewett, Freeman, Wharton, and Gilman." *Approaches to Teaching Gothic Fiction.* Eds. Diane Long Hoeveler and Tamar Heller. New York: MLA, 2003. 208–14.

Golden, Catherine. "'Overwriting' the Rest Cure: Charlotte Perkins Gilman's Literary Escape from S. Weir Mitchell's Fictionalization of Women." *Critical Essays on American Literature.* Ed. Joanne B. Karpinski. New York: G. K. Hall, 1992. 144–58.

Jackson, Rosemary. "Introduction." *What Did Miss Darrington See?* Ed. Jessica Amanda Salmonson. New York: Feminist Press, 1988.

Jackson, Shirley. "Home." *Just an Ordinary Day.* Eds. Laurence Jackson Hyman and Sarah Hyman Stewart. New York: Bantam, 1998.

——. "My Uncle in the Garden." In *Just an Ordinary Day.* Eds. Laurence Jackson Hyman and Sarah Hyman Stewart. New York: Bantam, 1998.

Killoran, Helen. *The Critical Reception of Edith Wharton.* Rochester, New York: Camden House, 2001.

Lawson, Richard. *Edith Wharton and German Literature.* New York: Ungar, 1977.

McDowell, Margaret B. "Edith Wharton's Ghost Stories." *Criticism* 12 (1970): 133–52.

Murphy, Bernice M. *The Rural Gothic in American Popular Culture: Backwoods Horror and Terror in the Wilderness.* New York: Palgrave, 2013.

Murray, Margaret P. "The Gothic Arsenal of Edith Wharton." *Journal of Evolutionary Psychology* 10.3.4 (1989): 315–21.

Nevius, Blake. *Edith Wharton: A Study of Her Fiction.* Berkeley: University of California Press, 1953.

Oates, Joyce Carol. "The Doll." In *Haunted: Tales of the Grotesque.* New York: Plume, 1995: 26–48.

——. "Five Prefaces." Rpt. *(Woman) Writer: Occasions and Opportunities.* New York: Dutton, 1988. 365–82.

Oppenheimer, Judy. *Private Demons: The Life of Shirley Jackson.* New York: Putnam's, 1988.

Parks, John G. "Chambers of Yearning." *Twentieth Century Literature* 30 (1984): 15–29.

Singley, Carol J. and Susan Elizabeth Sweeney. "Forbidden Reading and Ghostly Writing: Anxious Power in Wharton's 'Pomegranate Seed'." *Women's Studies* 20.2 (1991): 177–203.

Stengel, Ellen Powers. "Edith Wharton Rings 'The Lady's Maid's Bell." *Edith Wharton Newsletter* 7.1 (1990): 3–9.

Voller, Jack G. "Mary Wilkins Freeman." In *Gothic Writers: A Critical and Bibliographical Guide*. Eds. Douglass H. Thomson, Jack G. Voller, and Frederick S. Frank. Westport, CT: Greenwood, 2002. 120–25.

Waid, Candace. *Edith Wharton's Letters from the Underworld: Fictions of Women and Writing*. Chapel Hill: University of North Carolina Press, 1991.

Weinstock, Jeffrey Andrew. *Scare Tactics: Supernatural Fiction by American Women*. New York: Fordham University Press, 2008.

Welter, Barbara. "The Cult of True Womanhood: 1820–1860." *American Quarterly* 18 (1966): 151–74.

Wharton, Edith. "The Duchess at Prayer." *Scribner's Magazine* 28 (Aug. 1900): 151–64.

The Ghost Stories of Edith Wharton. [GS] New York: Simon & Schuster, 1937; rpt. 1973.

"The House of the Dead Hand." *The Collected Short Stories of Edith Wharton*. Digireads.com Books, 2011. 360–77.

Wharton's New England: Seven Stories and Ethan Frome. Ed. Barbara A. White. Lebanon: University of New Hampshire Press, 1995.

The Writing of Fiction. 1925. Rpt. New York: Octagon Books, 1966.

White, Barbara A. *Edith Wharton: A Study of the Short Fiction*. New York: Twayne Publishers, 1991.

8

ARDEL HAEFELE-THOMAS

Queer American Gothic

"Gothic has, in a sense, always been 'queer'"
(Hughes and Smith 1).[1]

Introduction

Netflix's 2015 original series, *Sense8*, a Gothic science fiction program created by Lilly and Lana Wachowski and J. Michael Straczynski, takes the viewer into the lives of eight different people around the globe. Through their mental/emotional connection, these "sensaters" have the ability to occupy each other's bodies, minds, and hearts regardless of their actual physical location. They are, in a sense, one another. Nomi, one of the eight, played by transgender actress Jamie Clayton, portrays a white transgender lesbian living in San Francisco. There is no explanation nor is there anything sensational about her "coming out" as either lesbian or transgender; rather, she completely embodies a queer and proud identity which enables her character to "get on" with the business of being human like everyone else. The queer Gothic science fiction structure allows Nomi to be Nomi.

Reality shows and news media in American popular culture have, over the last fifty years, tended to treat queer people as curiosities at best or as monstrosities at worst. Susan Stryker writes, "I find a deep affinity between myself as a transsexual woman and the monster in Mary Shelley's *Frankenstein*. Like the monster, I am too often perceived as less than fully human due to the means of my embodiment" ("My Words" 245). Even with the visibility of transgender celebrities like Caitlyn Jenner, American culture continues to sensationalize queer people's realities, thereby adding to the cultural confusion about queer identities. *Sense8*, however, simply presents Nomi in her loving relationship with Amanita, her cisgender African American partner.[2] *Sense8* exemplifies precisely the ways that Hughes and

Smith argue that queer Gothic embraces difference as it interrogates cultural "norms."

Gothic is a subgenre often labeled as pulp and relegated to the margins; therefore, authors who write Gothic often find that they have more room to take on uncomfortable social and cultural issues not written about in "polite" society. More specifically, American Gothic, like American Blues, is able to capture all of the complicated layers of various social and cultural concerns like racism and the after-effects of colonialism, genocide, and slavery; sexism and classism in the wake of the early Salem Witch Trials; homophobia and transphobia perpetuated by sodomy laws, anti-crossdressing laws, and the demonization of people suffering from AIDS.

American Gothic through a queer lens gives us a way into understanding the changing social, cultural, and political landscape where Lesbian, Gay, Bisexual, Transgender, and Queer (LGBTQ) rights are concerned in the United States. Historically, Gothic has been used as a mode to make the queer monstrous. One need only look to authors like Henry James (*The Turn of the Screw* 1898), Robert Bloch (*Psycho* 1959), Shirley Jackson (*The Haunting of Hill House* 1959), and Thomas Harris (*Silence of the Lambs* 1988) for examples of both overt and covert queer monstrosity often equated with mental illness.[3] This essay will not specifically address these types of queer Gothic tales, although they certainly help inform the queer and resistant texts explored here.

In considering queer Gothic from the mid-twentieth century onward with a focus on queer authors writing within and expanding the Gothic genre, which often embraces intersecting identities, we can see the ways that Gothic has served as a safe space to investigate deeper cultural chasms. These queer authors have chosen Gothic as a mode to explore the social layers of cultural "difference" that divide all of us. Queer American Gothic gives voice to people and stories often silenced by hegemonic cultural production.

Queer Southern Gothic

Truman Capote's first novel, *Other Voices, Other Rooms*, published in 1948, takes the reader on thirteen-year-old Joel Knox's journey from New Orleans into rural Mississippi (on the Southern American Gothic, see Crow [Chapter 10] in this volume; on the intersection of Capote with modernism, see Riquelme [Chapter 4] in this volume). Upon the death of his mother, Joel's estranged father writes and asks the boy to leave everyone and everything he knows to come live at Skully's Landing, a decrepit plantation haunted with the ghosts of a Confederate past. The novel is semi-autobiographical in its depiction of the effeminate, decadent, and queer young Capote.

Capote's novel drips with the stifling air that pervades much Southern Gothic; land and water converge in the literal and metaphoric swamp of liminal spaces that map out the American South as a queer and unsettled place still impoverished and battle-weary from the Civil War. Joel hitches a ride with Radclif, a racist white man who is also deeply suspicious of the boy's effeminacy: "Radclif eyed the boy over the rim of his beer glass, not caring much for the looks of him ... He was too pretty, too delicate and fair-skinned; each of his features was shaped with a sensitive accuracy, and a girlish tenderness softened his eyes" (4). With these first impressions, Capote upends the stereotype of the monstrous queer by making the "normal" man grotesque and contemptible.

Capote's landscape is populated with queer characters like Idabel Thompkins, who another character describes as a "freak" who never wears dresses (17), and his cousin, Randolph, who is an out transvestite. Although the author was certainly a product of his Southern upbringing in terms of race relations, it is interesting to note that his queer white characters often socialize with African Americans since both groups are relegated to the margins of Mississippi society.

Carson McCullers, who encouraged Truman Capote to write his first novel, offers us another example of a queer white Southern Gothic writer. In her 1951 novella, *The Ballad of the Sad Café*, McCullers explores three social outcasts: the androgynous and racially ambiguous Miss Amelia, the hunchback Cousin Lymon, and Miss Amelia's ex-husband, Marvin Macy. Miss Amelia is described as dark, tall, and freakish in her masculinity; racial tensions underscore queer tensions and vice versa. McCullers portrays Cousin Lymon as someone differently abled, and thus read within the confines of the small town, as a "freak."[4] Lymon also transgresses a gender and species binary in that nobody is certain if he is fully human. In fact, of the three, Marvin Macy is the only "typically" gendered and normative person. The three make up a queer love triangle that starts with Miss Amelia and Cousin Lymon until he leaves her, in front of everyone in the cafe, for the arms of her ex-husband, Marvin Macy.

Not only are the relationships in McCullers' grotesque story painted as queer, but the space of the cafe itself functions as both the town's carnival-like side show *and* a safe space for social outcasts: "But the new pride that the café brought to this town had an effect on almost everyone, even the children ... There, for a few hours at least, the deep bitter knowing that you are not worth much in this world could be laid low" (55). The cafe functions much like its urban queer counterparts of 1950s America – underground gay bars populated by racial, gender, and sexual outlaws.[5]

McCullers' queer story ends with a shift of the town's gathering space from the cafe to a dusty road on the outskirts of town. There, crowds gather to hear the prison chain gang. Here, in a haunting allusion to enslaved African and Irish ancestors, twelve men – black and white together – raise their voices to sing in a way that makes "the listener grow cold with ecstasy and fright" (71). Within the monotonous sound of the pickaxes striking the earth, the voice of a beautiful interracial and homosocial group rises above the August heat: "And what kind of gang is it that can make such music? Just twelve mortal men, seven of them black and five of them white boys from this county. Just twelve mortal men who are together" (72).

Capote and McCullers' queer identity set them outside of genteel mid-century Southern white culture. Although they both certainly enjoyed white privilege, they were less afraid of breaking the rules, particularly where race relations were concerned, than some of their heterosexual counterparts. Readers can see that within their queer Gothic frameworks, both authors attempt to grapple with early cross-cultural conversations on the edges of society.

While the effects of slavery may haunt the margins of Capote and McCullers' queer Southern Gothic stories, it is never dealt with head on. Queer African American authors Randall Kenan and Jewelle Gomez utilize the Gothic as a way to unflinchingly explore slavery in the past and present. In *A Visitation of Spirits* (1989), Kenan's protagonist, sixteen-year-old Horace Cross, spends a long night fighting with spirits of good and evil. Within his struggle, he is also coming to terms with his desire for other boys as a young African American intellectual already deeply marginalized in American culture.

Horace steps out of bounds in terms of his sexual orientation, but also within the confines of a racist Southern culture that demands that the black/white binary not to be crossed: "There had been five of them. Four white boys and Horace. Five boys who did not fit into the archaic, close-knit, rural ways of York County" (236). This description recalls the specter of McCullers' interracial and homosocial "twelve mortal men."

As Horace Cross grapples with his angels and demons in spirit form, his enslaved ancestors make an appearance to remind him of the middle passage. In his attempt to look away from the horror, Horace "saw clearly through a glass darkly and understood where he fit ... Never had he felt such self-loathing" (234–35). When his friend, Jimmy, reaches Horace, it is too late; the spirits have demanded that Horace give up his queer identity. Just before he puts the gun to his own head, Horace tells Jimmy, "You see, life the way Horace wants it ain't condoned" (252–53). In this Southern Gothic landscape, there is no room for the young queer African American man.

Jewelle Gomez' 1991 *The Gilda Stories* is a queer vampire novel comprising several short stories. The opening tale, "Louisiana: 1850," introduces the reader to a young runaway slave who, in a barn on the outskirts of New Orleans, stabs a white man to death when he tries to rape her. She is discovered by an old and strange white woman named Gilda who, in the first tense moments, the girl fears will sell her back into slavery. Instead, the elder soothes her through her thoughts in an instantaneous psychic connection between them: "She had heard of people who could talk without speaking but never expected a white to be able to do it. This one was a puzzlement to her: the dark eyes and pale skin ... she wore men's breeches and a heavy jacket" (13). Gilda's unladylike appearance marks her as different from the mythical white Southern Belle needing to be protected from the slaves. Instead of a plantation, Gilda operates an unusual establishment on the borders of New Orleans. During the day, Gilda's home, not unlike Miss Amelia's cafe, becomes a safe space for outcasts – in this case it is a homosocial gathering place for women. At night, Gilda's home functions as an illegal speakeasy.

Gilda's lover, Bird, is Lakota, and together, as a queer interracial vampiric couple, they are able to save runaway slaves who find themselves in danger in one of the biggest slave ports in the United States. Much of this story revolves around Gilda training the young girl to become her replacement so that she, tired from centuries of living, can go to her final rest. "Louisiana: 1850" concludes with Gilda bestowing her name on the girl, something that was usually done when white slave owners "freed" their slaves. In this case, however, Gomez radically revises history and changes power dynamics in creating a white character who gives up her own life so that the young runaway slave can become empowered through eternal life.

Gomez deftly ties her reimagined vampire mythos to social justice work and the nourishment of all people; her vampires become a sort of proverbial "neighborhood watch" group situated around the world in different eras always at the ready to help save those most vulnerable. With the new Gilda and Bird, who remains with her as a mentor, these stories turn the stereotypical lesbian vampire motif around to reconceptualize a queer vampiric community that empowers themselves while saving others.[6]

Camp Gothic: Humor and Empowerment

We generally understand Gothic as a genre that deals with horror and fear, but there are a growing number of theorists who have begun to focus on the comedic within Gothic.[7] Some queer American Gothic writers look to "camp" humor in particular as a way of highlighting and reexamining deep cultural tragedies. Susan Sontag describes "camp" as a "love of the unnatural: of artifice and exaggeration ... Camp is esoteric – something of a private code, a badge of identity even, among small urban cliques."[8] Over the past half century, "camp" has moved beyond these typically urban gay male parameters, but it still functions as a coded queer language that underscores social inequalities and hypocrisies.

Monica Palacios' short story "La Llorona Loca: The Other Side," rewrites the Chican@ folklore of La Llorona, the ghost of the crying woman who drowned her children and forever haunts riverbanks throughout the desert Southwest; she is a figure often used to scare children into obedience.[9] La Llorona exemplifies a stereotype of the "bad mother," an indigenous woman who cannot take care of her children, so Western Christianity steps in and recreates her as a witch. Over the centuries, the colonial roots of La Llorona's creation have almost been forgotten.

Beyond larger colonial concerns, Palacios also takes the opportunity in this story to use camp Gothic as a means to critique dominant Anglo-European culture as well as dominant heteronormative narratives that erase queer lives. In her retelling, Caliente, the most beautiful unmarried woman in the village, falls under everyone's suspicion because she refuses to date men. The townspeople gossip that she is "different" because "she wears spurs – on her house slippers" and they speculate that she might be "a PE teacher!" (49). The author's eye for camp shines through as the locals speculate about her sharp slippers; Palacios also points to the cultural stereotype that gym teachers are always lesbians. One day, a tall, dark, and handsome woman, La Stranger, rides into town and whisks Caliente away – the author notes they were in a rush because they were being chased "by many macho Mexican dudes" (50); a curandera (witch) in Tijuana marries them, and they settle down in Bakersfield, CA, in married bliss until La Stranger cheats on Caliente while she is at her Latin@ empowerment group and, in the ensuing fight, they both drown in the river. In Palacios' world, Chican@ lesbians, rather than a mother who has drowned her children, haunt the riverbank.

Palacios creates a violent death and a subsequent haunting, but throughout she also laces this ghost story with camp humor, which not only critiques mainstream heteronormative culture, but white queer, Chican@ queer, and Chican@ "straight" culture as well. The story makes fun of stereotypes about white lesbian fashion and Chican@ lesbian encounter groups. The specter of colonial violence and the erasure of women and specifically queer women haunts the text, but the camp humor also serves to give voice to and empower the specific audience for this story: Chican@ lesbians.

Camp humor can also be found in Gothic tales that focus on AIDS. It is crucial to remember that in the early 1980s in the United States, AIDS was labeled a "gay" disease. To this day, a queer taint envelops our notions about

AIDS in America, which continues to adversely affect people who are HIV+ or who have AIDS. In many communities, we still see immense homophobic shame tied to AIDS. Over the past three decades, a number of authors and artists, including Ron Athey, David Wojnarowicz, and Bill Sherwood, have created Gothic works that address the epidemic; however, playwright Tony Kushner's Pulitzer Prize-winning *Angels in America: A Gay Fantasia on National Themes* (1993) takes a different approach to the medical and cultural nightmare by using camp humor within a Gothic framework (on Tony Kushner and Gothic theatre, see Heather S. Nathans [Chapter 14] in this volume).

In *Angels in America*, AIDS becomes the vehicle through which Kushner explores over two hundred years of oppression in America from slavery and Jim Crow through McCarthyism and the Supreme Court's 1986 upholding of states' rights to continue to criminalize queer people.[10] Kushner's characters who battle against physical or mental illness often hallucinate and interact with ghosts. In one such vision, Prior Walter, the play's protagonist who has AIDS, enters into a fevered dream sequence that begins with his sitting at a bureau, where he gazes into the mirror and applies makeup:

> Prior: "I'm ready for my closeup, Mr. DeMille."
> One wants to move through life with elegance and grace, blossoming infrequently but with exquisite taste, and perfect timing, like a rare bloom, a zebra orchid ... But one so seldom gets what one wants, does one? One ... dies at thirty, robbed of ... decades of majesty ... I look like a corpse. A corpsette. Oh my queen; you know you've hit rock-bottom when even drag is a drag. (36–37)

Prior's reference to the infamous last scene in Hollywood's 1950 *Sunset Boulevard*, which was not only a serious film but has been from its release a steadfast camp classic, speaks in code to a particular queer audience. The fact of the scene's starting with this line flags it for this very specific audience; we can expect the rest to also be underscored with camp humor, which it is.

Teleported into this hallucination, Harper, a Mormon housewife addicted to valium and married to a closeted gay man, dogmatically replies to the male stranger in make-up, "In my church we don't believe in homosexuals" (38), only to be completely charmed by Prior's retort, "In my church we don't believe in Mormons" (38). From this moment on, the absurd and gothic setting allows Harper and Prior to connect on a deeper, more human level outside of the parameters of reality and the social restrictions that would be placed on them as two people whose paths should not cross. In this hallucinatory imagined realm beyond the boundaries of "normal," they offer compassion to one another as Harper tells Prior that something deep in his core is not sick at all, but healthy. In turn, Prior shows warmth and understanding for her drug addiction and imprisonment in a loveless marriage.

Throughout *Angels in America*, Kushner lines the camp with the Gothic and the Gothic with camp through recognizable Hollywood references that a mainstream audience would understand, but that a queer audience would also read on another level of coded language. At every moment when we are ready to lose hope along with Prior – when we are ready to slip into the gothic nightmare that is AIDS in the 1980s – camp rescues us.

Gothic in Queer Independent Presses

Angels in America offers an example of a mainstream play that operates on several levels in that it reaches out to the general American theatre-going audience while also incorporating coded queer language. Unlike Kushner's play, the writing explored in this section comes from popular queer independent presses set up solely by and for people who identify as LGBTQ. As such, these books do not aim to reach out to a heteronormative audience, although they certainly may be of note to people who identify as allies.

Brenda Weathers' *The House at Pelham Falls* (1986), published by Naiad Press, and Yvonne Heidt's *Sometime Yesterday* (2012), published by Bold Strokes Books, utilize haunted house motifs to explore contemporary lesbian relationships that must progress in order to set free another spectral lesbian couple from the past. Weathers' Dr. Karen Latham is a closeted anthropology professor on the run from Maggi England, an out and proud documentary filmmaker. Karen fears losing her esteemed position because of her queer identity, which she has been able to keep private. Rather than confronting her college's systemic sexism and homophobia as well as her own internalized self-hatred, she flees to the nether reaches of coastal Maine, where she purchases an abandoned Victorian house perched on a cliff overlooking the Atlantic. Heidt's heroine, Natalie, leaves a loveless marriage to a man and, in her quest to reestablish herself, stumbles upon a Victorian house on a remote section of coastal Northern California. In each story, the house is haunted by a long-dead lesbian couple whose relationship was tragically cut short. The eerie coastal homes become the site where the ghosts must use the bodies of the contemporary live women to consummate their past sexual relationships cut short by violent death.

The lesbian couples are not the only queer components in these novels. For both Weathers and Heidt, an older woman – a heterosexual ally – practices witchcraft in order to release the trapped souls. In the case of Heidt's story, Natalie's mother, who practices Wicca, has to break the evil spell on the house and save the dead women from the abusive father figure who has murdered and buried them in the backyard *because* they are queer. In this case, a past hate crime has to be replayed within the walls of the haunted house, but with a different and positive outcome. Weathers' novel presents an elderly and eccentric neighbor, Etta, who also has to work magic through the body of the contemporary woman, Karen, in order to dispel the ghost of Amelia who was killed in a winter storm by a falling tree only to leave her bereaved lover, Blessing, to haunt the house for the next century.

Jeffrey Ricker's short story, "Blackout" (2012), employs themes similar to both Weathers' and Heidts' tales. A gay male couple, Jason and David, decide to leave the frenetic city and buy an old house in the country. Unlike the lesbian couples, however, Ricker's men occupy the haunted house as an already established couple. In this tale, the house is haunted by the ghost of the former homophobic owner. Like Heidt's demonic ghost, this one, too, is bent on destroying the gay men.

As this story unfolds, the ghost kills David, the man who originally wanted to move to the country, by forcing the tree he is cutting to fall and kill him. The ghost voice then tells Jason "you're next, faggot" (177). Unlike the works of Weathers and Heidt, this story's concern is solely contemporary; David's murder is a hate crime although the culprit is spectral. As an early snowstorm rages outside, Jason drinks himself into a stupor as the ghost continues to taunt him. Power lines go down, Jason's firewood runs out, and without a vehicle, he cannot run for his life. As Jason awaits the hateful apparition to kill him, he becomes aware of another ghost, his dead partner, in the room fighting to save his life. David wins and Jason is released from the house's spell.

In all of these contemporary popular queer ghost stories, the writers imagine older heterosexual allies. Weathers and Heidt focus on elderly women who work magic. Ricker's story includes an older heterosexual couple who continually check in on their new neighbor. They nurse Jason back to health once David's ghost saves his life. The authors use the Gothic to make a social commentary on the necessity of parental figures whose unconditional love can protect and nurture their socially marginalized children. These elders represent the families that so many outcast queer people wish they had; their very presence interrogates the rigid ideals of heteronormative family structures that have no room to welcome queer children and their partners at the table. In using these kind and gentle allies, the authors also open up their books to a much wider audience. Within their queer Gothic framework, Weathers, Heidt, and Ricker point the way toward social healing beginning at home with family.

Conclusion

For many LGBTQ children throughout America, "home" and families of origin still represent the most terrifying place to be queer. Annually in the United States, thousands of children (so hundreds who will struggle to come out of the closet later) are taken by their families to evangelical Halloween haunted "Hell Houses" that function as fundraisers for churches. Here, they are treated to scenes of transgender youth and young lesbians committing suicide and young gay men lying in hospital beds writhing in pain and dying of AIDS in a pool of gore as Satan stands by laughing. Within the walls of these exhibits, the scenes depicted are largely medical, which underscores a notion that being queer relates to being sick – in this case physically and morally.[11]

In the second episode of Netflix's *Sense8*, "I Am Also a We," our transgender protagonist, Nomi, who has been injured in a motorcycle accident during the San Francisco LGBTQ Pride Parade, wakes up in a hospital room to find her mother and sister staring at her. Nomi's mother refuses to refer to her by her chosen name or gender identity, opting instead for masculine pronouns and her birth name, Michael. The mother has also made sure that Nomi's door remains locked and that Amanita has no access to her. Nomi's confusion and fear is palpable. This fear turns to abject terror when "the doctor" enters the room to explain Nomi's diagnosis. He argues that she needs immediate neurosurgery to cure her sickness (a lobotomy is on order). And, although the Western medical practitioner claims that the "disease" is a brain tumor, the underlying message is clear: Here is another sick queer in need of treatment.

With *Sense8*, though, the Wachowskis revisit and subvert the tropes found in much American Gothic horror that writes the queer figure as monstrous and sick – this is evident, for example, in Robert Bloch's 1959 novel *Psycho*, adapted for film by Alfred Hitchcock the following year, which underscores the notion that Norman Bates' true monstrosity is not that he has murdered a young woman who has stolen money from her boss. Rather, Bloch takes the homophobic stereotype of the "mama's boy" as a sissified effeminate man and infuses it with transphobia by turning a psychotic Norman Bates into his mother. The audience feels relieved when Western medicine makes its diagnosis and the doctors cart a gibbering Bates off in a straightjacket. In Foucauldian terms, however, the doctor's diagnosis "is an act of violence" precisely because it is a misdiagnosis (8). The true sickness – the true monstrosity – is the Western medical institutions' abuse of power; the Wachowskis expose this in the lie that Nomi is told about a brain tumor and the barring of her partner from the hospital room. Nomi becomes so convinced by her birth mother and the doctor that she is terminally ill that she thinks Amanita's call on her hospital room phone is the beginning of the hallucinations she has been told to expect. During this call, Amanita tells Nomi that she will burn down the hospital in order to free her. And, in the third episode of *Sense8*, "Smart Money's on the Skinny Bitch," Amanita does just that: She sets the hospital on fire so the two women can escape the gothic monstrosity that Western medicine has used to imprison queers. This scene serves as the Wachowskis' antidote; this is their answer to Bloch's doctors who pathologized Norman Bates. It's too bad Norman did not have an Amanita at the ready.

NOTES

This essay is dedicated to Paulina Palmer.

1. See William Hughes and Andrew Smith's *Queering the Gothic*. Hughes and Smith argue for definitions of queer both inside of and outside of sexual relations. Hughes and Smith claim that "queer" signifies difference and disruption of cultural assumptions of "the norm." See also Ardel Haefele-Thomas' *Queer Others in Victorian Gothic: Transgressing Monstrosity*. In *Queer Others* and for the purposes of this essay, I utilize "queer" to mean difference in much the same ways that Hughes and Smith do – difference that interrogates societal "norms" such as racial stereotypes and categorizations, gender "normativity" that follows an essentialist gender binary of man/woman, and heteronormativity that assumes that rigid structures of heterosexuality are not only normal but preferred (which alienates a large portion of people who identify as heterosexual who do not necessarily conform to these ideals). I also use the word "queer" as an umbrella term to denote Transgender, Bisexual, Lesbian, and Gay identities, people, and political struggles. "Queer" encompasses non-binary gender identities and expression such as trans* and genderqueer as well. "Queer" always interrogates hegemonic discourses.
2. Cisgender defines a person whose sex assigned at birth and gender identity line up. Please see Susan Stryker's *Transgender History* for one of the first and most detailed definitions of cisgender.
3. Please see George Haggerty's groundbreaking book *Queer Gothic* for an excellent discussion of James and Jackson in particular.
4. Please see Rachel Adams' essay, "'A Mixture of Delicious and Freak': The Queer Fiction of Carson McCullers" in *American Literature* for an outstanding discussion on the connections between Carson McCullers' own disabilities and identity as a "freak" and the ways that she translates this into her fiction.
5. See Audre Lorde's biomythography *Zami: A New Spelling of My Name*, in which she writes about 1950s gay bars in Harlem, NY, Lorde discusses the notion that being queer was a common denominator and that in many of the gay bars, white queers, Latin@ queers, and African American queers, in particular, were already in discussions with one another about intersecting identities and marginalization.
6. For a reading of this story within a queer feminist Gothic context please see my essay "Queering the Female Gothic" in Avril Horner and Sue Zlosnik, *Women and the Gothic*.
7. Please see Avril Horner and Sue Zlosnik's *Gothic and the Comic Turn* and Catherine Spooner's *Post-Millennial Gothic: Comedy, Romance and the Rise of 'Happy Gothic.'*
8. Susan Sontag's "Notes on 'Camp'" first appeared in 1964 in the *Partisan Review*. Although the essay is over fifty years old, it is still one of the most respected and definitive essays to consider "camp" as an underground form of gay urban humor that, through exaggeration, can quite subversively underscore deep cultural problems.

9. Recent queer scholarship has pointed out that using the term Chicano/a still frames the term within a gender binary. To make the word more accessible and accepting for all genders, the terms Chican@ and Latin@ are often used at this point. For more on this, please see Sandra Soto's book *Reading Chican@ Like a Queer: The De-Mastery of Desire*. There are also some academic departments that have taken on this name such as the University of Wisconsin and the University of San Francisco.
10. In 1986, the US Supreme Court had the opportunity to strike down the sodomy laws that remained on the books in a number of states. The Georgia sodomy case, Bowers v. Hardwick, came down to a 5–4 decision in favor of upholding the sodomy laws. In 1986, the United States was in the early and worst stages of the AIDS epidemic and the decimation of the gay men's community. The sodomy laws in the United States were not struck down until the 2003 Supreme Court case, Lawrence v. Texas.
11. Please see Sarah Kennedy and Jason Ciancotto's online booklet from The Task Force that discusses the connections between the evangelical "Hell Houses" and the rise in bullying and hate crimes against LGBTQ youth.

WORKS CITED

Adams, Rachel. "'A Mixture of Delicious and Freak': The Queer Fiction of Carson McCullers." *American Literature* 71.3 (1999): 551–83.

Bloch, Robert. *Psycho*. 1959. New York: The Overlook Press, 2010.

Capote, Truman. *Other Voices, Other Rooms*. 2nd edn. New York: Vintage, 2012.

Foucault, Michel. *The Birth of the Clinic: An Archaeology of Medical Perception*. Trans. A. M. Sheridan Smith. New York: Vintage Books, 1975.

Gomez, Jewelle. *The Gilda Stories*. Ithaca: Firebrand, 1991.

Haefele-Thomas, Ardel. "Queering the Female Gothic." *Women and the Gothic*. Eds. Avril Horner and Sue Zlosnik. Manchester: Manchester University Press, 2016. 169–83.

Queer Others in Victorian Gothic: Transgressing Monstrosity. Cardiff: University of Wales Press, 2012.

Haggerty, George. *Queer Gothic*. Urbana: University of Illinois Press, 2006.

Heidt, Yvonne. *Sometime Yesterday*. Valley Falls: Bold Strokes Books, 2012.

Horner, Avril and Sue Zlosnik. *Gothic and the Comic Turn*. London: Palgrave Macmillan, 2005.

Hughes, William and Andrew Smith. "Introduction." *Queering the Gothic*. Eds. William Hughes and Andrew Smith. Manchester: Manchester UP, 2009. 1–10.

"I Am Also A We." *Sense8*. Netflix. 5 June 2015. Television.

Kelly, Daniel W. *Rise of the Thing Down Below*. Valley Falls: Bold Strokes Books, 2014.

Kenan, Randall. *A Visitation of Spirits*. New York: Vintage Books, 1989.

Kennedy, Sarah and Jason Cianciotto. "Homophobia at 'Hell House': Literally Demonizing Lesbian, Gay, Bisexual and Transgender Youth." *The Task Force*. Web. 15 Oct. 2015.

Kushner, Tony. *Angels in America: A Gay Fantasia on National Themes*. New York: Theatre Communications Group, 1995.

"Limbic Resonance." *Sense8*. Netflix. 5 June 2015.

Lorde, Audre. *Zami: A New Spelling of My Name – A Biomythography*. Berkeley: The Crossing Press, 1982.

McCullers, Carson. *The Ballad of the Sad Café and other Stories*. 1951. New York: Bantam Books, 1981.

Palacios, Monica. "La Llorona Loca: The Other Side." *Chicana Lesbians: The Girls Our Mothers Warned Us About*. Ed. Carla Trujillo. Berkeley: Third Woman Press, 1991. 49–51.

Ricker, Jeffrey. "Blackout." *Night Shadows: Queer Horror*. Ed. Greg Herren and J. M. Redmann. Valley Falls: Bold Strokes Books, 2012. 167–85.

Roen, Paul. *High Camp: A Gay Guide to Camp and Cult Films, Vol. 1*. San Francisco: Leyland Publications, 1994.

"Smart Money's on the Skinny Bitch." *Sense8*. Netflix. 5 June 2015. Television.

Sontag, Susan. "Notes on 'Camp'." 1964. *Faculty Georgetown U*. Web. 15 Oct. 2015.

Soto, Sandra. *Reading Chican@ Like a Queer: The De-Mastery of Desire*. Austin: University of Texas Press, 2010.

Spooner, Catherine. *Post-Millennial Gothic: Comedy, Romance and the Rise of "Happy Gothic."* London: Bloomsbury Academic, forthcoming.

Stryker, Susan. "My Words to Victor Frankenstein above the Village of Chamounix: Performing Transgender Rage." *The Transgender Studies Reader*. Eds. Susan Stryker and Stephen Whittle. New York: Routledge, 2006. 244–56.

Transgender History. Berkeley: Seal Press, 2008.

Weathers, Brenda. *The House at Pelham Falls*. Tallahassee: The Naiad Press, Inc., 1986.

9

ELIZABETH JANE WALL HINDS

American Frontier Gothic

Toni Morrison's *Paradise* (1997) begins at the end: "They shoot the white girl first," we learn, before we learn why she or the other "girls" are shot, or who "they" are doing the shooting (3). This chapter will follow Morrison's lead, beginning by reading the late-twentieth-century *Paradise* as a case study in frontier Gothic, before looking back at some of the earliest instances of frontier Gothic in America – at Cotton Mather's *Wonders of the Invisible World* (1693), Mary Rowlandson's *Sovereignty and Goodness of God* (1682), and two of Charles Brockden Brown's novels (1798–99) – to then explore the changes in frontier Gothic as the frontier itself changed through the nineteenth and twentieth centuries. The frontier, it is commonly said, is always shifting; so too do the characteristics of the frontier Gothic genre. Still, there have remained over these centuries some remarkably stable through-lines: Frontier Gothic texts are those that invoke uncanny fear or terror through the active participation of their wilderness, or liminal, or borderland settings. What makes those settings so unsettled and unsettling – their locations haunted by their histories – is the subject of this chapter.

The "they" of the first chapter of *Paradise* are the men of nine families of Ruby, Oklahoma, a small, African American town established after WWII. Ruby is itself the follow-up town to Haven, founded in Oklahoma Territory during Reconstruction as a safe haven against post-Civil War violence against and exclusion of blacks in the South. Ruby could be a paradise, and its families mean it to be: They are church-going and financially successful; they have tidy flower gardens grown by women with little to do but tend them; their houses are seldom locked. But Ruby is not a paradise. They have replicated the outside world inside the supposedly safe circle. Here, they have created a place if not technically incestuous, definitely insular and inward looking: Nine families control everything in Ruby from street names to bank loans. The original founders were rejected along the road to Ruby by both white and black communities. Yet they have brought with them exclusionary habits from this outside world: "the 'utopian' community of Ruby is constantly undone by the community's insistence on sustaining itself through various horrific, 'protective' patriarchal acts" (Wester 379).

Just a few miles away, several women live at a location equally burdened by the past. The Convent, originally "an embezzler's folly" (3) built on the frontier beyond a town itself located on a frontier, is a huge, baroque mansion created as a haven from the world of law. It was later an actual convent that included one of the many schools for "Indian girls" throughout the West and Southwest during the late nineteenth-century Removal era. In the novel's present, the 1970s, only the Mother Superior and her ward, now aging and codependent, live there, but they are joined, one by one, by women who, like the citizens of Ruby, have all run away from abuse: from spousal beatings, abandonment, sexual slavery, and the like. The Convent might be a paradise, with women free to develop their own desires and heal the traumas of the past. But as Ruby changes – young people openly disagreeing with their elders, the Black Nationalist fist appearing on the town's shrine of a central oven – the patriarchs blame the Convent women; the Ruby men's point of view "marks the women as grotesque and witch-like, given their assumed worship and child sacrifice, and turns what is really just an unkempt house into a Gothic nightmare" (Wester 388). The Convent women are, to be sure, emotionally damaged. From one point of view, they are insane, peopling the gothic house – like Poe's House of Usher, it rises out of a mist when the men come to slaughter the women – with what looks like hallucinations and "deviant" behavior. From another point of view – that of many of the novel's women – the gothic terror stems from violence against and oppression of women. As Jeffrey Andrew Weinstock elaborates, the Gothic can illuminate "disenfranchisement suffered by women in American culture ... to highlight the terrors of the *known*, including abuse by fathers and husbands, economic dependency, the demands of motherhood, and circumscribed possibilities for self-actualization" ("American Monsters" 48, emphasis added). Ruby is haunted by an enemy within, the Convent by an enemy outside. There are two frontiers in *Paradise*, as there are two utopian spaces. Between these two frontiers is the history of frontier Gothic in America.

The "frontier" of frontier Gothic might be defined by the presence of standard Gothic tropes – the hint of the supernatural, female victims, graphic violence – set beyond "civilized" space, where the mind affects and is affected by the landscape. "On the edge of territories both enticing and terrifying ... psychic frontiers" become inseparable from geographical ones (Kerr *et al.* 1–2). Landscape isn't only a symbol or a setting. As James Folsom puts it, "both the land and its inhabitants are ... primarily projections of internal states of mind as well as reflections of external states of being" (30). The terrors of the "other" both inside and outside the charmed circle of Satan and his minions, of uncanny doubles, objects and events that appear to or actually do violate the laws of nature – these and other Gothic features are enhanced at the frontier, a misty area in a hazily perceived border between the known world and the unknowable, frightful wilderness. At the frontier, law and the safety of civic structures have no power. These are not the standard castles and specters associated with British Gothic, but the kind of terrors hidden in a seemingly open landscape.

The frontier is not only a spatial borderland, but a temporal one as well, incorporating layered, overlapping periods of time. The frontier defies our understanding of place – of *a* place – by hosting not one set of events but more than one. This space seems to violate some basic law of physics by which only one thing can happen in one place at one time: "The fantastic forms of the gothic landscape ... are the immanent portents of the past ... that exist in a parallel reality juxtaposed to the inscribed history of the present culture" (Mogen *et al.* 17). Indeed, the gothic effect arises from just this multiplication of time and space that is uncannily possible and impossible at once. The women of *Paradise* occupy just such an uncanny space: When a main character, Connie, begins to see more light and shadow as she goes blind, or when the Convent women appear, one by one, after they've been murdered, the novel produces an ontology both strange and familiar, home-like and unhomelike (Freud's *Heimlich* and *Unheimlich*, "The Uncanny"). The Convent is, after all, a palimpsest of past and present – rich man's dream house, sacred space and school, and home to marginal, "throwaway people" (3).

Blending time, space, and psyche, frontier Gothic has from the beginning offered a commentary on America itself, early in Anglo-American experience considered a vast wilderness, unpeopled and ready for settlement – unpeopled, of course, by disregarding Native Americans, as often happened. But the repressed always returns, as Freud tells us, and frontier Gothic enacts that terrifying return. It is "a literature of intersecting borderlands and failed repression, of a haunted national psyche" (Sivils 89). As Carol Margaret Davison writes of *Paradise*, "Ruby is prone to the myth of exceptionalism that informed America's sense of its origins and which underpins a 'self' and 'other' binary that produces the body of all 'others' as monstrous" (385). Women, Africans, African Americans, and Native Americans have all served as "other" in this literature, as the abjected, rejected, and repressed who continue to haunt the present: These ghosts refuse to stay in their graves, despite the American myth of progress and perfection that would prefer to deny the past.

Puritan Frontier Gothic

Two of the earliest American documents to use the structure and tropes of frontier Gothic, and uncannily parallel in their frontiers to *Paradise*, are Cotton Mather's 1693 *The Wonders of the Invisible World* and Mary Rowlandson's 1682 *Sovereignty and Goodness of God*. In his "record" of the Salem Witch Trials, "Mather famously figures the American wilderness as 'devil's territories'... reinforcing the characterization of Native Americans as diabolic agents," as does Rowlandson (Weinstock, "Monsters" 43). Like Morrison's Convent women, the "others" of *Wonders* and Rowlandson's narrative are tropologically blended with the wilderness itself, with its animals and misty outlines. Thus the "Divil," when given a chance, unleashes his "Mastives of Hell" on the Puritans of Salem (*Wonders* 11). Rowlandson writes, "Oh the roaring, and singing and dancing, and yelling of those black creatures [Indians] in the night... made the place a lively resemblance of hell" (17). Mather's Salem community has had "a Hedge about us," but the disruptive and unholy can invite the devil in through a "Breach" (11). Beyond the "Hedge" is the frontier, "fill'd with vast Herds of Salvages" (12).

In "herds," like mastiffs, these devil-"savages" are also animals; as Leslie Fiedler had it, at the frontier "unlikes turn into likes... things become their own opposites," the danger being that Puritan may become Indian and/or animal (31). David Mogen explains: "To Puritan eyes Indian religion was clearly a form of witchcraft... which not only threatened invasion from without but which, more insidiously, sought allies within their own constantly threatened communities" (95). Indians/animals/witches blend together in the Puritan gothic imagination, fed by their typological historiography that envisioned a recurrence of events and people. New England Puritans were types of Christ, or Moses, or both as their "errand into the wilderness" reiterated both Moses' and Christ's wandering in the "desert."[1] Through this temporal layering, it follows that the Native Americans are a type of the devil, antagonists of Christ's followers. Biblical history, then, predicted the seventeenth-century present, as this present reenacted and completed layered cycles of history. If the past can reappear at any time, then people can be, uncannily, more than one thing. Natives are devils; witches are "neighbors" *and* Satan's helpers; both Natives and witches can also be animals, the lowest, least civilized form of life to appear in Puritan texts. Such metamorphoses gothicized the threat in and of the frontier, as the sheer shiftingness of character, setting, and plot makes for a "spectralization of setting, the derealization of plot, and the ambiguation of character" (Jarraway 92).

Rowlandson's story is gendered differently from Mather's. She casts herself at times as a gothic damsel in distress, a victim of the violence and unknowing of her captivity among the Wampanoag during King Philip's/Metacomet's war with the English over property. She sees herself typologically as Job, passively suffering by God's direction at the hands of the devil's followers. "Because of the literal-mindedness with which she embraces her theology, the journey into the wilderness is a gothic encounter with the other world" (Mogen 96). Further, Rowlandson undergoes regular periods of mental instability threatening total dissolution of the self. She all but comes unhinged at the death of her child: "I must and could lie down by my dead babe, side by side all the night after. I have thought since of the wonderful goodness of God to me in preserving me in the use of my reason and senses in that distressed time, that I did not use wicked and violent means to end my own miserable life" (22). The association of women and madness will become a major gender marker in later Gothic, as we have seen with *Paradise*. Rowlandson's experience leaves her emotionally damaged, her sense of reality upended even many years after the experience: "I remember in the night season, how the other day I was in the midst of thousands of enemies, and nothing but death before me. It is then hard work to persuade myself, that ever I should be satisfied with bread again" (69). Rowlandson's experience of both time and space has become confused, such that "now" and "then," "here" and "there" surreally blend.

Charles Brockden Brown

These early American texts developed through a number of influences to become the full-blown frontier Gothic: "melding of Indian captivity tales, local history, wilderness environments, and select conventions of European works resulted in Frontier Gothic," which, "as it slowly evolved into the Western – would come to embody the myth of America itself" (Sivils 84). These seventeenth-century texts deployed Gothic tropes through a religious sense of the numinous, a felt sense of the presence of a supernatural world. Roughly a hundred years later, Charles Brockden Brown advanced this use of frontier Gothic for fictional purposes (on Brown, see also Ringel [Chapter 1] in this volume). Brown, the first US author to make a living by writing, developed the Gothic numinous not *through* religious supernaturalism but *in dialogue with it* as religious belief had morphed and diffused throughout the century. His *Wieland; or, the Transformation* (1798) exemplifies American Gothic in representing religious faith and mystical experience at the same time both are severely questioned by events of the novel. Clara Wieland, narrator and very type of the rational, Enlightenment ideal, undergoes several encounters with seemingly supernatural, numinous presences, as does her brother, to violent and tragic effect.

The Wieland family has a history of religious mania and possible insanity. The father of the novel's present generation, Theodore Wieland, Sr., catches fire in a burst of light, seeming to spontaneously combust while in prayer at his "temple," an outdoor, stone structure at some distance from his house and near a wilderness. This prelude to events of the novel's present appears only loosely connected, since the now-adult Wieland children, Clara and Theodore, Jr., have established an entirely different life than their parents had. Altered into an emblem of Enlightenment values, the temple has become a kind of playhouse, where they read, converse, and put on dramas. The temple, however, like the Wieland family, will not release the past so easily. Theodore, Jr. begins to "hear" commands from God to kill his family, the voices possibly produced by villain Francis Carwin. Theodore also tries to kill Clara before turning her penknife on himself. It has long been clear that Theodore inherited his father's melancholy disposition, his "calvinistic inspiration," and that he believes unflaggingly in a supernatural deity who directs human action (25). Clara, too, exercises an irrational faith in supernatural powers. She believes, for example, that one of Carwin's voices is her protector. Thus Enlightenment rationality collapses.

Wieland prefigured by two hundred years *Paradise*'s duality of frontier, utopian spaces. The temple, originally a "hedge" against the world for Wieland, Sr.'s worship practices, in the next generation becomes another utopia – of art and learning. Clara's house is similarly situated on the outer fringes of the family property, Mettingen. The temple, site of Wieland, Sr.'s death, now becomes haunted by mysterious voices; Clara's house, supposedly her safe haven, becomes the stage for voices in her closet threatening her death and rape; for her confrontation with Carwin; and finally for the insane Theodore, his wife murdered in Clara's bed, and his death. The past of these locations will not stay past. Clara's own repressions – of her secret love for Pleyel, of her mysterious sexual attraction to Carwin, and of her near-incestuous dream of her brother beckoning her over a pit – return in her "safe" home, where each of these men violates her safety and destabilizes her sense of self. Clara can only break the spell of the past by moving to Europe with an uncle, far from the failed utopias of the Wieland family.

Brown subtitled *Wieland* "An American Tale," and indeed the novel can be read as an allegory of American ideologies from which Native American Removal and westward expansion were constructed. Building and repurposing structures at America's frontiers aimed, in this view, to expunge any past on which the "enlightened" present might be staged. Enlightenment principles of reason and progress were, however, severely questioned by frontier

Gothic in America, which "frequently unsettle(s) the discourses of redemption, progress, and other ideological versions of histories" (Procházka 29). As identities and places begin to shift and transform in *Wieland*, the sureties of reason and intellect fail to protect against the return of the family's history of madness.

In his "To the Public" prefacing *Edgar Huntly* (1799), Brown more directly pointed his readers to a national allegory interpretation. He compares his novel to the then-popular British Gothic novels, with their "[p]urile superstition [and] Gothic castles and chimeras," concluding that American settings and events better capture interests "peculiar to ourselves": "The incidents of Indian hostility, and the perils of the western wilderness, are far more suitable [for Americans]; and, for a native of America to overlook these, would admit of no apology" (3). *Edgar Huntly* is Brown's novel most directly about the frontier. Set in the wilderness area just west of Philadelphia, its titular character wanders both asleep and awake, most often at night, in search of his close friend's murderer. Through much of the novel, Edgar pursues Clithero Edny, a sleepwalker whom Edgar believes might be the murderer, or at least believes can benefit from sympathetic understanding. In the end, Edgar could not be more mistaken about Clithero *and* himself. Clithero is revealed to be a mercurial character, not Waldegrave's murderer but nevertheless irrationally criminal in the past and the present. After waking in a pit at the bottom of a cave, engaging with (and killing) several Delaware Indians, and rescuing a captive, Edgar eventually has to be told by his mentor, Sarsefield, that he was himself sleepwalking. His first interpretation was more supernatural: "Had some mysterious power snatched me from the earth, and cast me, in a moment, into the heart of the wilderness?" (171). In this critique of Enlightenment certainty about the reasoning self, however, the case is worse than supernatural: "Disastrous and humiliating is the state of man! By his own hands, is constructed the mass of misery and error in which his steps are forever involved," Edgar declares; "How total is the blindness with regard to our own performances!" (278). As Bill Christopherson writes, "we are all blind to our inner self – a self that ... may be as depraved as our Calvinist forefathers thought" (23). The "light" of Enlightenment progress is either invisible to the sleepwalker or hidden by the darkness in which most of this novel takes place.

Edgar Huntly's frontier setting is gothicized by an ongoing irruption of the past into the present. Edgar, walking almost constantly through the novel, seems uneasy in space. Huntly farm, it turns out, is located on Delaware Indian land, more or less robbed by Pennsylvania founder William Penn's sons through the deceitful 1737 Walking-Purchase treaty. Though Edgar knows the history of Huntly farm, he, "blind" to his own family's responsibility, never quite understands the reasons for Native attacks on the Anglo Huntlys. Past actions in *Edgar Huntly* explode violently into the present in the form of Delaware characters, who, as Norman Grabo notes, "come from some nightmare without words" (68). As in *Paradise*, the gothically irrational doubling of objects, events, and characters in *Edgar Huntly* embodies the surreal superimposition of the present on a history of abjection of the racial "other," or as Sivils remarks, "[e]ntering the American Gothic wilderness, then, is as much about risking dehumanization and insanity as it is about the threat of Native Americans or animals. It is about the spiritual peril of traversing a land haunted by the specters of national injustice and hypocrisy" (91). *Edgar Huntly* is as much about property rights as was Rowlandson's captivity experience, as both Native Americans and English immigrants seek to occupy the same space.

Edgar Allan Poe

Brown's Gothic novels were of great interest a generation later to Edgar Allan Poe, whose fictions even more starkly represented the mutually defining fields of mind, geography, and history (on Poe, see also Bendixen [Chapter 2] in this volume). Indeed, the extensive doubling, darkness, and irrationality of Brown's characters move toward the outright supernatural in Poe's works, motivated by what Brown's fictions rendered as irrationally self-harming actions and what Poe famously named "the perverse." While most of Poe's Gothic fiction is rather housebound, his *Narrative of Arthur Gordon Pym* (1838) adopts and extends this and other Gothic characteristics in the liminal and deceptive space of the open sea, a frontier Charles L. Crow calls "sea-Gothic" ("Fear" 133). An early episode in this short novel, when Pym and his friend/double Augustus drunkenly sail a small boat called the *Ariel* to open sea and are run over by a ship, prefigures the entire plot involving two shipwrecks, starvation, a mutiny and a counter-mutiny, cannibalism, an encounter with the *Flying Dutchman*, and more unnameable, unworldly adventures south of the eighty-fourth parallel, Southern latitude (a frontier that had not been crossed when *Pym* was first published). The *Ariel* disaster, instead of curing Arthur's desire for sea adventures, makes him perversely long for them all the more: "My visions were of shipwreck and famine; of death or captivity among barbarian hoardes; of a lifetime dragged out in sorrow and tears, upon some grey and desolate rock, in an ocean unapproachable and unknown" (57).

Arthur's "visions," in the dream-logic of *Pym*, are played out to the letter. Below the eighty-fourth parallel, Arthur and Dirk Peters, a half Indian looking remarkably like an ape, eventually are the only survivors of an attack by deceitful, very black natives on the island of Tsalal, "la last" before the South Pole. Arthur and Peters manage to escape with a native hostage, then float southward through an increasingly white sea-wilderness toward the Pole, where they are soon engulfed by "a shrouded human figure, very far larger in its proportions than any dweller among men. And the hue of the skin of the figure was of the perfect whiteness of the snow" (239). A Southern white man, Poe dramatizes here a nightmare vision of slave insurrection, just six years after Nat Turner's rebellion in Virginia (on race and the American Gothic, see also Weinauer [Chapter 6] in this volume). In Poe's hallucinatory vision, the violence of slavery in America's past returns to punish those in power, reversing the American hierarchies so tentatively kept in place during these antebellum years.

On the surface, the frontier of *Pym* is a blank slate, a place where the American psyche meets a stubbornly literal sea topography to blend mind and place in mutual definition. However, this "unapproachable and unknown" location so perfectly reenacts and inverts the slavery in America's past that it would be hard *not* to see the locations, particularly Tsalal and points south, as reinscriptions of American places. Like Brown's *Wieland* before it, and *Paradise* after, Poe's frontier returns the repressed in terms exponentially more horrifying than the original events. But the quality of violence in this short novel is both more horrific and less motivated than in writers before Poe. Narrator Pym dwells on, for instance, the brutality, bludgeoning, shooting, and knifing involved in the counter-mutiny on board the *Grampus*, whereas only the aftermath of the Theodore's murders in *Wieland* is described. Also, violence happens to Pym not because he is seen as a devil, as the Salem Puritans saw their "witches," or because someone is tricking him with disguised voices, but simply because he is so often in the wrong place at the wrong time. Horrific things in *Pym* seem to originate with a rather malevolent universe, and this unmotivated violence highlights in relief the *very* motivated violence performed by black characters. The black cook on the ship, Pym says, "in all respects was a perfect demon" (84). On Tsalal, the natives trap the crew (minus Pym and Peters) in a gorge to murder them. Though they are uniformly described as "black," these natives have all the characteristics of earlier literary Native Americans who fulfilled the role of devils: these "blackskin warriors," "savages," act on "brute rage," "skulking among the bushes" on the island (214–15).

In her 1992 *Playing in the Dark: Whiteness and the Literary Imagination*, Toni Morrison describes Poe's *Pym* and other white writers' use of black characters as "others" toward the consolidation of whiteness during the nineteenth century. Morrison's idea of "American Africanism" examines these roles as literary tropes against which the power of whiteness was created. "The subject of the dream is the dreamer [the white writer]. The fabrication of an Africanist persona is reflexive; an extraordinary mediation on the self; a powerful exploration of the fears and desires ... longing and terror" of white "writerly conscious" (17). This Gothic "registers slavery as the cultural contradiction that haunts the Atlantic world's myths of freedom" (Goddu 71). The frontier seascape in *Pym* provides for both the repression of America's past and its return.

Twentieth-Century Frontier Gothic

Despite historian Frederick Jackson Turner's famous declaration that the American frontier was closing around 1900, American Gothic representation of frontiers has, if anything, proliferated since the turn of the twentieth century.[2] The Western, for example, became in the twentieth century a fantasy genre reformulating the terror, violence, and mythology of gothicized everyday landscapes (84). Many realistic short stories and novels, too, have blended the Gothic with the everyday world. To name just a few: Charlotte Perkins Gilman's 1892 "The Yellow Wallpaper," Edith Wharton's 1917 *Summer*, several William Faulkner novels, James Dickey's 1970 *Deliverance*, and Peter Matthiesson's *Watson* trilogy (1990–1999), the latter of which includes a Gothic history of mixed-race characters, murder, rape, and incest. These latter examples, beginning with Faulkner, reinscribed the American South as a terrifying frontier of wilderness settings, doubling of character and event, and the uncanny repetitions of perverse self-harm we have seen in much of the earlier literature.

To look at just one novel from this later, Southern frontier genre (on the Southern Gothic, see also Crow [Chapter 10] in this volume), Cormac McCarthy's 1973 *Child of God* bears a remarkable similarity to its literary forebears in these respects. Its protagonist, Lester Ballard, has mental deficits to begin with, then is rendered less capable by a severe beating during the auction of his property. Lester has no "place" to thrive, even as a child, after his father's suicide (his mother abandoned them early in Lester's life). Lester is both helpless and criminal, a victim and a monster. He degenerates to near-animal status as he moves away from Sevier County, Tennessee, and goes underground; like Brown's Edgar Huntly, he more or less wanders into mountain caves. But unlike Huntly, he stays there, begins practicing necrophilia – a rather Poe-esque trope – and murder to support his necrophilia habit. He ends in a mental institution, where, at his death, his body is brutally and graphically dissected for study, a clear parallel to his murder victims. Lester is a modern, terrifying, isolated individual, left to his own resources: We have seen this trend from *Edgar Huntly* through *Arthur Gordon Pym*. Those novels hinted at a dark outcome of the Enlightenment, a "free" individual whose freedom could spin out of control into absolute savagery, where later novelists like McCarthy follow such characters through to monstrous criminality. In Lester's regression, *Child of God* brings to the foreground what was implied in earlier frontier Gothic such as *Edgar Huntly* and Rowlandson's captivity: simultaneous fear of *and* attraction to becoming the "savage" other.

Modern frontier Gothics of the South, along with works like Morrison's *Paradise*, expand the earliest American theme of exclusive or utopian community as against the mysterious "devils" that live outside the circle. There is in these more recent texts, however, more self-consciousness about the complicity of the hegemonic order in creating and maintaining the monstrous, unknown "other" in the attempt to bury the past of dispossession. No less than fictions involving Native American-English warfare over land, *Child of God* is about a property dispute: Displacement uproots, unsettles, and finally criminalizes the frontier Gothic antihero. The community that dispossesses Lester, precisely like the men of Ruby who "purge" the Convent of *Paradise* of its witchy women, has reappeared in the modern world. *Child of God* "reveals how acts of violence are sanctioned by the normative community that instigates, mythologizes, and perhaps even needs a figure such as Lester" (Walsh 148). Poe's white America both needed and scorned black people to confirm their own sense of self, but Poe's awareness of this fact appears only in the refracted terms of the subconscious.

Frontier Gothic has long dramatized perverse self-harm, doubling, and other uncanny repetitions that raise a sense of nightmare, the return of repressed and abjected others from the past in a palimpsest of temporal "locations." It is possibly the most violent of Gothic modes, with guns being the murder weapon of choice at America's lawless frontiers. Native Americans used guns to capture (and to kill some of) Mary Rowlandson's family. *Paradise* begins with the men of Ruby bursting into the Convent to shoot the women there. Edgar Huntly is well-known for his fusil and tomahawk; more symbolic, however, is what he takes from a Native American he has just killed: in "some freak of fancy, I stuck his musquet in the ground, and left it standing upright in the middle of the road" (203). Lester Ballard recalls Edgar Huntly, slinking around the countryside in *Child of God* with his gun always at his side. The gun is clearly, for American Gothic, a fetishized object with near-magical powers. Its violence marks what Weinstock describes in his canny assertion that "The long path of the American Frontier Gothic stretches back in time to a gun planted in the middle of a road alongside a dead Indian" (*CBB* 43).

NOTES

1. A jeremiad, Mather's *Wonders* excoriates those considered to have fallen away from the original settlers' exemplary holiness. The "Young ones," especially, in Reiner Smolinski's editorial commentary "have become extravagantly and abominably Vicious" (see Mather xi), calling the devil's mastiffs into the midst of their utopian project, like the younger generations of Ruby, Oklahoma, who, according to its patriarchs, have come under the influence of the Convent witches.
2. The Turner thesis held that the westward movement of Anglo-American settlement across the United States created a moving frontier, and that a frontier mentality had come to define Americans: independent, violent, and democratic. Turner believed that the American frontier was free for anyone to "settle" ("The Significance of the Frontier in American History," delivered at the American Historical Association meeting in 1893 in Chicago).

WORKS CITED

Brown, Charles Brockden. *Edgar Huntly: or, Memoirs of a Sleep-Walker*. Ed. Sydney J. Krause. Kent, OH: Kent State University Press, 1984.

Wieland; or, The Transformation: An American Tale and Memoirs of Carwin the Biloquist. Ed. Alexander Cowie. Kent, OH: Kent State University Press, 1977. 1–310.

Christopherson, Bill. *The Apparition in the Glass: Charles Brockden Brown's American Gothic*. Athens: University of Georgia Press, 1994.

Crow, Charles L., ed. *Companion to American Gothic*. Hoboken, NJ: John Wiley & Sons, 2013.

"Fear, Ambiguity, and Transgression: The Gothic Novel in the United States." *A Companion to the American Novel*. Ed. Alfred Bendixon. Hoboken, NJ: Wiley-Blackwell, 2012. 129–46.

Davison, Carol Margaret. "Charles Brockden Brown: Godfather of the American Gothic." *Companion to American Gothic*. Ed. Charles L. Crow. Hoboken, NJ: John Wiley & Sons, 2013. 110–23.

Fiedler, Leslie. *Love and Death in the American Novel*. New York: Criterion Books, 1960.

Folsom, James K. "Gothicism in the Western Novel." *Frontier Gothic: Terror and Wonder at the Frontier in American Literature*. Eds. David Mogen, Scott P. Sanders, and Joanne B. Karpinski. London and Toronto: Associated University Presses, 1993. 28–41.

Freud, Sigmund. "The Uncanny." *The Standard Edition of the Complete Psychological Works of Sigmund Freud*, Vol. XVII (1917–1919). Trans. James Strackey. London: Hogarth Press, 1955.

Goddu, Teresa. "The African American Slave Narrative and the Gothic." *Companion to American Gothic*. Ed. Charles L. Crow. Hoboken, NJ: John Wiley & Sons, 2013. 71–83.

Grabo, Norman. *The Coincidental Art of Charles Brockden Brown*. Chapel Hill: University of North Carolina Press, 1981.

Jarraway, David R. "'Divided Moment' Yet 'One Flesh': The 'Queer' Contours of American Gothic Today." *Gothic Studies* 2.1 (2000): 90–103.

Kerr, Howard, John W. Crowley, and Charles L. Crow, eds. *The Haunted Dusk: American Supernatural Fiction 1820 – 1920*. Athens: University of Georgia Press, 1984.

Mather, Cotton. *Wonders of the Invisible World: Observations Historical as well Theological, upon the Nature, the Number, and the Operations of the Devil.* Ed. Reiner Smolinski. Digital Commons@University of Nebraska-Lincoln: Electronic Texts in American Studies. Paper 19. Web. 15 July 2016.

McCarthy, Cormac. *Child of God*. New York: Random House, 1973.

Mogen, David, Scott P. Sanders, and Joanne B. Karpinski. Introduction. *Frontier Gothic: Terror and Wonder at the Frontier in American Literature*. Eds. David Mogen, Scott P. Sanders, and Joanne B. Karpinski. London and Toronto: Associated University Presses, 1993.

Morrison, Toni. *Paradise*. New York: Plume, 1997.

Playing in the Dark: Whiteness and the Literary Imagination. New York: Vintage Books, 1992.

Procházka, Martin. "American Ruins and the Ghost Town Syndrome." *Companion to American Gothic*. Ed. Charles L. Crow. Hoboken, NJ: John Wiley & Sons, 2013. 29–40.

Poe, Edgar Allan. *The Narrative of Arthur Gordon Pym of Nantucket*. 1838. New York: Penguin Classics, 1986.

Rowlandson, Mary. *The Soveraignty and Goodness of God… Narrative of the Captivity and Restauration of Mrs. Mary Rowlandson. In Early Americas Digital Archive*. University of Maryland Technology in the Humanities, 2002. Web. 15 July 2016.

Sivils, Matthew Wynn. "Indian Captivity Narratives and the Origins of American Frontier Gothic." *Companion to American Gothic*. Ed. Charles L. Crow. Hoboken, NJ: John Wiley & Sons, 2013. 84–95.

Walsh, J. Christopher. *In the Wake of the Sun: Navigating the Southern Works of Cormac McCarthy*. Knoxville: Newfound Press, 2010.

Weinstock, Jeffrey Andrew. "American Monsters." *Companion to American Gothic*. Ed. Charles L. Crow. Hoboken, NJ: John Wiley & Sons, 2013. 41–55.

Charles Brockden Brown. Gothic Authors: Critical Revisions. Cardiff: University of Wales Press, 2011.

Wester, Maisha L. "Toni Morrison's Gothic: Headless Brides and Haunted Communes." *Companion to American Gothic*. Ed. Charles L. Crow. Hoboken, NJ: John Wiley & Sons, 2013. 378–91.

10

CHARLES L. CROW

Southern American Gothic

Much Southern American Gothic writing is about slavery and its legacy. However, we need to draw some careful distinctions. First, it is too easy to displace onto the South a "race question" that clearly is a national, not a regional issue. Second, race is not the only concern of American or of Southern Gothic. Pushing back against Leslie Fiedler's assertion in *Love and Death in the American Novel* that, "the proper subject for America gothic is the black man"[1] (397), Justin Edwards notes that this "negates gender, homosexuality, incest, genocide, rape, war, murder, religion, and class as 'proper' subjects of the nation's gothic literature" (xxvii). Indeed, the list could be extended to include, for example, disease, addiction, physical deformity, and degeneration or atavism. All of these issues appear in Southern Gothic. Nonetheless, the history of the South is distinctive, including slavery, Indian removal, rebellion, proud defeat, reconstruction, a long and bitter struggle to justify and restore white supremacy, and the erosion of the system of segregation into our own time. The conflicted narratives southerners have built from this history are the basis of Southern Gothic.

Origins

The South did not have a great Gothic novelist like Charles Brockden Brown at its literary beginnings (on Brown, see Ringel [Chapter 1] and Hinds [Chapter 9] in this volume), but it had, in William Byrd and Thomas Jefferson, keen observers of the social and historical conditions that would produce the Southern Gothic literature of the next century. Louis P. Simpson (xi) traces the origins of Southern Gothic to Byrd's *History of the Dividing Line Betwixt Virginia and North Carolina* (written following the surveying of the line in 1728 but not published until 1841) and Jefferson's *Notes on the State of Virginia* (1787).[2]

Byrd's *History*, with its rowdy and satirical twin, *The Secret History* (written on the spot for the author's amusement), are accounts of the official surveying party that established the boundary between the two colonies (Virginia and North Carolina) in 1728. In his descriptions of the Great Dismal Swamp and the poverty of its disease-ridden swamp dwellers, Byrd provides a first look at enduring Southern archetypes. Swamps are sometimes beautiful, but they are inherently dangerous, messy, and resistant to the attempts of humans to impose order upon them. They are ready-made symbols for dark and uncontrolled human emotion, and for, in a telling word spoken in George Washington Cable's *The Grandissimes* (1880), "Dissolution" (264). Swamps are enduring settings of the Southern Gothic, from Henry Clay Lewis' early story "A Struggle for Life" (1850) through Cable and Faulkner, and into fiction of our own time, from Cormac McCarthy's *The Outer Dark* (1968) to Peter Matthiesson's *Shadow Country* (2008) and Karen Russell's *Swamplandia!* (2011).[3]

In the swamp dwellers, Byrd portrays the rural poor whites who, with their hill-dwelling counterparts, almost constitute a fourth race, with blacks, indigenous Americans, and "respectable" whites, in the Southern hierarchy. Left behind by the passing frontier in remote pockets, these survivors cling to frontier ways, refusing or unable to evolve into successful farmers or citizens of orderly villages. They live lives of squalor and laziness. They eat only pork, and have become "hoggish in their Temper, & many of them seem to Grunt rather than Speak in their ordinary conversation" (Byrd 55). Byrd reports they are "devoured by musketas" (74), are subject to diseases that "kill abundance of People," and, in a chilling phrase, "make the rest look no better than Ghosts" (84).

Certainly the lives of impoverished and diseased squatters are a long way from that of the simple yeomen that Thomas Jefferson would celebrate in his Query XIX of his *Notes on the State of Virginia* as central to his vision of republican virtue. For Jefferson, as for the mid-Atlantic J. Hector St. John de Crèvecoeur,[4] the industry of the yeoman, who worked his own land and lived a life of simplicity and virtue, was essential to republican order. Rude frontiersman might be tamed or displaced by the advance of settlements and agriculture. The continuance of such backwoods folk and their brutish ways, however, disrupts the national, as well as Southern, narrative of progress, and suggests the inversion of progress: atavism or degeneration. They would be shown as objects of amusement, or fear, or sympathy. Their comic value is shown in the tradition of Old Southwest Humor, of which *The History of the Dividing Line* is a foundational text. The tradition of what Bernice Murphy calls "Rural Gothic," almost always set in the South, shows the backwoodsman as a figure of menace (as in James Dickey's *Deliverance* [1970]). Recent Gothic fiction by such writers as Dorothy Allison, Daniel

Woodrell, Karen Russell, Ron Rash, and Wiley Cash, however, depicts the rural figure, especially the backwoods woman, as a victim.

But if the degenerates described by Byrd were far from Jefferson's yeoman, so too were the lives of the slave-owning plantation owners such as Byrd himself and (two generations later) Thomas Jefferson. In the remarkable Query XVIII of *Notes on the State of Virginia*, which is the chapter before his celebration of the yeoman, Jefferson laments the inevitable corruption of the morals of the slave owner: "The whole commerce between master and slave is a perpetual exercise of the most boisterous passions, the most unremitting despotism on the one part, and degrading submissions on the other" (288). Jefferson's outburst identifies slavery as the original sin, the fatal flaw in Southern culture. It is an expression of guilt and of fear of a divine accounting to be paid, of the return of the repressed. And there is more, easily glimpsed beneath Jefferson's allusion to the "boisterous passions" of masters and "degrading submissions" of slaves: the sexual exploitation of enslaved women. We read this passage today knowing that DNA testing has confirmed the persistent reports of Jefferson's fathering of children upon his slave Sally Hemings. Behind Jefferson's Query, then, barely visible, are the mixed race people who are so important to Southern Gothic, their suppressed genealogies, the guilt of their fathers, and the fear of their retributive rage.

Before the War

In the antebellum years of the nineteenth century, white Southerners favored the historical fiction of Walter Scott and imitators such as William Gilmore Simms, whose narratives presented a reassuring vision of class and racial privilege. However, this sense of security was disrupted by the revolution in Haiti, by slave revolts in the South itself, by narratives of escaped slaves, and by the beginnings of Southern Gothic fiction.

The Haitian revolution of 1791–1804, cumulating in the massacre of some five to seven thousand whites organized by revolt leader Jean-Jacques Dessalines in early 1804, was the South's nightmare made real. Slave revolts in the South, like that of Nat Turner in 1831, inevitably evoked Haiti, but still were nearly unthinkable, since they denied the Southern narrative of the contented, loyal slave. For many Southerners, Turner must have been a monster, a madman, who misled his followers. Simms' *The Yemassee* (1835), published just four years after Turner's revolt, reinforces the core belief in the faithful and grateful slave. Hector, the slave of the hero Charles Craven, is developed as a parallel character to Craven's faithful dog, Dugdale. Hector and other slaves are faithful allies in putting down the rebellion of the Yamassee Indians, thus justifying both slavery and the Indian Removal Act of 1830.

If a slave who rebels must be mad or deluded, so too was a slave who escaped to the North. Conservative Southerners claimed both before and after the Civil War that escaped slave narratives were slanders, fabricated by abolitionists. Yet among the hundreds of escaped slave narratives are many with real and enduring power, such as *The Narrative of Frederick Douglass* (1845), Solomon Northrup's *Twelve Years a Slave* (1853), William Craft's *Running a Thousand Miles for Freedom* (1860), and Harriet Ann Jacobs' *Incidents in the Life of a Slave Girl* (1861). Teresa Goddu demonstrates how such narratives, while realistically documenting the cruelties of slavery, fall naturally into Gothic discourse (see Goddu 133–52).

Meanwhile, the earliest known short story by an African American, "Le Mulâtre" ("The Mulatto"), written in French by Victor Séjour in 1837, was a Gothic work inspired by the revolution in Haiti. Séjour was of Haitian and Louisianan mixed-race ancestry. Born a free black in Louisiana, he emigrated to France and worked primarily as a playwright. In "The Mulatto," a visitor to Haiti is told the story of Georges, who killed his master. Avenging the death of his wife, Georges learns only at the moment of his master's death that he has killed his own father. Séjour's melodramatic tale displays most of the themes of later American racial Gothic that were implied in Jefferson's Query: miscegenation, incest (at least symbolically, in the master's sexual menacing of his daughter-in-law), suppressed genealogies, and, especially, retribution. Since the story, even in its framing present, is set before the Haitian revolution, it stands as a warning of what is to come. The old slave who tells the story of Georges to the narrator proclaims that, if a slave "continues to live, it can only be for vengeance; for soon he shall rise ... and, from the day he shakes off his servility, the master would do better to have a starving tiger raging beside him than to meet that man face to face" (2).

Images of slave revolt can also be found in the one major writer of the prewar South who might seem to transcend sectional difference, Edgar Allan Poe (on Poe, see also Bendixen [Chapter 2] and Hinds [Chapter 9] in this volume). Yet his fables reveal the fears of his own time, as well as those that might seem universal. In "Hop Frog" (1849), for example, a dwarf jester suffers abuse from the king and his court until his lover is humiliated, and he seeks revenge. Hop-Frog's burning alive of the suspended king and his ministers is a Janus-faced image, recalling both slave rebellions and the lynching of blacks. Similarly, Poe's only novel, *The Narrative of Arthur Gordon Pym* (1838), suggests, in the attack of the coal-black people of Tsalal, both colonial wars and slave rebellions.

Yet the work by Poe that has the greatest resonance for Southern Gothic may be one that has no apparent connection with the South. "The Fall of the House of Usher" (1839) is set in the familiar geographically ambiguous Poescape, and its principle characters, the narrator and Roderick and Madeline Usher, seem European or British. But Poe's account of the collapse of a house, in both senses, as a dynasty and a structure, would echo through the literature of the postwar South as one of its most powerful images. We shall see this house, collapsing and often burning, again and again.

The Gothic and Local Color: The Plantation School

Poe's otherworldly and allegorical "The Fall of the House of Usher" could become the basis for so much Southern fiction only by being joined to the tangible, observable reality of the postwar South. The fallen house could be seen everywhere in the burned ruins of plantation manors, and the unpainted and decaying great houses that survived the war. W. E. B. Du Bois, in *The Souls of Black Folk* (1903), takes us on a tour of the Georgia black belt at the end of the century, and sketches the stories of several of these buildings: some abandoned, some still inhabited by families of former slave owners, and some of these even surviving with the help of their former slaves. He writes, "So we ride on, past phantom gates and falling homes, – past the once flourishing farms of the Smiths, the Gandys, and the Lagores, – and find all dilapidated and half ruined, even there where a solitary white woman, a relic of other days, sits alone in state among miles of Negroes and rides to town in her ancient coach each day" (449).

Clearly, there were many narratives to be spun about these intertwined families, both white and black. But in the decades after the war, the taste of most Americans was not for stories about decaying manor houses, and especially not for mixed race characters who were the legacy of slavery. Rather, readers wanted historical fiction about the time when the manor houses were bright with fresh paint, and filled with cavaliers, and belles in hoop skirts. If black people were shown, either in pre- or postwar settings, they were likely to be picturesque and kindly, telling folk tales to white children, or nostalgic for the life on the old plantation. The mood of Uncle Remus and the songs of Stephen Foster predominated.

The Southern Gothic of the decades after the Civil War usually subverts the dominant narrative that the South was attempting to construct as part of its campaign to restore white supremacy. But because writers are complex and follow their own impulses, rather than the patterns imposed by critics, we find some surprising inconsistencies in this. Thomas Nelson Page, for instance, is usually considered a member of the plantation school of local color,[5] as represented by his often-anthologized story, "Marse Chan" (1884). Yet in "No Haid Pawn" (1887), Page produced an astonishingly effective Gothic tale about a supposedly haunted house in a swamp and an escaped slave, with memorable images of the cost in blood of the construction of the abandoned plantation. Similarly, Grace King began her career as an apologist for the pre-war slave-owning Creole culture of Louisiana. Some of her stories, nonetheless, are frank and powerful in their depiction of racial issues. "The Little Convent Girl" (1893) shows the destruction of a mixed-race child when her protective father dies and she is thrown unsuspectingly into the racial and sexual world of her black mother's New Orleans.

George Washington Cable, however, though he had served in combat in the Confederate cavalry, was a consistent advocate of civil rights for black Americans, a position that ultimately obliged him to leave the South. Like Mark Twain, Kate Chopin, and Charles Chesnutt, Cable subverted the plantation school, and often drew on the Gothic for his exploration of racial themes. *The Grandissimes* (1880), like his short story collection *Old Creole Days* (1879, expanded 1883), was set in the pre-war past, and does indeed contain a gallery of picturesque characters and is spiced with New Orleans Creole dialect. But the novel begins specifically in 1803, the time of the transition from French to US rule. The analogy to the return of Louisiana to Union authority after the Civil War is obvious, and suggests that the issues of the novel are not to be softened with a nostalgic glow. When the German immigrant, pharmacist Joseph Frowenfeld, enters the Mississippi River from the Gulf, he sees "A land hung in mourning, darkened by gigantic cypresses, submerged, a land of reptiles, silence, decay" (9). *The Grandissimes* will show, before ending with the expected marriages and distribution of rewards, the terrible story of Bas Coupé, the mutilated African king, a voodoo curse, the death of a black woman at the hands of a mob, several other murders, deaths by duel, and a suicide.

The Grandissimes is a novel about identity and concealment. It begins, suitably, with a masked ball. The novel's main point-of-view character, the outsider Frowenfeld, is not present at the ball, but soon enters a Creole culture that is essentially masked. Frowenfeld struggles to untangle relationships of, between, and within the Creole families. For a long time he thinks Aurora and Clotilde are sisters, rather than mother and daughter. He does not understand until a quarter of the way into the narrative that there are two characters named Honoré De Grandissime, and not until later does he learn that the two Honorés are brothers, and that one of them is black. Frowenfeld feels that he has become "involved among shadows, and ... seemed at length almost to gasp in a atmosphere of hints, allusions, faint unspoken admissions, ill-concealed antipathies, unfinished speeches, mistaken identities and whisperings of hidden strife" (96).

Cable takes this ambiguity and makes it a narrative principle – as do other writers, white and black, of Southern Gothic. Sometimes one instance of suppressed genealogy will be revealed, but others not, and readers are invited to apply the principle and make their way through the hints and unvoiced admissions. Thus we are told – finally – that the two Honorés are brothers, but never told that Aurora and her servant Palmyre are sisters. Once seen, however, the symmetry is apparent and much guarded innuendo is explained.

Similar patterns appear throughout Southern Gothic, especially in narratives set in the time of slavery and the later nineteenth century. We are admitted only partially into a society where secrets are known – especially by slaves and their descendants – but not revealed. In Kate Chopin's "Desiree's Baby" (1893), for instance, we learn, in a concluding twist worthy of Maupassant, that Armand has African blood, and that his heritage is responsible for the appearance of the baby. However, we are not told that the child of the fair-skinned slave "La Blanche" was also fathered by Armand: Only the careful reader, alert to the story's ironies and symmetries, will see this. In Charles Chesnutt's "The Marked Tree" (1924), we understand only through hints and innuendo that the slave Isham, who was sold to pay for the wedding of young Johnny Spencer, was Johnny's brother.

Chesnutt's *The Marrow of Tradition* (1901) is a meditation on race at the beginning of the twentieth century. It was written at a bitter time when white supremacy had been restored in the South, and in the immediate aftermath of the Wilmington, North Carolina, riots of November 1898, when white mobs burned black-owned businesses and homes, killed black citizens, and expelled legitimately elected officials. *The Marrow of Tradition* is a realistic novel that accurately depicts the conspiracy of white supremacists who planned and executed this coup. It is also a Gothic novel deploying a full range of Gothic devices, including twins and doubles, hidden or destroyed legacies, and the now-familiar patterns of concealed genealogies. At the novel's core is the relationship between Olivia and Julia, her sister, who are so similar that they are often confused, though Julia is black, and disinherited through the theft and destruction of her father's last will and testament. The pattern of doubling is repeated, more subtly, with male characters. The novel's villain, Tom Delamere, wears blackface and impersonates his black servant Sandy at a cakewalk, and later in this disguise commits the robbery and murder for which Sandy is accused. As Eric Sundqvist has noted, Chesnutt drops a number of subtle hints that the impersonation is successful in part because of family resemblance (434). We meet old Mr. Delamere,

Tom's doting grandfather, and visit his crumbling plantation house, but are never given details of young Tom's parentage.

Chesnutt in *Marrow* is signifying on Mark Twain's *Pudd'nhead Wilson* (published in novel form in 1894), where there is also a doubling theme and a mixed race villain named Tom, who passes for white, disguises himself as black, and commits robbery and murder. But Clemens pushes his novel back into the period before the war, the time of his other "matter of Hannibal" novels, whereas Chesnutt probes the still-bleeding wounds of the present.

Chesnutt ends with words of guarded hope and warning: "There's time enough, but none to spare" (329). Literally, there is time for Dr. Miller, Julia's husband, to save the life of his white nephew. But, in a larger sense, reconciliation between divided Americans must occur. If not, there is the example of Josh Green, whose father was killed and his mother driven insane by the Klan. Green dies in extracting revenge on his father's killer. He is an implacable figure of black memory and fury, a raging tiger in the line going back to Séjour's Georges and Cable's Bas Coupé.

Southern Gothic and Modernism

The modernist project, with its experiments in time and consciousness, was well suited to Southern Gothic's concern with history and guilt. William Faulkner, especially, built fragmented narratives depicting tormented characters, usually young men, trying to understand or escape the burden of Southern history. Faulkner describes the full range of peoples in his fictional Yoknapatawpha County, from the Chickasaw Indians and their white and black descendants, enslaved and free blacks, country folk who are usually poor but sometimes rising, and the planter class that once rose and then fell. One of Faulkner's great themes is the decline of the county's pre-war aristocracy, as represented by his Sartorises, Compsons, McCaslins, and Sutpens.

Absalom, Absalom! (1936) is a fully formed modernist Gothic (see also Riquelme [Chapter 4] in this volume), with a complex hero villain in Thomas Sutpen, who pursues his object – a tainted version of the American dream – as ruthlessly as Ahab did his white whale in Melville's monumental *Moby-Dick* (1851). Sutpen is a demon according to Miss Rosa, and also a grand protagonist, a self-made man of tremendous courage and energy. At the end, he is trying to defeat time, and it is symbolically appropriate that he is cut down by a scythe. The fall of the House of Sutpen unfolds over many decades, set in motion by his original mistake, or sin, of denying his mixed race wife and son in Haiti. Quentin Compson, heir to his own collapsing dynasty, tells the story of Sutpen's Hundred to his Canadian Harvard roommate, answering a request to explain the South. Quentin witnesses the last act of the Sutpen tragedy, the burning of the decayed Sutpen mansion with the elderly Henry Sutpen and his black half-sister Clytie inside.

Like Quentin, young Isaac McCaslin in Faulkner's *The Bear* (1942) confronts his legacy, found in the cracked and dusty ledgers kept by his father and uncle. There, Isaac learns the secret of his grandfather's incest with his own enslaved daughter. Isaac seeks to escape the weight of guilt – not just his family's but the South's – by renouncing his inheritance, and living, Christlike, as a humble carpenter. Quentin, of course, escapes by suicide.

As Barbara Ladd notes (37–38), the characters in the fiction of Eudora Welty do not share this historical guilt. Welty, Faulkner's great Mississippi contemporary, generally describes a narrow range of time, and characters concerned with their own moment, not the burden of Southern history. Nonetheless, in "The Burning" (1955), Welty describes one of the events that loom in Southern lore, the firing of a plantation house by federal soldiers. But we do not reconstruct this event from the perspective of a haunted character – an Ike McCaslin – in a future time. We see it as it unfolds in front of us, in a continuing present. Or, rather, we see bits of the action through Welty's strangely redacted narration, like a highly edited film. We witness the intrusion of Federal soldiers into the home of Miss Theo and her sister Miss Myra. Miss Myra may be raped, and perhaps the housemaid Delilah. The house is looted by soldiers and the family's slaves, and set alight.

Also burned in the fire is the child Phinney, the secret of the house that must not be revealed. The old cook tries to tell the soldiers about "the trouble here" (468), but no one will listen or understand. Is Phinney white or black? The father may be the missing brother Benton, but who is the mother? Is it the simple-minded Myra, or is it the slave Delilah? The hints are contradictory and irresolvable. Miss Myra and Miss Theo hang themselves, and at the end of the story Delilah disappears, carrying Phinney's blackened bones wrapped in a cloth. The tragedy will cast no shadow, because no one will tell of it. We have the fragments of a Southern Gothic tale that hints at parody of Faulkner, or even, like much Gothic, of self-parody.

Writers of Southern Gothic after Faulkner are much less concerned with the fall of the houses of the antebellum aristocrats. The haunted house in Toni Morrison's great novel *Beloved* (1987) is the home of a former slave. (In portraying the humble home of a black woman, rather than the plantation house, as the site of haunting, Morrison had the precedent of Chesnutt's story "Po' Sandy" [1888].) The haunted house in Anne Rivers Siddons' *The*

House Next Door (1978) is set in an Atlanta suburb that could be anywhere, and has little historical context.

Queer, the Outsider, and the Grotesque

If the dominant narrative of America is one of heteronormative success, health and progress, and happy families, there is a disruptive counter-narrative about loneliness, failure, disease, the misfit, the outsider, the freak, and the sexually different. The South's narrative is different than that of other regions, more nostalgic and more skeptical of progress. But the South also has its queer and lonely disruptions, and some of the most notable examples of American Gothic lie within them (on queer Gothic, see also Haefele-Thomas [Chapter 8] in this volume).

Carson McCullers' fiction is filled with characters who are sexually ambivalent and physically strange. In *The Heart is a Lonely Hunter* (1940), there is a kind of same-sex marriage of the deaf mutes Singer and Antonapoulous, while the owner of the diner, Brannon, dresses secretly in the clothing of his late wife. In *The Ballad of the Sad Café* (1951), the strange triangle joining the dwarf Lymon, the sexually ambivalent Miss Amelia, and her husband Marvin Macy ends with Amelia physically beaten and turned into a kind of zombie, who haunts the ruined, soon-to-collapse structure of the title.

The works of Tennessee Williams and Truman Capote are replete with familiar emblems of Southern Gothic: the lost Belle Reve in Williams' *A Street Car Named Desire* (1947), the crumbling Cloud Hotel and the partially burned Skully's Landing in Capote's *Other Voices, Other Rooms* (1948), the surreal greenhouse in Williams' *Suddenly, Last Summer* (1958). Throughout the works of Williams and Capote there is a resistance to and satire of the conventional, as represented by Bricks' brother and horrible family in Williams' *Cat on a Hot Tim Roof* (1955), and by the brutality with which norms are enforced, as in the mob that kills Val in Williams' *Orpheus Descending* (1957). Heterosexuality generally is associated with violence and rape, as shown in Stanley's rape of Blanche in *Street Car* and in the gang rape of Zoo in *Other Voices*. Opposed to such heterosexual brutality, Williams and Capote valorize the outsider, the artist, the grotesque, and the queer.

Capote's *Other Voices, Other Rooms* is a queer Gothic *Bildungsroman*. The novel has many images of fragmented identity, like the distorted mirrors and looking glass in Skully's Landing. Skully's Landing is a plantation house, once a symbol of paternal authority, now inhabited by a disabled, impotent father, a homosexual man, a weak-willed white woman (Miss Amy), a strong sensuous young black woman (Zoo), and, with the arrival of Joel, a sexually ambivalent boy. Confused and divergent sexual identity is everywhere. Neighboring children Isabel and Florabel are identical twins, yet one is a tomboy (Isabel, based on Capote's childhood friend Harper Lee), and the other is assertively feminine. Above all, there is the "queer lady" seen by Joel in the window, who is revealed to be his cousin Randolph in Mardi Gras costume. While the novel's ending has Joel embracing his gay identity, it is not without sinister undertones. The developing relationship of Joel and the deceitful Randolph is troubling, since Randolph becomes a substitute father, while Joel's real father has been paralyzed by Randolph's gunshots. Presumably the boy and the middle-aged man are to become lovers, a symbolically incestuous relationship, and it is difficult not to see Joel as a victim.

Southern Theological Gothic

The South's dominant evangelical Protestantism, with its several variants and cults, provides the background for much Southern Gothic. In Wiley Cash's *A Land More Kind Than Home* (2012), the evil, lecherous evangelist of a snake-handling cult serves the same function as the evil monk of early European Gothic. The preacher, Carson Chambliss, once dealt in methamphetamine before discovering the addictive power of religion.

Flannery O'Connor, a Catholic, took her Pentecostal fellow Southerners as her subject in such novels as *Wise Blood* (1952) and *The Violent Bear It Away* (1960). Her fiction is filled with Gothic imagery, such as doubles and shadows, violent death, grotesque figures, and burnings. Yet she saw her novels essentially as comedies in the tradition of the Biblical Book of Jonah, in which her characters make themselves grotesque in their evasions of God's grace and His will. It is an indication of the strangeness (to most readers at least) of O'Connor's vision that she apparently regards the drugging and homosexual rape of young Tarwater in *The Violent Bear It Away* by a creature that may be a vampire, as a comic event. At the end, as young Tarwater burns the rustic home of his great uncle, Old Tarwater (a scene clearly meant to evoke Poe), he is at last ready to embrace his destiny as a prophet of the Lord.

A very different sort of theological Gothic can be seen in the early Southern novels of Cormac McCarthy, whose vision of an anarchic, possibly Manichean, universe owes something to Herman Melville. In *The Outer Dark* (1968), a young man, Culla, takes the baby just born to him by his sister, Rinthy, and exposes it in a wood. A wandering peddler retrieves the infant. McCarthy thus establishes, and will frustrate, the reader's expectation of a familiar myth or folk tale. The baby does not grow up to be Moses or Oedipus. The peddler is not a kindly mentor. Culla wanders the landscape, attempting to find his missing sister, while Rinthy searches for the lost boy. Meanwhile, a nameless trinity of horsemen rampage through the countryside murdering at will. The horsemen seem to represent a principle of chaos, or perhaps simply evil, and anticipate the judge of McCarthy's later Western novel, *Blood Meridian* (1985).

The two plot lines – the quests of Culla and Rinthy, and the havoc of the horsemen – touch at only one point, when the horsemen come upon the peddler and the baby, murder both, and, in unholy sacrament, drink the blood of the child. At the novel's end, Culla's miserable quest ends at the edge of an endless swamp, the bleakest of all in Southern Gothic, evoking Eliot's *Wasteland*: "Late in the day the road brought him into a swamp. And that was all. Before him stretched a spectral waste out of which reared only the naked trees in attitudes of agony and dimly hominoid like figures in a landscape of the damned. A faintly smoking garden of the dead that rounded away to the earth's curve" (142). Where O'Connor's insists on God's grace, and the world seems grotesque only because of human failure to recognize and receive it, McCarthy's world disrupts our attempts to see it as ruled by a benign deity.

Decadence, and the Rural Poor as Monsters and Victims

A core Southern nightmare has been the pollution of white bloodlines, most commonly though race mixing, as we have seen. A second version of this nightmare is degeneration or atavism. Through inbreeding or genetic accident, the highborn family declines, reverts, becomes an unspeakable Other. In Ellen Glasgow's story "Jordan's End" (1923), a once proud family is dragged down by hereditary insanity. In Erskine Caldwell's *Tobacco Road* (1932), the Jeeters have so degenerated that the reader watches their antics with mingled mirth, disgust, and pity, recalling William Byrd's attitude toward the swamp dwellers.

Byrd, one of a large party of armed men, never feared the pig-people of the swamp. But in the Southern Gothic of our time, the backwoodsman often rises up in fury against unwary outsiders. *Deliverance*, both James Dickey's novel (1970) and the movie (1972, directed by John Boorman), is a prime example of Southern Rural Gothic. The typical narrative, as in *Deliverance*, introduces a naïve group of tourists into a rural setting, where they are victimized by monsters in bib overalls. The story has endless variations in movies such as *The Texas Chainsaw Massacre* (1974) and *Southern Comfort* (1981).

There is an alternate version of the Southern Rural Gothic, however, that portrays the rural characters themselves as victims. They have lived in marginal areas functioning as internal colonies of the nation, especially in Appalachia, where wealth has been siphoned away for generations. Their Gothic tales, like all Gothic tales, involve family secrets and crimes, here modified by poverty, pride, and regional customs often inherited from their Scottish and Scotch-Irish ancestors.

Sometimes, in this tradition, which we might call "the Gothic of rural entrapment," there is a supernatural element. In Lori Roy's *Let Me Die in His Footsteps* (2015), some of the women of the rural Kentucky community possess the "know-how," a gift of heightened intuition. This trait, however, is of minor importance in this two-generation mystery involving a presumed rape, a lynching, and murder. There are typical Gothic doublings (a pair of girls in each time level), and a story of suppressed genealogy. The novel is also the coming-of-age story of Annie, the central character of the later time level, who learns the secret of her paternity.

More squarely in the tradition of Gothic realism, Dorothy Allison's *Bastard Out of Carolina* (1992) is the brutal *Bildungsroman* of a girl who is physically abused and raped by her stepfather, and struggles to establish an identity with the help of her extended Boatwright clan. Similarly, the adolescent Ree Dolly, in Daniel Woodrell's *Winter's Bone* (2006), set in Missouri's Ozarks, attempts to support her family in the absence of her father. In an uncanny sequence, she is taken blindfolded to a frozen pond, where she receives the severed hands of her dead father.

The characters in the Gothic of rural entrapment are caught by poverty, and snared often by their means of attempted escape. Too often the escape involves methamphetamine, the successor to moonshine in rural America. Meth cooking is the cottage industry in Ree Dolly's community in *Winter's Bone* (2006).

In "Those Who Are Dead Are Only Now Forgiven" (2013), Ron Rash draws together these themes and joins them to a moving version of the haunted house motif, the last we will examine. "The Shakleford house was haunted," the story begins. "In the skittering of leaves across its rotting porch, locals heard the withered misery of ghosts" (227). Lauren and Jody often visit the abandoned house to make love. They are talented high school seniors who seem poised to escape their depressed community for the university and a life in the greater world. When Lauren, at the last minute, decides not to leave, we infer that she is already in the grip of addiction. Returning at Christmas, Jody finds Lauren living at the Shakleford house, cooking meth with two high school dropouts. Unable to persuade Lauren to leave with him, Jody draws his remaining college money from the bank, and moves into the haunted house. Earlier, Lauren had dared the ghosts of the house to show themselves. Now they have claimed their last victims.

Conclusion

The South is both peripheral and paradoxically essential to the United States. Its hauntings continue to haunt us all through some of our most enduring texts. Southern Gothic has changed, of course, since the time of William Byrd and Thomas Jefferson, and even since Faulkner, Welty, and the other great writers of the mid-twentieth century. While race, or rather racism, remains as the master trope of American nightmares, other issues, always present, emerge as from a mist, and clarify: issues of poverty, class conflict, gender identity, child abuse, and addiction, among others. The South's Gothic remains, however, a reliable, if distorted, mirror of the cultural anxieties that shape our national conversation.

NOTES

1. Fiedler's book was very influential in its broadening and clarifying the definition of American Gothic.
2. The borders of the South are permeable, but here are defined as including the states of the Confederacy, plus Kentucky, Maryland, and the Missouri Ozarks.
3. To this list one might add *Dred: A Tale of the Great Dismal Swamp* (1856) by New Englander Harriet Beecher Stowe.
4. In *Letters from an American Farmer* (1782). Crèvecoeur, like Jefferson, has an important place in the history of American Gothic (see Ringel [Chapter One] in this volume). In his Letter IX, he visits a plantation in South Carolina, and discovers a slave dying in an iron cage, his eyes picked out by birds, an event that disrupts and overturns his narrative of republican virtue.
5. Local color writing, which was especially popular in the decades after the Civil War, stressed the customs, dialect, and other peculiarities of regions of the country. The plantation school (or school of Southern nostalgia), usually presented slaves or former slaves as simple and affectionate, and thus justified the reactionary southern position that slavery was not as cruel as portrayed by abolitionists, and that the federal reconstruction program was unnecessary.

WORKS CITED

Byrd, William. *William Byrd's Histories of the Dividing Line Betwixt Virginia and North Carolina*. New York: Dover, 1967.
Cable, George Washington. *The Grandissimes*. New York: Penguin, 1988.
Chesnutt, Charles W. *The Marrow of Tradition*. (1901). Ann Arbor: University of Michigan Press, 1969.

Du Bois, W. E. B. *The Souls of Black Folk*. In Du Bois, *Writings*. New York: The Library of America, 1986. 357–546.
Edwards, Justin D. *Gothic Passages: Racial Ambiguity and the American Gothic*. Iowa City: University of Iowa Press, 2003.
Fiedler, Leslie A. *Love and Death in the American Novel*. New York: Stein and Day, 1960. Rev. edn., 1966.
Goddu, Teresa A. *Gothic America: Narrative, History, Nation*. New York: Columbia University Press, 1997.
Jefferson, Thomas. *Notes on the State of Virginia*. In Jefferson, *Writings*. New York: The Library of America, 1984. 123–325.
Ladd, Barbara. *Resisting History: William Faulkner Zora Neale Hurston, and Eudora Welty*. Baton Rouge: Louisiana State University Press, 2007.
McCarthy, Cormac. *The Outer Dark*. New York: Random House, 1968.
Murphy, Bernice M. *The Rural Gothic in American Popular Culture: Backwoods Horror and Terror in the Wilderness*. Houndsmill: Palgrave Macmillan, 2013.
Rash, Ron. "Those Who Are Dead Are Only Now Forgiven." *Nothing Gold Can Stay*. New York: HarperCollins, 2013. 127–43.
Séjour, Victor. "The Mulatto." Tr. Philip Barnard. Web. 21 Dec. 2015.
Simpson, Louis P. Introduction. *3 by 3: Masterworks of the Southern Gothic*. Atlanta: Peachtree Publishers, 1985. vii–xiv.
Sunquist, Eric J. *To Wake the Nations: Race in the Making of American Literature*. Cambridge, MA: Harvard University Press, 1993.
Welty, Eurdora. "The Burning." *The Collected Stories of Eudora Welty*. New York and London: Harcourt Brace Jovanovich, 1980. 482–49.

11

LEONARD CASSUTO

Urban American Gothic

When literary critics talk about the Gothic, they're engaging in an extended analogy. That's because the Gothic originated in a different medium from literature: art and architecture. When scholars in those fields speak of the Gothic, they can be very precise, for Gothic is a particular term of art that refers to distinct visual elements that remain familiar to the viewers of medieval European cathedrals. Though Gothic architecture is still being created, it's very much derived from a place in time.[1] When we speak of Gothic literature, on the other hand, we can bring none of that precision to bear because the Gothic was not originally imagined in literary terms.

Gothic architects aimed at evoking a specific emotional response from the viewer. That response was a combination of fear and awe that was considered appropriate to one standing in the presence of God. Gothic cathedrals are imposing because they were supposed to inspire a submission to God. Gothic architecture didn't stay rooted in the church though. It spread to other structures, such as castles and palaces, which borrowed exemplary visual elements without the requirement that they bring viewers to their knees. The religious mission was shifted and distilled to a sense of pure intimidating effect.

Gothic literature does something similar. It takes elements from the Gothic architectural scheme, but not its religious mission. Roughly speaking, it secularizes and transports the visuals to another medium, and it does so figuratively – which is what makes it an analogy.

In practice, Gothic literature is marked by an elaborate, darkly lighted architectural setting that creates fear and apprehension in the characters who inhabit it. (Also the reader.) The crossing by the Gothic from architecture to literature gave flexibility to its practitioners, particularly as to location. Removed from actual houses of worship, the fear inspired by the Gothic no longer had to be a fear of God; it could now be brought on by ghosts, vampires, or flesh-and-blood murderers. Gothic literature began as verbal expression that *felt* something like Gothic architecture – and fundamentally, that's what it still is.

That analogy creates ambiguity, and that ambiguity is centered on subjectivity. That is, whether a work of literature should be labeled Gothic or not depends upon the associations and especially the sensations that the work creates in the reader. Unlike Gothic architecture, Gothic literature has no set list of ingredients – and that's what allowed Charles Brockden Brown, for example, to transform Gothic conventions and thereby transport Gothic effects to the American frontier in his 1799 novel, *Edgar Huntly* – which has no tolling bells, trapdoors, or flickering candles but instead their wilderness equivalents. Castles became caves, and ghosts became wild animals.[2]

If the literary Gothic is an analogy, then the urban Gothic is an analogy of that analogy that distills it further. The urban Gothic is located in a city setting, of course – that's definitional. But what exactly do we find in the urban Gothic setting? An effect consistent with the effects of traditional Gothic literature. The sense of darkness and foreboding in an urban setting is what characterizes the urban Gothic. In other words, the urban Gothic is marked not by ornate arched vaults and flying buttresses, but rather by a secularized version of the fear and foreboding that such architecture could create, sensations duplicated in mainstream Gothic literature.

Foreboding is not exactly fear. Fear has a direction. Instead, the urban Gothic readily produces anxiety, a sense of danger whose location can't be pinpointed. When danger pervades the atmosphere but can't be confronted directly, that lack of direction creates anxiety, an emotion that can be much harder to manage than fear.[3] We have a name for that effect in the literature, and especially the film, of the city: We call it noir.

"Noir" literature represents another analogy, this one from film – though the first *film here noirs* were themselves adapted from crime literature, so it's a double cross-pollination.[4] In the pages that follow, I'll trace the emergence of urban Gothic literature in the American antebellum period, but I'll spend most of my time examining its distinctive formations in the noirish crime literature of the twentieth century. Finally, I'll suggest that the psychopaths who dominate crime literature of the contemporary era are special creatures of the city's darkness, monsters of the urban Gothic.

The Antebellum American Gothic

The most important progenitors of the urban Gothic in US literature were Edgar Allan Poe and George Lippard. These two 1840s horror masters rendered the city as a shrouded and terrifying place. In doing so, they exploited the fact that the city was already little-known to most Americans. Nearly 90 percent of the US population lived in rural areas in 1840, and travel was cumbersome, difficult, and expensive.[5] Very few photos of urban landscapes circulated (as photography was still a new mass medium). Nor was the city a favored subject of American painters – it would not become one until the age of Realism later in the century.[6]

Poe's florid urban settings set the stage for some of his best-known and most influential short stories (on Poe, see Bendixen [Chapter 2] in this volume). In "The Man of the Crowd" (1840), for example, the narrator follows the title character into "the most noisome quarter of London," where "dim light" shows "antique, worm-eaten, wooden tenements" that are "tottering to their fall" where "paving-stones lay at random, displaced from their beds by the rankly-growing grass." Departing from this surrounding of "horrible filth "and "desolation," the narrator sees in the title character "the type and the genius of deep crime": a creature who, in his refusal of solitude, embodies the spirit of the city itself (395–96). The anonymous man of the crowd is indistinguishable from the city, and from the criminal doings within it.[7]

Poe's famous detective, Auguste Dupin, is likewise introduced as a creature born of the decadent and decayed city. Poe invented the genre of detective fiction – that is, he set out what would become the genre's main parameters – with his three Dupin stories. Poe begins the first of these stories, "The Murders in the Rue Morgue" (1841), by setting the detective up in a haunted house in Paris, a "time-eaten and grotesque mansion, long deserted through superstitions."[8] Like the tenements in "The Man of the Crowd," Dupin's house is also "tottering to its fall" amid "desolate" surroundings (400–401). We should not overlook Poe's explicit repetition from "The Man of the Crowd" of "tottering" buildings in a "desolate" milieu: In the earlier story, Poe identifies this surrounding as part of the domain of crime. From Poe's use of the exact same words to describe Dupin's neighborhood, we can therefore see that Dupin, who detects crime, originates in the same precincts as the crimes he solves. When the "true Darkness" falls, Dupin and the narrator emerge from their cavernous house to walk the streets "amid the wild lights and shadows of the populous city": here is noir, *avant la lettre* (401).

George Lippard, an admirer of Poe, took his own cue from such descriptions. Lippard suggests that the city is not only scary but also specifically threatening: Its moral corruption entangles the young and innocent. Some of the most prominent of the many plotlines in *The Quaker City, or The Monks of Monk Hall* (1845) center on schemes of seduction and murder that ensnare gullible youth. Thus does Lippard channel anxiety about the dangers that the city might hold.

In *The Quaker City*, Lippard portrays a dark and decadent Philadelphia cityscape that cloaks lurid and murderous doings. Monk Hall, the nucleus of the urban underworld, is a mansion "falling to decay" with chimneys that make "fantastic shapes" by moonlight. "The general effect," says the novel's narrator, "was that of an ancient structure falling to decay." Like Poe's urban scene, Monk Hall looks "desolate" and "time-worn" (50). Indeed, Lippard's descriptors are virtually the same as Poe's.

But Monk Hall is anything but desolate: Behind its doors hums a beehive of criminal activity conducted by some of the city's leading citizens. (That they are upstanding by day and nefarious by night goes to Lippard's angry satirical purpose, including his scabrous description of them as "monks.") The ringleader of these merry perpetrators of thievery and debauchery is the grotesquely ugly and homicidal proprietor of the place, who is known as "Devil-Bug." Devil-Bug is inextricably linked to Monk Hall: "It's the body," he declares of the building, and "I'm its soul!" He bonds with the architecture itself ("these old walls have been my friends!" and "the trap-doors know me") and he even merges with the place: "It's full of nooks and corners and dark places; so is my natur'!" When I die, he says, the building "must go with me!" (299).

Importantly, the setting produces the criminal here, and the two are inextricable. The criminality in *Quaker City* can't be separated from the place – nor may the criminals be understood apart from their urban milieu. When Devil-Bug has an extended dream of Judgment Day, he realizes immediately that the setting for the dream "must be in the Quaker City" (373). He watches the dream unfold before him as an apocalypse, an extended vision of the fall of Sodom as it might have been pictured by Hieronymus Bosch, with fighting zombies and "columns of hot vapor rising from the heaving earth" (391). This devastating retribution results not from Devil-Bug's own iniquities, but rather from "the city's crimes" to which Devil-Bug bears witness (393).

The criminal, the crime, and the city setting thus become indistinguishable. This physical union of criminal, crime, and location forms the thematic through-line for urban Gothic literature.

Hard-Boiled Gothic

These examples of Lippard and Poe have proved both influential and enduring, but the urban Gothic flowered in American literature around the time the United States became an urban nation. The 1920 census marked the tipping point of national urbanization: More Americans now lived in cities than outside of them.[9] The 1920s was also when the hard-boiled style, with its emphasis on urban settings, revolutionized American crime fiction. The timing is surely not a coincidence.

Hard-boiled storytelling has long been distinguished for its laconic, clipped emotional style. Its avatars are detectives, policemen, and also criminals who bury their emotions in order to act decisively – and often violently. They construct their own moral rules (a "code") by which they navigate their fallen world.

Hard-boiled fiction caught on immediately in the American popular market. It quickly dominated the pulp magazines and, led by Dashiell Hammett, soon established a permanent beachhead in the world of literary fiction. Though the style has evolved over the generations, it is still easily recognizable in today's crime literature, and remains ascendant in popular mystery and suspense fiction not only in the United States but also much of the world.[10] Hard-boiled stories written these days might take place almost anywhere, but in the decades beginning in the 1920s, when hard-boiled style first transformed American crime fiction, these new stories were virtually always set in cities.

Much early hard-boiled fiction advanced a populist reform agenda aimed at overthrowing urban corruption. The term "mean streets" was actually made popular by Raymond Chandler in a 1944 essay that exalted hard-boiled crime stories as a return to socially conscious realism in the genre ("Simple Art," 991). These stories were, says literary critic Sean McCann, "a popular critique of a decadent society" (40).

That decadent society as rendered by hard-boiled writers was frequently housed in a Gothic city. One pungent example is Leslie T. White's "City of Hell," a story about vigilante justice carried out by rogue cops that first appeared in *Black Mask* magazine in 1935. When the erstwhile police decide to take the law into their own hands, they engineer a makeshift courtroom "in the bowels of the earth, a abandoned sewer" where "ghostly shadows danced on the brick walls." The space is "more like a dungeon than a courtroom," with "only one door – a sort of arch" (120, 124). The dungeon comparison and the arch make the Gothic roots of this image particularly clear.

Some of the most memorable hard-boiled literature traffics in similar imagery. Raymond Chandler turns Los Angeles into a contemporary urban Gothic landscape in his fiction. In *Farewell, My Lovely* (1940), for example, detective Philip Marlowe is imprisoned in "a raw and modernistic" psychiatric hospital building, an "eyrie" atop a canyon where "nobody would be able to hear any screams" (874). Behind Marlowe's captivity is a femme fatale whose tongue "was a darting snake between her teeth" (866). This reptilian villainess intended, Marlowe later observes, "to kill anybody she had to kill" (980).

Chandler's urban Gothic could be seamy. His portrait of a decrepit office building in *The Big Sleep* (1939) is worth quoting at some length:

> I turned into the narrow lobby of the Fulwider Building. A single drop light burned far back, beyond an open, once gilt elevator. There was a tarnished and well-missed spittoon on a gnawed rubber mat. A case of false teeth hung on the mustard-colored wall like a fuse box in a screen porch. I shook the rain off my hat and looked at the building directory ... Plenty of vacancies or plenty of tenants who wished to remain anonymous ..... [S]mall sick businesses that had crawled there to die ... A nasty building ...
>
> An old man dozed in the elevator, on a ramshackle stool, with a burst-out cushion under him. His mouth was open, his veined temples glistened in the weak light ... The fire stairs hadn't been swept in a month. Bums had slept on them, left crusts and fragments of greasy newspaper, matches, a gutted imitation-leather pocketbook. In a shadowy angle against the scribbled wall a pouched ring of pale rubber had fallen and had not been disturbed. A very nice building. (717–18)

Marlowe reacts to these surroundings mainly with contempt mingled with disgust – indeed, the false teeth and used condom make for a squalid spectacle. (Though there is a trace of pity for the elevator operator whose shoe is "slit across a bunion" [718].)

But the Fulwider Building is not just grimy – it's also dangerous. Its darkness harbors Lash Canino, one of Chandler's cruelest villains, a man who would "bump a guy off between drinks" (715). Marlowe hears Canino's "heavy purr" from an adjoining office. It is "as false as an usherette's eyelashes and as slippery as a watermelon seed," and it leaves "a rictus of death" on the face of a grifter whose honesty had earlier appealed to Marlowe (718, 721, 725). When Marlowe confronts Canino later in the novel, the space is literal noir: "small, shut in, black. A private world for Canino and me" (740).

Canino's meticulous sadism is matched in the novel by the casual sadism of the fallen rich. A ruined city backyard oilfield festers behind the home of the novel's murderess. It's a wreck, with oil wells "no longer pumping" and "a pile of rusted pipe, a loading platform that sagged at one end, half a dozen empty oil drums lying in a ragged pile" (754). Beside a pool of "stagnant, oil-scummed water," the scion of a fallen family tries to kill Marlowe. Chandler renders her as an amoral child, and a different kind of monstrous villain: a female vampire.[11]

These examples from Chandler, one of the best-known and most-admired hard-boiled writers, are entirely consistent with the early work of Poe and Lippard. In particular, they show how the urban Gothic in fiction produces not simply lawlessness but monstrous lawlessness – and monstrous criminals. Indeed, that monstrousness is what separates the urban Gothic from a city setting that is simply tough and gritty. Hard-boiled writers rendered the city in all kinds of ways, but they have always been attentive to the possibilities of the Gothic to create human monsters. This awareness was clear almost from the beginning with, for example, the sadistic, seemingly unkillable title character in one of the first hard-boiled novels, Carroll John Daly's *The Snarl of the Beast* (1927).

It would be impossible – and not very useful – to track every instance in which American writers recreate Gothic effects in an urban setting. (For one thing, crime writers had no monopoly on the effect.[12]) Instead, I want to show how the development of the urban Gothic, which pollinated and was pollinated by film noir, created a breeding ground for the fiction that finally produced the most notorious of American monsters: the sexually psychopathic serial killer.

Gothic Psychopaths

Let us first look at some of the monsters that cleared the field for rampant sexual psychopathy. These human monsters of the urban Gothic can't be separated from the social conditions that produced them, so their stories make up an overtly socially conscious literature. Richard Wright's *Native Son* (1940) is an indelible example. Inspired by Poe and also by "cheap pulp tales" to "weav[e] fantasies about cities I had never seen," Wright invents a brutal murderer, Bigger Thomas, whose crimes are utterly interwoven with his degraded urban environment (*Black Boy*, 151, 156). (On Wright and race in the American Gothic, see also Weinauer [Chapter 6] in this volume.)

The Chicago of Bigger Thomas is dark and dangerous, rendered in a Gothic palette of blacks and whites, of "dark and whirling snow" (184). On the run with his girlfriend, Bessie, after the first of his murders, Bigger takes refuge in "a tall, snow-covered building whose many windows gaped blackly, like the eye-sockets of empty skulls" (231). Wright here gestures explicitly toward Poe's famous House of Usher – the resemblance of Bigger's fleeting refuge to the "vacant eye-like windows" of Poe's well-known Gothic edifice is clear ("Usher," 317).[13] The Chicago building is "black inside" with a "sharp scent of rot" (231). Wright continues to draw heavily on Gothic conventions as the police close their cordon on Bigger. On the run in the Chicago winter, Bigger cuts through alleys as "street lamps glowed through the murky air, refracted into mammoth balls of light" (254). As the police close in, Bigger breaks into a tenement "through a narrow loft" and a "trapdoor" (257–58). When he is finally caught, he is "swallowed in darkness" (270).

The segregated city, says Bigger's lawyer, Boris Max, stands for a larger "dislocation of life involving millions of people" (387). It traps Bigger from the start, and Wright argues that these surroundings make Bigger into the murderer he becomes. Max suggests that "the mere act of understanding Bigger Thomas" unveils Gothic horror, "a dragging of the sprawling forms of dread out of the night of fear" (383). Bigger's way of life is rendered as monstrous, "stunted and distorted" (388). He is, Wright elsewhere writes, a character whom the reader must face "without the consolation of tears" ("How Bigger Was Born," 454).

Wright portrays horrified Chicagoans questioning Bigger's humanity as a result of his deeds. One of Wright's contemporaries, Chester Himes, aims the same questions at a white antagonist in a different kind of murder story published a generation after Wright's novel. A crime novel of almost pure chase, Himes' *Run, Man, Run* (1966) makes the white man into the inhuman murderer. Walker, a homicidal police detective, kills out of unrestrained racial hatred, and then pursues an innocent black witness through the streets of Harlem. The tension of the unceasing chase shrinks the city for the man being pursued. New York becomes a tight, anxious place, one long "pitch-dark corridor" like the literal corridor that he flees into early on (33). Catalyzed by drink, the detective is possessed by a "frenzy of rage" that makes one of his victims believe "he had come face to face with the devil" (16). Himes describes him as rabid, with "teeth bared like a vicious dog's" and "red-tinted eyes that looked completely insane" (30). The prostitute he visits decides that he is "not quite human" (114). Like Bigger, he is an unsympathetic criminal whose violence arises from the conflicts that surround him.

Racial animus may produce vicious criminals then, but of course they may arise from other sources also. A generation further on, Lawrence Block's Matthew Scudder series presents numerous vivid examples of how the urban Gothic lends itself to criminals of monstrous sexual savagery. Scudder, a former policeman, begins the series as a shaky recovering alcoholic who works as an unlicensed private investigator in New York City. (He later joins Alcoholics Anonymous, and his recovery gains momentum as the series goes on.) Like Poe's Dupin, Scudder's damaged identity is inseparable from the city itself: His life broke apart years earlier when, as a policeman, he fired a shot at an escaping criminal and it ricocheted and killed a young girl.

The criminals Scudder pursues are among the most vicious in contemporary crime fiction. In *A Ticket to the Boneyard* (1990), for example, Scudder must fend off a "reptilian" revenge killer with a taste for sadistic rape named James Leo Motley (32). Motley visits his victims repeatedly, kills them when they are "used up," and then replaces them (265). Like Himes' New York in *Run, Man, Run*, the city becomes constricted and anxious for Scudder when he must locate Motley without being located himself, and protect his girlfriend from Motley at the same time. Motley seems to be able to materialize on the other side of doors, and she imagines him looking at her wherever she is, "perched up somewhere with a pair of binoculars" (42). Scudder's under-the-table cases lead to below-the-radar solutions. Put simply, he is a vigilante as well as a detective. When he kills Motley at the end of *Boneyard*, he says simply, "I just don't want you to be alive anymore" (321).[14]

Raymond Chandler lauded the hard-boiled crime story in 1944 for returning murder to the "people that commit it for reasons" ("Simple Art," 989). But as the form evolved, the foregoing examples suggest, the Gothic offshoots of the hard-boiled story give birth to murderers whose motives have little to do with reason. Wright portrays Bigger Thomas as someone who literally does not think. Instead, Bigger is a creature of impulse who feels and reacts. Only at the end of *Native Son*, when a newly reflective Bigger faces execution, does Wright have Bigger use the phrase "I think" (428). Similarly, Himes's rogue detective Walker is possessed by his anger and hatred. He kills because he hates, as a random impulse and not as part of a plan for advancement.

Characters such as these are the forefathers of the serial killer, a sexual psychopath who kills for pleasure, not gain. Sexual psychopaths appear in crime stories with increasing frequency in the second half of the twentieth century, first in the United States and then – as a successful export – in the rest of the world's crime stories too. Cultural critics have argued about what has led to their proliferation, and the reasons are surely myriad: Serial killers are a cultural symptom with many possible causes.[15] Mark Seltzer's idea of "wound culture" seems most pertinent to this discussion. Seltzer ties the rise of the serial killer to a collective addiction to violence and the social damage it wreaks. Stemming from Seltzer's previous work on automation and standardization of the natural (what he has called "machine culture"), wound culture holds up the serial killer as a radical example of human mechanization: He's an apparently interchangeable social cog, a man who looks and acts like everyone else except for the fact that he repeatedly kills other people.[16] Lacking an interior life and empty of everything but addictive, sadistic appetite, the serial killer is a horrifying vision of typicality itself. Seen in light of Seltzer's idea, the serial killer is perforce an urban character. Only in the city may the serial killer blend in as an updated version of Poe's "Man of the Crowd." Because the serial killer can be anyone, he stands as a Gothic specter who essentially embodies anxiety itself.

The most famous fictional serial killer is surely Thomas Harris' Hannibal Lecter, a supporting character in *Red Dragon* (1981) who emerges as the antihero of *The Silence of the Lambs* (1988). (Lecter's story peaks in the latter novel, and then loses momentum, as Harris continues to follow the character forward and back in time, beyond the point of interest in both directions.[17]) Lecter ("Hannibal the Cannibal") is tied to the urban Gothic from the start. He begins *Lambs* incarcerated in a Baltimore hospital far from "natural light" (12). In the memorable film adaptation, a brilliant neo-noir, director Jonathan Demme depicts these surroundings as a Gothic crypt, a dungeon full of monsters. Demme's heavy reliance on urban Gothic imagery fits with Harris's own. The Memphis courthouse from which Lecter escapes, for example, is a "massive, Gothic-style structure" that "looked like a medieval stronghold" (221). The other serial killer in the novel, "Buffalo Bill," maintains his own dungeon in which he stores his victims prior to killing them.

Lecter is a modern medieval monster whose behavior Harris repeatedly describes in vampiric terms. When he tantalizes a female senator with false hope of a clue to her daughter's abduction, he "took a single sip of her pain and found it exquisite" (201). When the young detective Clarice Starling meets Lecter for the first time, she "felt suddenly empty" afterwards, "as though she had given blood" (24). When Lecter extracts from Starling the story of screaming lambs that gives the novel its title, Demme films it as a sexual consummation, and then adds a telling detail: He has Lecter order rare lamb chops afterwards by which to symbolically consume his prey.

These sadistic affectations have become standard fare for fictional serial killers – that is the measure of Harris' influence. These sexual psychopaths are the worst horror of the urban Gothic, a monster who captures and tortures people, all while hiding unseen in the background of the city. In this respect, the serial killer is the apotheosis of the urban Gothic style.

Fade to Black

The Gothic city can be located anywhere, including the future. *Blade Runner*, Ridley Scott's stunning 1982 urban Gothic neo-noir loosely based on a novel by Philip K. Dick, is set in a futuristic Los Angeles whose particulars – such as flying cars – may be alien, but whose urban alienation registers as deeply familiar. A story of the pursuit of rogue "replicants" (manufactured beings) who rebel against their own enslavement, *Blade Runner* climaxes in and atop an old Gothic hotel that symbolizes the fallen and decadent society that devalues the human life it creates.

The urban Gothic has received some of its most evocative modern renderings in film. *Blade Runner* builds on a noir tradition that began in the 1940s. Classic noirs like Billy Wilder's *Double Indemnity* (1944) and Joseph H. Lewis' *The Big Combo* (1955), to name two of many, portray Los Angeles, a spread-out city, as strikingly closed-in. The city, say Silver and Ursini, essentially becomes a character itself in these movies. This first generation of noirs were themselves inspired by books, and the films in turn inspired a second generation of hard-boiled writers to produce their own urban Gothic literature. The claustrophobic city streets rendered by David Goodis in many novels in the 1950s and 1960s, for example, owe much to the films noirs he admired. So *Blade Runner* and its relations are part of a literary tradition of the urban Gothic, not just a cinematic one.

With a focus on human rather than supernatural monsters, the urban Gothic links traditional Gothic horror and the literature of realism. Unlike haunted houses, cities are real places – and as the example of Wright's Bigger Thomas shows perhaps most clearly, people who behave monstrously are still people whose motives beg for explanation.

The focus on human monsters brings immediacy to the social focus that the Gothic has always shared with crime fiction. But if the fantastic monsters of the Gothic place a prism between the observer and reality, the urban Gothic keeps the focus on people and the situations that made them the way they are. The urban Gothic refuses to separate whodunit from the setting that produced the criminal. The creatures of the urban Gothic are made monstrosities in a dark city laboratory.

NOTES

1. On the Gothic and architecture, see Nick Groom's "Gothic Antiquity: From the Sack of Rome to *The Castle of Otranto*," Chris Brooks' *The Gothic Revival*, and Kenneth Clark's *The Gothic Revival: An Essay in the History of Taste*.
2. Jeffrey Andrew Weinstock makes the case in *Charles Brockden Brown* that Brown pioneers the urban Gothic subgenre in his two 1799 novels, *Ormond, or, The Secret Witness* and *Arthur Mervyn; or, Memoirs of the Year 1793*. On Brown, see also Ringel (Chapter 1) and Hinds (Chapter 9) in this volume.
3. See May, *The Meaning of Anxiety*.
4. On the origins and themes of film noir, see Homer B. Pettey and R. Barton Palmer's collection *Film Noir*, William Luhr's *Film noir*, and Mark Bould's *Film noir: From Berlin to Sin City*.
5. For US Census data on urban/rural population split, see www.census.gov/population/censusdata/table-4.pdf.
6. A number of urban engravings date from the 1840s and thereabouts; these images tend toward the picturesque. When photographers first started capturing the city, they saw it in bleaker terms.
7. Speaking of a specific kind of criminal, Karen Halttunen describes the confidence man as an urban creation facilitated by the anonymity of the city as compared to the small town.
8. Poe's other two Dupin stories are "The Mystery of Marie Rogêt" (1842–43) and "The Purloined Letter" (1844).

9. US Census data.
10. For more on the movement of hard-boiled fiction from pulp magazines to high-toned literary books published by the likes of Alfred A. Knopf, see Cassuto, "Raymond Chandler."
11. For more on Chandler's vampiric portrayal of the femme fatale, see McCann, 168–70.
12. Shirley Jackson and Stephen King are two horror writers who have exploited the urban Gothic with dexterity. See, for example, King's *The Stand* (1978, 1990), or Jackson's brilliant "The Tooth" (in *The Lottery and Other Stories* [1949]).
13. The nod to Poe is not surprising; Wright acknowledged Poe's influence and, in a 1940 essay on the origins of *Native Son*, he said that, "if Poe were alive, he would not have to invent horror; horror would invent him" ("How Bigger Was Born," 462).
14. For a fuller discussion of Scudder's vigilantism, see Cassuto, *Hard-Boiled Sentimentality*, 197–200.
15. For a discussion of some of the competing theories of why serial killers have flooded American crime literature, see Cassuto, *Hard-Boiled Sentimentality*, chapter 9, esp. 259–72.
16. For a related take on the serial killer's relationship to contemporary bureaucratic capitalism, see Annalee Newitz's *Pretend We're Dead: Capitalist Monsters in American Pop Culture*. Newitz sees the serial killer as a distorted version of a worker who produces dead "commodities."
17. Later productions include Harris's novels *Hannibal* (1999) and *Hannibal Rising* (2006), and a television show called *Hannibal* that ran from 2012 to 2015.

WORKS CITED

Block, Lawrence. *A Ticket to the Boneyard*. New York: William Morrow & Co., Inc., 1990.

Bould, Mark. *Film noir: From Berlin to Sin City*. London: Wallflower Press, 2005.

Brooks, Chris. *The Gothic Revival*. London: Phaidon, 1999.

Cassuto, Leonard. *Hard-Boiled Sentimentality: The Secret History of American Crime Stories*. New York: Columbia UP, 2009.

"Raymond Chandler." *The Cambridge Companion to American Novelists*. Ed. Timothy Parrish. Cambridge: Cambridge University Press, 2013. 168–78.

Chandler, Raymond. *Farewell, My Lovely. Raymond Chandler: Stories & Early Novels*. New York: the Library of America, 1995. 765–984.

The Big Sleep. Raymond Chandler: Later Novels & Other Writings. New York: The Library of America, 1995. 587–764.

"The Simple Art of Murder." *Raymond Chandler: Later Novels & Other Writings*. New York: The Library of America, 1995. 977–92.

Clark, Kenneth. *The Gothic Revival: An Essay on the History of Taste*. Harmondsworth: Penguin, 1962.

Groom, Nick. "Gothic Antiquity: From the Sack of Rome to *The Castle of Otronto*." *Terror and Wonder: The Gothic Imagination*. Ed. Dale Townshend. London: The British Library, 2014. 38–67.

Halttunen, Karen. *Confidence Men and Painted Women: A Study of Middle-Class Culture in America, 1830–1870*. New Haven and London: Yale University Press, 1982.

Harris, Thomas. *The Silence of the Lambs*. New York: St. Martins, 1988.

Himes, Chester. *Run, Man, Run* (1966). New York: Carroll & Graf, 1995.

Lippard, George. *The Quaker City or, The Monks of Monk Hall* (1845). Rpt. Amherst: University of Massachusetts Press, 1995.

Luhr, William. *Film noir*. Malden, MA: Wiley-Blackwell, 2012.

May, Rollo. *The Meaning of Anxiety* (1950); rev. edn. New York: W.W. Norton & Co., 1996.

McCann, Sean. *Gumshoe America: Hard-Boiled Crime Fiction and the Rise and Fall of New Deal Liberalism*. Durham: Duke University Press, 2000.

Newitz, Annalee. *Pretend We're Dead: Capitalist Monsters in American Pop Culture*. Durham: Duke University Press, 2006.

Petty, Homer B. and R. Barton Palmer, eds. *Film Noir*. Edinburgh: Edinburgh University Press, 2014.

Poe, Edgar Allan. "The Fall of the House of Usher." *Edgar Allan Poe: Poetry and Tales*. New York: The Library of America, 1984. 317–36.

"The Murders in the Rue Morgue." *Edgar Allan Poe: Poetry and Tales*. New York: The Library of America, 1984. 397–431.

"The Man of the Crowd." *Edgar Allan Poe: Poetry and Tales*. New York: The Library of America, 1984. 388–96.

Seltzer, Mark. *Serial Killers: Death and Life in America's Wound Culture*. New York: Routledge, 1998.

Silver, Alain, and James Ursini. *L.A. Noir: The City as Character*. Santa Monica, CA: Santa Monica Press, 2005.

U.S. Census, Population 1790–1990. www.census.gov/population/censusdata/table-4.pdf.

Weinstock, Jeffrey Andrew. *Charles Brockden Brown*. Cardiff: University of Wales Press, 2011.

White, Leslie T. "City of Hell!" (1935). Rpt. *The Black Lizard Big Book of Pulps*. Otto Penzler, ed. New York: Vintage, 2007. 112–32.

Wright, Richard. *Black Boy (American Hunger)*. (1945); rev. edn. 1993. New York: Harper Perennial: 1993.

"How Bigger Was Born" (1940). *Native Son* (1940; rev. ed. 1991). New York: Harper Perennial, 1993. 431–62.

Native Son. (1940; rev. edn. 1991). New York: Harper Perennial, 1993.

PART III

Genre and Media

12

KAREN COATS

The Gothic in American Children's Literature

A stroll through the children's section of any bookstore or library in the United States, especially in the month of October, will reveal displays of colorful picture books featuring an array of ghosts, witches, monsters, haunted houses, and the like. But what browsers will quickly notice is that these images that are supposed to haunt our dreams are all drawn in styles that make them appear cute, cuddly, or comical. The scenes pictured on the covers of books for middle grade readers, by contrast, are more likely to be images that conventionally inspire fear and disgust – creepy ventriloquist dummies or dolls with bulbous eyes, weapons dripping with gore, noxious-looking vines populated by oversized insects. Wander over to the young adult section, and you'll find that the creatures, now most likely humanoid in form, are more sexy than frightening, draped in shadows, exuding an appealing whiff of danger behind their preternatural good looks. Clearly, Gothic tropes and motifs are treated very differently for readers of different ages.

What is striking beyond the content differences in books for different ages is the sheer number of books that focus on scary things. These books are obviously a publishing mainstay for young readers; whether they are written for preschoolers, middle graders, or young adults, scary stories *sell*. Even nonfiction for young readers borrows tropes from the Gothic, honing in on the gross and disturbing aspects of human existence with titles like *How They Croaked: The Awful Ends of the Awfully Famous* (Bragg, 2011) and *What's Eating You?: Parasites – The Inside Story* (Davies, 2007), and compelling true stories that mirror Gothic horror, such as *The Borden Murders: Lizzie Borden and the Trial of the Century* (Miller, 2016). In fact, it's not going too far to say that the literature of fear has become the dominant aesthetic category in youth publishing today.

Such enormous popularity raises questions about Gothic literature for young readers that we don't typically ask about such literature for adults. No one asks, for instance, whether the latest adult horror novel is too scary for its readers, and yet we do ask that question about books for children.

When we think back to our own childhood attitudes toward frightening texts, or recall intensely felt experiences like storytelling at a sleepover, visiting a staged haunted house at Halloween, or fighting our bedtime fears, most of us have memories that fall into conflicting emotional categories. On the one hand, we may remember enjoying a "good scare." On the other hand, we can likely recall some terrifying experience that still makes us shudder before we wave it away with an embarrassed laugh. This ambivalence in our personal experience prompts us to have strong opinions about the presence of Gothic themes in literature for young readers; basing our assessment on our own experiences, we tend to practice a kind of moral or ethical criticism with regard to the monsters, witches, ogres, paranormal lovers, and other denizens of the underworld that populate literature for children and young adults.

Such moralizing tendencies are grounded in our attitudes toward childhood itself. While literary critics of peer literature – that is, literature written for adult readers by adult writers – can focus on the content of texts without considering the developmental needs of their audience, people who take children's literature seriously have to factor in a certain asymmetry in the way adults and children process stories. Marah Gubar has noted that this asymmetry usually takes one of two forms – either a "deficit model" or a "difference model" (450). Under a deficit model, adult thinking and behavior is both the norm and the goal, and children are thought of as unfinished adults, "lacking the abilities, skills and powers that adults have" (451). Adherents to such a model might worry that children can't "handle" Gothic literature, that they lack strategies for managing the fear it evokes, and that they will suffer harm from exposure to scary stories. A difference model, by contrast, positions children as "a separate species, categorically different from adults," about which we can know nothing until they magically emerge out of their cocoons into their adult forms (Gubar 451). People who work within this model focus entirely on the children who are imagined in and by the texts themselves. Since real children are ultimately unknowable, adult authors and critics impose their fantasies of who children are and how they speak and think on their readers, believing that children's responses will be exactly what they wish them to be. In this model, children can't talk back, disagree, or present an alternate interpretation of what the story is presenting to them.

Gubar proposes instead that we adopt a "kinship model" (453) that would enable us to understand that children and adults are similar but not the same; that they have similar fears, anxieties and desires but that they may deal with these differently; and that children have some skills and abilities that adults no longer have. The kinship model is therefore an important rapprochement in thinking about the Gothic in children's literature because the images, motifs, and themes of the Gothic symbolize fears, anxieties, and desires that are just as recognizable to children as they are to adults. Juliann Fleenor, for instance, argues that the Gothic world is "one of nightmare, and that nightmare is created by the individual in conflict with the values of her society and her prescribed role" (10). Though referring specifically to adult women, her assessment is particularly apt for children and teens, whose values and roles within society are always under active negotiation. The toddler, for instance, has no respect for social propriety, and no real power (other than the public tantrum) to change the fact that he or she has to follow rules adults insist on. Adolescents aren't all that different. The power imbalance between large bodies and small ones, legal citizens and dependents, turns even the most beloved and carefully nurtured child into a victim of the way things are. And this is of course to say nothing of the very real threats that less fortunate young people may be exposed to in their daily lives.

So whether their chief terrors are metaphorical or existential, children recognize in Gothic literature fears of being consumed, lost, victimized, or overwhelmed that have their seeds in childhood but persist into adulthood. In addition, the Gothic also transcribes desires common to both adults and children, in particular the desires for mystery and transcendence – for a responsive, enchanted universe outside the material world that we access through our senses. As our walk through the bookstore indicates, however, there are some important differences in the treatment of Gothic themes in literature for children than in literature produced for adults or even teens, and there are certainly differences in the way children respond to fantasy and threat. At the risk of being overly simplistic, I would suggest that the goal of Gothic literature for young children is to achieve mastery over turbulent emotions, most often through humor and the domestication of personified inner demons; the goals of middle grade books are to help readers imagine transcendence and inspire heroism in the face of threats; and the goals of young adult literature bring these two together and add to them the goal of negotiating the fraught and often frightening transition into adult bodies, identities, and social roles.

I make these claims from a presentist perspective – that is, they arise out of my observations of the kinds of Gothic literature that are widely read today, and out of recent developments in our understanding of how children's brains and minds process literary texts. However, in order to understand where we are now, it is important to look at how we got here.

An Overview of the Development of American Children's Gothic

Theorists of storytelling suggest that stories arose out of our need to negotiate the challenges of social life in harsh environments.[1] Stories enable us to simulate conflicts and, through a combination of empathy and analysis, practice the skills we need to recognize and cope with threats. In order for this storytelling work to be effective, stories often have to go to dark places and stage dramatic conflicts with tragic outcomes as warnings. As Charles Baxter puts it, "Hell is story-friendly" (133). Throughout the history of children's literature, high-minded censors have tried to keep children away from dark stories, seeking instead to provide a steady diet of mild-mannered children making good decisions. But life isn't always happy, and children aren't always interested in being good, so they and their allies seek out the stories they need anyway, stories that introduce elements that stimulate their imaginations by introducing elements of conflict and even terror that are not part of their daily lives, but could be in some form or other, and forcing them to engage in problem-solving along with the protagonists in order to escape dangers and emerge triumphant.

Still, many adults, at least since John Locke penned his opinions on education in 1693, have had strong objections to children's insatiable appetite for the gruesome. Locke was famous for his theory that children are blank slates, born with neither sense data nor innate rules for processing sensory input, and that these things are learned entirely through experiences. Among the most dangerous of those experiences, Locke proclaimed, was the exposure to scary stories, lest such tales "shatter" their spirits beyond hope of recovery (176). One hundred years later, this attitude was fully endorsed by Dr. Thomas Furlong Churchill in his *General Guide to Health*, who argued that early exposure to frightening tales could lead to misery, insanity, and even premature death (Plumptre 15).

While it is tempting to scoff at such overwrought pronouncements, the early writers and reviewers of children's literature took them very seriously. Dale Townshend notes that the stories Locke and Churchill object to are not strictly speaking "Gothic" since this category hadn't been invented yet, but he highlights a curiously parallel development of properly Gothic novels and a distinctive children's literature that excludes all ghostly and supernatural superstitions. As the genre of Gothic literature developed in Europe in the 1700s, a concomitant strand of the "explained supernatural" appeared in literature for children, wherein a seemingly paranormal event is given a rational, human explanation, a twist that we are well familiar with today through the exploits of Scooby-Doo. Townshend goes on to catalogue the strenuous efforts of eighteenth-century writers and critics not merely to resort to the "explained supernatural" in their tales, but to expunge all mention of the supernatural from children's books, including those in biblical narratives, using scissors if necessary! The goal was to evict all manner of supernatural beings from the central realm of belief to the outlying realm of unbalanced imagination.

But in the unforgettable words of Carol Anne (Heather O'Rourke) in Brian Gibson's *Poltergeist II* (1986): "They're baaack."

In fact, the return of the supernatural in American children's literature came through Evangelical texts in the early 1800s, which deployed conventions we now consider Gothic in order to drive home the horrors of hell and damnation. The folk narratives that Locke found objectionable and the rational texts written in reaction to them were British in origin, but the book-loving Puritans brought their own Gothic imaginations to the American shores. Consumed as they were with the demonic elements of the supernatural, the stories Puritans shared with children had to have a healthy dose of Hell to contrast with the glories of Heaven in order to seduce children into repentance. This religious impulse, combined with the terrors, real and imagined, of the violent confrontations with indigenous and enslaved people and the Romantic literature that was both imported and produced locally led to Gothic motifs seeping into Mark Twain's tales of American boyhood, Louisa May Alcott's *Little Women* (1868–69), Frances Hodgson Burnett's *The Secret Garden* (1911), the works of Canadian writer L. M. Montgomery, and the Little House books of Laura Ingalls Wilder. In addition, as has always been the case, literature written for adults, such as Washington Irving's and Edgar Allan Poe's tales, was eagerly consumed by children and eventually became part of youth culture through school assignments and screen versions in the twentieth century.

The impulse of the Gothic in this new crop of North American stories was not to walk readers through Hell on the road to salvation, however. These works were secular, and their writers wrote to support themselves financially, so the need to entertain children was paramount if they were going to gain a wide readership. Alcott's Jo March, for instance, "rashly took a plunge into the frothy sea of sensational literature" (553), selling Gothic tales to a publication called the "Weekly Volcano," whose editor assures her that "[m]orals don't sell nowadays" (551). However, she is shamed into quitting this endeavor by Professor Bhaer, who opines, "I would rather give my boys gunpowder to play with than this bad trash" (563), advice that Alcott herself must have taken to heart once she hit on a financially successful formula for morally uplifting children's books and could give up writing sensational potboilers under a pseudonym. Beyond making money, though, Alcott and others were self-consciously participating in the creation of a national mythology that, while it carried the traditions of the past forward, altered those traditions considerably. The ghosts, witches, and warlocks of American fairy tales, for instance, have no use for royalty and often use their power to effect social critique of the wealthy (Lurie 8). L. Frank Baum, in his introduction to *The Wonderful Wizard of Oz* (1900), took particular exception to the transmission of what he felt were outdated European sensibilities into his new ideas about what American children's books should look like, saying that "the time has come for a series of newer 'wonder tales' in which the stereotyped genie, dwarf and fairy are eliminated, together with all the horrible and blood-curdling incidents devised by their authors to point a fearsome moral to each tale" (5). Despite Baum's call to replace "heartaches and nightmares" with "wonderment and joy" (5) in children's fantasy, however, the Gothic remained a significant part of child culture in the late 1800s and early decades of the twentieth century. Walt Disney certainly flirted with the genre in his early work, offering Gothic fear in quick, animated bites; several of the Silly Symphonies produced in 1929 are decidedly Gothic; Mickey Mouse himself visits a haunted house in 1929, and a segment of *Fantasia* (1940) offers young viewers a storyline of restless demonic spirits summoned to a midnight revel before morning's light and a line of monks reclaim the cathedral.

In addition, new landscapes as well as encounters with people from other cultures and religious traditions through colonization and slavery offered expanded visions for the representation of fear in realistic American children's literature as well as in wonder tales. The Gothic, an insatiably hungry genre that gobbles up anything it can use, welcomed these new monsters and locales into the New World stories. Working through symbols that represent the repression of sexual anxiety and a fear of the "other," the Gothic intrudes in these early adolescent texts through singular moments in the course of ordinary lives, however, rather than treating the entire story as a Gothic nightmare. Twain's Huck Finn and Tom Sawyer, for instance, are consumed with superstitions and tales of violence and horror, and Tom has his Gothic moment when he is lost in the cave with Becky Thatcher and, possibly, Injun Joe – a variant of the Gothic trope of being buried alive. June Cummins points to a nightmarish Gothic moment in Laura Ingalls Wilder's *These Happy Golden Years* (1943) when Laura awakens to find her landlady about to murder her husband with a knife. Cummins places this episode within the tradition of the Female Gothic as an externalization of Laura's conflicts and anxieties about her own sexuality and her socially prescribed role in the lead-up to her marriage. (On the Female Gothic, see Hoeveler [Chapter 7] in this volume.) While Cummins argues that the other books in the series have no similar Gothic motifs, the Gothic does in fact appear earlier in the series when, in *Little House on the Prairie* (1935), Laura and her family spend an anxious night listening to the eerie sound of Native Americans preparing for war. The moments of terror in these books reflect the ways both adult sexuality and the "other" – and in these cases it is notable that the other is specifically encoded in the American imagination as the indigenous and enslaved people victimized by white settlers – haunt the child characters on their own paths to adulthood.

Montgomery and Burnett deploy Gothic tropes to more romantic ends. Montgomery's heroines are avid readers of Gothic romances, as was Montgomery herself. Kathleen Miller argues that, as a result, Montgomery advocates for an embrace of Gothic sensibility as a form of female empowerment. Though she sometimes parodies the excesses of Gothic literature, Montgomery ultimately comes down on the side of showing "what can be achieved through a good Gothic imagination that is allowed to go a little wrong" (141). Burnett's setting in *The Secret Garden* of a large manor house with a haunting secret has been mined for its Gothic tropes as well.[2] As with Montgomery, Burnett's invocation of the Gothic has positive outcomes: The protagonist, ten-year-old Mary Lennox, braves an encounter with her brooding uncle, investigates the eerie sounds of a boy crying in the dark, and opens the locked garden, thus bringing light and life back to the house and its inhabitants.

Such mastering of Gothic adventures on the way to redemption and empowerment may perhaps be indebted to earlier Puritan sensibilities, as the pattern sometimes surfaces in literature aimed at setting to rights the sins of America's past and present, particularly in the tradition of Southern Gothic (on the Southern Gothic, see Crow [Chapter 10] in this volume). In R. A. Nelson's *Days of Little Texas* (2009), for instance, a young faith healer joins forces with a ghost girl to do battle with the devil on the grounds of a defunct plantation where horrendous atrocities were perpetrated against the slaves; his frightening supernatural ordeal exposes the villains and brings about healing and retroactive justice. Rosemary Clement-Moore's *Texas Gothic* (2011) draws on spooky local history and lore, contemporary ghost-hunting techniques, and an appetite for heroines with psychic powers to attack greed and environmental abuse. Lesley M. M. Blume's *Tennyson* (2008) follows a less energetic though no less moralistic path through its Southern Gothic landscape as its main character, shunted off to her grandmother's crumbling old plantation while her father searches for her wayward mother, begins to write about the house's troubled history, which is revealed to her in dreams; like many texts in this tradition, the emphasis is on the character coming to terms with her own power and responsibility as she takes up a more adult role within a family with a troubled legacy.

This more positive developmental inflection on the Gothic might also reflect a trajectory for girls' growth modeled on the proto-Gothic myth of Persephone. Although it is generally understood that Persephone is not a willing party to her marriage with Hades, variants of the myth question the degree to which she is complicit. In some versions, for instance, she disobediently plucked the one flower that would allow the earth to open up so that Hades could capture her, and while in the underworld she ate several pomegranate seeds knowing that this would doom her to stay there. So while her mother does rescue her by working out a deal whereby she would stay part of the year above ground with her mother and part of the year as the Queen of the Underworld, the character of Persephone provides a perfect metaphor for a young girl's ambivalent desire for a dark, powerful lover played against her desire for a life lived in the light and under the protection of her mother. Holly Virginia Blackford locates this Gothic pattern of American girls descending into underworlds, flirting with broody boys, doing battle with controlling mothers, and emerging into womanhood in texts such as *Little Women, The Secret Garden*, Stephenie Meyer's *Twilight* (2005), and Neil Gaiman's *Coraline* (2002) among others. Indeed, today's teen girls who regularly fall in love with tortured vampires, sexy werewolves, malevolent fairies, and misunderstood demons could well have their own Gothic reality show entitled The Real Housewives of Hell, but that is getting ahead of my history.

American Gothic in print literature for children went into something of a remission during the mid-twentieth century. Realism and historical fiction dominated youth publishing in the States, and what fantasies were produced, such as those by Edward Eager, were mild tales of pleasant wish-fulfillment. But the '70s, '80s, and '90s ushered in an explosion of American fear literature for young readers. Despite appearing regularly on banned and challenged books lists, Alvin Schwartz's collections of scary stories drawn from folklore and urban legends have become elementary school staples since the first book, *Scary Stories to Tell in the Dark*, was published in 1981. Richard Peck and Robert Cormier introduced the psychological grotesque into young adult literature with novels such as *Are You in the House Alone?* (1976), *We All Fall Down* (1991), and *Tenderness* (1997), which feature teenage girls terrorized by mentally unbalanced men. Christopher Pike and R. L. Stine adopted a publishing strategy that was working well for other kinds of genre fiction by producing a book a month in their horror series for middle graders and young adults. The Goosebumps series, in particular, brought Gothic horror into suburbia, with its white, middle-class protagonists encountering monstrous intrusions into their ordinary lives. Children's literature critic Perry Nodelman suggests that it is the marketing of these books that is the real monster; each book encourages ownership by including an excerpt from the next book and having a number on its spine, making a gap in the collection noticeable (118). But he goes on to suggest that the worse horror of these books is their affirmation of the white, egocentric, amoral, consuming child as the desirable norm, as that child gleefully takes on the mantle of "most frightening of all" (122).

This more recent inscription of the monstrous as desirable has come to fruition, according to Victoria Nelson in what she explores as the "rehabilitat[ion of] supernaturalism as an aesthetic mode – brighter, more Romantic, and more culturally heterodox"; the Gothic genre, she argues, has evolved "from horror story to fairy tale" (xi–xii). Certainly, the monsters of twenty-first century American children's picture books are more sympathetic than their predecessors, *Sesame Street* critters notwithstanding. In fact, more often than not, the monsters are in need of understanding and friendship, as is the case in Katherine Tegen's *Dracula and Frankenstein are Friends* (2003), where the monstrous buddies work through a difficult social situation, and Mo Willem's *Leonardo, The Terrible Monster* (2005), where Leonardo is not so much a terrible monster as he is terrible at *being* a monster. Amanda Noll's *I Need My Monster* (2009) tells a tongue-in-cheek story of a boy who can't sleep because the monster who lives under his bed has gone fishing, and no slimy substitute will do. And as the children grow into teens, these amiable monsters move from under their beds to in them, as vampires are redeemed into brooding Byronic heroes who regret their appetites, and witty, amoral, smokin' hot demons, apparently, make awesome boyfriends.

This is not to say that horror has disappeared completely from Gothic fiction for the young. To the contrary, the dark stories, such as Daniel Kraus' *Rotters* (2012) and *Scowler* (2013), Dia Reeves' *Slice of Cherry* (2011), and Andrew Smith's *The Marbury Lens* (2010), are as terrifying as any adult horror novel, and perhaps even more so given the uncanny innocence of children and teens as both victims and perpetrators of unthinkable acts of violence. These novels often fall into the category of the psychological grotesque, with the evil located in disordered minds rather than in eruptions of the supernatural. In addition, traditional Gothic novels in the form of adaptations of or homages to the classics appear with frequency. Lynn Messina's *Little Vampire Women* (2010), for instance, teases out latent Gothic themes in its source text with uncanny and creepy precision, while April Lindner's *Jane* (2010) offers a contemporary revision of *Jane Eyre* (1847) that works weirdly well with Rochester's character transformed into an aging rocker who has damaged his first wife through excessive drug use before falling in love with his pragmatic teen nanny. Teen zombies, on the other hand, almost can't help being funny, so they most often appear in social satire, upsetting proms and exposing adult corruption and corporate malfeasance.

This litany of the many faces of the Gothic in youth literature could go on *ad infinitum*, as each of the types and genres treated in this volume are represented many times over in youth literature. Generally speaking, however, we can summarize by saying that contemporary books written for very young children and middle grade audiences tend to be brighter, or at least resolve into endings where the child protagonists are safe and the evil is contained. Young adult novels, on the other hand, tend to be evenly split between the bright Gothic, where traditional villains are redeemed, and its darker twin, where the extremes of human and supernatural evil are relentlessly explored. The outcomes of young adult novels are also less cheerful; as in the last book of J. K. Rowling's Harry Potter series (*Harry Potter and the Deathly Hallows*, 2007), good ultimately wins, but not without significant loss.

Children and the Gothic Imagination

The robust presence of the Gothic throughout the history of children's literature proves that it is perennially appealing, but doesn't answer why children are attracted to scary stories or ones with more complexly veiled Gothic themes. It helps here to know something about the way children's thinking differs from that of adults. Without going into the weeds of cognitive science, I will pull out two salient differences that affect our engagement with the Gothic. First, empirical research shows that preschool children are much better at metaphorical thinking than they will be after that age (Gardner and Winner 130). The Gothic relies heavily on symbols and images that allegorize things that might be too disturbing to look at straight on. Frankenstein's monster stands in for the fragmented self and the anxiety of one's origins; a crumbling old house full of ghosts might represent the fragility of the past and the shame of buried secrets; a mansion with many sealed-off rooms may symbolize the complexity of the mind as it represses some things and seeks to open up others; a looming figure stands in for anyone who has power over a child or poses a threat. Hence, the scary stories that attract young children are those that stage mastery over these fearful elements, and they don't need to be literal to be effective; in fact, it probably helps more if they aren't. When Max goes into his imagination and has a wild rumpus with his Wild Things, he is experiencing the purgative value of the Gothic imagination; he transforms his aggression and anger at his mother's reprimand into monsters and becomes their master (Sendak n.p.). Other stories that domesticate scary creatures or treat them with warmth and humor, such as Samantha Berger's *Crankenstein* (2013) and Adam Rex's *Frankenstein Makes a Sandwich* (2006), place child readers in a position of either empathy or superiority, giving them options for metaphorical mastery over emotions that threaten to overwhelm them. In fact, Michelle Knudsen's *Marilyn's Monster* (2015) strongly indicates that kids *need* inner monsters for comfort and to manage bullies. Moreover, it is a downright adorable affirmation of how a Gothic imagination can lead to female empowerment, as young Marilyn, tired of waiting for her perfectly suited monster to find her, must seek him out on her own.

A second difference in the way children process stories is related to the sometimes overwhelming power of emotion. At birth, our limbic systems are more fully developed than our prefrontal cortexes. This has interesting implications for understanding how children work with fiction. The limbic system is largely responsible for the generation and expression of emotion, while the prefrontal cortex is the brain's CEO, in charge of functions like regulating behavior, performing reality checks, assessing risk, and suppressing emotional or sexual urges. The upshot of this is twofold: First, children process stories with their emotions rather than with cool-headed reason. This continues through their teenage years, when the flood of hormones augments the desire for sexy melodrama. Second, the underdeveloped prefrontal cortex allows children to enter into fantasy more fully, because there isn't that pesky inhibitory function that tells them something is impossible or unreal. This is not to say that children don't know when they are pretending, but it is to say that they can be more fully absorbed in the world of fiction; they have a greater capacity for belief. As they enter middle childhood, this capacity starts to close down, which may be why they seek transcendence and mystery in their fictions – to hold on to belief, but also to sort out the differences and connections between belief and imagination. As Nelson argues, "outside the purview of organized religion, the genre of supernatural horror [and, I would add, bright supernatural Gothic as well] has been the preferred mode, or even the only allowed one, a predominantly secular-scientific culture such as ours has for imagining and encountering the sacred, albeit in unconscious ways" (xi).

When we put these things together, we have a better understanding of the draw and power of Gothic literature to help children manage existential fears, anxiety, and desire. In their real worlds, young children have very little power; in their fictions, they can have monsters composed of their own aggression who do their bidding, giving them practice in the beneficial exercise of power as well as protection from being overwhelmed by their emotions. In their physical worlds, middle graders and teens are limited by what they can see; in their Gothic fictions, they can encounter transcendence. In their social worlds, teens feel trapped in confining roles and unruly bodies; in their fictions, these roles and bodies are parodied, transformed, and acknowledged for the horrors they sometimes are. Hell may indeed be story-friendly, but the effects of Gothic stories can lead young readers out of the shadows.

NOTES

1. See Boyd; Gottschall; Gregory.
2. See Krüger; Silver.

WORKS CITED

Alcott, Louisa May. *Little Women*. Boston: Roberts Brothers, 1868–1869.
Baum, L. Frank. *The Wonderful Wizard of Oz*. Chicago: Geo. M. Hill Co., 1900.
Baxter, Charles. *Burning Down the House: Essays on Fiction*. St. Paul: Graywolf, 1997.
Berger, Samantha. *Crankenstein*. Illus. Dan Santat. New York: Little, Brown, 2013.
Blackford, Holly Virginia. *The Myth of Persephone in Girls's Fantasy Literature*. New York: Routledge, 2011.
Blume, Lesley M. M. *Tennyson*. New York: Random House, 2008.
Boyd, Brian. *On the Origin of Stories: Evolution, Cognition, and Fiction*. Cambridge, MA: Harvard University Press, 2009.
Bragg, Georgia. *How They Croaked: The Awful Ends of the Awfully Famous*. Illus. by Kevin O'Malley. New York: Bloomsbury USA, 2011.
Bronte, Charlotte. *Jane Eyre*. London: Smith, Elder & Co., 1847.
Burnett, Frances Hodgson. *The Secret Garden*. New York: Frederick A. Stokes, 1911.
Clement-Moore, Rosemary. *Texas Gothic*. New York: Delacorte, 2011.
Cormier, Robert. *We All Fall Down*. New York: Bantam Doubleday, 1991
  Tenderness. New York: Bantam Doubleday, 1997.
Cummins, June. "Laura and the 'Lunatic Fringe': Gothic Encoding in *These Happy Golden Years*." *Children's Literature Association Quarterly*. 23.4 (Winter 1998): 187–93.
Davies, Nicola. *What's Eating You?: Parasites—The Inside Story*. Illus. by Neal Layton. Somerset, MA: Candlewick, 2007.
Fantasia. Dir. James Algar, Wilfred Jackson, Hamilton Luske, et al. Walt Disney Productions, 1940. DVD.
Fleenor, Juliann, ed. Introduction. *The Female Gothic*. Montreal: Eden, 1983. 3–28.
Gaiman, Neil. *Coraline*. New York: HarperCollins, 2002.
Gardner, Howard, and Winner, Ellen. "The Development of Metaphoric Competence: Implications for the Humanistic Disciplines." Ed. Sheldon Sacks. *On Metaphor*. Chicago: University of Chicago Press, 1979. 121–40.
Gottschall, Jonathan. *The Storytelling Animal: How Stories Make Us Human*. New York: Houghton Mifflin Harcourt, 2012.
Gregory, Marshall. *Shaped by Stories: The Ethical Power of Narratives*. South Bend, IN: University of Notre Dame Press, 2009.
Gubar, Marah. "Risky Business: Talking about Children in Children's Literature Criticism." *Children's Literature Association Quarterly* 38.4 (Winter 2013): 450–57.

Knudsen, Michelle. *Marilyn's Monster*. Somerset. MA: Candlewick, 2015.
Kraus, Daniel. *Rotters*. New York: Random House, 2012.
— *Scowler*. New York: Random House, 2013.
Krüger, Stefanie. "Life in the Domestic Realm – Male Identity in *The Secret Garden*." Eds. Marion Gymnich and Imke Lichterfeld. *A Hundred Years of the Secret Garden: France Hodgson Burnett's Children's Classic Revisited*. Goettingen: Bonn University Press, 2012. 69–76.
Lindner, April. *Jane*. New York: Little, Brown, 2010.
Locke, John. *Some Thoughts Concerning Education*. 1693. Eds. J. W. Yolton & J. S. Yolton. Oxford: Clarendon, 1989.
Messina, Lynn. *Little Vampire Women*. New York: HarperTeen, 2010.
Meyer, Stephenie. *Twilight*. New York: Little, Brown, 2005.
Miller, Kathleen. "Haunted Heroines: The Gothic Imagination and the Female Bildungsromane of Jane Austen, Charlotte Brontë and L. M. Montgomery." *The Lion and the Unicorn* 34.2 (Apr. 2010): 125–47.
Miller, Sarah. *The Borden Murders: Lizzie Borden and the Trial of the Century*. New York: Random House, 2016.
Montgomery, L. M. *Anne of Green Gables*. Boston: L. C. Page and Co., 1908.
Nelson, R. A. *Days of Little Texas*. New York: Knopf, 2009.
Nelson, Victoria. *Gothicka: Vampire Heroes, Human Gods, and the New Supernatural*. Cambridge, MA: Harvard University Press, 2012.
Nodelman, Perry. "Ordinary Monstrosity: The World of Goosebumps." *Children's Literature Association Quarterly* 22.3 (Fall 1997): 118–25.
Noll, Amanda. *I Need My Monster*. Illus. by Howard McWilliam. New York: Flashlight Press.
Peck, Richard. *Are You in the House Alone?* New York: Viking, 1976.
Plumptre, James. *The Truth of the Popular Notion of Apparitions, or Ghosts, Considered by the Light of Scripture: A Sermon*. Cambridge: James Hodson, 1818.
Poltergeist II: The Other Side. Dir. Brian Gibson. MGM Distribution, 1986. DVD.
Reeves, Dia. *Slice of Cherry*. New York: Simon Pulse, 2011.
Rex, Adam. *Frankenstein Makes a Sandwich*. New York: HMH, 2006.
Schwartz, Alvin. *Scary Stories to Tell in the Dark*. New York: Harper & Row.
Sendak, Maurice. *Where the Wild Things Are*. New York: Harper & Row, 1963.
Silver, Anna Krugovoy. "Domesticating Bronte's Moors: Motherhood in *The Secret Garden*." *The Lion and the Unicorn* 21.2 (1997): 193–203.
Smith, Andrew. *The Marbury Lens*. New York: Feiwel and Friends, 2010.
Tegen, Katherine. *Dracula and Frankenstein Are Friends*. Illus. by Doug Cushman. New York: HarperCollins, 2003.
Townshend, Dale. "The Haunted Nursery: 1764–1830." *The Gothic in Children's Literature: Haunting the Borders*. Eds. Anna Jackson, Karen Coats, and Roderick McGillis. New York and London: Routledge, 2007. 15–38.
Wilder, Laura Ingalls. *Little House on the Prairie*. New York: Harper, 1935.
— *These Happy Golden Years*. New York: Harper, 1943.
Willems, Mo. *Leonardo, The Terrible Monster*. New York: Hyperion, 2005.

13

TRAVIS D. MONTGOMERY

Gothic American Poetry

So powerful was the taste for dark fiction during the early years of the American republic that Philadelphian man of letters Joseph Dennie felt compelled to point out the ill effects, and in his 1803 essay, "On Gothicism," Dennie declared that reading the works of Ann Radcliffe and her tribe "enfeebles the mind," "induces a habit of melancholy," and "strengthens frantic fear" (476). Madness was, of course, a key Gothic theme, as American authors working in the mode well understood. Exploring "the dark and irrational side of the human psyche," Gothic writers portrayed the world in ways that troubled Enlightenment sensibilities (Ringe 11). Often at the mercy of malevolent powers beyond their control, the obsessive villains and the terrified victims featured in Gothic tales did not embody the values of a responsible, republican citizenry celebrating self-reliance and the power of reason, but despite the animadversions of Dennie and others, Gothicism remained a powerful force in American literary expression. As Charles L. Crow has observed, many writers used this mode to create an "oppositional literature, presenting in disturbing, usually frightening ways, a sceptical, ambiguous view of human nature and of history" (2). Written against the grain of Jeffersonian optimism regarding America and its people, Gothic tales revealed that all was not well in America.[1]

Many scholars recognize the contrarian character of such writing, but these critics tend to focus on prose works rather than poetry. For this reason, Gothic verse produced in America, with the exception of Edgar Allan Poe's and Emily Dickinson's contributions, has been an understudied subject, even though many American poems feature Gothic elements that readers find in the fictional works of writers such as Nathaniel Hawthorne and Toni Morrison. The appeal of the mode transcends barriers of gender, race, class, and political allegiance, but through this remarkable diversity runs a common thread: American Gothic poetry is, for the most part, critical. Its purpose is unsettling and upsetting readers, driving them away from the comforts of received ideas and popular pieties.

The Eighteenth Century

For eighteenth-century poets working in the Gothic vein, balladry offered thematic material and formal models. Of particular significance were the Border Ballads, many of which were folksongs from the Scottish Lowlands. In these lyrics, treachery, murder, lost love, and the uncanny were common themes, and the standard metrical form was alternating lines of iambic tetrameter and iambic trimeter arranged in quatrains. Such poems were especially influential in Britain, where the Ballad Revival began during the eighteenth century. A key event in this movement was the publication of Bishop Percy's *Reliques of Ancient English Poetry*, a compendium including a number of Border Ballads. This poetic collection appeared in 1765, one year after Horace Walpole's *Castle of Otranto* saw print. Thus, the Ballad Revival and emergence of literary Gothicism were coeval, and the thematic correspondences between spooky ballads and Gothic tales were striking.[2] These affinities were not lost on poets, as "The Battle of Lexington," an undated ballad by Lemuel Haynes, indicates. In this poem, which memorializes those who perished in the 1775 fight between Massachusetts militiamen and British regulars, the British are "Tyrants fill'd with horrid Rage" who "slay the innocent," the "unhappy Victims ... unpitied by those Tribes of Hell" (lines 13, 16, and 25–7). Describing the King's soldiers as ungovernable demons, Haynes transforms these Redcoats into Gothic monsters, against which he pits the "Sons of Freedom," the enlightened defenders of liberty (line 20).[3]

Haynes' successors employed imagery in similar ways, identifying threats to self and society, but unlike Haynes, these later poets frequently dwelled on *internal* threats rather than external ones, pointing out domestic problems that required attention. For example, Philip Freneau also used Gothic devices for poetic effect. In "The House of Night," he dramatizes the final agonies of a personified Death, who envisions a mélange of supernatural horrors, and with its descriptions of a tumulus filled with funerary objects, "The Indian Burying Ground" (1788) is comparably morbid. Written in alcaic verse similar to the stanza form of traditional ballads, the latter poem has, however, a subversive edge. Here Freneau suggests that American landscapes are haunted, filled with the spirits of indigenous people wandering the earth under "midnight moons" and "o'er moistening dews" (line 33). These ghosts are irrepressible reminders of the history of white settlement, which was, in part, a record of illegitimate land seizures and usurpations carried out by freedom proclaimers. In this poem, Freneau, who supported the revolutionary cause, checked the self-congratulatory spirit of the times, pointing out the ways in which tyranny works its seductive power not only abroad but also at home.

The Antebellum Period

As the eighteenth century faded into the nineteenth, the Gothic themes of balladry kept captivating poets, British and American. In 1798, William Wordsworth and Samuel Taylor Coleridge released their *Lyrical Ballads*, the collection in which that Gothic touchstone, "The Rime of the Ancyent Marinere," premiered. Two years later, no less a terror writer than Matthew Gregory Lewis published a two-volume set of ballads entitled *Tales of Wonder*, and a short time thereafter, Sir Walter Scott's *Minstrelsy of the Scottish Border* appeared.[4] Such collections fired the imaginations of poets across the Atlantic, and William Cullen Bryant was one American poet of the antebellum period who found inspiration in the ballad tradition preserved by his British forebears. Although he contemplated death and decay in poems such as "Thanatopsis" and "The Prairies," Bryant was not a thoroughgoing Gothicist, but he did produce some dark pieces, one of which was "The Murdered Traveller" (1825). Written in ballad meter, this poem depicts the discovery of a skeleton in the greenwood. Contemplating the bleached bones, the speaker imagines that while the family of the ill-fated wanderer awaited his return, wild animals "stole/ To banquet on the dead" (lines 23–24). Significantly, this gruesome situation recalls a similar one in "The Twa Corbies," a Border Ballad wherein two ravens anticipate eating the body of "a new slain-knight" abandoned by "his hawk, his hound, and lady fair" (lines 6 and 8). Through comparable imagery, Bryant suggests that the natural world is inimical or at least indifferent to humanity. A reminder about the limits of human power, "The Murdered Traveller" probably surprised American readers drunk on their successes in the wake of two military triumphs over Great Britain and full of pride in technological progress heralded by the steamboat and other inventions.

A contemporary of Bryant, the Southern poet William Gilmore Simms also employed the Gothic elements of balladry in his verse. For example, "The Hunter of the Calawassee: A Legend of South Carolina" (1838) is the story of a proud hunter named Kedar, who recklessly chases a strange buck with a single horn through the South Carolina wilds. Ignoring the warnings of his aged slave Lauto, Kedar meets his death in a "gloomy stream" while his quarry, a ghostlike, "failing shadow," disappears into the thick woods (lines 123 and 128). "The Hunter of Calawassee" consists of sixteen eight-line stanzas, but each of the lines contains a four-iamb phrase and a three-iamb phrase separated by a caesura. In short, the poem exhibits a modified form of ballad meter, and Simms' use of this rhythmic pattern complements the Gothic themes in "The Hunter of Calawassee." Many ill-fated villains of Gothic fiction share Kedar's "satanic pride," and the hunter's arrogance has dreadful consequences (Fisher 65). Thus, the story has a cautionary message for readers who, like Kedar, had an "irreverent attitude toward nature," a reservoir of spiritual power that humans could neither understand nor control (Kibler 367). For Simms, this power merits respect, and misguided attempts to subdue it wholly were doomed to failure. Such dreams of control were products of Enlightenment hubris, for which the Gothic imagination operated as ideological redress.

Often associated with the optimism of "Psalm of Life" or the sentimentality of "The Village Blacksmith," Henry Wadsworth Longfellow was not unaware of the dark side of American life, which he occasionally communicated in Gothic terms. Like Bryant and others, Longfellow considered the ballad form a powerful medium for such expression, and one of his most famous poems, "The Wreck of the Hesperus" (1841), bears a striking resemblance to "Sir Patrick Spens," an oft-anthologized Border Ballad (Arvin 69).[5] Longfellow's story is not, however, a simple rehash. While Sir Patrick reluctantly departs on the voyage that results in his death, the prideful sea captain in "The Wreck of the Hesperus" disregards reports of bad weather and foolishly sets sail, whereupon he and his daughter perish at sea. Furthermore, "Sir Patrick Spens" lacks the ghoulish details of Longfellow's piece, in which the poet describes the skipper's "frozen corpse," which is "[l]ashed to the helm, all stiff and stark" while the light from a lantern shines "[o]n his fixed and glassy eyes" (lines 48–9 and 52). This Gothic imagery gives the poem an admonitory power: Longfellow warns readers against the folly of skipper, whose excessive self-reliance exhibits a destructive contempt for external forces that thwart human endeavors. With its New England setting, "The Wreck of the Hesperus" was a rebuke to many nineteenth-century Americans who embraced an excessively rugged individualism.

Although Gothic devices appeared occasionally in Longfellow's works, Gothicism pervaded the verse of Edgar Allan Poe (see also Bendixen [Chapter 2] in this volume). The theme of madness especially fascinated him. Three of his most famous poems, "The Raven," "Ulalume," and "Annabel Lee," showcase troubled speakers overwhelmed by grief, and to convey their mental distress, Poe, a master of prosody, employs hypnotic metrical patterns and rhyme for emotional effect, drawing readers into the inner worlds of these bereaved souls. In so doing, he suggests that everyone is susceptible to such madness, especially the derangement resulting from helplessness in the face of death, which is, as Poe suggests in "The Conqueror Worm" (the first version of which appeared in the 1838 tale "Ligeia"), the inevitable end of all struggles to transcend worldly limitations. Such forebodings did not, however, destroy the creative aspirations of Poe, who believed that "poetry ... must specialize in aesthetic transcendence, eschewing" whatever "might entangle it with this present world," where all was subject to decay (Wilbur xxii–xxiii). Longings for escape through art were, however, problematic for professional writers, who could not afford to ignore market realities.[6] This situation irritated Poe the poet, who expressed his creative angst through Gothic means, as "The Doomed City" (1831) illustrates.[7] In this piece, a personified Death sits enthroned in a ruined city without residents but full of fabulous sculptures, architectural marvels, and idols with precious stones for eyes. Amid these art wonders are, however, signs of decay such as "Time-eaten towers" and "open graves" (lines 10 and 31). Ruled by Death himself, the city is certainly a Gothic space, and Poe's portrayal of the town may indicate his anxiety about the future of literature in a world where commerce, a force that could kill creative independence, is king.

Responsive to the uncanny themes in folklore, John Greenleaf Whittier pursued supernatural topics in poems such as "Birchbrook Mill," "The Demon of the Study," and "The Witch of Wenham," to name only three. The poet derived his impressive knowledge of the weird from patient inquiries into local traditions, and these studies led Whittier to publish *Legends of New England* (1831) and *The Supernaturalism of New England* (1847), both of which evinced the author's interest in things paranormal.[8] The Quaker poet clearly admired Charles Brockden Brown (on Brown, see Hinds in this volume); in an essay entitled "Fanaticism," Whittier discusses *Wieland*, a seminal text of American literary Gothicism, and calls Brown, the author of the 1798 novel, "a writer whose merits have not been sufficiently acknowledged" (108). Taken together, the aforementioned poems and prose works reveal a fascination with Gothic material that spanned the years of Whittier's creative life. The poet found the Gothic mode especially effective for dramatizing the corrupting effects of slavery, which he felt poisoned whatever it touched and undermined the nation's commitment to freedom. To expose the nefarious designs of the Slave Power, which he represented as an evil force possessing the soul of the republic, Whittier relied on Gothic devices throughout "Ichabod" (1850).[9] Written in response to Daniel Webster's efforts on behalf of the Compromise of 1850, which included a Fugitive Slave Bill that pleased Southern politicians, this poem expresses deep grief over the Massachusetts senator's appeasement of the South, a surrender Whittier likens to Lucifer's fall. To convey his horror at Webster's treachery, Whittier plies Gothic imagery, calling the statesman "A bright soul driven, / Fiend-goaded, down the endless dark, / From hope and heaven" (lines 14–16). For Whittier, the fallen Whig orator has a "Dishonored brow," and of this outcast once "loved and honored, naught / Save power remains" (lines 20 and 25–26). Thus, Webster resembles the tormented figures of Gothic fiction such as Charles Maturin's Melmoth, the outcast who wanders the earth after making a Faustian bargain. By linking the senator to such characters, Whittier emphasizes the great man's inner transformation, the corruption of his noble soul.[10]

For female poets of the nineteenth century, writing in the Gothic mode was a way to challenge patriarchal control over literary expression. As Sandra M. Gilbert and Susan Gubar have argued, such authors labored under an "anxiety about the impropriety of female invention" (50). Popularity would not erase this fear, for even successful American women poets worked within a society that directed women to a private, domestic world outside the literary marketplace. Thus, writing women who published simply violated the established order of things. Against this regime stood Lydia Sigourney, whose antebellum poem "The Suttee" was a protest redolent of Gothicism (on the Female Gothic, see Hoeveler [Chapter 7] in this volume). In this piece, a young widow seated "on the pile by her dead lord" awaits her ceremonial immolation (line 1). "An infant's wail" interrupts the proceedings, and recognizing the cry of her child, the woman begs "the flame-kindlers" to let her nurse it (lines 7 and 15). They comply but quickly grow impatient, seizing the baby and letting out a "wild, demonic shout" accompanied by "the thundering yell/ Of the infernal gong" before setting the woman ablaze (lines 42 and 43–44). Memories of the event torment the participants, who often hear in their dreams the "burning mother's scream" (line 50). The sacrificial victim here stands for the woman writer, whose calling puts her at odds with the patriarchal order. Truly subversive is the inclusion of the crying child, which represents the voice of the female creator. For Sigourney, a woman's pursuit of creative fulfillment is *natural*, as natural as a mother caring for her baby, and with the image of the mother/artist cradling her child/creative power, the poet attacks the idea that the life of writing is unsuitable for women. While Sigourney enjoyed fame as the Sweet Singer of Hartford for her sentimental verse, "The Suttee," a truly Gothic production, revealed her bitter awareness that some considered her professional pursuits offensive.[11]

The Gothic idiom proved equally important for writers of temperance songs, poems that drew attention to substance abuse in America. These lyrics were shaped by the sensational reform rhetoric of the Washingtonians, which "was often violent and lurid in its renderings of alcohol's ravages, and people were eager to read and hear about the degeneracy and wickedness they supposedly protested" (Rosenthal and Reynolds 4). The popular songwriter Jesse Hutchinson, Jr. also viewed intemperance as a form of possession, as his Gothic piece "King Alcohol" (1843) reveals. This king is "a beast of many horns," an infernal demon who "catches men," and the monarch's minions include various liquors that make up "a fiendish crew/ As ever a mortal knew" (lines 3, 4, and 12–13). Popular writing of this kind was important to the young Walt Whitman, who penned a temperance novel entitled *Franklin Evans* (1842), and according to David S. Reynolds, the sensational techniques and themes of temperance writers had some influence on Whitman's poetics.[12]

Civil War Years and the Postbellum Era

Two startling events, the 1859 appearance of Charles Darwin's *The Origin of Species* and the outbreak of the Civil War in 1861, forever changed American life, and as he mused over the fallout, Herman Melville wrote many gloomy poems.[13] Drawing on the work of nineteenth-century geologists and biologists, Melville took a sledgehammer to anthropocentric notions about nature that inflated human pride. In "The New Ancient of Days, or The Man of the Cave of Engihoul," which was published long after Melville's death, the poet describes a fossilized "ogre of bone" who mocks the pretensions of humanity by suggesting that people descended from sponges and apes and "grin[ning] for his godless fee" (lines 71 and 72). According to Melville, this gleeful skeleton, a Gothic Ancient of Days, has ousted Jehovah of old, the deity who created humans in his image and made them masters over creation. Smiling grimly, the new god has a troubling message: People are not as important in the scheme of things as they had assumed. Melville also expresses deep pessimism about the Civil War and its fruits in his 1866 poem "The House-top" (appropriately subtitled "A Night Piece"), an account of the New York Draft Riot of 1863. During this orgy of fire and murder, brute instincts triumph over moral restraint as "man rebounds whole æons back in nature" (line 16). Degeneration of this kind has Gothic correlatives such as the corruption of Ambrosio in M. G. Lewis' *The Monk* (1796). Initially a respected figure, Ambrosio the monk becomes a perpetrator of horrible crimes. Creatures of impulse like Lewis' cleric, the rioters in "The House-top" are brutal, demonic figures, and the poem is powerfully subversive. Pondering the lawlessness on display during the New York uprisings, Melville judges such behavior a "grimy slur on the Republic's faith implied,/ Which holds that Man is naturally good" (lines 25–26). This realization undermined the moral arrogance that allowed some Americans to consider the Civil War a crusade in which, as Julia Ward Howe put it in "The Battle Hymn of the Republic," "our God is marching on."

Long recognized as a purveyor of Gothicism, Emily Dickinson worked during this tumultuous time, capturing the anxious mood of the era in her poetry, most of which she wrote during the 1860s. Dickinson mentions specters repeatedly, and Death is ubiquitous in her verse, a body of writing replete with sepulchral images such as coffins and gravestones. She famously characterizes madness as "a Funeral, in my Brain" (line 1), and throughout her work, "Dickinson stresses the interior, psychological aspect of gothicism" that points to "one's own deepest capacities for self-destruction" (Eberwein 120). The poet did not, however, confine her investigation of madness to the individual. Keenly aware of the irrational side of human nature, she explored insanity as a social label, pointing out the ways in which "sane" people terrorize outsiders in the name of reason and order. "Much Madness is divinest Sense – " involves such a turning of the tables. In this poem, Dickinson offers a grim view of society, which she portrays as a group of mad dungeon keepers punishing the nonconformist "with a Chain" (line 8 and Crow 62). Like Melville, Dickinson also uses Gothic techniques to debunk old pieties about the natural world. In "A narrow Fellow in the Grass," she depicts a boy's sudden discovery of a snake while walking barefooted through a field. To create an atmosphere of anxiety, Dickinson employs slant rhyme in all of the stanzas save the last, in which the speaker reveals that what he had mistaken for "a Whip Lash/Unbraiding in the Sun" was, in fact, a serpent (lines 13–14). These imperfect rhymes alerted readers that something was not right, and the problem that Dickinson brings into focus is the dangerous impulse to claim fellowship with "Nature's People," to believe that the wild world is a place where humans can be completely at home (line 17). The bone-chilling discovery of the snake, which elicits "tighter Breathing" (line 23), is a "gothic scare," a terrible reminder that the universe is an uncanny place (Wardrop 82).

As a prophetic poet, Stephen Crane followed in the footsteps of Melville and Dickinson. Rejecting the expansionist brag of the postbellum period, Crane suggested that Americans, for all their pride in national power, were repeating the mistakes of their forebears, and in *War Is Kind* (1899), he marshals Gothic imagery while censuring heedless militarism. This collection of poetry includes "Fast rode the knight." Here a warrior plunges into battle, crying "To save my lady!," but the poem ends with a gruesome image of the knight's mount, "A horse,/Blowing, staggering, bloody thing/ Forgotten at the foot of castle wall" (lines 4 and 11–13). Published during the last year of the Spanish-American War, "Fast rode the knight" features a charge similar, in some respects, to the dash of Theodore Roosevelt and his volunteer Rough Riders up a hill to the San Juan Heights, an event that Crane witnessed.[14] While such daring acts could secure military objectives, terror and bloodshed were their inevitable results, and Crane warns against martial adventurism, a destructive approach to foreign policy that was, he suggested, simply medieval.

1900–1945

At the dawn of the twentieth century, some poets explored the hidden horrors of quotidian existence. Taking a cue from Edwin Arlington Robinson, whose verse exposed the misery that everyday people hide from others, Edgar Lee Masters wrote *Spoon River Anthology* (1915), a collection of dramatic monologues in which many dead people from a small American town brood over their disappointments or rage against the wrongs they suffered, giving vent to their pent-up feelings. In "Margaret Fuller Slack," the titular speaker, who "would have been as great as George Eliot/ But for an untoward fate," laments her marriage, which left her saddled with unwanted children (lines 1–2). Overworked and weighed down with domestic cares, she "died from lock-jaw, an ironical death" representing her lost independence, and the poem closes with a warning: "Sex is the curse of life!" (lines 15 and 17). Such dispatches from the grave show that contentment was not necessarily the lot of people who lived away from cities, calling into question the pastoral myths that have long influenced national life. The Gothic vision also fascinated Robert Frost, whom Lionel Trilling famously called "a terrifying poet," a writer insistent that "the actual America is tragic" (378 and 379). "Two Witches" revealed Frost's curiosity about the supernatural, but Gothic themes also turn up in better-known pieces such as that grim portrait of a dying marriage, "Home Burial," and "Out, Out—," a shocking poem about a boy who dies shortly after a freak accident with a saw.

Gothicism was also an important tool for modernist poets worried about cultural decline. Intrigued by the macabre, Amy Lowell produced a book of poems entitled *East Wind*, which contains various "portraits of desperate and deranged people" (Benvenuto 92), but before publishing that volume, she had put her Gothic predilections to work in "The Captured Goddess" (1914), an imagist piece. Here Lowell describes the speaker's pursuit of a rainbow-winged goddess who enchants her surroundings with color. Within a "narrow-streeted city," this divine wonder worker falls into the hands of men who bind her and put her up for sale (line 29). The harrowing sight of the naked goddess shivering and weeping terrifies the speaker, who runs away in fear while "the grey wind hissed" (line 42). Filled with Gothic imagery of bondage and rape, this poem conveys Lowell's profound anxieties about the commodification of art, that perennial source of wonder and delight, in a world where money was fast becoming the only measure of value (Hovey 78). Such a place was, Lowell indicates, a carceral space, the narrow streets representing the imaginative constraints under which twentieth-century poets labored. The conception of the modern world as a nightmarish wasteland was, of course, central to the works of Ezra Pound and T. S. Eliot, and in "Ode to the Confederate Dead," Allen Tate presents "a kind of Southern analogue to" that vision (Hirsch 65). Hart Crane also struggled with the challenges of modern authorship, revealing his anxieties in *The Bridge* (1930). The section entitled "The Tunnel," a remarkable cache of Gothic imagery including "brilliantly particular snapshots of city demoralization," is especially revelatory (Berthoff 107). Amid these terrors, Crane inserts a description of Edgar Allan Poe's face, which appears "[b]elow the toothpaste and dandruff ads" in the New York City subway (line 74). This juxtaposition indicates that the literary productions of geniuses like Poe had become mere commodities, and the tenebrous scene painting of "The Tunnel" left few doubts about how Crane viewed that state of affairs.

In the early twentieth century, some African American writers turned out Gothic poems exposing racial violence that sullied the nation's history. The brutality of lynching was the subject of Paul Laurence Dunbar's "The Haunted Oak" (1903), in which a tree tells the story of a black man hanged from one of its boughs. Murdered by masked men, this "guiltless victim" dangled in "the moonlight dim and weird," letting out a "gurgling moan" before his struggles ceased (lines 8, 7, 10). The bough later withered, after which the tree declared itself accursed and stood as an uncanny reminder of the atrocious act. Paranormal machinery in this poem highlights Dunbar's message: Past injustices haunt America. Claude McKay, a luminary of the Harlem Renaissance, makes a similar point in "The Lynching" (1920), a terrifying sonnet wherein "little lads, lynchers that were to be,/ Danced round" a charred corpse "in fiendish glee" (lines 13–14). For McKay, racial violence is a transformative power that turns children into demons. Ending this evil, passed from generation to generation, requires Americans to acknowledge the dangers of racism, and poetry is a vehicle for catching the conscience of the nation.

Another outlet for Gothic expression was weird poetry, which flourished in the decades before the Second World War. For writers of the weird school, the true universe was a world of horrors concealed by false appearances, a place sublime and terrifying. George Sterling's "A Wine of Wizardry" (1907) exemplifies the style. Drunk on "dusky wine," the speaker enters a dreamlike space beyond the workday world, and many of the sights there are deeply disturbing (line 3). To mention two examples, Satan paws "a screaming thing his fiends have flayed" before a "demon altar," and a "blue-eyed vampire, sated at her feast,/ Smiles bloodily against the leprous moon." (lines 157–58, 156, and 196–97). These dark scenes suggest that things are not what they seem, for forces beyond human ken operate within the universe, a place unknown and possibly unknowable. Whereas realism empowered readers, weird writing terrified them with a sense of their fundamental impotence. Convinced "of the cosmic insignificance of humanity in a boundless universe" (Joshi 132), H. P. Lovecraft, the horror writer famous for creating the tentacled monster Cthulhu, advanced this belief in *Fungi from Yuggoth*, a posthumously published sonnet sequence in the weird tradition. Here the speaker discovers a "book that told the hidden way/ Across the void and through the space-hung screens/ That hold the undimensioned worlds at bay" ("III. The Key": lines 5–7). Terrifying visions follow and, at one point, the speaker declares, "I ceased to hope – because I understood" ("XVII. A Memory": line 14). For the weird poet, understanding means recognizing the futility of human striving, a deeply subversive move. The notion of a weird universe makes triumphalism of any kind ridiculous.

1945–Present

During the second half of the twentieth century, the Gothic imagination proved its staying power as poets recorded their forebodings about America's future. In *Howl* (1956), Allen Ginsberg also paints a bleak picture of postwar America, a world where Moloch, a "sphinx of cement and aluminum" named after a pagan deity, seized visionaries, "bashed open their skulls[,] and ate up their brains and imagination" (line 79). Associated with industry, finance, and war, this monster, "whose breast is a cannibal dynamo," pursues power and wealth with machinelike regularity (line 83). Moloch's depredations are not, however, confined to tormented poets at odds with modernity; the suffering he inflicts is widespread: "Children screaming under the stairways! Boys sobbing in armies! Old men weeping in the parks!" (line 80). For Ginsberg, the forces that made America a superpower were snuffing out real happiness and freedom, and his Gothic vision of Moloch reveals the hidden costs of prosperity. A contemporary of Ginsberg, Sylvia Plath was also sharply critical of the world she inhabited. Blending images of Nazi tyranny and vampirism in "Daddy," she attacked patriarchal violence, physical and psychological, against women, but, as Kathleen L. Nichols has argued, an idiosyncratic Gothicism shaped many of Plath's other poems, which documented "the real-life horrors of her own historical era" such as nuclear warfare and genocide (329).

A great deal of popular music produced after 1950 was also leavened with Gothic imagery and themes. Noting the recurrence of the word "sin" in the songwriter Bob Dylan's lyrics, Christopher Ricks has said that "Dylan's [was] an art in which sins [were] laid bare" (3 and 2), and social sin was on display in

"Tombstone Blues," a song about poverty and grief in a town where the local Chamber of Commerce welcomes Jack the Ripper and ghostly figures from American history haunt the streets. Here, Dylan suggests that modern America is a hotbed of corruption, a decadent place far removed from its heroic origins.[15]

The Gothic mode remained important throughout the following decades. With their black-clad front men and pyrotechnic displays, many heavy metal bands of the 1970s and 1980s surrounded themselves with Gothic accoutrements, and their music exposed dark impulses at work within self and society. During the waning years of the Reagan administration, the group Guns-N-Roses released "Welcome to the Jungle" on an album entitled *Appetite for Destruction* (1987), the cover of which was skull-studded. The paradise of sadists described in that song provided a reality check for those who believed it was, as President Reagan had said, "morning in America." In the early years of the twenty-first century, the Gothic impulse also found expression in rap lyrics such as Jay-Z's "Lucifer" (2003), which sheds light on the grim realities of living in the inner city, where many people struggled to preserve life, protect liberty, and pursue happiness.

Far from an exhaustive account, this essay offers only a general survey of Gothicism in American poetry, but the range of writers mentioned above demonstrates how pervasive Gothic expression is in the nation's verse productions. Contrarian writing of this kind bears some resemblance to the dark psalms of the Bible, those terrifying poems expressing despair, outrage, and grief, lyrics so different from the consoling devotional verse that inspires many contemporary believers. Calling these grim poems "psalms of disorientation," Walter Brueggemann considers them a necessary part of a community's "conversation with God," which demands an "honest facing of the darkness" (176 and 12). In a secular context, the dark psalms of American poetry serve a similar role. These pieces discourage facile patriotism, suggesting that national pride is useful only insofar as it encourages Americans to live up to their cherished ideals. That process requires seeing things as they are, and Gothic verse, which often reveals exceptionalist distortions, is an indispensable aid for national soul-searching.

NOTES

1. An important study of subversive elements in antebellum Gothic prose is *Gothic America: Narrative, History, and Nation*, in which Teresa A. Goddu demonstrates how Edgar Allan Poe, Harriet Jacobs, and other writers challenge "America's national myth of new-world innocence by voicing the cultural contradictions that undermine the nation's claim to purity and equality" (10). For more on the early American Gothic, see Ringel (Chapter 1) in this volume.

2. For the Ballad Revival, see Douglass H. Thomson's introduction (13–36) to *Tales of Wonder*. For the original ballads and their influence, see William Beattie's introduction (13–25) to *Border Ballads*.
3. The text cited here is the version prepared by Ruth Bogin, whose "'The Battle of Lexington': A Patriotic Ballad by Lemuel Haynes" features a transcription of the manuscript.
4. For the rise of the "Gothic ballad," a literary form based on folk models, see Douglass H. Thomson's introduction (13–36) to *Tales of Wonder*.
5. See also Lawrence Buell's Penguin edition of Longfellow's verse. Here Buell calls the poem "[a] New World rendition of the medieval ballad of 'Sir Patrick Spens'" (387). According to Samuel Longfellow, the poet's brother, "The Wreck of the Hesperus" belonged to the Gothic ballad tradition, for the first published version featured "marginal notes after the manner of Coleridge's *The Ancient Mariner*" (*Works of Henry Wadsworth Longfellow* 53). Gothic elements in "The Wreck of the Hesperus" were also evident to Horace Gregory, who detected in the poem's "tears, pathos, and melodrama" the influence of a "Gothic Muse" (xv–xvi). For Longfellow and balladry, see pages 247–50 of Virginia Jackson's "Longfellow in His Time," which appears in *The Cambridge History of American Poetry*.
6. For Poe and the publishing world of nineteenth-century America, see chapter 6 of William Charvat's *The Profession of Authorship in America: 1800–1870* and Terence Whalen's *Edgar Allan Poe and the Masses: The Political Economy of Literature in Antebellum America*.
7. This poem is an early version of "The City in the Sea."
8. According to Edward Wagenknecht, who prepared an edition of *The Supernaturalism of New England*, "There can be no doubt that young Whittier's tastes were Gothick" (9). For Whittier and the Gothic, see also Faye Ringel's "New England Gothic," which includes observations on Gothicism in the poetic works of New England writers such as Henry Wadsworth Longfellow, Emily Dickinson, Amy Lowell, and Robert Frost.
9. The poet's vision of the peculiar institution as a destructive force tallies with the ideas of antislavery politicians such as Salmon P. Chase, who "believed in the existence of a conspiratorial 'Slave Power' which had seized control of the federal government and was attempting to subvert the Constitution for its own purposes" (Foner 9).
10. The Whittier section of this essay derives from a paper that the author presented at the 2014 American Literature Association Conference, which took place in Washington, DC.
11. Nina Baym has called readers to recognize the breadth of Sigourney's artistry. For Baym, the poet "was obviously an important [writer] in her own time, and we will understand that time better if we abandon a social construction of Sigourney based on a limited awareness of her work" (166). For information about "the Poetess," a label that has shaped the reception of Sigourney's writings, see Jackson's "The Poet as Poetess," which appears in *The Cambridge Companion to Nineteenth-Century American Poetry*.
12. Whitman's novel was published in 1842, one year before Hutchinson's song appeared, but both texts were the products of Washingtonian influence. For Whitman's debts to temperance literature, see chapters 2 and 3 of David S.

Reynolds' *Beneath the American Renaissance: The Subversive Imagination in the Age of Emerson and Melville.*

13. For a brief account of creative responses to midcentury controversies, scientific and religious, and to the violence of the Civil War era, see chapter 6 of Drew Gilpin Faust's *The Republic of Suffering: Death and the American Civil War.* Among the writers that Faust discusses are Dickinson and Melville.
14. For Crane's experiences in Cuba during the war, see chapter 23 of Paul Sorrentino's *Stephen Crane: A Life of Fire.*
15. For subversive Gothic material in Dylan's "Blind Willie McTell," see David Punter's "Gothic, Theory, Dream" (17–18 and *passim*).

WORKS CITED

Arvin, Newton. *Longfellow: His Life and Work.* Boston: Little, Brown and Co., 1963.

Baym, Nina. "Reinventing Lydia Sigourney." *Feminism and American Literary History: Essays.* By Nina Baym. New Brunswick, NJ: Rutgers University Press, 1992. 151–66.

Beattie, William. "Introduction." *Border Ballads.* Ed. William Beattie. Harmondsworth: Penguin, 1952. 13–25.

Benvenuto, Richard. *Amy Lowell.* Twayne: Boston, 1985.

Berthoff, Warner. *Hart Crane: A Re-introduction.* Minneapolis: Minnesota University Press, 1989.

Bogin, Ruth. "'The Battle of Lexington': A Patriotic Ballad by Lemuel Haynes." *William and Mary Quarterly* 42.4 (1985): 499–506. *JSTOR.* Web. 28 Sept. 2015.

Bryant, William Cullen. "The Murdered Traveller." *The Poetical Works of William Cullen Bryant.* Ed. Parke Goodwin. 1883. Vol. 1. New York: Russell & Russell, 1967. 120–21.

Brueggemann, Walter. *The Message of the Psalms: A Theological Commentary.* Minneapolis: Augsburg, 1984.

Buell, Lawrence, ed. *Selected Poems.* By Henry Wadsworth Longfellow. New York: Viking-Penguin, 1988.

Charvat, William. *The Profession of Authorship in America: 1800–1870.* Ed. Matthew J. Bruccoli. New York: Columbia University Press, 1992.

Crane, Hart. "VII: The Tunnel" from *The Bridge. The Complete Poems of Hart Crane.* Ed. Marc Simon. Centennial Edn. New York: Liveright, 2001. 95–101. Print.

Crane, Stephen. "Fast rode the knight" from *War Is Kind. Stephen Crane: Complete Poems.* Ed. Christopher Benfey. New York: Library of America, 2011. 85.

Crow, Charles L. *American Gothic.* Cardiff: University of Wales Press, 2009.

Dennie, Joseph. "On Gothicism." *Literature of the Early Republic.* Ed. Edwin H. Cady. New York: Holt, Rinehart, and Winston, 1950. 474–77.

Dickinson, Emily. "A narrow Fellow in the Grass." *The Poems of Emily Dickinson: A Reading Edition.* Ed. R. W. Franklin. Cambridge: Belknap-Harvard University Press, 1999. 443–44.

"I felt a Funeral, in my Brain." *The Poems of Emily Dickinson: A Reading Edition.* Ed. R. W. Franklin. Cambridge: Belknap-Harvard University Press, 1999. 153.

"Much Madness is divinest Sense -." *The Poems of Emily Dickinson: A Reading Edition*. Ed. R. W. Franklin. Cambridge: Belknap-Harvard University Press, 1999. 278.

Dunbar, Paul Laurence. "The Haunted Oak." *The Collected Poems of Paul Laurence Dunbar*. Ed. Joanne M. Braxton. Charlottesville: Virginia University Press, 1993. 219–20.

Eberwein, Jane Donahue. *Dickinson: Strategies of Limitation*. Amherst: Massachusetts University Press, 1985.

Faust, Drew Gilpin. *The Republic of Suffering: Death and the American Civil War*. New York: Vintage Civil War Library-Random House, 2009.

Fisher, Benjamin F. "'To Shadow forth Its Presence': Simms's Gothic Narrative Poems." *Southern Quarterly* 41.2 (2003): 60–72.

Foner, Eric. *Free Soil, Free Labor, Free Men: The Ideology of the Republican Party Before the Civil War*. 1970. Oxford: Oxford University Press, 1995.

Freneau, Philip. "The Indian Burying Ground." *Poems of Freneau*. Ed. Harry Hayden Clark. New York: Hafner, 1929. 355–56.

Gilbert, Sandra M. and Susan Gubar. *The Madwoman in the Attic: The Woman Writer and the Nineteenth-Century Literary Imagination*. 2nd edn. New Haven: Yale University Press, 2000.

Ginsberg, Allen. *Howl*. *Howl and Other Poems*. San Francisco: City Lights, 1959. 9–26.

Goddu, Teresa. *Gothic America: Narrative, History, and Nation*. New York: Columbia University Press, 1997.

Gregory, Horace. "Introduction." *Evangeline and Selected Tales and Poems*. By Henry Wadsworth Longfellow. Ed. Horace Gregory. New York: Signet-Penguin, 1990. vii–xxiv.

Hirsch, Edward. "Helmet of Fire: American Poetry in the 1920s." *A Profile of Twentieth-Century American Poetry*. Eds. Jack Myers and David Wojhan. Carbondale: Southern Illinois University Press, 1991. 54–83.

Hovey, Jaime. "Lesbian Chivalry in Amy Lowell's *Sword Blades and Poppy Seed*." *Amy Lowell, American Modern*. Eds. Adrienne Munich and Melissa Bradshaw. New Brunswick, NJ: Rutgers University Press, 2004. 77–89.

Hutchinson, Jesse, Jr. "King Alcohol." *Stephen Foster & Co.: Lyrics of America's First Great Popular Songs*. Ed. Ken Emerson. New York: Library of America, 2010. 76–77.

Jackson, Virginia. "Longfellow in His Time." *The Cambridge History of American Poetry*. Eds. Alfred Bendixen and Stephen Burt. Cambridge: Cambridge University Press, 2015. 238–58.

"The Poet as Poetess." *The Cambridge Companion to Nineteenth-Century American Poetry*. Ed. Kerry Larson. Cambridge: Cambridge University Press, 2011. 54–75.

Joshi, S. T. *A Dreamer and a Visionary: H. P. Lovecraft in His Time*. Liverpool: Liverpool University Press, 2001.

Kibler, James Everett. "Explanatory and Textual Notes." *Selected Poems of William Gilmore Simms*. Ed. James Everett Kibler. Twentieth Anniversary Edn. Columbia: South Carolina University Press, 2010. 329–441.

Longfellow, Henry Wadsworth. "The Wreck of the Hesperus." *The Works of Henry Wadsworth Longfellow*. Ed. Samuel Longfellow. 1886. Vol. 1. New York: AMS Press, 1966. 60–64.

Lovecraft, H. P. *Fungi from Yuggoth. The Ancient Track: The Complete Poetical Works of H.P. Lovecraft*. Ed. S. T. Joshi. New York: Hippocampus Press, 2013. 80–95.
Lowell, Amy. "The Captured Goddess." *Sword Blades and Poppy Seed*. Cambridge: Riverside Press, 1914. 31–33.
Masters, Edgar Lee. "Margaret Fuller Slack." *Spoon River Anthology*. Ed. Jerome Loving. New York: Penguin, 2008. 60.
McKay, Claude. "The Lynching." *Complete Poems*. Ed. William J. Maxwell. Urbana: Illinois University Press, 2004. 176–77.
Melville, Herman. "The House-top." *Tales, Poems, and Other Writings*. Ed. John Bryant. New York: Modern Library-Random House, 2002. 346.
"The New Ancient of Days, or The Man of the Cave of Engihoul." *Tales, Poems, and Other Writings*. Ed. John Bryant. New York: Modern Library-Random House, 2002. 321–23.
Nichols, Kathleen L. "The Cold War Poetry of Sylvia Plath." *A Companion to American Gothic*. Ed. Charles L. Crow. West Sussex: Wiley-Blackwell, 2014. 328–39.
Poe, Edgar Allan. "The Doomed City." *The Collected Works of Edgar Allan Poe*. Ed. Thomas Ollive Mabbott. Vol. 1. Cambridge: Belknap-Harvard University Press, 1969. 199–200.
Punter, David. "Gothic, Theory, Dream." *A Companion to American Gothic*. Ed. Charles L. Crow. West Sussex: Wiley-Blackwell, 2014. 16–28.
Reynolds, David S. *Beneath the American Renaissance: The Subversive Imagination in the Age of Emerson and Melville*. 1988. New York: Oxford University Press, 2011.
Ricks, Christopher. *Dylan's Visions of Sin*. New York: ECCO-HarperCollins, 2003.
Ringe, Donald. *American Gothic: Imagination and Reason in Nineteenth-Century Fiction*. Lexington: Kentucky University Press, 1982.
Ringel, Faye. "New England Gothic." *A Companion to American Gothic*. Ed. Charles L. Crow. West Sussex: Wiley-Blackwell, 2014. 139–50.
Sigourney, Lydia. "The Suttee." *American Women Poets of the Nineteenth Century: An Anthology*. Ed. Cheryl Walker. New Brunswick, NJ: Rutgers University Press, 1992. 14–16.
Rosenthal, Debra J. and David S. Reynolds, eds. *The Serpent in the Cup: Temperance in American Literature*. Amherst: Massachusetts University Press, 1997.
Simms, William Gilmore. "The Hunter of Calawassee: A Legend of South Carolina." *Selected Poems of William Gilmore Simms*. Ed. James Everett Kibler. Twentieth Anniversary Edn. Columbia: South Carolina University Press, 2010. 97–101.
Sorrentino, Paul. *Stephen Crane: A Life of Fire*. Cambridge: Belknap-Harvard University Press, 2014. Print.
Sterling, George. "A Wine of Wizardry." *The Thirst of Satan: Poems of Fantasy and Terror*. Ed. S. T. Joshi. New York: Hippocampus Press, 2003. 145–52.
Thomson, Douglass H., ed. *Tales of Wonder*. By Matthew G. Lewis. Ontario: Broadview Press, 2010.
Trilling, Lionel. "A Speech on Robert Frost: A Cultural Episode." *The Moral Obligation to Be Intelligent: Selected Essays*. Ed. Leon Wieseltier. New York: Farrar, Straus and Giroux, 2000. 372–80.

"The Twa Corbies." *Border Ballads.* Ed. William Beattie. Harmondsworth: Penguin, 1952. 127.

Wagenknecht, Edward. "Whittier and the Supernatural—A Test Case." *ESQ* 50.1 (1968): 8–11.

Wardrop, Daneen. *Emily Dickinson's Gothic: Goblin with a Gauge.* Iowa City: Iowa University Press, 1996.

Whalen, Terence. *Edgar Allan Poe and the Masses: The Political Economy of Literature in Antebellum America.* Princeton: Princeton University Press, 1999.

Whittier, John Greenleaf. "Fanaticism." *Literary Recreations and Miscellanies.* Boston: Ticknor and Fields, 1854. 107–12.

———. "Ichabod." *Complete Poetical Works of John Greenleaf Whittier.* Ed. Horace Scudder. Boston: Houghton, Mifflin and Co., 1894. 186–87.

Wilbur, Richard, ed. *Edgar Allan Poe: Poems and Poetics.* New York: Library of America, 2003.

14

HEATHER S. NATHANS

Gothic American Drama

In his *Annals of the New York Stage*, George C. Odell marks the 1790s as the period that "began an outbreak of Gothic horror hitherto unparalleled in the New York theatre, and of a magnitude sufficient to satisfy the imagination of Horace Walpole, Mrs. Radcliffe, or Kotzebue" (22). Odell's description of the "dark-browed villains," "unearthly visitants," wandering heroines, and "hired assassins," summarizes the mania for the Gothic that has gripped American audiences since the late eighteenth century. While it may seem incongruous that a genre traditionally featuring ruined castles and feuds between ancient families should settle in the resolutely democratic American landscape, playwrights, performers, and theatre managers found numerous opportunities to reimagine Gothic spectacles for US theatre-goers.

Since the end of the eighteenth century, audiences have imbibed vernacularized visions of European Gothic dramas, filtered through American sensibilities and recalibrated to trace Gothic vistas onto emerging American frontiers. From the now long-lost dramas of the 1790s and the age of melodrama, to the more familiar works of Susan Glaspell, Tennessee Williams, Sam Shepard, Tony Kushner, August Wilson, and Stephen Sondheim, the Gothic has cast a long shadow over the American theatre. By the twentieth century, playwrights invoked the Gothic to peel back layers of the "mysterious, grotesque and desolate" aspects of American life, exposing the savagery concealed beneath the façade of the ordinary (qtd. in Keith xvi). This chapter explores the incursions of the Gothic into the history of American drama, emphasizing the impact of the spectacular on audiences wrestling with issues of race, gender, class, and cultural identity as they played out on the national stage. It surveys some of the highlights of the history of the Gothic in the American theatre, while exploring lesser-known works that reveal the subversive power of the genre as well.

Stung with Lust of Power

Before the Revolution, many American audiences relished theatre as a tangible link with the distant British cosmopolitan center. Plays from London brought a flavor of sophisticated culture, as greedily devoured by theatre-goers as the imported tea and other goods shipped into colonial ports. By 1774, wartime edicts banished theatre from American shores as a frivolous distraction from nation-building. After the war, theatrical troupes returned to their former colonial haunts, seeking to persuade audiences that theatrical entertainments could instill principles of good citizenship. Dramas such as *Gustavus Vasa*, which played at the 1794 opening of Boston's Federal Street Theatre, were aimed at the "genuine lover of liberty" (*The British Drama* 378). However, theatre managers and proprietors quickly discovered that selling only civic virtue made for poor box office receipts. Moreover, early theatre companies were composed largely of British-born actors trained to perform British plays. And in the absence of new American dramas (with a few notable exceptions from authors such as Royall Tyler, Susannah Rowson, William Dunlap, and Judith Sargent Murray), the national stage quickly reverted to a largely European repertoire. While managers excised overtly British references in scripts so as not to offend democratic sensibilities, trends in European drama continued to shape American tastes and theatrical practices over the next several decades. Thus, the "national" drama would incorporate the Gothic creations streaming from Europe into American settings. Indeed, the term "Gothic" became a selling point for theatre managers eager to capitalize on the popularity of the genre. As theatre scholar Susan Anthony notes, the label has been variously attached to historical tribes, the medieval era (particularly its architecture), barbaric atrocities, and stories featuring the supernatural (6). Thus, a contemporary scholar researching "Gothic" American dramas finds eighteenth- and nineteenth-century theatrical advertisements promising audiences Gothic temples, halls, dungeons, bed-chambers "ornamented with ancient portraits," abbeys, and gates "in the Gothic style."[1] And while the moniker frequently applied to scenic effects, scholars Amy Hughes, Shirley Samuels, Ellen Malenas Ledoux, and others argue that these productions had complex agendas that addressed issues of race, class, and gender through the medium of Gothic spectacles. As Hughes contends, "The spectacular instant offered producers, reformers, audiences, and consumers a unique opportunity to articulate ideas" (45).[2] Despite this, as Benjamin F. Fisher notes, historians of American theatre have often been reluctant to label early national dramas as "Gothic." The stigma attached to the genre has long reduced it to a collection of exaggerated effects, and scholars have classified the "sensational" aspect of Gothic drama as mere commercial excess, a "passing fad," or as an embarrassing relic of a more primitive era (B. Fisher 99).

To do so risks overlooking the ways in which the sensational spectacles of Gothic drama invited American audiences to reimagine their roles in contemporary culture, whether in the eighteenth century or the twenty-first. Hughes' "heightened, fleeting, and palpable" moments of performance that "captivate the spectator through multiple planes of engagement" presented a range of embodied *choices* for American audiences (8). As they trembled on the precipices of literal and figurative cliffs, Gothic characters and the actors who portrayed them presented moments of suspended tension in which the outcomes of events were far from certain. The resolution of Gothic dramas required the same kind of decisive action and deliberate choices necessary to create a new culture. They juxtaposed the will of the individual against the drive for the common good: a critical struggle during an era in which the desire for power was seen as antithetical to the health of the emerging democratic state.

One of the earliest American Gothic dramas to showcase an individual's fight to put the greater good before his own interests is William Dunlap's *Fontainville Abbey* (1795). Indeed, Benjamin Fisher suggests that the seeds of American Gothic writing may be found not in the novels of Charles Brockden Brown, but in the popular dramas "of his friend William Dunlap" (100). Dunlap, often called the "Father of American Drama," was the manager of the Park Street Theatre in New York and a prolific playwright and translator. His hit *Fontainville Abbey* derives from the work of Ann Radcliffe, the celebrated British novelist.[3] David Grimsted describes it as a "salty taste of the tide that was to engulf the stage for over half a century" (16). Set in a ruined Gothic abbey, it follows the adventures of La Motte, a hero torn between virtue and a thirst for vengeance against his enemy, the Marquis de Montalt. The two struggle over the beautiful Adeline (the daughter of de Montalt's murdered brother). In the end, justice overtakes the Marquis, while La Motte is cleared of his crimes and Adeline is restored to her rightful place. Oral Sumner Coad describes it as "more thoroughly Gothic than any of its dramatic precursors in England," and abounding in the kind of "terroristic machinery" that was unequaled on the American stage until the sensational spectacle of Matthew Lewis' *The Castle Spectre* (154). Given Dunlap's talent for painting and his painstaking attention to spectacular details, it seems hardly surprising that the settings and stage machinery accompanying the drama would attract audiences.[4] While some critics of the period viewed the excess of Gothic drama as a betrayal of Enlightenment ideals, American audiences recognized in the turbulent emotions, violence, and sordid family plots the messy struggles that the champions of classical republicanism sought to conceal in cities dotted with cold marble temples to liberty.

What strikes the historian most forcibly is the inability of its severest critics to successfully *contain* the Gothic. In 1798, the same year that Odell marks as the "outbreak" of the Gothic on the New York stage at the Park Theatre, the city's bookshops brimmed with tempting fare such as *The Mysteries of Udolpho*, *The Haunted Cavern*, *The Haunted Priory*, and *Count Roderick's Castle, or Gothic Times*.[5] Theatre managers promised audiences sensational spectacles with dramas including Matthew Lewis' *Evelina, or The Castle Spectre*, claiming, "No piece ever produced in London has attracted such curiosity or such than any dramatic representation ever seen in America."[6] Indeed, Lewis' tragedy proved an unprecedented commercial (if not critical) hit with both British and American audiences. The 1798 production of *The Castle Spectre* at Boston's Federal Street Theatre featured a "Gothick Chamber" and "subterraneous caverns."[7] In addition to its spectacular scenery, the play's plot enthralled audiences. The beautiful Evelina is murdered by the treacherous Osmond, but returns as a ghost to save her daughter, Angela, her husband, Reginald, and Angela's fiancé, Edric (secretly the Earl of Northumberland). In the climax of the play, Osmond attempts to murder Reginald, only to be stopped by Evelina's ghost. Angela snatches the very dagger that stabbed her mother so many years ago and uses it to wound Osmond (Lewis 98). The play also features the character of Hassan, Osmond's slave, stolen from his family in Africa. As Lewis observes in a note to the reader, "Hassan is a man of violent passions, and warm feelings, whose bosom is filled with the milk of human kindness, but that milk is soured by despair" (101). While Lewis may have intended Hassan as a comment on the British anti-slavery movement then gaining momentum in London, for American audiences familiar with the horrors of the Saint Domingue uprising (later Haiti) that began in 1791, Hassan's ferocity might have suggested the unresolved "spectre" of slavery looming within their own borders.

Even as American readers and audiences roamed exotic gothic terrains in plays and novels, in their politics they conjured the Gothic as a more malignant force. A 1798 article in the *New York Commercial Advertiser* (1 March) bemoaned the divisive party politics roiling in the House of Representatives when the situation overseas – including the XYZ Affair of 1797–1798 in which French diplomats demanded bribes to cooperate with American officials, the threats to American citizens by Barbary pirates, and the bloody French Revolution – seemed likely to unleash a "gothic reign" as "hideous as any that ever blotted the page of history." But the Gothic was also a form that, even as early as 1801, gave itself to political parody – particularly with regard to American leaders "stung with lust of power," as the *New York Commercial Advertiser* lamented (1 March, 1798). For example, J. Horatio Nichols' closet dramas, *Jefferson and Liberty, or Celebration of the Fourth of March* (1801) and *The Essex Junto, or, Quixotic Guardian* (1802), invoke familiar staples of Gothic dramas to satirize what some Democratic-Republicans viewed as the excesses of the Federalist party. In *The Essex Junto*, the evil Duke of Braintree (John Adams) and the lustful General Creole (Alexander Hamilton) kidnap the daughter of the Old Patriot (George Washington). The lovely Virginia is torn from her fiancé, Monticello (Thomas Jefferson), and imprisoned. Nichols' playlet sets scenes in remote castles, rustic cottages, lonely prisons, and even one locale entitled the "caverns of delusion" (Nichols, *The Essex Junto* 12). Like Lewis' *The Castle Spectre*, Nichols' work also invokes the threat of escaping slaves. And, as Michelle Granshaw notes, Nichols paints Alexander Hamilton as the evil Federalist villain "General Creole." In so doing, Nichols draws on negative stereotypes of native West Indian characters as intemperate, violent, prospective seducers. The image would have resonated with American audiences and certainly with negative Democratic-Republican representations of Hamilton (Granshaw 3). His other play, *Jefferson and Liberty*, also features wild romantic forests and dungeons in which republican heroes lie imprisoned, mourning the fate of liberty (see Nichols' *Jefferson and Liberty*).

If Nichols highlighted the dangers of despotism through satirical Gothic dramas burlesquing the clichés of the genre, Jewish American playwright Samuel B. H. Judah used exotic settings to convey messages about the dangers of class warfare. In Judah's *The Rose of Arragon, or, the Vigil of St. Mark* (1822), Prince Aurelio has deserted his court to woo a country maiden, Rosaline, leaving the country prey to the treacherous Count Laranda. Laranda captures both Rosaline and Aurelio. As rescuers rush to free the imprisoned pair, Rosaline stabs the count and saves the day. The final tableau closes on the lovers embracing while Rosaline's rescued father, Benorio, looks on benevolently (Judah 38).

Judah's drama emerged at a moment when urbanization, early westward expansion, and the growth of the slave economy were challenging the image of Thomas Jefferson's simple "yeoman farmer." While 1807 marked the official end of the Atlantic slave trade, slavery itself remained the foundation of the nation's commerce. Judah's New York was still five years away from realizing its gradual emancipation project, and residents felt the tension in ongoing debates between working class white citizens and growing populations of free blacks vying for resources and cultural authority. Moreover, although Judah came from a well-established family, as a Jewish American he was still marginalized because of his faith. Indeed, Jews often found themselves accused of crimes equal to those of any Gothic villain (such as draining the blood of Christians to bake into Passover cakes), and the figure of the Wandering Jew appeared frequently in Gothic novels and on stage around the turn of the nineteenth century.

In addition to its story of class struggle, Judah's drama underscores the dangers of political and patriarchal despotism, a theme also highlighted in James Nelson Barker's 1824 Gothic melodrama, *Superstition, or the Fanatic Father*. Barker's play unfolds during the Salem Witchcraft Trials. It explores the dangers of religious extremism, and is noteworthy for the creation of Reverend Ravensworth, whose plotting leads to the death of his daughter's fiancé, Charles Fitzroy.[8] As Wendel Craker suggests, with its diatribes against mob rule, the play "roams the unstable ideological borders between zealotry and fanaticism," as it "others" those characters – whether Caucasian or Native American – who do not conform to a particular ideal (490). Scholars of American Gothic literature such as Peter K. Garrett, Charles L. Crow, Robert K. Martin, and Eric Savoy have noted that Puritanism and rural New England eventually provided fodder for authors such as Nathaniel Hawthorne, Edgar Allan Poe, Edith Wharton, and Eugene O'Neill. But while the cold desolation of the northern landscape offered settings for supernatural sensations, elsewhere emerging urban environments exposed another aspect of the American Gothic: moral corruption.

Atrocities Almost Too Horrible for Belief

As Karen Haltunnen, Tyler Anbinder, John Frick, Patricia Cline Cohen, and others have argued, the rapid urbanization of the United States in the 1820s–1850s complicated social relationships between the emerging middle classes and ever-expanding populations of working class and urban poor. Shadowy specters of criminals, prostitutes, and disenfranchised young men lurked on the fringes of bourgeois awareness, examples of what might happen to those who strayed from the paths of rectitude. These shadows crept into theatres as urban-underworld dramas of crime and temperance gained popularity on the national stage. By the 1840s, a new genre of American city-mysteries, popularized by French author Eugène Sue, showed audiences all walks of city life. David Reynolds argues that these stories, "reflected the profound fears and fantasies" of urban Americans. He characterizes them as more "nightmarish and stylistically wild" than their European counterparts, "envisioning unbridled depravity among the rich and squalid wretchedness among the urban poor" (82).

Perhaps not surprisingly, during this period urban theatres grew more segregated by class. For example, in New York, urban elites retreated to plush enclaves such as the Astor Place Opera House, while middle class audiences embraced the Park Street Theatre or Niblo's Garden, and lower classes flocked to the Bowery Theatre. Moral reform melodramas such as *The Drunkard* (1844) became popular fare, but they often incorporated sensation scenes reminiscent of early Gothic dramas to attract audiences. However, when the stories depicted onstage invoked sensations too close to home, scandal and furor ensued. American theatregoers tacitly acknowledged elements of gothic corruption among particular segments of society, but protested when they became too familiar.

Thus, a tremendous theatrical *non*-event took place in Philadelphia on 11 November 1844. George Lippard's *The Quaker City, or The Monks of Monk Hall*, a scandalous Gothic novel that drew on the controversial trial of Singleton Mercer who had been acquitted for the murder of his sister's seducer, was adapted for the stage and proposed for the Chestnut Street Theatre in Philadelphia. Readers had devoured Lippard's version of the tale (which Lippard dedicated to Charles Brockden Brown; for more on Lippard, see Cassuto [Chapter 11] in this volume). It opens with a dying lawyer confiding a mysterious packet to his protégé. In them lie tales of unavenged crimes, secret murders, and "atrocities almost too horrible for belief" (Lippard 3). How could the dramatized version, which promised salacious scenes of corruption and revenge, fail to entice audiences? According to the *New York Herald* (13 November 1844), rumors of the play's debut sent "ladies into hysterics" and "gentlemen swore" as everyone alternated between "tantalizing suspense and agonizing despair." The *Herald* claimed that several of the prominent citizens mentioned in the play had approached Philadelphia's mayor to shut down the show. He pressured the manager, Francis C. Wemyss, who substituted a comedy for that evening's performance. Wemyss may have been concerned that the throngs gathering around the playhouse would destroy it if he failed to give in. The article describing the uproar warns New York theatregoers against any attempt to bring the show to that city. Describing it as "trashy, verbose, soporific," the *Herald* dismissed it as "one of those abortive and flatulent imitations of the absorbing Mysteries of Paris" (13 November 1844). However, as Aaron Tobiason and Sari Altschuler suggest, Wemyss transgressed not only in producing the play, but in proposing to share it with working-class and African American audiences whom he encouraged to attend his theatre. Perhaps the real danger of Lippard's Gothic melodrama lay in Wemyss' crossing of racial and class boundaries. Though the play itself does not survive, the playbill promises a scene in which a Negro character known as "Devil-Bug" dreams of a dystopian world one hundred years in the future (Altschuler and Tobiason 269). How might local Philadelphia audiences still reeling from violent race riots in Moyamensing earlier that year react to a futuristic vision of a city that might be dominated by African American leaders?

The Spell of Impending Doom

Playwright, abolitionist, and former slave William Wells Brown claimed that "Slavery has never been represented. Slavery never *can* be represented" (qtd. in Ernest 1). Yet Brown and other nineteenth-century authors turned to the Gothic to convey some small sense of slavery's horrors (on this point, see also Weinauer [Chapter 6] in this volume). As Maisha Webster argues, "Slaves' use of Gothic conventions brings them to the point of the unknowable" (40). Brown's play *The Escape, or a Leap for Freedom* (1858) intertwines the familiar Gothic trope of the innocent woman menaced by a powerful man with a more subversive commentary on slavery, since the heroine, Melinda, is a slave, and the man who threatens her with rape is her "master," Gaines. He cloisters her in a secluded cabin in a dark forest – an image that would have resonated with American audiences accustomed to Gothic spectacle, with the added onstage tension of interracial conflict.

Similarly, George Aiken's adaptation of Harriet Beecher Stowe's blockbuster novel *Uncle Tom's Cabin* invoked Gothic spectacle to heighten its impact on viewers. Stowe's original novel incorporated Gothic elements of the supernatural.[9] For example, escaping slaves Cassie and Emmeline disguise themselves as ghosts to trick superstitious slaveholder Simon Legree. Aiken's stage adaptation layers in another Gothic element that explains Legree's credulity. Near the end of the play, after Legree orders a savage beating for Tom, Legree's henchmen hand him a piece of paper in which Tom had wrapped one of Little Eva's curls. The sight recalls Legree's dead mother. He shudders as he recollects, "Often in the deep night ... I have seen that pale mother rising by my bed-side, and felt the soft twining of that hair around my fingers 'till the cold sweat would roll down my face and I would spring from my bed in horror." Cassie revels in his fright, calling it "a spell of terror and remorse" (Aiken 438). Aiken uses the mother's ghost to lend credibility to Cassie's trick later in the play *and* to suggest that Legree already suffered from a guilty conscience. The Gothic, with its emphasis on the power of the imagination, offered the ideal tool for conveying the "invisible" horrors of slavery to white, Northern theatregoers.

The Last of the Old Gothic Strain

By the late nineteenth century, the American fetish for the Gothic had largely given way to a taste for Realism and Naturalism, inspired by trends in European drama led by artists of the Théâtre Libre and playwrights such as Henrik Ibsen and August Strindberg. Within the United States, images from Jacob Riis' *How the Other Half Lives* (1890) and novels such as Stephen

Crane's *Maggie, A Girl of the Streets* (1893) stripped urban life of its picturesque Gothic qualities (see Elbert and Ryden [Chapter 3] in this volume). Onstage, the Gothic shifted to parody or the decorative, as in now-forgotten comedies such as *Katty O'Sheal* (1870) and *Barney the Baron* (1880). And a different kind of spectacle emerged in musical extravaganzas such as *The Black Crook* (1866), which dazzled audiences with leggy dancers in tights.

Elements of the Gothic resurfaced with the rise of the Little Theatre Movement, most notably in the works of Susan Glaspell and Eugene O'Neill. One of the founders of the Provincetown Players, Glaspell gained renown as a playwright, journalist, and novelist. The stripped-down aesthetic of the Little Theatre Movement, the small spaces in which artists performed, and the minimal budgets of those fledgling companies eliminated the option for the same sensational scenic effects that had thrilled earlier audiences. Thus, Glaspell, O'Neill, and other early twentieth-century American playwrights relied on language and symbols to generate a Gothic atmosphere. While nineteenth-century playwrights incorporated Gothic elements to inspire moral reform and to reinforce unwritten codes of Christian paternalism,[10] early twentieth-century writers deployed the Gothic to call attention to social injustice. As Linda Ben-Zvi notes of Glaspell's murder-mystery drama, *Trifles* (1916), the author "externalizes" the desperation of farm wife Minnie Wright who has strangled her husband in response to his long history of mental and/or physical abuse. The "trifles" of the play, including the shattered jam jars, the mangled birdcage, the dead bird, and the disrupted kitchen, reflect the "broken, cold, imprisoning" world the character endures (Ben-Zvi 154). These elements create what Ben-Zvi describes as a "dark, foreboding, gothic scene" that set the stage for an audience to acquit Minnie Wright of her husband's murder and to "see what might cause women to kill" (154).

While Eugene O'Neill often explored the darker side of the human psyche by invoking contemporary psychology or models from classical Greek theatre, many of his works also feature sensational elements that reflect the legacy of the nineteenth-century Gothic stage. For example, scholars have noted that O'Neill's one-act *The Emperor Jones* (1920) juxtaposes the contemporary movement toward expressionism alongside relics of the Gothic. Jones is an African American laborer who reinvents himself as emperor of a small island only to be toppled from power and driven into the island's forest by his former subjects. There he finds not only his enemies but the ghosts of his own past and those of the whole African American people. The blend of the expressionistic and the Gothic appears most notably in Jones' forest encounter with the "Little Formless Fears" that O'Neill describes as "black, shapeless, only their glittering little eyes can be seen. If they have any describable form at all it is that of a grubworm about the size of a creeping child" (O'Neill *The Emperor Jones*). While these figures owe much to the language of psychoanalysis circulating in early twentieth-century American culture, they also recall the specters described in *Uncle Tom's Cabin* in their effort to paint the legacy of racism.

O'Neill's opening stage description for *Desire under the Elms* (1924) paints another classic Gothic scene: "Two enormous elms are on each side of the house ... There is a sinister maternity in their aspect, a crushing, jealous absorption. They have developed from their intimate contact with the life of man in the house an appalling humaneness" (1). The phrase "an appalling humaneness" suggests a re-envisioning of the Gothic on the American stage, as dramatists such as O'Neill, Glaspell, and others used it to reveal America's darker legacies of racial and gender discrimination. By the 1940s and 1950s, American playwrights would turn to the Gothic to explore the nation's history of homophobia as well.

Scholars of American drama have long acknowledged traces of the Gothic imagination in Tennessee Williams' plays, with his penchant for claustrophobic settings and characters haunted by the ghosts of their pasts. In *Queer Gothic*, George Haggerty discusses the power of the Gothic to encode performances of "perverse pleasure" and sexual transgression on stage (indeed, he traces this phenomenon all the way back to *The Castle Spectre*). For Haggerty, the Gothic enables a "revolution in the coding and decoding of sexual identities" (84). Amanda in *The Glass Menagerie* (1944), Blanche in *A Streetcar Named Desire* (1947), and Violet Venable in *Suddenly Last Summer* (1958) are haunted by the ghosts of the men they have betrayed or driven away. While the ghosts never appear onstage, Williams summons them using the same kind of spectacular language and even some of the same kinds of effects used on the nineteenth-century stage. For example, Violet Venable, whose closeted son Sebastian was cannibalized by the young men he wanted to seduce, lives in a "mansion of Victorian Gothic style" crusted with Gothic trappings that border on the burlesque. In the opening scene, Williams describes the mansion's greenhouse as teeming with "violent" colors and "massive tree-flowers that suggest organs of a body, torn-out, still glistening with undried blood." The garden crackles with "harsh cries and sibilant hissings and thrashing sounds" (Williams 5). While the Gothic has never been a genre noted for its subtlety, Williams seems to incorporate it to call attention to the "underlying dreadfulness in modern experience," and the things that had to be left unsaid in 1950s American culture, which still criminalized homosexuality and still ostracized openly gay men and women (Bak 227). (For more on the queer Gothic, see Haefele-Thomas [Chapter 8] in this volume; see Crow in this volume [Chapter 10] for more on Tennessee Williams.)

The Great Work Begins

The experimentalism of the 1960s and 1970s brought an influx of new artists to the American stage, including playwright Sam Shepard, whose poetical dramas reflect the popularity of drug culture and the disaffected voice of young Americans disgusted by the Vietnam War, Watergate, and widespread political corruption. Additionally, by the mid-1970s, a slowing international economy, a worldwide oil crisis, and rising inflation produced an economic depression that hit working- and middle-class Americans hard. It undermined the postwar economic boom of the 1950s, and destabilized notions of the "American Dream."

This disillusionment appears in Shepard's *Buried Child* (1979), which recalls nineteenth-century Gothic tales with its story of a young man's return to his long-abandoned home where his family remains haunted by the terrible secret of a murdered child (the product of an incestuous relationship between mother and son). Shepard often turned to the supernatural to expose what Herbert Blau describes as the "equivocal violence" and terror of the "empty incognito" in the American dream. Blau imagines Shepard's Gothic scenarios as a comment on the capitalist machine mowing down the remains of the American frontier. Shepard's landscapes are haunted not by ruined castles as in earlier Gothic dramas, but with an "overgrowth of nature gone to seed" (Blau 525–26). Similarly, Stephen Sondheim's 1979 *Sweeney Todd: The Demon Barber of Fleet Street* imagines the Gothic as a mechanized force of darkness. Set in industrialized London, the musical depicts capitalism as a device that literally grinds its victims into sausage, as Todd slashes the throats of his patrons and Mrs. Lovett bakes them into pies. But its horror exposes the struggle of the poor to survive, as Todd sings, "The history of the world my sweet/Is who gets eaten and who gets to eat."[11]

By the 1990s, American playwrights turned to the Gothic to help exorcise the ghosts of the nation's troubled past. August Wilson's 1990 drama, *The Piano Lesson*, chronicles an African American family's slave legacy. Boy Willie wants to sell the family's piano to purchase the land where his family once lived in bondage. The piano is carved with the faces of family members sold in exchange for the instrument. His sister, Berniece, claims that the piano represents their only link with those lost ancestors. At the climax of the play, Boy Willie encounters the ghost of the slaveholder, Sutter, and finally faces the demons that haunt his family. Kathleen Brogan has described Wilson's drama as a new kind of "cultural haunting" that emerged in the latter decades of the twentieth century. As Brogan argues, Wilson and other playwrights "turn to the supernatural to examine the troubled transmission of immigrant, slave, or native cultures" (Brogan 4).

Tony Kushner looks at cultural hauntings in the "melting pot where nothing melted" through his 1993 drama *Angels in America* (10). Exploring the impact of AIDS in 1980s America, he presents characters struggling with the consequences of their histories and their choices. Kushner depicts McCarthy-era attorney Roy Cohn as a "marvelous Gothic hero-villain," facing the ghosts of his past, including Ethel Rosenberg, a woman he helped condemn for treason (Edmundson 169). Cluttered with outlandish special effects, *Angels* comes full circle to the "outbreak of Gothic horror" on America's post-Revolutionary stage two centuries before. Kushner incorporates the sensational spectacles of early American melodrama, simultaneously revealing the mechanisms behind the effects, as when an angel crashes through the ceiling of a dying Prior Walter, proclaiming, "The great work begins" (Kushner 290). As critics have noted, Prior's response, "Very Steven Spielberg," simultaneously acknowledges the impact of the sensation while underscoring its manipulative quality (J. Fisher 49).

Far more than a passing fad, the Gothic ultimately proved curiously adaptable for American playwrights, and perhaps the greatest measure of its success lies in its persistence throughout contemporary American culture. As Catherine Spooner notes, it can be "progressive or conservative, nostalgic or modern, comic or tragic, political or apolitical, feminine or masculine, erudite or trashy, transcendentally spiritual or doggedly material, sinister or silly" (Spooner 156). Whether blatantly sensationalistic or more subtly spectacular in its effects, the Gothic developed as a form that allowed audiences to confront fears about racism, sexism, political corruption, and homophobia, revealing both an "appalling humaneness" and an appalling humanity as well.

NOTES

1. From various ads for theatrical entertainments in newspapers such as *The Gazette of the United States* [Philadelphia, PA] 7 Apr. 1800; *The American Citizen* 3 July 1810; and *The Boston Gazette* 28 Mar. 1811.
2. Also see Ledoux and Malenas; Samuels.
3. The title of the play is sometimes given as *Fontainville Forest*, and Fisher notes that Dunlap may have been aware of the 1794 British version of the novel by James Boaden, *Fontainville Forest*. Advertisements sometimes conflate the two.
4. See the review in the *Boston Polar Star* 28 Oct. 1796.
5. Titles recorded in *The Weekly Museum* [New York, NY] 6 Jan. 1798.
6. *Russell's Gazette* [Boston, MA] 28 Nov. 1798.
7. *Russell's Gazette* [Boston, MA] 28 Nov. 1798.
8. For a detailed discussion of Barker's drama, see Miller's *Entertaining the Nation*.
9. See Haltunnen's "Gothic Imagination and Social Reform: The Haunted Houses of Lyman Beecher, Henry Ward Beecher, and Harriet Beecher Stowe."

10. For an extended discussion of the role of paternalism in the shaping of nineteenth-century bourgeois melodrama, see McConachie's *Melodramatic Formations*.
11. As Erin Bone Steele writes, Sondheim's version of *Sweeney Todd* represents one of many over the past century. For more, see Steele, "Melodramatic Borrowings."

WORKS CITED

Aiken, George L. *Uncle Tom's Cabin*. Early American Drama. Ed. Jeffrey H. Richards. New York: Penguin, 1997. 368–443.
Altschuler, Sari and Aaron M. Tobiason. "Playbill for George Lippard's *The Quaker City*." *PMLA* 129.2 (2014): 267–73.
American Citizen. America's Historical Newspapers. Web. 5 Feb. 2016.
Anthony, Susan M. *Gothic Plays and American Society, 1794–1830*. Jefferson: McFarland & Co., 2008.
Bak, John S. "'Sneakin' and Spyin' from Broadway to the Beltway: Cold War Masculinity, Brick, and Homosexual Existentialism." *Theatre Journal* 56.2 (2004): 225–49.
Ben-Zvi, Linda. "'Murder, She Wrote': The Genesis of Susan Glaspell's *Trifles*." *Theatre Journal* 44.2 (1992): 141–62.
Blau, Herbert "The American Dream in American Gothic: The Plays of Sam Shepard and Adrienne Kennedy." *Modern Drama* 27.4 (1984): 520–39.
Boker, George Henry. *Leonor De Guzman*. Philadelphia: J. B. Lippincott & Co., 1883. Literature Online. Web. 5 Feb. 2016.
Boston Gazette, America's Historical Newspapers, Web. 5 Feb. 2016.
Brogan, Kathleen. *Cultural Haunting: Ghosts and Ethnicity in Recent American Literature*. Charlottesville: University Press of Virginia, 1998.
Coad, Oral Sumner. *William Dunlap: A Study of his Life and Works and his Place in Contemporary Culture*. New York: DeVinne Press, 1917.
Craker, Wendel D. "Spectral Evidence, Non-Spectral Acts of Witchcraft in Salem in 1692." *New Perspectives on Witchcraft and Demonology*. Ed. Brian P. Levack. London: Routledge, 2001.
Edmundson, Mark. *Nightmare on Main Street: Angels, Sadomasochism, and the Culture of Gothic*. Cambridge, MA: Harvard University Press, 1999.
Ernest, John, ed. *The Oxford Handbook of the African American Slave Narrative*. New York: Oxford University Press, 2014.
Fisher, Benjamin F. "Early American Gothic Drama." *A Companion to American Gothic*. Ed. Charles L. Crow. New York: Wiley Blackwell, 2014.
Fisher, James. *Understanding Tony Kushner*. Columbia: University of South Carolina Press, 2009.
Gazette of the United States. Web. 5 Feb. 2016.
Granshaw, Michelle. "General Creole: Jon H. Nichols's Political Plays in the Early American Republic." *New England Theatre Journal* 21 (2010): 1–23.
Grimsted, David. *Melodrama Unveiled: American Theater and Culture, 1800–1850*. 1968. Berkeley: University of California Press, 1987.
Haggerty, George E. *Queer Gothic*. Urbana: University of Illinois Press, 2006.
Hughes, Amy E. *Spectacles of Reform: Theater and Activism in Nineteenth-Century America*. Ann Arbor: University of Michigan Press, 2012.

Judah, Samuel B. H. *The Rose of Arragon, or, The Vigil of St. Mark: A Melo-drama in Two Acts*. New York: S. King, 1822.

Kushner, Tony. *Angels in America: A Gay Fantasia on National Themes*. New York: Theatre Communications Group, 2013.

Lewis, M.G. *The Castle Spectre: A Drama in Five Acts*. London: Printed for J. Bell, 1798. University of Michigan Digital Library Text Collections. Web. 2 Feb. 2016.

Lippard, George. *The Quaker City, or The Monks of Monk Hall*. Philadelphia: Leary, Stuart & Company, 1876. Archive.org. Web. 5 Feb. 2016.

Murphy, Brenda. *The Theatre of Tennessee Williams*. New York: Bloomsbury, 2014.

New York Commercial Advertiser. America's Historical Newspapers, Web. 5 Feb. 2016.

New York Herald. America's Historical Newspapers, Web. 5 Feb. 2016.

Nichols, J. Horatio. *Jefferson and Liberty: Or, Celebration of the Fourth of March*. n. p., 1801. Early American Imprints, Series 2. Web. 2 Feb. 2016.

The Essex Junto, or, Quixotic Guardian. Salem: Printed by Nathaniel Coverly, 1802. Early American Imprints, Series 2. Web. 2 Feb. 2016.

O'Neill, Eugene. *Desire Under the Elms*. 2nd edn. New York: Boni and Liveright, 1925. Project Gutenberg. Web. 5 Feb. 2016.

O'Neill, Eugene. *The Emperor Jones*. O'Neill.com. Web. 5 Feb. 2016.

Odell, George C. *Annals of the New York Stage*. Vol. 2. New York: Columbia University Press, 1927.

Reynolds, David S. *Beneath the American Renaissance: The Subversive Imagination in the Age of Emerson and Melville*. New York: Oxford University Press, 2011.

Russell's Gazette [Boston, MA]. America's Historical Newspapers. Web. 5 Feb. 2016.

Spooner, Catherine. *Contemporary Gothic*. London: Reaktion Books, 2007.

The British Drama: A Collection of the Most Approved Tragedies, Comedies, Operas, and Farces in Two Volumes. London: Jones and Company, 1824. Archive.org, 5 Feb. 2015.

Webster, Maisha L. *African American Gothic: Screams from Shadowed Places*. New York: Palgrave Macmillan, 2012.

Weekly Museum, America's Historical Newspapers, Web. 5 Feb. 2016.

Williams, Tennessee. *Suddenly Last Summer*. New York: Dramatists Play Service, 1986.

15

CAROL MARGARET DAVISON

Gothic American Film & TV

America's century-long dark romance with the Gothic on the big and small screens has been culturally compelling, visceral, and commercially successful. These distinctive productions have been characterized by technological innovation, which has served to intensify graphic realism aimed to thrill and repulse, as well as an increasing reflexivity and capacity for sociopolitical and cultural critique. American Gothic cinema and television are driven, putatively, by the primary objective of horrifying/terrifying their viewers with what may be described as a "controlled" (because imaginary) nightmare that generates for many, like its Gothic literary counterpart, a pleasurable terror. More compelling, however, for cultural scholars is the special lens these cultural productions cast on America, interrogating that nation's conception of itself as a utopia already achieved (Baudrillard 77) while bringing its changing individual and collective dreams and nightmares over the course of decades – classifiable under such regional and subject categories as the Southern Gothic (see Crow [Chapter 10] in this volume), the urban Gothic (see Cassuto [Chapter 11] in this volume), and "Hillbilly Horror" – into sharper, more disturbing focus.

This chapter assesses developments in Gothic film and television from a periodized perspective, mainly by decade, honing in primarily on the changing cautionary, culturally constructed figure of the monster that is frequently employed to mediate various primal yet sublime terrors and taboos, and the often consanguineous concepts of monstrosity and evil. Foremost among these terrors and taboos, and consistent across the century, is the fear of death that is evoked by the sublime, according to Edmund Burke, the philosopher and cultural critic who theorized about pleasurable terror in the mid-eighteenth century (96). In an increasingly death-denying American culture, the sublime terror of death, as variously manifested, inheres in the figure of the death-defying, death-wielding "monster," whether human or supernatural, and his/her/its abjected/spectral/monstrous body. Meditations about the sources, nature, and attractions of evil as socially and religiously defined and proscribed are likewise mediated through the monster/monstrous.

The voyeuristic, vicarious engagement with evil has long been a key attraction in Gothic cinematic and televisual productions. Stephen King, for example, describes the appeal of the horror movie in *Danse Macabre* as offering "an invitation to indulge in deviant, antisocial behavior by proxy – to commit gratuitous acts of violence, indulge our puerile dreams of power, to give in to our most craven fears. Perhaps more than anything else, the horror story or horror movie says it's okay to join the mob, to become the 'total tribal being, to destroy the outsider" (31). King's theory about audience identification with the monster fails to recognize the complex representation of this figure as filmmakers often promote audience identification with the community combating the monster. His statements nevertheless go to the heart of longstanding debates about spectatorship and the perspective of the "monster"/killer, a perspective frequently – and contentiously – deemed to be gendered, like horror cinema more generally, as male (Jancovich, "1940s" 248). They also tap into concerns about Gothic cinema's potentially pernicious influence, concerns that have consistently given rise to censorship laws and codes designed, since the first appearance of these works, to restrict and police them. As far back as 1915, during the early days of silent film, the United States Supreme Court denied free speech protection to cinema based on the medium's putative capacity "for evil, having power for it, the greater because of the attractiveness and manner of exhibition" (Gunning 22). King's observation also suggests the violation of the (in)famous Motion Picture Production (Hays) Code of 1930 that delineated a specific set of "moral" regulations, and restricted representations ranging from miscegenation and homosexuality, to the deterrence of audience identification with evildoers.

As in the case with Gothic literature, Gothic film and television generate terror by playing on anxieties about boundaries of the self that extend to boundaries of the family, community, and nation. The theme of transformation and/or annihilation of subjectivity/individuality where, as Eugenia C. DeLamotte claims, "[w]hat was x becomes y, the line dividing them dissolving" (21) constitutes the principal threat. As the American Gothic repeatedly reveals in its fixation on antisocial forces either invading from without or being bred from within (homegrown terrorism), and antifamily values' acts like incest and matricide, transgression of the boundary between x and y is a two-way street: The self may be threatened by an Other and/or revealed itself to be Other. The threats in the twentieth and twenty-first centuries are but new adaptations of the monstrous terrors of the eighteenth- and nineteenth-century Gothic: Internal and external threats are made against an individual's self-control, self-awareness, subjectivity, autonomy, and agency as rendered most intimately and immediately through the body. While a shift occurs from the 1930s/1940s Creature Features and 1950s alien-invasion films that spotlight the spectacularized monster/alien as an external threat to the last quarter of the century where the monster is increasingly humanized and psychologically dissected yet socially dangerous, various forms of late twentieth-century body horror – slasher, splatter, and "torture porn" films – position the human body as itself monstrous and alien. Filtered through a Gothic lens and assuming such forms as vampirization, zombification, and demonic/alien/technological possession, this Othered body is vulnerable to such threats and terrors of advanced capitalism as invincible viruses, mass surveillance and censorship, and various forms of literal objectification and consumption.

From Silent Terror to the 1950s

American Gothic cinema of the silent era (the 19-teens and 1920s) established gloomy mise-en-scènes, its diverse cultural influences ranging from German Expressionist cinema to the American freak show. Drawing on a wide range of narratives, especially Anglo-American Gothic literature (including Poe) and contemporary works of terror, and employing such enticing themes as mesmerism and the supernatural, these early silents, like the 1930s Creature Features that followed, focused on the spectacular physical/visual nature of the monster, and evoked brooding atmospherics, effects that were accomplished with the assistance of German film luminaries who fostered Expressionism like Friedrich Murnau (*Nosferatu*, 1922), Fritz Lang (*Metropolis*, 1927), Paul Leni (*The Cat and the Canary*, 1927), and Karl Freund (*The Golem*, 1920), all of whom emigrated to Hollywood in the 1920s and 1930s.

Although the "motion" picture was rendered more compelling as a result of its transformation into the "talking" picture at the close of the 1920s, many 1930s horror-talkies appear slow and stilted, having begun life – like Tod Browning's *Dracula* (1931) – as stage plays. Experimenting, in the style of seminal French filmmaker Georges Méliès, with the cinematic apparatus as a mesmerizing modern technology that self-reflexively represented mesmerizing monsters by way of superimpositions, dissolves, split screens, intercutting, and point-of-view, filmmakers tried different monsters on for size. This was especially true at Universal Studios, "a factory of horror" (Browning 235) that saw the production – on the heels of *The Hunchback of Notre Dame* (Wallace Worsley, 1923) and *The Phantom of the Opera* (Rupert Julian, 1925), both starring Lon Chaney – of such classics as Tod Browning's *Dracula* (1931), James Whale's *Frankenstein* (1931) and *The*

Invisible Man (1933), and Karl Freund's *The Mummy* (1932). While these creatures satisfied the need for audience escapism in the devastating face of the Great Depression, they often promoted sympathy for the unjustly alienated monsters who, according to Noel Carroll, "signaled the depression anxiety of being cast out of civil society due to impoverishment" (215). Like classic Anglo-American Gothic works of the late eighteenth century, these Creature Features also repeatedly registered the collision of superstitious Old World ideas and those of the rational, scientific New World, an ideological battle that resonated with immigrant viewers who were themselves wrestling with such conflicts – Old World superstitions and legends usually being granted legitimacy in order to enhance their terrifying effects and increase box-office returns. Anticipating the more reflexive horror films of the late twentieth century, Browning's quintessentially American yet bizarre *Freaks* (1932), banned in Britain for three decades, promoted the sympathetic monster theme of the 1930s while turning the camera back uncomfortably on its audiences, forcing them, as suggested by the freaks' famous "One of us!" chorus, to reflect on the concept of the monster and the public taste for "monstrous" spectacle.

Drawing on longstanding views dating back at least to the Salem Witch Trials, fin-de-siècle British Gothic literature, and the popular Anglo-American spiritualist movement, films like *Dracula* (1931), *Frankenstein* (1931), and *White Zombie* (Victor Hugo Halperin, 1932) associated women with the supernatural/superstitious, their minds and bodies a battlefield between seductive forces and patriarchal males (often rational scientists, men of faith, and fiancés). Amid the creation of the second cycle of Universal horror films, and such wartime propaganda horrors featuring Nazi and Japanese villain-scientists as *The King of the Zombies* (Jean Yarbrough, 1941) and *Black Dragons* (William Nigh, 1942) starring Béla Lugosi, anxieties about the control over women's bodies were ramped up as significant numbers of women entered the workforce. The demand for films to satisfy female audiences grew in conjunction with the entry of more women screenwriters into Hollywood (Hanson 9).

This cataclysmic shift in the national labor force, in conjunction with the anxieties it incited about women's new-found economic and – as it was socially perceived – sexual freedom, also left its mark on the movie industry, especially Gothic cinema, which exhibited a growing fascination with character psychology. The detective aspects of the film noir mystery thriller, with its magnetically seductive femmes fatales and contrasting chiaroscuro mise-en-scènes that captured a character's inner turmoil, were extended in horror film to the psychological probing of haunted heroes/heroines and the darker side and motives of human "monsters"/killers, fixations retained in Gothic cinema into the twenty-first century. Such mysteries as David O. Selznick's *Jane Eyre* (1943), advertised as a "romantic horror tale" (Jancovich *Horror*, 242), and Alfred Hitchcock's *Rebecca* (1940), a rewrite of *Jane Eyre* later classified as a "woman's film," employed a Female Gothic recipe that retained the romance plot while registering marital fears of the husband turned prison-master/murderer. (For more on film noir, see Cassuto [Chapter 10] in this volume; for more on the Female Gothic, see Hoeveler [Chapter 7].)

Rebecca was influential to the terror/thriller branch of American Gothic cinema, serving as the breeding ground for the more subtle, psychologically suggestive terror crafted by Val Lewton who worked as Selznick's story editor. Subsequently secured to set up RKO's horror unit, Lewton produced, among other films, *Cat People* (1942), and *I Walked with a Zombie* (1943), both directed by Jacques Tourneur, works retrospectively described as "stand[ing] out as chamber music against the seedy bombast of the claw-and-fang epics of the day" (Clarens 111). Marked by a "distinctive use of light and shade" (Tudor 34), *Cat People* tells the story of a young Serbian woman who believes she turns into a cat when sexually aroused. It plays out, through the distorted lens of horror, contemporary American medical debates about the source of and cure for female frigidity – either physical or psychoanalytic – during a decade that saw the popularization of Freudian psychoanalysis. *I Walked with a Zombie* follows suit, featuring another psychiatrically medicalized wife, a woman caught in an "incestuous" love triangle between two brothers, where the supernatural is granted veracity and associated with a foreign, atavistic Other who signals sexual desire and tension. In an era that witnessed the beginning of the American love affair with psychology and other behavioral sciences then being used to shape domestic, foreign, and military policy, psychiatry is notably at the forefront of many horror films, the discourse through which its "monsters" are identified and pathologized.

In a manner paralleling the advent of British fin-de-siècle invasion scare narratives like Richard Marsh's Gothic science-fiction work *The Beetle* (1897), and H. G. Wells' *The War of the Worlds* (1897), the disillusioned 1950s postwar era saw the rise of the hybrid science-fiction horror film. It registered Cold War and McCarthyite fears about a (crypto-)Communist invasion. This is exemplified in Don Siegel's *Invasion of the Body Snatchers* (1956), which chronicles the invasion and transformation of Americans into evil, replicant "pod people" in the suburbs, the new "bourgeois utopia" (Fishman 50–51), the site of the valorization of the nuclear family, the reification of gender identities and spheres (Beuka 2–3), and the consolidation of a collective, mythic national identity of shared goals and values. Perhaps most fascinating is the explanation given by a psychiatrist, after being transformed into pod form, to the medical doctor protagonist, that the "epidemic mass hysteria," probably caused by "worry about what's going on in the world," is "cured" by the pods who eliminate the pain associated with love, ambition, and faith, thereby allowing people to be "reborn into an untroubled world where everyone's the same." Thus is the dark side of the "American (conformist) Dream" that annihilates individuality equated with the leveling effects of Communist infiltration, a terror then being used to justify America's "containment strategy," its imperialist interventions in Third World nations.

This post-Hiroshima/Nagasaki era's other primary terror was the impact of chemical experimentation on human beings. In Japan, this anxiety relating to nuclear scientific technologies and their attendant threats of apocalypse was expressed in Ishiro Honda's famous *Godzilla* (1954), which featured an enormous, aggressive, primordial sea monster awakened and empowered by nuclear radiation. Dozens of updated Creature Features like *The Werewolf* (Fred F. Sears, 1956), however, centered on human-to-monster transformations by immoral, experimenting "Atom-age scientists." Notably, countless other slimy monsters of the deep proliferated in 1950s sci-fi/horror films. The *Attack of the Giant Leeches* (Bernard L. Kowalski, 1959), Roger Corman's *Attack of the Crab Monsters* (1957), and *The Alligator People* (Roy Del Ruth, 1959) were all used to suggest the huge contrast, along evolutionary lines, between the ultra-primordial and the "civilized," a gulf readily and horrifyingly breeched due to the atavistic instincts and practices underpinning "advanced" nations and technologies. The objective of producing a graphic, more realistic terror was also at the forefront of 1950s horror movies, resulting in such 3D films as *House of Wax* (Andre DeToth, 1953), *It Came from Outer Space* (Jack Arnold, 1953), and *The Creature from the Black Lagoon* (Jack Arnold, 1954).

1960s and 1970s Terror

Produced by CBS, Universal's television company, *Alfred Hitchcock Presents* (1955–1965) marked one of the first entries of the Gothic into American television. Debates about the Gothic's effectiveness in that medium have been contentious and ongoing. Lenora Ledwon deems television an ideal medium for the Gothic, surpassing film, given its uncanny, ghostly effects: this "mysterious box [is] simultaneously inhabited by spirit images of ourselves and inhabiting our living rooms" (260). Others maintain that, "horror in the modern cinematic sense is not well suited to mainstream television due to broadcasting restrictions" (Robson 242). Such restrictions, however, have sometimes bred innovation – bizarre progeny that combine the Gothic with the soap opera, the family melodrama, and the situation comedy (sitcom). A mix of mysteries, dramas, and Gothic thrillers, Hitchcock's series shared a fascination with human psychology and delighted in revealing the fault lines and vulnerabilities of his middle-class audience and their suburban ideal as expressed in such popular sitcoms as *Leave It to Beaver* (1957–1963), *Ozzie and Harriet* (1952–1966), and *Father Knows Best* (1954–1960). His exposé of a morally bankrupt, monetarily obsessed society in thrall to the Rat Race and underwritten by ruthless competition and destructive conformity in his tales of criminal double-dealing paved the way for later Gothic television series like David Lynch's *Twin Peaks* (1990–1991). This critique is especially in evidence in his frequent representation of women as sexually promiscuous, greedy, deadly, and anti-maternal, alongside his portrait of the embattled institution of marriage as a site of discord, repression, and secrecy, which resonated with the American public given the legal possibility of divorce.

Such 1960s and 1970s "magicoms" – fantastic family sitcoms (Marc 107) – as *The Munsters* (1964–1966) and *The Addams Family* (1964–1966) likewise exposed the inconsistencies of the American suburban ideal while running to another modal extreme with the comic and the camp. Humor has been present in American Gothic film, to varying degrees, since its inception, where it has served "as an undercutting agent to counter-balance its more horrific moments" (Brophy 284). It especially proliferated in the 1970s when the "saturated" genre of horror cinema became marked by "horrality," a neologism coined by Philip Brophy to signal a "combination of horror, textuality, morality, [and] hilarity" (277). Presenting typical middle-class concerns in a defamiliarized way – namely, from the unique perspective of two families of monsters trying to live their conventionally deviant lives in what are represented as the intolerant suburbs – *The Munsters* and *The Addams Family* exposed the suburbs as a hyperconformist, even anti-American locale given its xenophobia and threat to individualism. Concerns about antisocial isolationism were consistently indicted in the Gothic since its advent.

Such anxiety-inducing ideas found expression in other televisual productions of the 1960s and 1970s. In its exploration of the secret lives, traumas, and transgressions of an American family over the course of two centuries, the cult phenomenon *Dark Shadows* (1966–1971), America's first Gothic soap opera, reconfigured key elements and plot lines from the rich Anglo-American Gothic tradition to speak, in its 1225 episodes, to the 1960s counterculture zeitgeist with its drive for liberation – sexual and political – and quest for alternative spiritualties. In this, and its action-packed storyline involving power struggles between warlocks, zombies, werewolves, and otherworldly creatures, it served as a wellspring of ideas for later American small-screen productions like *Buffy the Vampire Slayer* (1997–2003) and

True Blood (2008–2014). By way of two mansions on the Collins estate signifying the Old (Britain) and New Worlds (America), in combination with the unique 1950s science fiction-inspired elements of parallel universes and time-travelling sequences over two centuries, *Dark Shadows* engaged with questions of history, filiation, and inheritance, damningly reminding young Americans of their consanguinity with their forefathers. In a similar fashion, Barnabus Collins, its 175-year-old haunted, melancholic vampire who yearns to resurrect his lost lover in favor of an originary romantic ideal, registers the quintessentially Gothic tension between Old World values and New World "free love" sexual practices and mores. In this latter aspect, *Dark Shadows* also flirted with Queer Gothic (see Ardel Haefele-Thomas [Chapter 8] in this volume) in destabilizing distinct sexual identities and encouraging its audience to identify with different characters and subject positions (Benshoff, *Dark Shadows* 35–36).

American Gothic horror on the big screen in the 1960s was marked by various anxieties, the first exemplified by George A. Romero's independent black-and-white *Night of the Living Dead* (1968). This low-budget masterpiece, featuring people combating a zombie/"ghoul" attack on their town, like Siegel's *Invasion of the Body Snatchers*, employed horror to craft a trenchant social commentary. Romero's critique is dual, being directed at 1960s American domestic and international race relations in the form of the Civil Rights Movement at home and the Vietnam War abroad. Although African Americans are not implicated in the evil attack, the unheroic extermination of Ben, its assertive, smart, and articulate African American protagonist, who is swiftly dispatched by rifle-carrying white men who misidentify him as a zombie, carries forward the established link in the genre between African Americans and zombies. This closing scene is sociopolitically pointed and disjunctive as the narrative moves from Ben's survivalist heroism indoors to his reduced, denigrated position when seen, and objectified, by the posse of lynching, white vigilantes outside who summarily slaughter then hook him onto a bonfire, captured in the film's final arresting documentary photographs. *Night of the Living Dead* thus exposes – without advocating – the perpetuation of the racist American view of African Americans as mindless, enslaved but threatening monsters such as was advanced in earlier zombie films like Victor Halperin's *White Zombie* (1932), and Lewton's *I Walked With a Zombie*.[1]

Notably, while films like *King Kong* (Merian C. Cooper and Ernest B. Schoedsack, 1933) and *Candyman* (Bernard Rose, 1992) engage with race relations in America and identify miscegenation as a particularly terrifying yet titillating social transgression for which retribution occurs, some directors used the Gothic to different ends. The blaxploitation horror film *Blacula* from the early 1970s, for example, by black director William Crain, features the sympathetic Mamuwalde, a dignified African Prince used to celebrate "the Afrocentric cultural politics adopted by some branches of the Black power movement" (Medovoi 14). After calling for an end to slavery in 1780 at a dinner party at the film's opening, Mamuwalde is brutally victimized by a virulently racist Dracula, and tragically separated from his beloved wife, Luva, thus setting off a centuries-long quest for reunion. The specter of slavery and violent race relations that assume a major role in American Gothic literature, particularly in the Southern Gothic where the frequently Africanized South serves as the "repository for everything from which the nation wants to disassociate itself" (Goddu 3), sometimes remain unreferenced and unrepresented in American Gothic productions on the big screen. Despite its all-white suburban setting, for example, John Carpenter's *Halloween* (1978), featuring the psychopathic Michael Myers as the embodiment of faceless evil, was inspired, according to Carpenter, by the many random acts of extremely radicalized violence he witnessed growing up in Bowling Green, Kentucky.

The second major anxiety registered in big screen sf horror productions of the 1960s and 1970s responded to the Equal Rights Amendment (1972), Second Wave feminism, and such medical breakthroughs as the birth control pill, which disrupted established power relations by granting women more control over their bodies. In *Rosemary's Baby* (Roman Polanski, 1968), *The Exorcist* (William Friedkin, 1973), *The Stepford Wives* (Bryan Forbes, 1975), and *Carrie* (Brian De Palma, 1976), the contested terrain is the monstrous/abjected and medicalized body, especially as experienced by young women undergoing (demonic) transformations into/during womanhood and motherhood. Following from Stoker's *Dracula* (1897), terror is evoked in relation to the sexually desiring female body and the need for its social policing/control, a fear filtered through a supernatural lens, the Biblical trope of women's body as the devil's gateway being frequently literalized. Read through a feminist lens, these works chronicle contemporary Anglo-American Female Gothic fears about the monstrous constraints of sexual biology, the terror surrounding pregnancy (tokophobia), and the associated idea of women being reduced to reproductive/copulating *machines*. The era's crop of films about demonic children, including *It's Alive* (Larry Cohen, 1974), *The Omen* (1976), *Demon Seed* (Richard Donner, 1977), and *Alien* (Ridley Scott, 1979), likewise imagine horrifying mutant pregnancies, births, and offspring on the heels of the thalidomide scandal. While women's constraining roles and the carceral domestic sphere were once the primary terrors in Anglo-American Female Gothic literature, such cultural productions in the late twentieth century figure women's bodies as the site of terror because they are biologically imprisoning. Although, according to Philip Brophy, "[t]he contemporary horror film tends to play not so much on the broad fear of Death, but more precisely on the fear of one's own body, of how one controls and relates to it" (280), the woman's body is an especially terrifying site of *memento mori* abjection.

Alfred Hitchcock's masterpiece, *Psycho* (1960) lent expression to the third deep-rooted anxiety of the era – namely, the physical indistinguishability of the homicidal maniac from the average American. In the figure of Norman Bates, inspired by the mother-fixated, necrophiliac serial killer and body-snatcher Ed Gein, *Psycho* invited its viewers to psychoanalyze the make-up and motives of an apparently "normal" monster. It also gave birth, in its iconic femicidal shower sequence, to the slasher film – the most popular horror film style from the 1970s to 1990s – that focused, suspensefully, on a serial killer's acts of predation and tactile, graphic bodily violence, by way of visually fetishized sharp instruments. With the institution of the MPAA ratings system in 1968 and in the wake of the Vietnam War, which brought the horrors of war into American living-rooms for the first time, American Gothic cinema became vastly more graphic, engendering "body horror," which is characterized by a heightened sense of the body's viscerality and the camera's pleasure in gruesomely defiling it without the aid of editing (Brophy 280–81).

Serial Killers, Haunted Houses, and Beyond

Although Tobe Hooper's surprise success, *The Texas Chainsaw Massacre* (1974), operated largely on a sense of dread and implied violence, it inspired such later slasher films as *Friday the Thirteenth* (Sean S. Cunningham, 1980) and *A Nightmare on Elm Street* (Wes Craven, 1984) and set the stage for the subsequent gruesomely graphic splatter film and "torture porn" films like *Saw* (James Wen, 2004) that sought to affectively unsettle the viewer by any means necessary: While the former sought "to mortify [its viewers] with scenes of explicit gore" (McCarty 1), the latter emerged after the 9/11 attacks on America and narrativized psychological manipulation to prompt individuals to torture and kill in graphic scenes of "creative" violence and dismemberment, thus reflecting the contemporary phenomenon of military torture and massacre at a remove.

Hooper's quintessentially American Gothic slasher film features a dysfunctional, family of depraved cannibalistic serial killers deprived, significantly, of living female members. Through the younger figure of Leatherface, whose individuality is grotesquely effaced by his wearing, Gein-like, the actual faces of his victims like a mask, the suggestion is made that the family itself serves as the Frankensteinian site of monster-making. Setting aside various contentious claims about this film as a sociopolitical critique of capitalism, Andrew Tudor has persuasively argued that the vengeful, sadistic killer's "psychosis is sexual in some way and that male aggression and misogyny are significant elements within it" (202). Notably, traditional forms of authority are presented as either ineffectual or the cause of the homicidal psychosis (Jancovich, *Horror* 108), and women are shown fighting back. In this, *The Texas Chainsaw Massacre* incorporates the Female Gothic convention Carol Clover calls the Final Girl (35), the young woman who ultimately escapes, which carries through to such psychological thrillers as *The Silence of the Lambs* (Jonathan Demme, 1991), another Gein-influenced narrative.

America's fascination with serial killers on both the small and big screens in the 1980s and 1990s, theories about whose nature – whether human or monster/machine – then proliferated in studies both scientific and psychoanalytic, are long established in that nation's literary tradition. In Charles Brockden Brown's *Wieland; or The Transformation. An American Tale* (1798), the very first American Gothic novel, Carwin the Biloquist, who goads Theodore Wieland, a religious fanatic, into killing his wife and children, considers how he may have "rashly *set in motion a machine*, over whose progress [he] had no control" (242, emphasis added; on Brown, see Ringel [Chapter 1] and Hinds [Chapter 9] in this volume). Rob Zombie's 2007 remake of Carpenter's *Halloween* (1978) likewise captures this fixation in its suggestion that Michael Myers, who seems supernaturally unstoppable like Freddy Krueger in 1984's *Nightmare*, is not "a normal man" but, rather, as his psychologist Dr. Loomis states, a dehumanized "soulless killing machine driven by pure animal instinct."

Poltergeist (1982), Hooper's other major directorial hit from the following decade, showcased the haunted house, perhaps "the most persistent site ... of American gothic's allegorical turn" (Savoy 9) that had been consistently featured in literature from Hawthorne's *The House of the Seven Gables* (1851) to Toni Morrison's *Beloved* (1987), and in films ranging from *The Dark House* (James Whale, 1932) and *The Haunting* (Robert Wise, 1963), to *The Amityville Horror* (Stuart Rosenberg, 1979) and the gory *The Evil Dead* (Sam Raimi, 1981). While channeling fears around control of the self and the family in the form of an anthropomorphized locale capable of monstrously possessing its inhabitants, haunted house horror also grants spine-chilling expression to spectral encounters of an intergenerational, other worldly kind born of personal and/or political historical transgressions and traumas.

Revolutionized technologically by way of special effects like CGI that enhanced representations of the supernatural, small screen productions of the 1990s presented a different perspective on evil, the origins and nature of the serial killer, and the social proliferation of violence. While David Lynch's

Twin Peaks (1990–1991) and Shaun Cassidy's *American Gothic* (1995–1996) may be stylistically and regionally distinct – the latter granting credibility to the supernatural and being set in the South – both deploy classic American Gothic motifs like the double, "the wilderness of the self," and father-daughter incest to implicate their audiences in a domestic violence and sexual abuse epidemic that has become, each suggests, as banal, normalized, and American as apple pie. In graphic and sensational episodes, they reveal that hyperconformity yields hidden depravities, intimating that terrorist (serial) killers are likely to be homegrown yet terrifyingly unidentifiable in a shape-shifting world where, as Sheriff Lucas Buck asserts in *American Gothic*, "No one is who they appear to be."

Twenty-first century audiences may be witnessing the golden age of American Gothic on the small screen. Regionally and stylistically varied and ideologically sophisticated, the most accomplished recent expressions are provocatively self-reflexive as they mine and market – to adapt a line from Poe – terrors of America and of the soul. Visionary Gothic guru Alan Ball's two epic series for the premium cable network HBO, *Six Feet Under* (2001–5) and *True Blood* (2008–2014), advance powerful philosophical meditations – ontological and metaphysical – on the American/human condition. Premiering in June of 2001, *Six Feet Under*, which follows the lives and relationships of the Fishers, a repressed white middle-class family who own and operate a funeral home in Los Angeles, was tragically timely for a death-denying, youth-obsessed nation on the cusp of the traumatic events of 9/11 and the aftermath of reflection and mourning. Ball's series engages head-on with Arnold Toynbee's claim that Americans see death as profoundly "un-American, an affront to every citizen's inalienable right to life, liberty and the pursuit of happiness" (131). While offering a wake-up call, Ball's series employs imagined reanimated corpses to probe questions about spiritual transcendence – a consistent preoccupation in American Gothic cultural productions – and to expose America's dark underbelly of homophobia, racism, and capitalism's corruption of human relationships.

Assuming a gory "horror Gothic" mode and featuring spectacular violence between various supernatural creatures, Ball's intertextual *True Blood* features an orphaned waitress – a telepathic "freak of nature" and hybrid human-fairy – as its unlikely heroine. It is set in a Southern Gothic environment steeped in the supernatural and hoodoo where vampires have recently "come out of the coffin" during what has become known as the "Great Revelation" to live peaceably among human beings thanks to the Japanese development of synthetic blood. Sociopolitical questions relating to national citizenship, immigration, identity, and belonging that have long plagued America but were heightened in the aftermath of 9/11, are paramount as vampires fall into two camps – those who advocate integration into human society and the attainment of equal rights, and those who resist, believing coexistence impossible due to their polarized natures. Thus does Ball purposefully reconfigure the miscegenation theme and invert the traditional human-vampire dynamic to offer a literally spectacular, often violent meditation on warlike, regressive humanity. He also engages such other issues as the cut-throat nature of consumer capitalist culture and the paradoxical make-up of our myriad addictions – drugs, media/technology, sex – "fixes" that have spawned their own distinct branches of Gothic literature and film.

On big and small American screens, the Gothic has proven to be – like the monsters it features and fetishizes – a stylistically protean, popular, and hybrid-friendly mode through which to convey entertaining, emotionally powerful, nationally relevant and reflective tales ranging in horror/terror intensity across a variety of styles. Several decades ago, the televisual and cinematic American Gothic was declared to be oversaturated and critically embarrassing. Such painstakingly crafted, self-contained mini-series as *American Horror Story* (2011–), however, have attracted new audiences and been infused with new life by technically savvy, experimental writers and cinematographers. While paying homage to such established motifs as the haunted house, witchcraft, and the freak show, they have staked out new, uncharted terrain, thus raising the Gothic's stakes as a powerfully expressive aesthetic. It will likely be some time before the Gothic rests in peace.

NOTE

1. Sympathetic, psychologically complex transmutations of the zombie – the current cinematic/televisual monster of choice – in Romero's various follow-ups have mirrored the vampires whose popularity surged in the 1980s and 1990s in the wake of the HIV epidemic.

WORKS CITED

Baudrillard, Jean. *America*. Trans. Chris Turner. London: Verso, 1968.
Benshoff, Harry M. *Dark Shadows*. Detroit: Wayne State University Press, 2011.
"Horror Before 'The Horror Film'." *A Companion to the Horror Film*. Ed. Harry M. Benshoff. Chichester, West Sussex: Wiley Blackwell, 2014. 207–24.
Beuka, Robert. *SuburbiaNation: Reading Suburban Landscape in Twentieth-Century American Fiction and Film*, New York: Palgrave, 2004.
Brophy, Philip. "Horrality – The Textuality of Contemporary Horror Films." *The Horror Reader*. Ed. Ken Gelder. London: Routledge, 2000. 276–84.
Brown, Charles Brockden. (1926), *Wieland, or the Transformation*. 1798. New York: Harcourt Brace Jovanovich, 1926.

Browning, John Edgar. "Classical Hollywood Horror." *A Companion to the Horror Film*. Ed. Harry M. Benshoff. Chichester, West Sussex: Wiley Blackwell, 2014. 225–36.

Burke, Edmund. *A Philosophical Enquiry Into the Origin of Our Ideas of the Sublime and the Beautiful*. 1757. London: J. Dodsley, 1767.

Carroll, Noël. "*King Kong*: Ape and Essence." *Planks of Reason: Essays on the Horror Film*. Eds. Barry Keith Grant and Christopher Sharrett. Lanham, MD: Scarecrow Press, 2004. 212–39.

Clarens, Carlos. *Horror Movies: An Illustrated Survey*. London: Panther, 1971.

Clover, Carol J. *Men, Women, and Chainsaws: Gender in the Modern Horror Film*. Princeton: Princeton University Press, 1992.

DeLamotte, Eugenia C. *Perils of the Night: A Feminist Study of Nineteenth-Century Gothic*. New York: Oxford University Press, 1990.

Fishman, Robert. *Bourgeois Utopia: The Rise and Fall of Suburbia*. New York: Basic Books, 1987.

Goddu, Teresa. *Gothic America: Narrative, History, and Nation*. New York: Columbia University Press, 1997.

Gunning, Tom. "Flickers: On Cinema's Power for Evil." *Bad: Infamy, Darkness, Evil and Slime on Screen*. Ed. Murray Pomerance. Albany: State University of New York Press, 2004. 21–38.

Hanson, Helen. *Hollywood Heroines: Women in Film Noir and the Female Gothic Film*. London: I. B. Tauris, 2007.

Jancovich, Mark. *Horror*. London: B. T. Batsford, Ltd., 1992.

"Horror in the 1940s." *A Companion to the Horror Film*. Ed. Harry M. Benshoff. Chichester, West Sussex: Wiley-Blackwell, 2014. 237–54.

King, Stephen. *Danse Macabre*. 1981. New York: Berkley Books, 1983.

Ledwon, Lenora. "*Twin Peaks* and the Television Gothic." *Literature/Film Quarterly* 21.4 (1993): 260–70.

Marc, David. *Comic Visions: Television Comedy and American Culture*. Malden and Oxford: Blackwell, 1997.

McCarty, John. *Splatter Movies: Breaking the Last Taboo of the Screen*. New York: St. Martin's Press, 1984.

Medovoi, Leerom. "Theorizing Historicity, or the Many Meanings of *Blacula*," *Screen* 39.1 (1998): 1–21.

Robson, Eddie. "Gothic television." *The Routledge Companion to the Gothic Novel*. Eds. Catherine Spooner and Emma McEvoy. London: Routledge, 2007. 242–50.

Savoy, Eric. "The Face of the Tenant: A Theory of American Gothic." *American Gothic: New Interventions in a National Narrative*. Ed. Robert K. Martin and Eric Savoy. Iowa City: University of Iowa Press, 1998. 3–19.

Toynbee, Arnold. "Changing Attitudes Towards Death in the Modern Western World." *Man's Concern with Death*. St. Louis: McGraw-Hill, 1968. 122–32.

Tudor, Andrew. *Monsters and Mad Scientists: A Cultural History of the Horror Movie*. Hoboken, NJ: Wiley-Blackwell, 1991.

16

TANYA KRZYWINSKA

Gothic American Gaming

Before considering American Gothic features of games, some preliminary consideration of the medium-specific qualities of games is necessary. Games require a physical level of engagement and many are designed to provide players with a sense of presence and agency in the game space. Often, gameplay is contextualized within an antagonistic, unfriendly environment over which players are invited to develop mastery.

While making use of conventions and forms found in other media, games also have some very specific properties that affect how such conventions are used. A game is designed to provide structures to support gameplay (often referred to by game developers as "mechanics").[1] As such, games construct story in ways different from other media. Story has to fit with gameplay and the two are often linked through the journey a player takes through the game. Given that games are principally organized around a set of "ideal" actions to be performed by a player, feedback mechanisms on that performance are important componentry. The organization of feedback mechanisms is central to a game's design, provided by a game's computing, its graphics, audio, and interface. Feedback is wide-ranging and includes seeing your own character or an enemy die as a result of your actions, hearing a droopy sound when you fail to complete a task, and the vibration of your controller when a weapon is fired. There are many other forms.

As King and Krzywinska have argued, games allow players varying degrees of freedom in terms of movement, action, and choice. Player-characters can, for example, roam around in an open environment as in *The Secret World* (Funcom, 2012–present), or their movement might be restricted as in arcade shooter franchise House of the Dead (Sega, 1996–present). In each of these games, players must rise to challenges that involve manipulating their characters to enable passage through the game. Even where some latitude for action and movement is afforded, as in *Alan Wake* (Remedy/Microsoft, 2010), it is often the case that player agency does not stretch to alteration of a storyline. We might call this restrictive "on-rails" approach to design the

"Ghost Train" format, wherein players experience the same predetermined ride. This approach differs from the type of game in which a player's actions influence the trajectory of story, as is the case with *Fable* (Lionhead, 2004) or the Mass Effect series. Many games prefer to limit the effects of player choice in order to preserve authorial control of a storyline and/or to keep production costs down.

Games then have their own distinctive qualities that must be kept in mind when considering their treatment of American Gothic. They are highly structured systems that respond to a player's activity. These include the moment-by-moment transactions effected as a player moves through a game and which may lead to larger, cumulative loops, represented as achievement points or progress bars. Much as a Skinner box works to affect the behaviors of rats, game loops train a player to understand and learn what a game requires her to do. Player agency and choice (or the lack thereof) are therefore central to the definition of a game. These properties are rich food for the Gothic imagination, with its preoccupation with paralysis and futility and *may* therefore be deployed to demonstrate that choice and agency, as taken-for-granted staples of games, are illusory.

Gothic Gaming

To address the American Gothic qualities of videogames, a comparison with other media may be initially helpful. Through its ensemble format and blatant postmodern mash-up of Gothic icons and texts, British-made TV serial *Penny Dreadful* (2014–2016) neatly encapsulates three core features of American Gothic material that are found in videogames. The first is *monstrosity*.

Ethan Chandler, played by actor Josh Hartnett, is one of *Penny Dreadful*'s main characters. He is an American come recently to Europe to escape the tyranny of his father and a dubious past. Following the transatlantic passage of other werewolves to Europe, he is an American werewolf in London. Chandler's father represents American colonial power and is demonstrably linked to the murder of indigenous people; becoming werewolf is an indication that Chandler too is implicated in such brutality. Even as he expresses honorable intentions, Chandler carries within a monstrosity that is blind to civilization and empathy. In Gothic media, monsters come in many forms – some do not know they are monsters, while others are more simply rendered; in games, too, monsters are multiform. Monstrosity provides not only spectacle and "flavor" (a term used by game developers to mean theme and/or genre), but as we'll see, may also serve a game's mechanics.

The second core feature of American Gothic gaming is *otherness*. As with actor Lon Chaney Jr.'s werewolf in the 1940s Universal Pictures Wolfman films, Chandler's angst brings pathos to the role of monster. He has the demeanor of a conventional hero, but his monstrosity provides the type of flaw expected of a tragic antihero. As a deeply conflicted character and exhibiting behaviors over which he has no conscious control, Chandler's compartmentalized monstrosity makes him "other" to himself. In the context of Gothic fiction, where opportunities are exploited to create a sense of hostility or discomfort, the "other" is not simply that which is not like us as a form of genial difference. Instead, it is a force or presence that works to undermine or harm us. This other might be embodied or not; and, as is the case with Chandler, it might not be characteristic of an antagonist.

Chandler also suffers. He has a strong sense of alienation and despair. Displaced and estranged, he has lost his coordinates, seeking solace and redemption. *Dislocation* is therefore our third feature of Gothic games: Characters who have strayed outside of their comfort zone are common in Gothic fiction generally and videogames are no different.

An examination of monstrosity, otherness, and dislocation can then be used as a means of understanding how games utilize Gothic conventions and provides a framework for the analysis of the key relationships in games among story, character, and game mechanics.

Monsters, You Monster, I Monster!

Monsters hold court in a large variety of games. They are drawn from a host of mythologies and take on a host of guises. Some are demons, others malformed humans. Some are born of twisted moral purpose, others embody rage or lust. Some are material, others made of more gauzy stuff. Some represent voracious appetite; others seek sadistic dominion over earth and humans. Aliens, zombies, and psychopaths are typical American Gothic monsters that populate games of different genres and are available for different platforms.

While in most fictions monstrosity is deployed as a narrative stratagem, in games monstrosity is a guise that gives meaning and form to logarithmic counting devices. These are built around the use of systematic distinctions and categories. Many game monsters are part of what can be thought of as a demonology – a system arranged around strength, behaviors, and representational form. Echoing medieval bestiaries and demonologies, game monster taxonomies are tied into the design of a player's experience of a game's structure. The strength of *The Secret World*'s monsters is handily and typically scaled in accordance with the abilities and capabilities afforded to a player as she is channeled to the relevant area of the game. A newly minted player-character arriving with few skill points at Kingsmouth is unlikely to be able to tackle killing the strong monsters that are hatched from the sea, but is well-equipped to deal with the weaker zombies that populate the area around the town. As the player-character grows in strength, she becomes able to tackle sea monsters and gain their loot. In most combat-based games, it is plain to see a game-based structure at work in the demonology. In service of this process, games take up real world mythological systems and translate them to a ludic agenda.[2]

A close parallel between Christian conceptions of demonic typologies and game monster typologies is therefore apparent, but not because of a universal notion of monstrosity; rather, typology itself gives structure and weight to the realization of a mythology. This aids in giving a fiction greater authority and depth, thereby increasing the potential for player suspension of disbelief. Games rely for their credibility with their audience on their ability to create coherent scaling systems that dovetail neatly with a game's feedback mechanics. Killing monsters might solicit many different types of pleasures, but at base monsters are convenient game mechanics.

The Cacodemons of *Doom II: Hell on Earth* (idsoftware, 1994) provide an early example – designed, as so many game monsters are, to be simply cannon fodder. Such monsters, however, play an important role. They serve to keep up a flow of action and act as feedback affirmation of a player's mastery and progress (or not!). Cacodemons are conventional game monsters. They are in effect puzzle-based "obstacles" designed to test a player's ability to master the weapons and tactics available. Combining elements of demonology with Lovecraftian alien lore, Cacodemons are denizens of Outer Space; as such they are linked to a well-worn frontier mythology. Cacodemons are, however, principally ludic rather than narrative devices.

Their ludic function is also echoed in their representational form. They float around the game space, providing therefore a less stable target than other monsters in the game. In addition, their wide toothy grins, which open to spit plasma bolts, taunt the unprepared player, upping the emotional ante. Cacodemons as well are large enough to nearly engulf a player's screen, making it hard to master the immediate game space, bucking the trend of the era where small sprites were far more common. Their sequel-evolved form in *Doom 3* (id software, 2004) presents a much fleshier body than their colorful predecessors, resembling more closely the medieval demons found in Hieronymus Bosch's paintings of Hell. As a game franchise, Doom's demonology can therefore be coopted as a visual lesson in game graphics technology evolution.

While Cacodemons in *Doom* are encountered singly or in small numbers, videogames regularly present players with hosts of monsters that move as a massed, repetitious swarming body: Zombies, animated skeletons, or aliens are common cannon fodder in games in which shooting or something equivalent is the core mechanic. Given the reliance on powerful visual feedback mechanisms including spectacle, alongside a ludic requirement to quantify player actions, it is perhaps not surprising that "shooting" legions of de-individualized monsters is called on so regularly by game developers. Massed examples of cannon-fodder monsters that roam any number of games gave rise to the term "mobs" (short for monster mobiles). Such monsters present a threat but also endorse a sense of a player's agency through their death. It is therefore not much of a leap from rows of space invaders marching down the screen toward a player in the classic *Space Invaders* (Taito, 1978) to the more visually and behaviorally complex monsters of the latest PlayStation 4 big-budget horror game such as *Until Dawn* (Supermassive/Sony, 2015).

In the development of Gothic gaming, the slow movement of zombies in particular suited games that had simple Artificial Intelligence (AI). *Dead Rising* (Capcom, 2006), for example, populated its game spaces with thousands of zombies, making use of the ubiquity of widescreen televisions to create visual impact. *Typing of the Dead* (Sega, 1999), in contrast, provided a variant of the shoot'em up format to dispatch its hordes of zombies in which players type words appearing above zombies' heads to dispatch them. Developments in game AI have generated smarter zombies that respond more receptively and idiosyncratically to situations, as in squad-based shooter *Left 4 Dead* (Turtle/Rock, 2008) where they create a greater sense of jeopardy, making for edgier game play.

In contrast to the relatively simplistic Cacodemons or easily dispatched legions of walking dead is the "big boss," the strongest monster in a game. Arguably the most iconic and idiosyncratic of all game monster big bosses is the relentless and unflinching Pyramid Head that stalks the Silent Hill games.[3] Strings of bulked muscle are juxtaposed with an anonymizing metal, angular helmet; Pyramid Head's contradictory form powerfully signifies a loss of humanity. He does not see; no facial expression is visible. In him, archetypal aberrational fairy tale monster meets the fearful symmetry of geometry. He is a monster for, and from, the game age: Flesh textures are fused with the polygonal forms that lie at the foundation of all 3D game characters, but which are conventionally hidden to create the illusion of real bodies. Blind to pity, relentlessly dragging his crude, oversized sword along the ground, players hear him before they see him. This is a boss designed not to face but from which to flee. In terms of narrative, and in the franchise's structural demonology, Pyramid Head remains enigmatic. It is never his story that is told – a narrative absence that strengthens his archetypal bogeyman status. Pyramid Head is therefore a highly individualized monster unlike the Cacodemons and the other cookie-cutter counterparts discussed above.

While principally mechanicals, game monsters are, however, more than that. Even as simple cannon fodder, they come heavily freighted with myth, meaning, and affect; their bodies speak story, in addition to being designed to delight, surprise, and disturb. Pyramid Head's form speaks of dehumanization and biological aberration for instance. In eco-terror games, such as the Resident Evil series, monsters are produced by careless human actions and technologies and their form reflects this often manifesting corruption or the perversion of the natural. Monsters then can be used to represent that which is marginalized or generally overlooked as inconvenient. They are therefore very often deployed in game narratives as cautionary figures, and monsters that serve a moral purpose are most common in games with complex narratives. Monsters functioning in this capacity are seen in *Alan Wake*, for example, where a more existential tack is taken rather than the apocalyptic one common to zombie games. While *Alan Wake* is populated by psychopaths, conjured out of backwoods red-neck horror films such as *Texas Chainsaw Massacre* (Tobe Hooper, 1974) and *Deliverance* (John Boorman, 1972), it is in fact Wake himself, whom the player plays, who is author of the game's antagonistic force and is therefore monster. A similar case is found in the second Silent Hill game, in which the protagonist is deeply implicated in evil acts of which he is seemingly unaware. In both cases, a model of repression is in play, providing therefore a far more genuinely Gothic twist on the usual Manichean mechanics of shoot'em up style games. Here it is the narrative context that throws a certain light on the mechanic – the mechanics are in themselves largely unaffected but the narrative context is what gives these their meaning.

In other instances, narrative mechanics can affect game mechanics profoundly. In *Spec Ops: The Line* (2012, Yager/2 K), narrative mechanics actively work against game mechanics and this produces a very interesting and unusual twist that positions and names the player, not just the player-character, as monster. This game looks at first to be a standard military shooter. The player-character leads a squad on a reconnaissance mission but acts in increasingly psychopathic ways. Over the course of the game, he turns from hero to monster. A player is likely to anticipate that the player-character will once again revert to that of hero. He does not. In this, *Spec Ops* toys with its players, goading them into not completing the game. Versed in the expectation that game is to be completed, few players give up. Loading screens display messages that are directed explicitly at the player, asking why she is still playing the game given the unconscionable actions of the character (the only way a player has agency over the character is to *stop* playing). The game strongly and directly positions the player as Monster, implicating her in the deaths on screen and perhaps even on the way that her game literacy desensitizes her to violence. In this, *Spec Ops* renders the player "other" and "monstrous" – a shift away from the more usual projection of the monstrosity onto other and othered people.

We have then gone from monsters as cheap cannon fodder that are not intended to cause a player any cause for moral concern, to individualized monsters, structurally positioned as "You, Monster," to a game that calls this precisely into question by positioning the player as "I, Monster." All these positions can be regarded as modalities of otherness, a concept that has a key presence in Gothic gaming.

other to Other

Otherness is a hot property of the Gothic and is purposed in games to structure narrative, to create atmosphere and stylistic coherence, and to generate emotional engagement. It resides mainly at the level of representation, also informing story and mechanics (although perhaps to a lesser extent). In keeping with post-Freudian psychoanalysis, the concept of the other can be divided into two distinctive categories. There is the other with a lower case "o," which refers to other people – those who are not me and therefore different to me. The property of otherness can, however, become exaggerated into not just other, but radically alien and different: an Other with a capital "O." This Other is threatening and terrifying, calling into question our sense of being and purpose. In addition, certain people or groups of people can be "othered," made more strange and different as means of ostracizing and marginalizing them. The Other is then grounded in our psychological and social relation with other human beings and its properties prove to be a valuable asset for Gothic fiction and games.

Monsters are direct embodiments of the Other, although what form this takes and the degree to which they are Other differs. The otherness of some game monsters is lightly and stereotypically sketched, serving ludic purposes more fully than narrative ones, providing a type of *functional* otherness. This is the case with cannon-fodder monsters that are designed to provide visual feedback of a player's mastery of the game, as an embodied form of progress bar. The otherness of zombies lies in their representational status as "no-longer" people; reduced to flesh and dumb appetite they are devoid of identity or humanity. They ask no ethical or compassionate questions of a player. Such functional monsters are infinitely replaceable and unlikely to appeal to empathy; they can therefore be hacked about, slashed, shot, and chainsawed with wild abandon. Often game monsters call on a visual quality of otherness through their presentation as malformations or perversions, providing therefore spectacle for players. Otherness is not always conveyed through twisted and strangely formed bodies, however; it can also be inflected through dress, accents, and or speech patterns, as with the red-neck psychopaths of *Dead Rising 2* (Capcom, 2010) or the deadly politeness of Bioshock's antagonist (2 K, 2007). Drawn from cultural stereotypes, such cues work to make these characters easy or desirable to "kill." Otherness in games is therefore laden with meanings that grow out of real-world inter-human relationships.

Otherness becomes most complex in American Gothic, where a game's player-character is herself marked out as Other. This configuration is largely confined to Gothic games and it is perhaps not a coincidence that many such characters are American, as in *Silent Hill 2, Alan Wake*, and *Spec Ops*. Manuel Aguirre uses the term "false hero" in Gothic fiction to describe protagonists that exhibit characteristics different from those of a standard hero. This may be a protagonist who does not conform to the rugged white male stereotype and who in some cases is revealed as monstrous in terms of bodies or actions (as in the games listed above). The use of the "false hero" allows otherness and monstrosity to be configured in such a way as to offer a departure from a conventional good-versus-evil narrative, as well as to question some of the norms of gaming, as in *Spec Ops*.

Gothic games clearly deploy monsters as "othered" obstacles to be defeated. Just as importantly, Gothic games also create mysterious and antagonistic spaces – other worlds – that dislocated players are challenged to navigate successfully. In Gothic games, space and location are themselves habitually rendered as Other. The design of game space is important to the creation of Gothic atmosphere and might be understood as translation of adjectives such as "leprous" or "eldritch" found in weird fictions such as H.P. Lovecraft's short stories. The challenge for game designers is that space also has to function as a context for action and must be tailored around gameplay. In a ludic sense, environments can also be employed to actively impede a player's progress through space, acting therefore as antagonist. As such, gamers often use the term "PvE" games to designate player versus the environment, in contrast to "PvP" games in which the contest is player versus player. In representational, narrative, and ludic senses, space in Gothic games becomes hostile and strange, in some cases no longer seeming to serve human agency or purpose. As in Richard Slotkin's description of the frontier, this can be a place where the known rules no longer function. In games, a player needs to discover and conform to what a space requires of her. In this sense, game space takes on the guise of the (capitalized) Other, operating as an outside force that dispassionately demands strict conformity from a player. Space can therefore be configured in an Othered way to provide players with a keen sense of dislocation through a disturbance from a proper or usual place or state. Otherness is thus a modality deployed in games that affects monstrosity – as well as dislocation, to be discussed below – investing each with their emotional and psychological power.

The Place of Dislocation in Games

The pairing of an American game setting with the Gothic usually results in some form of dislocation. As with the American werewolf in London in *Penny Dreadful*, dislocation is an inherently spatial dimension and game media is especially good at creating literalized spaces that players can seemingly occupy. Gothic games in particular work hard to give a player a sense of being in and inhabiting the space of the game. 3D graphics and first-person perspective heighten perceptual engagement, enhanced by VR headsets or other forms of Augmented Reality, to strengthen a sense of presence and immediacy. Game space is also important to the way story is delivered in games. Story is written into what the player is asked to do in a game space and cues for such are often found in the visual or auditory design of the space and objects within that space. I have identified three types of dislocation that are relevant to the American Gothic in games: the cultural, the temporal, and the psychological.

Cultural dislocation is a feature of some games using an American setting. These subdivide into two: games that are made within America that thematize cultural dislocation, as with *The Wolf among Us* and the Bioshock series (2 K Boston/Irrational, 2007–2013), and games that approach American landscapes and culture from another cultural perspective, such as the Silent Hill series (1999–2012) and *Deadly Premonition* (Rising Star, 2010), made in Japan. Both forms of cultural dislocation raise questions about just what "America" is, what purposes it serves, and for whom.

Turning first to American games that thematize cultural dislocation, *The Wolf among Us* is based on Bill Willingham's Fables comic book series and is a story-based point and click game. Known as "fables," the game's main characters are drawn from European fairy tales and have been forced to immigrate to America. They are required to mask their fantastical identities in order to pass as human. This is expensive and a black market has developed as a result. This economy is linked directly to the fables' dislocative situation and provides the source of the game's plot. In order to control frontier life, bureaucracy and law take shape. Bigby Wolf (a werewolf), the player-character, is tasked with the role of Sherriff and tacitly complicit with the process of "normalization" – certainly an upended role for a werewolf and once-upon-a-time Big Bad Wolf! Core then to the plot and overarching mythos is the difficulty of adapting to a new culture and the need to change – not just in terms of daily habits and adjusting to reduced social status but also in terms of embodiment – as a means to fit in and survive at the frontier. As we might expect, the usual cues and roles are no longer in place – a kind of social leveling has taken place that means it is much more difficult to ascertain previously extremely clear moral alignments. Bluebeard is shorn of the power to represent evil, for example. Bigby is now able to turn werewolf at will, helping his transformation from false hero to newly minted conventional hero (the reverse of the journey made by Ethan Chandler, the werewolf of *Penny Dreadful* mentioned at the start of the chapter).

Apocalyptic scenarios common within games also work with cultural dislocation, where norms and roles are disrupted. In *The Secret World* (2012–present), an elderly woman, Norma Creed, takes on the hero role, holding out against hordes of sea monsters and zombies, as well as acting as helper to new players by providing quests that will improve their standing in the game. In *The Last of Us* (Naughty Dog, 2013), the heroic status of the player-character is far from a given, and whether he has acted heroically or selfishly is very much open to a player's interpretation. Both these characters enact the roles of Gothic antiheroes.

A twist on conventional forms of cultural dislocation is present in games made by Japanese game developers that use an American Gothic small-town modality where normality is simply a thin veneer that barely covers over a seething chaos of the unconscionable as in the Silent Hill series and *Deadly Premonition*, a game that puts the player in the shoes of a psychic detective come from out of town to investigate the ritual murder of girls. There is therefore a transnational culturally dislocative dimension at work lending an additional layer of weird to Gothic games. In the cases of Silent Hill and, more specifically, *Deadly Premonition*, elements of American series such as *Twin Peaks* (David Lynch, 1990–1991) are read and repurposed to strange-making effect through Japanese cultural frameworks.

Temporal dislocation in American Gothic games similarly plays with and questions ideas of American identity and often results from a disturbance to the conventional order of things. Games do, of course, regularly break with linear time in any case, but this is now accepted as integral to the medium – you "die," then you respawn and try that tricky task over again. This tends to make death seem less real and therefore less of a temporal dislocation. However, certain games more consciously upend chronological time in aggressive or significant ways. Bother an ancient Indian burial site or find yourself at some kind of frontier (the Arctic, internet, deep space, or black holes) and hell breaks loose, making nonsense of linear organizations of time: ghosts, doubling, time loops, multiple worlds. *Deadly Premonition*, for example, makes temporal dislocation central to its game mechanic in which players must visit locations at certain times if they are to follow leads. As such, time acts as a strong determining "Other" in the game; the player must obey its dictates.

In American Gothic games, as in other Gothic media, ghosts in particular often function as indications or catalysts of temporal dislocatedness. As a form of small-town American fiction, The Sims series (Maxis/EA 2000–present) doesn't seem very Gothic on the surface, but it is nonetheless populated by ghosts. These might be dead Sims and pets, likely killed accidently or consciously by the player, who appear at night if their bodies have not been "properly" buried. Sims' ghosts are testimony not just to the effects of the games' internal life cycle and aging (a variable that can actually be turned off), but also act as commentary on the player's treatment of their Sims, providing a kind of return-of-the-repressed that is directly related to a player's choices and actions.

Ghosts also appear as emblems of the return of the repressed in other games including *Alan Wake*, where the eponymous character is haunted, self-referentially, by his own fiction. In *Bioshock Infinite* (2 k Games, 2014), Lady Comstock's ghost is something akin to Schrodinger's cat; her various guises are symptomatic of the game's multiple/parallel worlds concept, thereby drawing on a Weird Science model of American Gothic where time is rarely a stable constant. Lady Comstock's ghost is not only a demonstration of the concept of the "multi-verse" but also draws on an older, much-used Gothic convention: the return of that which has been repressed or suppressed. In a franchise that draws on the anti-ultraistic work of Ayn Rand, this ghost is testimony to what has been suppressed: ultra-nationalism and religious extremism.

Psychological dislocation, our final variant on Gothic dislocation, often occurs in conjunction with cultural and temporal dislocation. In *Max Payne* (Remedy, 2001), psychological dislocation occurs through the brutal murder of Payne's wife and child, which are represented by dislocated dream-like experiences in which the normal rule of space and time do not apply. This sequence, as well as similar scenes in *Deadly Premonition*, functions as a spectacle and storytelling device rather than a game space within which a player is able to act. These spaces are distinct from "normative" game spaces for orderly and regulated human/player agency – they are then spaces out of time and space and symptomatic of disordered minds.

Psychological dislocation in the general context of Gothic manifests itself very often as a form of paralysis – an inability to comprehend and/or act on a situation. As Eve Kosofosky Sedgwick explains in *The Coherence of Gothic Conventions*, claustrophobia sums up Gothic's emotional ethos. Introducing psychological dislocation into videogames creates a problem for game developers as games generally work toward giving players increasing mastery of over events – that is, overcoming paralysis and engaging in effective, goal-directed action. Alternative ways to balance Gothic inaction with engaging audiences as players have to be found. In *Call of Cthulhu: Dark Corners of the Earth* (Headfirst/Bethesda, 2005), players must avoid going mad. Actions must be surreptitious and measured if madness is to be avoided; if not, the player-character becomes paralyzed and unable to act.

Games that take a weird path often have a slow pace, a mode that frustrates players thrilled by low-effort actions that yield high-octane spectacle and high impact. However, it is common for games that take this left-hand path to use the first-person perspective expected of normative shooter-style games. This is because it is easier to create a more intense, psychologically dislocative experience for the player using first person perspective, enabling, for example, perceptual effects based on a limited vista to be used (less of a case of "it's behind you!" and "what's that behind me?!"); examples include all of the Doom games but perhaps is most unnerving in *Doom 3* (2004) and *Alien Isolation* (2014). Limiting a player's view affords her less control, creating an edgier and more sensation-driven experience. A heightened sense of immersive perceptual proximity is driving the new breed of immersive virtual-reality based games that delight in breaking through the fourth wall, as in the case of *Alone* (2015). Such games make use of the perceptual qualities of their hardware to enhance the sense of psychological dislocation for the player. In *Alone*, the player must turn her head to see what is behind her, made possible by the 360-degree immersion effect of the headset, and *Lost in the Rift* (2014) asks the player to escape a claustrophobic labyrinth creating a strong sense of psychological and spatial dislocation for a player that is not mediated through a character. Given that perspective is in first person, cut-away shots, used often in cinema or television, are not possible. This enhances the sense of presence, and allows no escape from the situation at hand. There is then no time or room for strategic appraisal, unlike in turn-based or strategy games.

In the main, psychological dislocation in games hinges around agency and its loss. Messing with perceptual cues is a core weapon in Gothic's armory as Gothic games that play with psychological dislocation seek to unbind us from the familiar and the easy. Making choices of what to do next in *The Stanley Parable* (Galactic Café, 2011/2013), for example, brings the player up short because the game does not employ the usual cue and conventions used within games. In this game, as with the Bioshock games and *Spec Ops*, the promise of player agency is exposed as a lie. This is built into the narrative of all these games but it extends beyond this to directly affect the player themselves, and not just the games' lead characters. In each of these cases the effect is to demonstrate that games encourage conformity, with players simply responding by rote to the stimuli proffered. These are then games that are in themselves monstrous and Other. They dislocate and undermine the normative and comfortable pleasures of agency and mastery provided by, and expected of, most other games. As a form of pervasive psychological dislocation, this Gothic gaming seeks to reveal the deterministic nature of the world and bodies we live in, exposing our sense of individuality, mastery, and control over ourselves and our lives as deception. The players of such games are thus staged as dysfunctional and impotent Gothic antiheroes.

Conclusion

American Gothic of whatever stripe is arguably at its most interesting in games where it departs from stable and melodramatic locations of good and evil, and moves toward a secular, dislocative "Weird" that is focused, like Mary Shelley's *Frankenstein* (1818), in upon our dislocated selves. Like *Penny Dreadful*'s Chandler, the player of such games is no longer an innocent bystander or the hero of the day, putting wrongs to rights, but is instead caught-up in her own narrative of self-deception. Monstrosity, Otherness, and dislocation provide the structures that give American Gothic games their character but they can be deployed to very different ends, from providing a strong sense of achievement and mastery of the game world to exactly the opposite. In all cases, however, examination of concepts of monstrosity, Otherness, and dislocation raise critical and existential questions relevant to human psychology, metaphysics, and morality. *Silent Hill 2*'s Pyramid Head heraldically presides over this complex space. A collaged exquisite corpse, rendered from Japanese folklore and computer-generated geometry, his estranged flesh speaks through the specific vocabulary of games to our collective desire to transcend both death and our fleshly incarnation. Pyramid Head is never defeated or fully explained across the full set of Silent Hill games; he thus remains supremely enigmatic, preserving his emblematic status as Monstrous Other with the rules of the game his to command.

NOTES

1. Game mechanics is a term often used within the game development community to refer to the various rules and procedures that determine how a player engages with a game.

2. The term Ludic is often used in Game Studies to refer to features of a game that relate to its rules and to that which facilitates gameplay. It comes from the Latin *Ludus*, which is used to refer to games, play, or sport.
3. Competing with Pyramid Head for preeminent big boss status is Psycho Mantis from the Metal Gear Solid games.

WORKS CITED

Aguirre, Manuel. "Gothic Fiction and Folk-Narrative Structure: The Case of Mary Shelley's Frankenstein." *Gothic Studies* 15.2 (Nov. 2013): 1–18.

King, Geoff and Tanya Krzywinska. *Tomb Raiders and Space Invaders: Videogame Forms and Contexts*. London: IB Tauris, 2006.

Sedgwick, Eve Kosofsky. *The Coherence of Gothic Conventions*. New York: Methuen, 1980.

Slotkin, Richard. *The Fatal Environment*. New York: Atheneum, 1985.

INDEX

Abrams, J. J., 80, 81
Adams, John, 205
Adams, Rachel, 125
adaptation, 179, 207, 212, 216
adulthood, 178
affect, 61, 63, 215
African American, 44, 128, 130, 209, 211, 222
Agassiz, Louis, 89
Aguirre, Manuel, 236
AIDS, 116, 120, 121, 122, 124, 126, 212
Aiken, George, 208
Alan Wake, 229, 234, 236, 239
Alcott, Louisa May, 41, 175
Alien Isolation, 240
Allison, Dorothy, 142, 153
Alone (video game), 240
Altschuler, Sari, 207
American Horror Story, 227
Anthony, Susan, 202
anthropocentricism, 190
anxiety, 52
apocalypse, 16, 18, 71
  post-apocalypse, 73
  zombie, 23, 73
Arthur Gordon Pym (character), 89
atemporality, 77–79
Atwood, Margaret, 110
Austin, William, 33

Babo (character). *See* Melville, Herman
  Benito Cereno
Ball, Alan, 226–27
Balzac, Honoré de, 104
Barnes, Djuna, 58, 60, 61, 65, 69
  Nightwood, 58, 61, 62–64
Baudelaire, Charles, 60, 62–63
Baum, L. Frank, 54, 176
Baxter, Charles, 174

BDSM, 192
Becker, Robin, 73
Beckett, Samuel, 64
Bell, Michael, 42
Beloved (character), 96
Bendixen, Alfred, 42
Ben-Zvi, Linda, 209
Bercovitch, Sacvan, 17, 23
Berger, Samantha, 180
Bergland, Renée, 42
Berkeley, Bishop, 17
Bible, 17, 195
Bierce, Ambrose, 40, 50, 51
Bigger Thomas (character), 94, 162–63, 164, 166
Bildungsroman, 31, 60, 61, 66, 67, 150, 153
Bioshock, 236, 237
Bioshock Infinite, 239
Bird, Robert Montgomery, 33
Black Dragons, 218
Blackford, Holly Virginia, 178
Blair Witch Project, The, 8
Blau, Herbert, 211
blaxploitation, 222
Bloch, Robert. *See Psycho* (novel)
Block, Lawrence, 163
blues (music), 116
Blume, Lesley M. M., 177
body politics, 25, 37, 75, 90, 102, 110, 111, 173, 181, 217, 223
Bogin, Ruth, 196
Border Ballad, 185–86, 187
Bosch, Hieronymus, 232
Botting, Fred, 2
Bould, Mark, 166
Braddon, Mary Elizabeth, 61
Bradford, William, 87
Brady, Matthew, 50

Brite, Poppy Z., 71
Brooks, Chris, 166
Brooks, Max, 71, 74
Brophy, Philip, 221, 224
Brown, Charles Brockden, xi, 1, 4, 9, 10, 15, 26, 86, 88, 128, 132–35, 141, 157, 166, 188, 203, 207
  Alcuin, 25
  Arthur Mervyn, 24–25
  Edgar Huntly (character), 137, 138
  Edgar Huntly, Or, Memoirs of a Sleepwalker, 4, 9, 10, 24, 26, 88, 134–35, 137, 138, 157
  Ormond, 24–25
  Wieland, 24, 25–26, 133, 136, 188, 225
Brown, William Wells, 92, 208
Browne, S. G., 72
Brueggemann, Walter, 195
Bryant, William Cullen, 33, 186
Buell, Lawrence, 196
Buffy, the Vampire Slayer, 221
Burnett, Frances Hodgson, 175, 177
Burnham, Michelle, 88, 96
Byrd, William, 141–43, 152, 154

C. Auguste Dupin (character), 110, 158, 163
Cable, George Washington, 142, 146, 148
Caldwell, Erskine, 152
Call of Cthulhu, Dark Corners of the Earth, 240
Cape Ann, 20
capitalism, 5, 33, 44, 46, 52, 54, 72, 75–76, 77, 78, 79, 107, 111, 167, 178, 211, 217, 221, 225, 226, 227
Capote, Truman, 10, 60, 61, 66–67, 68, 116–18
  Other Voices, Other Rooms, 58, 61, 66, 67, 116, 150–51
  queer identity, 118
Carroll, Noel, 218
Carruthers, William, 18
Cash, Wiley, 143, 151
Cat and the Canary, The, 217
Chandler, Raymond, 160–62, 164
  Big Sleep, The, 161
Chaney, Jr., Lon, 231
Chaney, Lon, 217
Chesnutt, Charles W., 52–54, 85, 94, 146, 147, 148
  Marrow of Tradition, The, 147
  "Po' Sandy," 149
Chicago, 162,
Chican@, 120, 127

childhood, 110, 151, 172–73, 175, 181
children's literature, 172, 173
  censorship, 174
  history, 174, 178, 180
  supernatural, 174
Chopin, Kate, 53, 146, 147
Churchill, Thomas Furlong, 174
civil rights, 74, 75, 146
Clara Wieland (character), 132–33
Clark, Kenneth, 166
class, 2, 5, 10, 23, 44, 59, 141, 143, 148, 184, 201, 202
  bourgeois, 206
  middle, 46, 48, 52, 206, 211, 221, 226
  social, 31, 32
  working, 51, 205, 206, 207, 211
classism, 116
Clayton, Jamie, 115
Clement-Moore, Rosemary, 177
Clover, Carol, 225
Clute, John, 15
Coleridge, Samuel Taylor, 186
Collins, Wilkie, 61, 62
colonialism, 86, 87
colonization, 176
Connecticut, 17, 18
Conrad, Joseph, 58, 60, 62
  Heart of Darkness, 57, 58, 62, 64
  Secret Agent, The, 60
consumer culture, 49, 72, 77
Cooper, James Fenimore, 8, 9, 26
Cormier, Robert, 178
Craft, William, 144
Crafts, Hannah, 92
  Bondwoman's Narrative, The, 92–94
Crane, Stephen, 50–52, 191, 197
  Maggie, A Girl of the Streets, 209
  Red Badge of Courage, The, 52
Crawford, F. Marion, 40
Creature From the Black Lagoon, The, 220
creepypasta, 76
crime fiction, 157
  hard-boiled, 159–62, 164
Crow, Charles L., 85, 135, 184, 206
Cthulhu (character), 194
culture, 6, 81, 86, 88, 115, 201, 202
  adaptation, 238
  anxiety, 2, 6, 72, 87, 154
  Creole, 146,
  difference, 116
  drug, 211
  transgression, 2, 11
Cummins, June, 176

INDEX

Daly, Carroll John, 162
Dana, Jr., Richard Henry, 8
Dangerfield, Rodney, 73
Danielewski, Mark Z., 80
danse macabre, 65
Dark Shadows (TV serial), 221, 222
Darwin, Charles, 190
Davenport, James, 17,
Davis, Rebecca Harding, 49
Davison, Carol Margaret, 130
de Crèvecoeur, J. Hector St. John, 22, 142
Dead Rising, 233
Dead Rising 2, 236
Deadly Premonition, 237, 238, 239
Declaration of Independence, the, 15
deficit model, 172
Deliverance (film), 152, 234
Deliverance (novel), 137, 142, 152
Demme, Jonathan. See *Silence of the Lambs, The* (film)
Dennie, Joseph, 184
Derrida, Jacques, 76
Dessalines, Jacques, 143
detective fiction, 158, 164
determinism, 44, 52, 54
Dick, Philip K., 165
Dickinson, Emily, 40, 184, 190
difference model, 172
digital media, 79
disability, 52, 74, 117, 121, 137
dislocation. *See also* video game
  cultural, 237–38
  psychological, 239–41
  temporal, 238–39
Disney, Walt, 176
domestication, 180
domesticity, 46, 47, 49, 50, 112, 120, 122, 123, 173
  abuse, 129
Doom 3, 232, 240
Doom II, 232–33
Dorst, Doug, 80, 81
Dostoevsky, Fyodor, 68
Douglass, Frederick, 93,
Dr. Moreau (character), 76
Dracula (1931 film), 217, 218
Dracula (character), 79
Dracula (novel), 5, 61, 223
Drake, Nathan, 16
Dreiser, Theodore, 51
Du Bois, W. E. B., 145
Dunbar, Paul Laurence, 85, 94, 96, 193
Dunlap, William, 26, 202, 203

Dustan, Hannah, 21
Dwight, Timothy, 18
Dylan, Bob, 194
dystopia, 207

Eager, Edward, 178
East India Company, 54
Edgar Huntly (character), 88, 134–35
Edwards, Jonathan, 6, 17,
Edwards, Justin, 9, 141
Egan, Jennifer, 79
Eggers, Robert, 7
eighteenth century, 1, 2, 6, 16, 18, 21, 22, 58, 71, 81, 88, 106, 174, 203, 215, 216, 218
  poetry, 185
  theatre, 202
Elbert, Monika M. and Bridget M. Marshall, 42
Eliot, T.S., 57–58, 60, 62–64, 65, 68, 69, 152, 193
  "Hollow Men, The," 62
Ellis, Bret Easton, 1
Ellison, Ralph, 61, 66, 95,
  Invisible Man, 9, 58, 60, 66, 68–69, 94
Enlightenment era, 1, 10, 15, 17, 132–34, 137, 184, 187, 203
Erdrich, Louise, 1
Ethan Chandler (character), 230
Europe, 15, 17
  feudalism, 15
  settlers, 15
exceptionalism, 195

Fable (video game), 230
fairy tale, 2, 175, 179
  monster, 233
Fantasia, 176
fantasy, 16, 110
Faulkner, William, 9, 39, 59–61, 66, 94, 137, 142, 154
  Absalom, Absalom!, 9, 60, 61, 65, 69, 148
  "Bear, The," 149
  Nobel Peace Prize speech, 68
  Sound and the Fury, The, 67
  Yoknapatawpha County, 148
feminism, 105, 112, 223
  Second Wave, 223
femme fatale, 160
Fiedler, Leslie, 1–2, 11, 16, 85, 131, 141,
  Love and Death in the American Novel, 1, 16, 41, 85, 154
film, 1, 71, 157, 175, 215, 221, 224
  audiences, 218

245

INDEX

film (cont.)
  camp, 119, 221
  censorship, 216
  Creature Feature, 217–18, 220, 231
  demonic children, 223
  female Gothic, 223
  noir, 162, 218
  silent, 216, 217
  slasher, 224
  torture porn, 224
Fisher, Benjamin F., 202, 203
Fleenor, Juliann, 173
Flying Dutchman, the, 33, 135
folklore, 188
Folsom, James, 129
Ford, Susan, 110
Foucault, Michel, 124
Fox, Andrew, 72
France, 102
  French Revolution, 16, 22, 34, 58, 204
Frankenstein (1931 film), 66, 74, 217, 218
Frankenstein (novel), 24, 61, 65, 66, 73, 115, 241
Frankenstein's monster (character), 180
Freaks, 218
Freeman, Mary E. Wilkins, 44, 46, 99, 100, 101, 111
  "Lost Ghost, The," 47, 100
  "Luella Miller," 47, 100
  "Wind in the Rose-bush, The," 47, 100
Freneau, Philip, 185,
Freud, Sigmund, 36, 73, 130, 219
  Heimlich, 130
frontier, 130, 142, 157, 211, 236, 237, 239
  American South, 137
  captivity narrative, 132
  civilization, 7–8, 21, 230
  definition, 129
  mythology, 232
  self-harm, 138
  wilderness, 132, 133, 134, 137
Frost, Mark. *See* Lynch, David
Frost, Robert, 192
futurism, 79

Gaiman, Neil, 178
game mechanics. *See* gameplay
Game Studies, 242
gameplay, 229, 234, 242
Garner, Margaret, 95
Garrett, Peter K., 206

gender, 2, 5, 10, 46, 47, 48, 49, 59, 102, 105, 108, 110, 130, 132, 161, 177, 181, 201, 202, 223
  androgyny, 117
  binary, 117, 125
  cisgender, 115
  female body, 110
  fluidity, 67
  norm, 120, 150
  normativity, 125
  sexism, 116, 122, 212
  transgender, 64, 124
  violence, 110
  women as victims, 39
geography, 6, 7, 8, 11, 105
ghost, 2, 8, 10, 20, 44–49, 50–51, 76, 79, 91–94, 100, 101–4, 108–10, 116, 120–23, 130, 142, 153, 156, 160, 171, 177, 180, 195, 204, 238–40
Giger, H.R., 5
Gilbert, Sandra M., 189
Gilman, Charlotte Perkins, 10, 45, 48, 101, 111, 137
  "Giant Wistaria, The," 51, 101
  Home, The, 46
  "Rocking-Chair, The," 51
  "Yellow Wallpaper, The," 46, 49, 101
Ginsberg, Allen, 194,
Glasgow, Ellen, 152
Glaspell, Susan, 201, 209–10, 213
Gliddon, George, 89
globalization, 72, 76
Goddu, Teresa A., 9, 11, 41, 86, 93, 94, 96, 144, 198, 223
Godwin, William, 24
Godzilla (1954 film), 220
Golem, The (1915 film), 217
Gomez, Jewelle, 118, 119,
Goodis, David, 166
Goosebumps (series), 178
Gothic. *See also* frontier; gender; identity; monster, Naturalism; theatre; urban
  anxiety, 7, 9, 10, 103, 172, 173, 181, 216, 222, 224
  architecture, 156, 159
  ballad, 196
  boundaries, 65, 89, 100
  British, 86, 134, 218
  camp, 119–22
  children's literature, 171–82
  desire, 2, 4, 6, 33, 34, 129, 137, 172, 173, 181, 241

246

INDEX

European, 24, 174
Female, 10, 24, 25, 49, 50, 51, 54, 93, 111, 189, 191, 210, 218, 219, 223, 225
feminist tradition, 40
frontier, 4–5, 6, 7, 21, 24, 128–38
geography, 7, 38
heroism, 2, 3, 5, 54, 58, 69, 94, 101, 164, 173, 177, 201, 222, 231, 234, 236, 238, 241
history, 38, 201
indigenous, 96
medievalism, 18
New England female writers, 99, 111
numinous, 132
parody, 204, 209
popular music, 194
power, 3, 10–11, 47, 49, 53
psychological, 4, 10, 24, 39, 54, 58, 60, 67, 68, 71, 85, 93, 101, 104, 111, 130, 132, 135, 187, 191, 208, 219, 240
revival, 81
romance, 3, 16, 22–23, 26, 38, 39, 44, 71
Southern, 117, 118, 141–54, 177, 215, 223, 226
technological, 76–79
terror, 23, 32, 35
textuality, 79–81
transgression, 57, 59, 216
trauma, 39
urban, 24, 25, 63, 67, 78, 79, 156–66, 188, 206, 215
victim, 39, 41, 103, 109, 111, 129, 143, 153, 173, 184, 189
villain, 22, 39, 61, 94, 148, 160, 161, 177, 180, 184, 201, 206, 212
Gothic Revival, 15, 27
Great Awakening, the, 17
Great Britain, 15, 16, 102, 186
  anti-slavery movement, 204
  Ballad Revival, 185
  colonists, 5
Great Dismal Swamp, the, 142
Grimsted, David, 203
Groom, Nick, 166
Gubar, Marah, 172
Gubar, Susan, 189
Guns-N-Roses, 195
Gustavus Vasa, 202

Hades (character), 178
Haggerty, George, 210
Haiti, 22, 148
  Revolution (1791–1804), 143, 144, 204

Halloween, 124, 172, 223
Halloween (1978 film), 225
Halloween (2007 film), 225
Hamilton, Alexander, 205,
Hammett, Dashiell, 160
Hannibal Lecter (character), 164, 165
Harris, Charlaine, 71, 72
Harris, Thomas, 5, 164, 165
Hattenhauer, Darryl, 106
Hawthorne, Nathaniel, 20, 26, 31, 32, 34, 37, 38, 39, 42, 71, 85, 184, 206
  Blithedale Romance, The, 39
  "Endicott and the Red Cross," 38
  "Gray Champion, The," 38
  House of the Seven Gables, The, 39, 71, 225
  Marble Faun, The, 39
  Scarlet Letter, The, 20, 39, 71
  "Young Goodman Brown," 8, 9, 32, 38, 88
Haynes, Lemuel, 185
Heidt, Yvonne, 122, 123
Hemings, Sally, 143
Hemingway, Ernest, 74
Hempstead, Joshua, 17
Henry Jekyll (character), 76
Himes, Chester, 163,
historical fiction, 145, 178
Hitchcock, Alfred, 124, 219, 221
  Alfred Hitchcock Presents, 220
  Psycho (1960 film), 224
Hogle, Jerrold, 81
Hooker, Samuel, 17
Hopkins, Pauline Elizabeth, 53, 54
horror, 49, 50, 80, 91, 95, 157, 171, 174, 176, 178, 179, 180, 193, 211, 215, 216, 219, 225, 227
  body, 217, 224
  boom, 22
  film, 216, 217, 218, 219, 221, 222, 224
  folklore, 20
  Gothic, 16, 21, 44, 46, 51, 54, 106, 111, 119, 124, 163, 165, 166, 171, 178, 201, 212, 222, 226
  hillbilly, 215, 234
  science fiction, 219, 220, 223
  slavery, 93, 95, 118, 208
  supernatural, 4, 20, 101, 181, 185, 194
  torture porn, 217
  tradition, 40
  video game, 233
House of the Dead series, 229
House of Wax (1953 film), 220
Howe, Julia Ward, 190

247

Howells, William Dean, 51
  influence on Realism, 52
  Rise of Silas Lapham, The, 54
Hughes, Amy, 202, 203
Hughes, William, 116, 125
human rights, 74
Hume, David, 6
Hunchback of Notre Dame, The (1923 film), 217
Hutchinson, Jr., Jesse, 189

I Walked with a Zombie, 219, 222
Ibsen, Henrik, 208
identity, 11, 38, 52, 58, 61, 62, 64, 69, 79, 116, 124, 125, 134, 153, 163, 173, 201, 235, 237, 238
  aristocratic, 32
  gender, 67, 219
  queer, 67, 118, 151
  racial, 89, 90
  sexual, 151, 210, 222
Iñárritu, Alejandro G., 5
individualism, 187, 203, 216, 221, 234
Interview with a Vampire (film), 71
Invasion of the Body Snatchers (1956 film), 219, 222
invisible man (character), 68–69
Invisible Man, The (1933 film), 218
Irving, Washington, 8, 26, 31, 32, 33, 175
  "Adventure of the German Student, The," 34
  "Devil and Tom Walker, The," 34
  "Legend of Sleepy Hollow The," 8, 31, 33, 34
  "Rip Van Winkle," 31, 32
It Came From Outer Space, 220

Jack Barnes (character), 73–75
Jack the Ripper, 195
Jackson, Rosemary, 100,
Jackson, Shirley, 1, 10, 106–9, 111, 167
  Haunting of Hill House, The, 10, 106, 116
  "My Uncle in the Garden," 106–7
  proto-feminism, 112
  We Have Always Lived in the Castle, 106
Jacobs, Harriet, 93, 195
  Incidents in the Life of a Slave Girl, 93, 144
James, Henry, 10, 41, 44–47, 102, 103, 109
  Aspern Papers, The, 104
  Turn of the Screw, The, 10, 45, 46, 109, 116
Jane Eyre (novel), 179
Jay-Z, 195

Jefferson, Thomas, xi, 89, 141, 142–43, 144, 154, 205
  Notes on the State of Virginia, 141, 142, 143
Jenner, Caitlyn, 115
jeremiad, 17, 23, 139
Jewett, Sarah Orne, 44, 46, 99, 104, 111
  Country of the Pointed Firs, The, 47, 99
  "Foreigner, The," 47, 48, 49
Joel Knox (character), 61, 66–68, 116, 117, 151
Joyce, James, 58, 67
  Portrait of the Artist as a Young Man, A, 66
  Ulysses, 66
Judah, Samuel B. H., 205–6

Karloff, Boris, 74
Keats, John, 103
Kenan, Randall, 118
Kierkegaard, Søren, 108
Killoran, Helen, 112
King of the Zombies, The, 218
King Philip's War, 5, 9, 17, 21, 27, 132
King, Grace, 146
King, Martin Luther, 74
King, Stephen, 1, 5, 8, 71, 74, 216
  Danse Macabre, 216
  Pet Sematary, 8
  Salem's Lot, 5, 74
  Stand, The, 167
kinship model. *See* Gubar, Marah
Knudsen, Michelle, 181
Kostova, Elizabeth, 79
Kraus, Daniel, 179
Ku Klux Klan, 148
Kuhn, Thomas, 74
Kushner, Tony, 10, 121, 201
  Angels in America, 121, 122, 212
Kyd, Thomas, 62

Ladd, Barbara, 149
Last of Us, The, 238
Latin@, 120, 125
Lawrence, D.H., 85
Ledoux, Ellen Malenas, 202
Ledwon, Lenora, 220
Lee, Harper, 151
Left 4 Dead, 233
Lewis, Henry Clay, 142
Lewis, Joseph H., 165
Lewis, Matthew Gregory, 186, 190, 204–5
Lindner, April, 179
Lippard, George, 157, 158–60, 161
  Quaker City, The, 158, 159, 207

Little Theatre Movement, 209–10
Lloyd-Smith, Allan, 8, 10
local color writing, 146
  definition, 154
  plantation school, 145, 146
Locke, John, 174–75
London, 51, 63, 158
London, Jack, ix, 4, 51
Longfellow, Henry Wadsworth, 187
  "Wreck of the Hesperus, The," 187
Lorde, Audre, 125
Los Angeles, 165, 226
Lost in the Rift, 240
Lovecraft, H. P., 20, 71, 80, 194, 232, 236
  Supernatural Horror in Literature, 4
Lowell, Amy, 192
Lugosi, Béla, 218
Luhr, William, 166
Lynch, David, 221
  Twin Peaks, 7, 225

Maberry, Jonathan, 73
madness, 41, 89, 93, 101, 109, 134, 184, 187, 191, 240
Marion, Isaac, 72
Marsh, Richard, 219
Martin, Robert K., 206
Marx, Karl, 44, 46
Marxism, 112
Mass Effect series, 230
Masters, Edgar Lee, 192
maternity, 47, 50, 210
Mather, Cotton, 6, 7, 8, 9, 16, 19, 20, 21, 22, 131, 132
  Magnalia Christi Americana (Vol. 2), 22
  Wonders of the Invisible World, 7, 8, 16, 128, 131
Mather, Increase, 17, 87
Matthiessen, Peter, 137
  Shadow Country, 142
Maturin, Charles, 188
Maupassant, Guy de, 40, 147
Max Payne, 239
McCann, Sean, 160
McCarthy, Cormac, 1, 71, 137, 151
  Blood Meridian, 152
  Child of God, 137, 138,
  Outer Dark, The, 142, 151
McCarthyism, 219
McCullers, Carson, 117–18, 150
  Ballad of the Sad Café, The, 117, 150
  disability, 125
  queer identity, 118

McDowell, Margaret, 112
McKay, Claude, 193
medievalism, 16
Méliès, Georges, 217
melodrama, 181, 207, 212
Melville, Herman, xii, 8, 41, 49, 92, 148, 151, 197
  Benito Cereno, 85, 90–92, 95
  Moby-Dick, 41
  "Paradise of Bachelors and The Tartarus of Maids, The," 49
  poetry, 190–91
Memoirs of the Bloomsgrove Family, 22
Messina, Lynn, 179
Metropolis, 217
Meyer, Stephenie, 71
Mickey Mouse (character), 176
Middle Ages, the, 15, 16
Miller, Kathleen, 177
Mitchell, Isaac, 23, 26
Mitchell, S. Weir, 45
modernism, 57–69, 116, 148–50, 192
  transatlantic, 57
  violence in Western culture, 59
Mogen, David, 21
monster, 2, 52, 54, 58, 61, 72, 73, 74, 75, 76, 81, 124, 125, 130, 143, 152, 161, 162, 163, 165, 171–72, 176, 178, 179, 180, 181, 194, 227, 235, *See also* video game monster
  demon, 231, 232
  digital, 77
  gendered, 216
  human, 215, 218, 231
  psychopath, 110, 111, 157, 163–64, 165, 234
  serial killer, 5, 80, 162, 164–65, 223, 224–26, 231
  supernatural, 166, 215
  sympathetic, 72–75, 218
Montgomery, L. M., 175, 177
Morrison, Toni, 1, 9, 15, 39, 42, 60, 64, 85, 86, 90, 96, 184
  Beloved, 9, 39, 85, 94, 95, 149, 225
  Paradise, 128–31, 133, 135, 138
  Playing in the Dark, 9, 86, 96, 136
  Sula, 60, 64
Morton, Samuel, 89
Morton, Thomas, 87
Morton, Timothy, 3
Motion Picture Production Code of 1930, 216
Mummy, The (1932 film), 218

INDEX

Murray, Judith Sargent, 202
mystery, 81

Nabokov, Vladimir, 1
Napoleonic Wars, the, 22
Native American, 5, 9, 42, 44, 86, 88, 119, 130–31, 133–35, 138, 142, 148, 176, 206
　"savage Indian" stereotype, 8, 136
　school, 129
Naturalism, 4, 8, 20, 32, 33, 44, 48, 49, 51, 52, 53, 54, 186
Naylor, Gloria, 1
Nazi, 218
Nelson, R. A., 177, 181
Nelson, Victoria, 179
neoliberalism, 78
neo-noir, 165,
New England, 40, 41, 49
　history, 38
Nichols, J. Horatio, 205,
Nietzsche, Friedrich, 36, 108
Night of the Living Dead, 222
Nightmare on Elm Street, 225
nihilism, 52
nineteenth century, 1, 8, 9, 18, 31–42, 57–59, 60, 61, 62, 79, 89–94, 110, 136, 138, 143, 147, 175, 208, 216
　Antebellum period, 186–90
　frontier, 128
　playwright, 209
　poetry, 20, 63, 189
　Realism, 62
　Removal era, 129
　Romanticism, 62
　theatre, 202, 206, 209, 210
Nodelman, Perry, 178
noir, 157, 158, 161, 165
Noll, Amanda, 179
nonfiction, 171
Norman Bates (character), 124
Norris, Frank, 4, 48, 51
　McTeague, 48, 52
　"A Plea for Romantic Fiction," 51
Northrup, Solomon, 144
Nosferatu, 217
Nott, Josiah, 89
nuclear family, 219

O'Brien, Fitz-James, 39, 40
O'Connor, Flannery, 151, 152
O'Neill, Eugene, 206, 209–10
　Desire Under the Elms, 210
　Emperor Jones, The, 209

Oates, Joyce Carol, 1, 10, 109–11
　"Accursed Inhabitants," 109
　Bellefleur, 110
　A Bloodsmoor Romance, 110
　"Doll, The," 110
　Haunted Tales of the Grotesque, 109
　My Heart Laid Bare, 110
　Mysteries of Winterthurn, 110
Odell, George C., 201, 204

Page, Thomas Nelson, 145, 146
Paine, Thomas, 74
Palacios, Monica, 120
Palahniuk, Chuck, 4
Palmer, Barton Palmer, 166
Parks, John G., 109
Patmore, Coventry, 100, 111
patriarchy, 3, 10, 49, 101, 102, 104, 105, 107, 111, 112, 129, 189, 218
　violence, 194
Paulding, James Kirke, 34
Peck, Richard, 178
Penny Dreadful, 230, 237, 238, 241
Percy, Bishop, 185
Persephone (character), 177, 178
Pettey, Homer B., 166
Phantom of the Opera, The (1925 film), 217
Phelps, Elizabeth Stuart, 50
Philip Marlowe (character), 160
photography, 50
picture books, 171, 179
Pike, Christopher, 178
Plath, Sylvia, 194
player, 230
　agency, 229, 230, 235, 241
　avatar, 229
　monster, 234, 235
playwright, 10, 26, 121, 144, 201, 208–12
podcasts, 76
Poe, Edgar Allan, 4, 8, 9, 26, 31, 33–38, 43, 71, 80, 90, 92, 95, 97, 129, 135–38, 144, 157–59, 161–62, 164, 175, 184, 188, 193, 206, 217
　"Black Cat, The," 4, 35, 109
　detective fiction, 35
　"Fall of the House of Usher, The," 35–37, 66, 145
　"Hop Frog," 144
　"How to Write a Blackwood's Article," 35
　"Imp of the Perverse, The," 4
　"Man of the Crowd, The," 158
　"Murders in the Rue Morgue, The," 158

250

INDEX

Narrative of Arthur Gordon Pym, The, 8, 9, 85, 89–90, 135–37, 144
"Philosophy of Composition, The," 35
poetry, 187
"Raven, The," 35, 187
satire, 35
"William Wilson," 4, 60, 101
poetry, 35, 62–64, 184–95
    Antebellum, 190
    female poets, 189
    form, 185, 191
    meter, 186,
    Romantic, 61
    temperance songs, 189
    weird, 194
Poltergeist, 225
Pope, Christine, 72
popular culture, 57, 73, 115
populism, 160
postindustrial, 78
postmodernism, 77, 109, 110
Pound, Ezra, 193
power, 2, 53, 59, 65, 66, 85, 92, 100, 102, 104, 105, 119–21, 124, 136, 145, 177, 181, 187, 194, 203, 223
    supernatural, 87
Psycho (film), 124
Psycho (novel), 124
psychology, 4
Punke, Michael, 5
Puritanism, 6, 7, 15, 16, 19, 21, 26, 38, 86, 87, 101, 131, 136, 175, 177, 206, *See* also Mathers, Cotton
    fears of Native Americans, 131
    frontier Gothic, 131–32
    jeremiad, 17
Pyramid Head (character), 233, 234, 241, 242

queer, 40, 61, 64, 66, 67, 69, 71, 150, 210
    ally, 122–23
    coming out, 115
    desire, 40, 118
    difference, 116
    fears, 40
    homophobia, 116, 122, 123, 124, 210, 212, 226
    monster, 116–17
    norm, 123
    transgender, 115
queer theory, 40
Quentin Compson (character), 61, 66, 148

race, 2, 5, 6, 8, 9, 10, 47, 52, 53, 59, 65, 66, 85–96, 111, 142, 143, 201, 202, 207
    ambiguity, 147
    antislavery texts, 85
    Atlantic slave trade, 25
    boundary, 207
    color line, 52, 92
    difference, 3, 8, 59, 88, 90
    hypodescent, 89
    identity, 52, 92
    institutional racism, 10
    miscegenation, 9, 66, 89, 144, 216, 222, 227
    passing, 53
    racism, 35, 53, 116, 117, 118, 122, 154, 193, 212, 226
    relations, 222
    riots, 207
    slavery, 3, 34, 35, 48, 66, 86, 88–89, 93, 94, 116, 118, 119, 141, 143, 145, 154, 176, 188, 204, 205, 208, 211, 223
    stereotype, 125, 147
    transformation, 94
    violence, 68, 94, 177, 193
    white violence, 88
    whiteness, 136
race theory, 88, 94
Radcliffe, Ann, 2, 3, 4, 23, 86, 90, 184, 201, 203
    Italian, The, 3
    Mysteries of Udolpho, The, 3, 5, 204
    Romance of the Forest, The, 26
Rand, Ayn, 239
rape. *See* sexaul violence
Rash, Ron, 143, 153
ratiocination, 35
rationality, 6, 11, 51
readers, 171
    child, 172, 174, 180,
    middle grade, 171, 173, 180
Realism, 44, 45, 46, 49, 51, 52, 54, 57, 58, 64, 69, 99, 129, 137, 153, 158, 160, 166, 178, 194, 215, 220
    children's literature, 176
Reeves, Dia, 179
religion, 3, 6, 10, 11, 66, 86–88, 99, 100, 107, 109, 120, 121, 124, 131–33, 151–52, 156, 175, 188, 206, 209, 223, 225, *See* also Puritanism; Satan
    Atheism, 87
    biblical narrative, 174
    extremism, 239
    Jesus Christ, 131, 149
    New Testament, 73
    Protestantism, 151

Resident Evil series, 234
Rex, Adam, 180
Reynolds, David, 206
Rice, Anne, 1, 71
Ricker, Jeffrey, 123
Ringe, Donald, 23
Roberts, Siân Silyn, 96
Robin Vote (character), 64, 67
Romanticism, 6, 31, 34, 44, 51, 175, 179
   children's literature, 177
Romero, George A., 74, 222
Roosevelt, Theodore, 191
Rowlandson, Mary, 5, 21, 85, 87, 92, 131, 132, 135, 138,
   Sovereignty and Goodness of God, The, 5, 128, 131
Rowson, Susannah, 202
Roy, Lori, 153
rural, 32, 67, 107, 112, 116, 118, 142–43, 152–54, 158, 166, 206
Russell, Karen, 143
   Swamplandia!, 142
Ryan, Carrie, 73

Samuels, Shirley, 202
Satan, 6–9, 17, 34, 87, 88, 106, 107, 124, 130, 131, 163, 177, 188, 193, 223
Savoy, Eric, 35, 86, 206
Scary Stories to Tell in the Dark, 178
Schwartz, Alvin, 178
science fiction, 40, 115
Scooby-Doo (character), 174
Scott, Ridley
   Alien, 5, 223
   Blade Runner, 165, 166
Scott, Walter, 143, 186
Secret World, The, 229, 231, 238
secularism, 175, 195
Sedgwick, Eve Kosofosky, 240
Séjour, Victor, 144, 148
   "Le Mulâtre," 144
Seltzer, Mark, 164
Selznick, David O., 219
semiotics, 80
sensationalism, 51, 175, 189, 202, 212
Sense8 (television), 115, 124
sensibility, 39
sentimentalism, 50
seventeenth century, 7, 62, 132
sex, 10, 68, 192
   desire, 219, 223
   difference, 10
   exploitation, 143

   freedom, 222
   urges, 181
sexual violence, 110, 112, 119, 133, 150, 153, 163, 192
sexuality, 6, 10, 49, 99
   fear, 40
   freedom, 218
   gender, 120
   lesbian, 64, 115, 119, 120, 122, 123
   norms, 10
   psychosocial, 112
   trauma, 110
Shakespeare, William, 16
Shelley, Mary. *See Frankenstein* (novel)
Shepard, Sam, 201, 211
Shining, The (film), 71
Shining, The (novel), 10
Siddons, Anne Rivers, 149
Sigourney, Lydia, 189,
Silence of the Lambs, The (film), 5, 225
Silence of the Lambs, The (novel), 5, 116
Silent Hill 2, 236, 241
Silent Hill series, 233, 234, 237
Silverman, Kenneth. *See* Poe, Edgar Allan
Simms, William Gilmore, 143, 186, 187
   Yemassee, The, 143
Simpson, Louis P., 141
Sims series, 239
Six Feet Under, 226,
sixteenth century, 62
Slender Man (character), 76, 77
Slotkin, Richard, 236
Smith, Andrew, 116, 125, 179
Smith, John, 87
Smith, L. J., 71
Smith, Samuel Stanhope, 89
Smith, Shawn, 89
Smith-Rosenberg, Carroll, 25
social media, 76, 78
socialism, 78
Sondheim, Stephen, 201, 211
Sontag, Susan, 119, 125
Southern Comfort, 152
Space Invaders, 233
Spec Ops, 234, 236
Spencer, Edmund, 74
Spofford, Harriet Prescott, 39–41, 46
   "Amber Gods, The," 40, 48
Spooner, Catherine, 212
Stanley Parable, The, 240
Steele, Erin Bone, 213
Sterling, Bruce, 77, 78
Sterling, George, 193

INDEX

Stern, Howard, 74
Stevenson, Robert Louis, 60
Stine, R. L., 178
Stoker, Bram. *See Dracula* (novel)
Stowe, Harriet Beecher, 9, 41, 93, 208
   Dred, A Tale of the Great Dismal Swamp, 154
Straczynski, J. Michael, 115
Straub, Peter, 1
Strindberg, August, 208
Stryker, Susan, 115
sublime, 5, 16, 193, 215
suburban, 80, 178
Sue, Eugène, 206
Sunset Boulevard (film), 121
supernatural, 33, 39, 47, 48, 100, 101, 105, 123, 129, 132, 153, 156, 174, 175, 179, 180, 188, 202, 206, 211, 217, 219, 223, 225, *See also* ghost
Swedenborg, Emanuel, 99
Sweeney Todd: The Demon Barber of Fleet Street (play), 211

Tate, Allen, 193
Tegen, Katherine, 179
television, 7, 71, 215, 220–22, 225
   camp, 221
   magicom, 221
   melodrama, 221
   sitcom, 221
   soap opera, 221
Texas Chainsaw Massacre (1974 film), 152, 224, 225, 234
theatre, 5, 10, 16, 64, 66, 121, 122, 201–12
   American, 201, 202
   audience, 207
   British, 202
   classical Greek, 209
   Elizabethan, 62
   European, 201, 202
   manager, 207
   managers, 201, 202, 204
   satire, 204–5
   troupe, 202
   urban, 206,
Thomas Sutpen (character), 61, 65–66, 148
Thoreau, Henry, 74
Tobiason, Aaron, 207
Tourneur, Jacques, 219
Townshend, Dale, 174
tragedy, 174
Transcendentalists, 37
trauma, 92, 110

True Blood, 71, 222, 226
Tudor, Andrew, 225
Turner, Frederick Jackson, 137
Turner, Nat, 143
Twain, Mark, 41, 54, 146, 175, 176
   Pudd'nhead Wilson, 148
twentieth century, 61, 69, 79, 111, 116, 128–30, 137–38, 157, 164, 175
Twilight (film), 71
Twilight (novel), 71, 178
Twin Peaks, 238
Tyler, Royall, 23, 202
Typing of the Dead, 233

Uncle Tom's Cabin (novel), 9, 41, 85, 93, 208, 210
Uncle Tom's Cabin (play), 208
United States of America, 3, 15, *See also* race
   AIDS epidemic, 122
   American Dream, 211, 220
   American Revolution, 22, 32, 38
   antebellum period, 157
   Civil Rights Movement, 222
   Civil War, 44, 45, 49, 50, 52, 59, 66, 94, 117, 128, 144, 145, 146, 154, 190, 197
   Federalism, 205
   Federalist period, 16
   Great Depression, 218
   imperialism, 54
   McCarthyism, 121
   New World, 15, 16, 18, 20, 21, 23, 176, 218
   politics, 204–5
   post-9/11, 224, 226
   post-Reconstruction era, 52
   post-WWI, 60, 62, 63
   post-WWII, 60, 66, 128, 220
   Progressive Era, 52
   race relations, 57, 69
   Removal era, 133, 141, 144
   urbanization, 206
   Victorian era, 52, 57, 111
   World War I, 59
   World War II, 59
United States Supreme Court, 216
Until Dawn, 233
urban, 78, 107, 117, 120, 158, 159, 160, 206
   anxieties, 158
   architecture, 157, 158, 161, 162, 164
   corruption, 160
   criminality, 159,
   desolation, 158, 159
   foreboding, 157

urban (cont.)
  lawlessness, 161
  poor, 206
  secularization, 157
urbanization, 159
utopia, 16, 17, 18, 128, 129, 133, 138, 215, 219

vampire, 5, 37, 47, 61, 71, 72, 151, 156, 161, 178, 217, 222, 226, 227
  queer, 119
Vampire Diaries, The (television), 71
Victor Frankenstein (character), 66, 74, 76
video game, 229–41
  agency, 229, 230
  arcade, 229
  augmented reality, 237
  big boss, 233
  character, 231
  first-person perspective, 240
  gameplay, 231
  ludology, 232, 236
  monster, 230–37
  narrative, 231, 232, 234
  obstacle, 232
  shooter, 233, 234, 240
  space, 236–41
Vietnam War, 211, 222, 224
Virginia, 142
Vlad the Impaler, 79

Wachowski, Lilly, 115, 124, 125
Wachowski, Lana, 115, 124, 125
Walpole, Horace, 15, 81, 86, 185, 201
  Castle of Otranto, The, 15, 81
War of the Worlds, The (novel), 219
Ward, Elizabeth Stuart Phelps, 46
Waste Land, The, 57, 62–64
Watergate, 211
Weathers, Brenda, 122–23
Webster, Daniel, 188,
Webster, Maisha, 208
Weinstock, Jeffrey Andrew, 24, 47, 87, 99, 103, 129, 138, 166
weird writing, 4, 193, 194, 236, 241
Wells, H. G., 219
Welty, Eudora, 149, 154
Werewolf, The, 220
Western (genre), 137
Wharton, Edith, ix, 10, 44, 45, 46, 54, 102–5, 111, 113, 137, 206
  "Afterward," 45, 54, 102
  "Angel at the Grave," 104

"Fullness of Life, The," 103
"Duchess at Prayer, The," 104
"House of the Dead Hand, The," 105
influences, 112
marriage, 103
Where the Wild Things Are, 180
Whig, 188
White Zombie, 218, 222
White, Leslie T., 160
whiteness, 178, 179
Whitman, Walt, 73, 75, 190
Whittier, John Greenleaf, 188
Wigglesworth, Michael, 6, 16
Wilde, Oscar, 58, 60–61, 62, 64, 65
  Picture of Dorian Gray, The, 60, 61
  Salome, 60
Wilder, Billy, 165
Wilder, Laura Ingalls, 175, 176
Wilder, Thornton, 5
Willems, Mo, 179
Williams, Tennessee, 201, 210
  Street Car Named Desire, A (play), 150
Willingham, Bill, 237
Wilson, August, 201
  Piano Lesson, The, 211
Wilson, Harriet, 92
Windham, CT, 21
Winthrop, John, 16, 20, 30
witch, 18, 129, 171, 172, 175
  Salem Witch Trials, 6, 9, 18, 20, 116, 131, 218
  witchhunt, 18, 19
witchcraft, 7, 54, 106, 122, 131, 138, 227
Wolf Among Us, The, 237
Wollstonecroft, Mary, 24, 74
Wood, Sally S. B. K., 22, 26
Woodrell, Daniel, 143, 153
Woolf, Virginia, 58, 60
Wordsworth, William, 186
Wright, Richard, 95, 164
  Native Son, 9, 94, 162–63
Wynne, Madeline Yale, 49

xenophobia, 221

yellow journalism, 51
young adult literature, ix, 73, 171, 172, 173, 178, 180
Young Goodman Brown (character), 8, 9
zombie, 63, 71–76, 150, 159, 179, 217, 221, 222, 231–33, 234, 235, 238

Cambridge Companions to ...

AUTHORS

Edward Albee edited by *Stephen J. Bottoms*
Margaret Atwood edited by *Coral Ann Howells*
W. H. Auden edited by *Stan Smith*
Jane Austen edited by *Edward Copeland and Juliet McMaster (second edition)*
Beckett edited by *John Pilling*
Bede edited by *Scott DeGregorio*
Aphra Behn edited by *Derek Hughes and Janet Todd*
Walter Benjamin edited by *David S. Ferris*
William Blake edited by *Morris Eaves*
Boccaccio edited by *Guyda Armstrong, Rhiannon Daniels, and Stephen J. Milner*
Jorge Luis Borges edited by *Edwin Williamson*
Brecht edited by *Peter Thomson and Glendyr Sacks (second edition)*
The Brontës edited by *Heather Glen*
Bunyan edited by *Anne Dunan-Page*
Frances Burney edited by *Peter Sabor*
Byron edited by *Drummond Bone*
Albert Camus edited by *Edward J. Hughes*
Willa Cather edited by *Marilee Lindemann*
Cervantes edited by *Anthony J. Cascardi*
Chaucer edited by *Piero Boitani and Jill Mann (second edition)*
Chekhov edited by *Vera Gottlieb and Paul Allain*
Kate Chopin edited by *Janet Beer*
Caryl Churchill edited by *Elaine Aston and Elin Diamond*
Cicero edited by *Catherine Steel*
Coleridge edited by *Lucy Newlyn*
Wilkie Collins edited by *Jenny Bourne Taylor*
Joseph Conrad edited by *J. H. Stape*
H. D. edited by *Nephie J. Christodoulides and Polina Mackay*
Dante edited by *Rachel Jacoff (second edition)*
Daniel Defoe edited by *John Richetti*
Don DeLillo edited by *John N. Duvall*
Charles Dickens edited by *John O. Jordan*
Emily Dickinson edited by *Wendy Martin*
John Donne edited by *Achsah Guibbory*
Dostoevskii edited by *W. J. Leatherbarrow*
Theodore Dreiser edited by *Leonard Cassuto and Claire Virginia Eby*
John Dryden edited by *Steven N. Zwicker*
W. E. B. Du Bois edited by *Shamoon Zamir*
George Eliot edited by *George Levine*
T. S. Eliot edited by *A. David Moody*
Ralph Ellison edited by *Ross Posnock*
Ralph Waldo Emerson edited by *Joel Porte and Saundra Morris*
William Faulkner edited by *Philip M. Weinstein*
Henry Fielding edited by *Claude Rawson*
F. Scott Fitzgerald edited by *Ruth Prigozy*
Flaubert edited by *Timothy Unwin*
E. M. Forster edited by *David Bradshaw*
Benjamin Franklin edited by *Carla Mulford*
Brian Friel edited by *Anthony Roche*
Robert Frost edited by *Robert Faggen*
Gabriel García Márquez edited by *Philip Swanson*
Elizabeth Gaskell edited by *Jill L. Matus*
Goethe edited by *Lesley Sharpe*
Günter Grass edited by *Stuart Taberner*
Thomas Hardy edited by *Dale Kramer*
David Hare edited by *Richard Boon*
Nathaniel Hawthorne edited by *Richard Millington*
Seamus Heaney edited by *Bernard O'Donoghue*
Ernest Hemingway edited by *Scott Donaldson*
Homer edited by *Robert Fowler*
Horace edited by *Stephen Harrison*
Ted Hughes edited by *Terry Gifford*
Ibsen edited by *James McFarlane*
Henry James edited by *Jonathan Freedman*
Samuel Johnson edited by *Greg Clingham*
Ben Jonson edited by *Richard Harp and Stanley Stewart*
James Joyce edited by *Derek Attridge (second edition)*
Kafka edited by *Julian Preece*
Keats edited by *Susan J. Wolfson*
Rudyard Kipling edited by *Howard J. Booth*
Lacan edited by *Jean-Michel Rabaté*
D. H. Lawrence edited by *Anne Fernihough*
Primo Levi edited by *Robert Gordon*

Lucretius edited by *Stuart Gillespie and Philip Hardie*
Machiavelli edited by *John M. Najemy*
David Mamet edited by *Christopher Bigsby*
Thomas Mann edited by *Ritchie Robertson*
Christopher Marlowe edited by *Patrick Cheney*
Andrew Marvell edited by *Derek Hirst and Steven N. Zwicker*
Herman Melville edited by *Robert S. Levine*
Arthur Miller edited by *Christopher Bigsby (second edition)*
Milton edited by *Dennis Danielson (second edition)*
Molière edited by *David Bradby and Andrew Calder*
Toni Morrison edited by *Justine Tally*
Alice Munro edited by *David Staines*
Nabokov edited by *Julian W. Connolly*
Eugene O'Neill edited by *Michael Manheim*
George Orwell edited by *John Rodden*
Ovid edited by *Philip Hardie*
Petrarch edited by *Albert Russell Ascoli and Unn Falkeid*
Harold Pinter edited by *Peter Raby (second edition)*
Sylvia Plath edited by *Jo Gill*
Edgar Allan Poe edited by *Kevin J. Hayes*
Alexander Pope edited by *Pat Rogers*
Ezra Pound edited by *Ira B. Nadel*
Proust edited by *Richard Bales*
Pushkin edited by *Andrew Kahn*
Rabelais edited by *John O'Brien*
Rilke edited by *Karen Leeder and Robert Vilain*
Philip Roth edited by *Timothy Parrish*
Salman Rushdie edited by *Abdulrazak Gurnah*
John Ruskin edited by *Francis O'Gorman*
Shakespeare edited by *Margareta de Grazia and Stanley Wells (second edition)*
Shakespearean Comedy edited by *Alexander Leggatt*
Shakespeare and Contemporary Dramatists edited by *Ton Hoenselaars*
Shakespeare and Popular Culture edited by *Robert Shaughnessy*
Shakespearean Tragedy edited by *Claire McEachern (second edition)*
Shakespeare on Film edited by *Russell Jackson (second edition)*
Shakespeare on Stage edited by *Stanley Wells and Sarah Stanton*
Shakespeare's First Folio edited by *Emma Smith*
Shakespeare's History Plays edited by *Michael Hattaway*
Shakespeare's Last Plays edited by *Catherine M. S. Alexander*
Shakespeare's Poetry edited by *Patrick Cheney*
George Bernard Shaw edited by *Christopher Innes*
Shelley edited by *Timothy Morton*
Mary Shelley edited by *Esther Schor*
Sam Shepard edited by *Matthew C. Roudané*
Spenser edited by *Andrew Hadfield*
Laurence Sterne edited by *Thomas Keymer*
Wallace Stevens edited by *John N. Serio*
Tom Stoppard edited by *Katherine E. Kelly*
Harriet Beecher Stowe edited by *Cindy Weinstein*
August Strindberg edited by *Michael Robinson*
Jonathan Swift edited by *Christopher Fox*
J. M. Synge edited by *P. J. Mathews*
Tacitus edited by *A. J. Woodman*
Henry David Thoreau edited by *Joel Myerson*
Tolstoy edited by *Donna Tussing Orwin*
Anthony Trollope edited by *Carolyn Dever and Lisa Niles*
Mark Twain edited by *Forrest G. Robinson*
John Updike edited by *Stacey Olster*
Mario Vargas Llosa edited by *Efrain Kristal and John King*
Virgil edited by *Charles Martindale*
Voltaire edited by *Nicholas Cronk*
Edith Wharton edited by *Millicent Bell*
Walt Whitman edited by *Ezra Greenspan*
Oscar Wilde edited by *Peter Raby*
Tennessee Williams edited by *Matthew C. Roudané*
August Wilson edited by *Christopher Bigsby*
Mary Wollstonecraft edited by *Claudia L. Johnson*
Virginia Woolf edited by *Susan Sellers (second edition)*
Wordsworth edited by *Stephen Gill*
W. B. Yeats edited by *Marjorie Howes and John Kelly*
Xenophon edited by *Michael A. Flower*
Zola edited by *Brian Nelson*

TOPICS

The Actress edited by Maggie B. Gale and John Stokes

The African American Novel edited by Maryemma Graham

The African American Slave Narrative edited by Audrey A. Fisch

Theatre History by David Wiles and Christine Dymkowski

African American Theatre by Harvey Young

Allegory edited by Rita Copeland and Peter Struck

American Crime Fiction edited by Catherine Ross Nickerson

American Gothic edited by Jeffrey Andrew Weinstock

American Modernism edited by Walter Kalaidjian

American Poetry Since 1945 edited by Jennifer Ashton

American Realism and Naturalism edited by Donald Pizer

American Travel Writing edited by Alfred Bendixen and Judith Hamera

American Women Playwrights edited by Brenda Murphy

Ancient Rhetoric edited by Erik Gunderson

Arthurian Legend edited by Elizabeth Archibald and Ad Putter

Australian Literature edited by Elizabeth Webby

The Beats edited by Stephen Belletto

British Black and Asian Literature (1945–2010) edited by Deirdre Osborne

British Literature of the French Revolution edited by Pamela Clemit

British Romanticism edited by Stuart Curran (second edition)

British Romantic Poetry edited by James Chandler and Maureen N. McLane

British Theatre, 1730–1830, edited by Jane Moody and Daniel O'Quinn

Canadian Literature edited by Eva-Marie Kröller (second edition)

Children's Literature edited by M. O. Grenby and Andrea Immel

The Classic Russian Novel edited by Malcolm V. Jones and Robin Feuer Miller

Contemporary Irish Poetry edited by Matthew Campbell

Creative Writing edited by David Morley and Philip Neilsen

Crime Fiction edited by Martin Priestman

Dracula edited by Roger Luckhurst

Early Modern Women's Writing edited by Laura Lunger Knoppers

The Eighteenth-Century Novel edited by John Richetti

Eighteenth-Century Poetry edited by John Sitter

Emma edited by Peter Sabor

English Literature, 1500–1600 edited by Arthur F. Kinney

English Literature, 1650–1740 edited by Steven N. Zwicker

English Literature, 1740–1830 edited by Thomas Keymer and Jon Mee

English Literature, 1830–1914 edited by Joanne Shattock

English Novelists edited by Adrian Poole

English Poetry, Donne to Marvell edited by Thomas N. Corns

English Poets edited by Claude Rawson

English Renaissance Drama, second edition edited by A. R. Braunmuller and Michael Hattaway

English Renaissance Tragedy edited by Emma Smith and Garrett A. Sullivan Jr.

English Restoration Theatre edited by Deborah C. Payne Fisk

The Epic edited by Catherine Bates

Erotic Literature edited by Bradford Mudge

European Modernism edited by Pericles Lewis

European Novelists edited by Michael Bell

Fairy Tales edited by Maria Tatar

Fantasy Literature edited by Edward James and Farah Mendlesohn

Feminist Literary Theory edited by Ellen Rooney

Fiction in the Romantic Period edited by Richard Maxwell and Katie Trumpener

The Fin de Siècle edited by Gail Marshall

Frankenstein edited by Andrew Smith

The French Enlightenment edited by Daniel Brewer

French Literature edited by John D. Lyons

The French Novel: from 1800 to the Present edited by Timothy Unwin

Gay and Lesbian Writing edited by Hugh Stevens

German Romanticism edited by Nicholas Saul

Gothic Fiction edited by Jerrold E. Hogle

The Graphic Novel edited by Stephen Tabachnick

The Greek and Roman Novel edited by Tim Whitmarsh

Greek and Roman Theatre edited by Marianne McDonald and J. Michael Walton

Greek Comedy edited by Martin Revermann

Greek Lyric edited by Felix Budelmann

Greek Mythology edited by Roger D. Woodard

Greek Tragedy edited by P. E. Easterling

The Harlem Renaissance edited by George Hutchinson

The History of the Book edited by Leslie Howsam

The Irish Novel edited by John Wilson Foster

Irish Poets edited by Gerald Dawe

The Italian Novel edited by Peter Bondanella and Andrea Ciccarelli

The Italian Renaissance edited by Michael Wyatt

Jewish American Literature edited by Hana Wirth-Nesher and Michael P. Kramer

The Latin American Novel edited by Efraín Kristal

The Literature of the First World War edited by Vincent Sherry

The Literature of London edited by Lawrence Manley

The Literature of Los Angeles edited by Kevin R. McNamara

The Literature of New York edited by Cyrus Patell and Bryan Waterman

The Literature of Paris edited by Anna-Louise Milne

The Literature of World War II edited by Marina MacKay

Literature and Disability edited by Clare Barker and Stuart Murray

Literature and Science edited by Steven Meyer

Literature on Screen edited by Deborah Cartmell and Imelda Whelehan

Medieval English Culture edited by Andrew Galloway

Medieval English Literature edited by Larry Scanlon

Medieval English Mysticism edited by Samuel Fanous and Vincent Gillespie

Medieval English Theatre edited by Richard Beadle and Alan J. Fletcher (second edition)

Medieval French Literature edited by Simon Gaunt and Sarah Kay

Medieval Romance edited by Roberta L. Krueger

Medieval Women's Writing edited by Carolyn Dinshaw and David Wallace

Modern American Culture edited by Christopher Bigsby

Modern British Women Playwrights edited by Elaine Aston and Janelle Reinelt

Modern French Culture edited by Nicholas Hewitt

Modern German Culture edited by Eva Kolinsky and Wilfried van der Will

The Modern German Novel edited by Graham Bartram

The Modern Gothic edited by Jerrold E. Hogle

Modern Irish Culture edited by Joe Cleary and Claire Connolly

Modern Italian Culture edited by Zygmunt G. Baranski and Rebecca J. West

Modern Latin American Culture edited by John King

Modern Russian Culture edited by Nicholas Rzhevsky

Modern Spanish Culture edited by David T. Gies

Modernism edited by Michael Levenson (second edition)

The Modernist Novel edited by Morag Shiach

Modernist Poetry edited by Alex Davis and Lee M. Jenkins

Modernist Women Writers edited by Maren Tova Linett

Narrative edited by David Herman

Native American Literature edited by Joy Porter and Kenneth M. Roemer

Nineteenth-Century American Women's Writing edited by Dale M. Bauer and Philip Gould

Old English Literature edited by Malcolm Godden and Michael Lapidge (second edition)

Performance Studies edited by Tracy C. Davis

Piers Plowman by Andrew Cole and Andrew Galloway

Popular Fiction edited by David Glover and Scott McCracken

Postcolonial Poetry edited by Jahan Ramazani

Postcolonial Literary Studies edited by Neil Lazarus

Postmodern American Fiction edited by Paula Geyh

Postmodernism edited by Steven Connor

The Pre-Raphaelites edited by Elizabeth Prettejohn

Pride and Prejudice edited by Janet Todd

Renaissance Humanism edited by Jill Kraye

The Roman Historians edited by Andrew Feldherr

Roman Satire edited by Kirk Freudenburg

Science Fiction edited by Edward James and Farah Mendlesohn

Scottish Literature edited by Gerald Carruthers and Liam McIlvanney

Sensation Fiction edited by Andrew Mangham

The Sonnet edited by A. D. Cousins and Peter Howarth

The Spanish Novel: From 1600 to the Present edited by Harriet Turner and Adelaida López de Martínez

Textual Scholarship edited by Neil Fraistat and Julia Flanders

Travel Writing edited by Peter Hulme and Tim Youngs

Twentieth-Century British and Irish Women's Poetry edited by Jane Dowson

The Twentieth-Century English Novel edited by Robert L. Caserio

Twentieth-Century English Poetry edited by Neil Corcoran

Twentieth-Century Irish Drama edited by Shaun Richards

Twentieth-Century Russian Literature edited by Marina Balina and Evgeny Dobrenko

Utopian Literature edited by Gregory Claeys

Victorian and Edwardian Theatre edited by Kerry Powell

The Victorian Novel edited by Deirdre David (second edition)

Victorian Poetry edited by Joseph Bristow

Victorian Women's Writing edited by Linda H. Peterson

War Writing edited by Kate McLoughlin

Women's Writing in Britain, 1660–1789 edited by Catherine Ingrassia

Women's Writing in the Romantic Period edited by Devoney Looser

Writing of the English Revolution edited by N. H. Keeble

The Writings of Julius Caesar edited by Christopher Krebs and Luca Grillo